WORDS MADE FLESH

*To Marsha,
Friend and Colleague,
Pittman*

SELECTED SERMONS BY
THE VERY REVEREND J. PITTMAN McGEHEE D.D.

Copyright © 2011 J. Pittman McGehee, D.D.
All rights reserved.

ISBN: 1452804532
ISBN-13: 9781452804538

For the people of Christ Church Cathedral
and
For my grandchildren: Finnegan, Baxter, and Clementine
…you are love made flesh.

ACKNOWLEDGEMENTS

Kay Pieringer deserves much credit for the genesis and production of this book. She volunteered to be the project manager, and she managed very well. The members of the selection committee each read and helped edit a year or two of sermons and contributed greatly to the final selection. Thanks go to the committee: Sidney Buchanan, Donna Boyd, Cece Fowler, Suzanne Jennings, Rick Newlin, and Kate Pogue. Further editing was done by Bonnie Fairbanks, Donna Fong, Sue Green, Gretchen Harwood, Ellen Luby, Sue Orrell, Marilyn Wolfe-Kirk, and Winnie Youngblood. To all, a great thanks. The lion's share of professional editing and interface with the publisher's editorial staff was done tirelessly by Donna Boyd.

Further acknowledgement to my family—Bobby, Pittman Jr., and Jarrett—who graciously shared their husband and father with the Cathedral family during my tenure as dean.

I must acknowledge my longtime secretary, Julia Crowder, who typed each of these sermons and helped administer my professional life. To Canon John A. Logan—subdean, mentor, and colleague—I offer recognition. I proclaimed many times how I led the Cathedral and John ran it. To all the priests who served with me in those years and to the administrative staff who supported us in our ministries, I offer thanksgiving.

Finally, I offer gratitude to my very creative daughter-in-law, Merrilee McCommas McGehee, for her cover design. Taking the original typed manuscripts and creating a mosaic of words beneath the Cathedral roodscreen provides a compelling image of the "words made flesh."

INTRODUCTION

I was dean of Christ Church Cathedral in Houston, Texas, from November 1980 until June 1991. These sermons were delivered at the Cathedral during that time. The Russian author and playwright, Chekhov, wrote to a friend: "A conscious life without a definite philosophy is no life, rather a burden and nightmare." Substitute for "philosophy" the word "theology" or "worldview" and you will know what I was attempting to develop for the people of Christ Church and most particularly for myself. These words made flesh come from an ordinary man who was called to an extraordinary task. When ordained, the new priest is given two symbols of his office: a Holy Bible and a chalice. The Church is essentially saying, "Keep the story alive and the mystery present." My preaching attempted to be faithful to that task. The theologian, Paul Tillich, wrote: "Sometimes I think it is my mission to bring faith to the faithless, and doubt to the faithful." I concur.

Between the birth we did not request and the grave we cannot escape, I hope these words may help us, in the meantime, to be able to find the extraordinary in the ordinary, the miraculous in the mundane, and the sacred camouflaged in the profane. And to help us remember that "the Word was made flesh and dwelt among us, full of grace and truth." (John 1:14)

1981

January 1981

There is a story told of a little girl from Kansas. Her name is Dorothy. Today, for a brief period of time, we are going to join Dorothy. We're off to see the Wizard—the Wonderful Wizard of Oz.

If you remember, Dorothy was a farm girl from Kansas, and in a summer cyclone was whisked away into the land of Oz. After she landed, she discovered many things about this strange country in which she found herself.

Oz was a country ruled by a wonderful wizard who lived in the center of the land. And the land was divided into four kingdoms ruled by witches. The witches of the north and south were good witches, and their counterparts in the east and west were evil witches.

As Dorothy and her trusty companion, her dog Toto, landed in the land of the east, Dorothy's house killed the Wicked Witch of the East. And Dorothy inherited her ruby slippers. In this land of the east, Dorothy was a heroine, and the people were at her service. The only thing Dorothy desired of the people of the east was to return to her home in Kansas. But it was not within their power to enable her to return home; only the great Oz could perform such a trick. So they informed her that she must travel to the Emerald City in the center of the land. How was she to get there? Simple: follow the Yellow Brick Road.

So Dorothy and her dog Toto start off to see the Wizard, the Wonderful Wizard of Oz. On her journey, she encounters three pathetic and lovable characters who join her in the journey down the Yellow Brick Road.

First she encounters a man of straw, the Scarecrow, who is stuck on a pole and wants more than anything to have brains. So Dorothy, out of her love and concern, takes him off the pole on which he is stuck and invites him to join her in her journey to Oz, with the hope that the Wizard can restore them both—Dorothy with a return to home and the straw man to a man with brains. But the Scarecrow is apprehensive. "What if the Wizard cannot give me brains?" Dorothy responds, "It is worth the risk, because if he doesn't, you will not be any worse off than you already are." So he joins her and stumbles along the road because he cannot think ahead to anticipate holes and obstacles in the road.

Next, they encounter a tin woodman who is frozen and rusted. Dorothy takes an oil can and frees him. He tells her that he wants more than anything to have a heart, because when you don't have a heart, the only thing you can care about is the fact that you don't have a heart. Dorothy then asks him to join her and her straw friend in their journey to Oz, in hopes that the Wizard will accomplish a threefold restoration of home, head, and heart. So the three set off, on their way down the Yellow Brick Road.

The next encounter is with a lion who has lost his courage. The king of beasts is only a kitten and desires to regain his courage. Dorothy and the others accept him as he is and invite him to join them in their separate approaches to the same source of hope—the Wizard of Oz.

So this motley crew moves together seeking a fourfold restoration of a home, a mind, a heart, and courage. On this journey to Oz, they encounter obstacle after obstacle, which are finally overcome by each offering what he has, until they finally reach the Emerald City and the home of Oz.

When they arrive at Oz's palace and are allowed to stand in his presence, he tells them that before he can grant them their wishes, they must travel to kill the only source of wickedness left in the kingdom, the Wicked Witch of the West. So off they travel again and overcome adversity after adversity reaching the witch. In the process, each offers what he has at a great price. The tin man is left bent and broken, the straw man is spread over the countryside, the lion is caged, and Dorothy is taken as a slave. The only thing that will kill the witch is water, and Dorothy accomplishes this task because, in her slavery, she is forced to wash the floor. One day, she takes a bucket of water and throws it on the witch, who is washed away. And because of the water, the tin man is patched up, the straw man is restored, the lion is uncaged, and the bonds of slavery are taken off of Dorothy.

They then return to the Wizard so that he can perform his miracle. The Wizard has never been seen by anyone, for he takes many forms. And when the four come into his presence for the last time, the Wizard is exposed. As it turns out, the Wizard is not a wizard after all, but just a man who had come to Oz quite by accident, much like Dorothy. The only power he has is the power people gave him. And, as you can imagine, the Cowardly Lion, the Tin Man, the Scarecrow, and Dorothy are disappointed that they will not receive their gifts. But Oz tells the lion that he already has courage, or he would not have arrived at Oz had he not had courage all along. And he repeats the same to the others. Oz's point is that the thing each seeks is already within each of them. But they ask Oz to symbolize for them the gifts they already have, and in fine fashion, he fills the Scarecrow's head with pins to symbolize that he is sharp, he places a silk heart in the breast of the Tin Man, and he pours a bottle of courage into a bowl for the Cowardly Lion to drink. And Dorothy finally discovers that the ruby slippers she has worn from the beginning are all she needs to take her home. So, all discover that what they wanted most was available to them all the time, and the wizardry of Oz is that he points this out to them through symbols.

Well, now the question comes. Why listen this morning to a children's story? We are Dorothy—we are straw men, tin men, and cowardly lions. Oz is our world. We are each of the characters, and they are each a part of who we are.

Let us start from the beginning. It is a cyclone of one type or another that finally forces us to find our way back home. Your cyclone may be death, pain, crises, or tragedy, but life has a way of whirling us around till we feel we are in a strange land where we can't think, feel, or have the courage to find our way back home. And when this happens, we look for a wizard—some hope of restoration—a Yellow Brick Road to follow so that we can return home.

We find ourselves on a pole like the Scarecrow; we can't think our way out of our predicament. And it takes someone to help us off so we can start our journey. We need our thinking function, but not it alone, to find our way. We need heart—that is our feeling function—or we are like the Tin Man, frozen, rusted, unable to move. And, it sometimes takes the love of others to oil us into mobility so that we may seek wholeness again. We need soul or courage to give us that depth to face obstacles on our journey to wholeness, or we are Cowardly Lions, phonies who look great on the outside but are empty inside. We need a loyal dog like Toto. He is our reliable instinct that barks when danger is near and, if trusted, will help us through trouble.

Oz is not God; he is only a man. He is like a priest. He only enables people to get in touch with what they already have. Oz didn't perform miracles; he was only a vehicle that enabled miracles to happen. One even happened to him. He used symbols (or sacraments) to allow the Scarecrow to accept and recognize the brains he had; the Tin Man, the heart and feelings he had; the Lion, the courage he had; and Dorothy, the ruby slippers which could take her home again.

The Emerald City is like the Church. It is the place where the priest is, and the people come to find the sacraments and symbols to get them in touch with the gifts of grace that are available to them once pointed out. And it is ironic that the thing that kills the Wicked Witch, the evil one in the story, is water. And in our own Christian story, it is water that washes away evil in baptism.

When we are in a cyclone and find ourselves in a strange land where we can't think, feel, or have courage to go on, thank God there is an Emerald City in the center of the land and a Yellow Brick Road to follow, or we would forever be lost. I know—I am Dorothy, I have been lost; I'm the Scarecrow, the frozen Tin Man, and the Cowardly Lion—and I found an Oz and the sacraments of life that helped me to love with all my heart and mind and soul, and to find a home, right here in the Church. And I am convinced that that is a possibility for all the Dorothys in the world—and that includes you.

<u>Oh, yeah. Where is God in all this? God wrote our story.</u>

Amen.

September 13, 1981

Adam Sesom was an ordinary man. He was thrust out of the gates of college some two decades ago, amidst his generational pack, with a corporate and aggressive ambition to catch the fluffy mechanical rabbit known as success. In the subsequent first quarter around the track, he acquired a wife, two children, an upward five-figure salary, and a chronic case of melancholia.

He was now at the age when that previous fluffy illusion of success had expanded the gap between where he was and where it was leading. His chronological age was not the only factor in his slower pace, but all that age about him, which could not be classified as body, seemed to resist the race and incline itself toward a different, new direction that could only be defined as an "other."

That instinctual inclination toward the "other" culminated in an experience that transformed Adam's world. One could call it luck, accident, fate, coincidence, or by a more substantial word like revelation, but by any name, the event was extraordinary. So much so that Adam's wife of twenty years was transformed from a confrontation to a person apart from, and a part of who he was. His two children were changed from intrusions into dual evolving mysteries within which he was both observer and actor. His vocation changed from something he did to an expression of something he was. He decided not only to leave the pack chasing success but also to finish the race at his own pace.

Now, to call this life-changing experience one event would be to call a galaxy one star. But the understanding of one star can define the galaxy. So, in this way, there was one event that symbolized the change of Adam Sesom.

For some time, Adam's only escape from the aggression and intrusion of life was reading. In the last few years, his reading had moved from syrupy fiction to history and philosophy. One night, late, while reading a book on the history of the American Indians of the West, his attention was struck by the description of an ancient tribal rite of passage. He read with increasing fascination the description of this curious tribal rite. The rite was simple: in order for young men to be elevated from the order of brave to warrior, they were first required to pass a series of tests and examinations. The last rite began with the chief instructing the brave to go into the desert, armed with only a skin of water, and to draw a circle in the sand, ten feet in diameter, and to take his place in the center. He was further instructed to remain in the center of that circle for twenty-four hours, mentally recording every event that took place in that twenty-four-hour period. He was then to return to the chief and tell his story and the story of his people using the events that occurred in that day. As Adam finished the ritual description, he felt physiological change. Amidst sweating palms and rapid breathing, he made a vow.

The following Saturday, he left before daybreak armed with only a thermos of water, a notebook, and a pencil. There was not a desert available to him, so he drove to a nearby forest, parked his car, and journeyed into the trees until he found a suitable clearing whereby he might reenact the ancient rite in some desperate act to reclaim the warrior in him.

Perhaps it would be best to let Adam speak for himself as he describes his twenty-four-hour stationary journey in his own journal.

"I have just taken my place in this clearing. I have drawn a circle, ten feet in diameter, and placed myself in the center. If one could image the circle as a clock, I am sitting with my back to the twelve o'clock and facing the six o'clock. The only distinguishing features of the clearing are small shrubs all about, with a lone pine tree at about seven thirty on the clock. I have only this pencil and paper, a thermos of water, and a desire to participate in this primitive ritual, hoping for some encounter with the taunting—'other.'

"The first event, now about one hour into my journey, was the majestic flight of a large bird who flew over the clearing from twelve o'clock to six o'clock. It was as if he was the conductor of the forest orchestra. I hope he has initiated the action for the tune of my time here.

"Just now, at about two o'clock on the circle, a small fawn ventured out into the clearing. Almost simultaneously, at about three o'clock, a black snake crawled from beneath a bush. The three of us, caught in the momentary electricity of unspoken awareness, drank in the threefold contradiction. Almost as quickly as he had come, the fawn darted back into the forest, and in his own time, the snake crawled into the quiet darkness out of which he came.

"As I reflect on this second event, I am reminded that I am a namesake. My thoughts rush to another Adam. The fawn is his unconscious innocence, much like my own early innocence. And the black snake that emerged out of the darkness, is reminiscent of the evil that entered me much like the occurrence in another garden, which set the stage for a continual rehearsal of innocence confronted with evil. Somehow that fawn was destined to see the snake, as I was to see them both, and myself reflected in their eyes.

"It is much later now and my thoughts run from the comedy of my action to the eternal nature of my time and space. As I laugh at myself, tears roll out a fantasy of my being every man who has had to confront himself, in fear and trembling, asking the ultimate questions in the center of unavoidable existence. The twelve o'clock is the birth I did not request and the grave I cannot escape and I am caught in the center laughing and crying trying to find meaning in mere being.

"There must be a pond nearby, because moments ago a mother duck and her ducklings sauntered across the circle at about five o'clock. They were a sight to behold. The mother was in tentative command and the ducklings waddled in an uneven cadence much like a teenage girl in her first set of high heels. My reflective chuckle takes me back to my own adolescence. I, too, followed my parents in uneven cadence testing my newfound legs of identity. In challenge to go my own way, I talked too loud and knew too much and had a body that was capable of more than I had experience to handle. My experience has now somehow caught up with my body, with sufficient external and internal scars for proof. In this moment I have the strong desire to return to that adolescent age of growth and wouldn't return if I could.

"I am now twelve hours into my journey. It is dark and has been raining for over an hour. I am cold, wet, and hungry and perhaps it is best that I don't have rain gear, heat, or food. Because this is my life. All the years before somehow did not prepare me for the dark journey of the soul whether in life at large, or in this limited circle. I agonize now, as I did at home, crying out of my darkness, 'Is there a light in this darkness or mere being?'

"I am only now able to write of the last event of my time here. My words are like the seismographic reading of my rapidly beating heart. Out of the midst of the darkness and rain, at about seven thirty on the circle, lightning struck the lone pine tree and in the intense energy of the flash the tree was consumed in flames. In that instant, I knew the quickness of death. My whole being wrenched in the power of the event. My soul and body were encased in the contradiction of light and darkness and I was somehow the mediator. The source of that light can be only the 'other.' I am somehow both victim and victor of a transformation ritual. If for only a moment, in that light there was no darkness at all. As my consciousness returns, I am aware that I was turned and I have turned. I am now sitting facing the twelve o'clock with my back to the six. I am not only different, I will never be the same again.

"It is now the end of my twenty-four hour lifetime. And at ten o'clock on the circle, a wise owl welcomes a new sunrise. As I re-read the accounts of my stationary journey, I realize that I have only recorded ordinary events of animals, weather, lightning, fire, and trees. Moses had his burning bush, St. Paul his blinding flash, and every man his Christ. Perhaps now I understand that what was great about them was not what happened to them, but that they were able to see the extraordinary in the ordinary.

"As I leave this place, I am reminded of the lines from that popular song, and I rewrite them for the new warrior, 'he was born in the summer of his fortieth year, going home to a place he'd never been before.'"

Amen.

November 1, 1981

Several weeks ago, I came into the parking lot to find against the front wheel of my car a piece of paper. In some knee-jerk reaction of cleanliness is next to godliness, I picked up that piece of paper with a resolve to throw it in the trash. I placed it on the seat next to me, knowing that as soon as I got home, I would take that piece of paper and put it in the wastebasket in the kitchen. The next morning, when I got into the car to come to work, there sat my friend, judging me with those things left undone. With equal resolve, I crushed my silent friend into a ball and placed that piece of paper in my glove compartment, knowing that as soon as I got to work, I would take that piece of paper and put it in the trash basket in my office.

Several days later, while looking for a map in my glove compartment, there sat my crinkled friend, smiling a crooked smile from side to side. With greater resolve, I pulled my mute friend from its compartment and put it in my coat pocket, knowing that as soon as I got out of the car, I would place it in the nearest trash basket. Several weeks later while at a cocktail party, a friend was complimenting me about something I had done, and in a familiar manner, I bowed my head in great humility, toed the carpet, and placed my hand in my right coat pocket, only to find myself brought back to reality about my human nature. That other side of me emerged when I found in my right-hand coat pocket that piece of paper, my crinkled friend. I marched directly, with great resolve, to the kitchen of that house, ready to throw the piece of paper away. When I did so, I decided that I might just take one glance at that piece of paper to see if there was something on it. Maybe…perhaps at last, God had communicated with me uniquely and directly. When I opened the piece of paper, I saw on it a marvelous child's drawing. It was a very primitive drawing of a house with smoke and windows. There was revelation in that to me, because I got in touch with—that is to say, I remembered through that piece of paper—a most wonderful poem by one of my great heroes. It is a poem entitled "Grace's House." It was written by that great mystical monk, Thomas Merton.

As most of you know, Thomas Merton was a Trappist monk at Gethsemane Monastery in Kentucky. I have been a fan of Merton for years. The depth and breadth of his writing and teaching makes him one of the great contemporary humanists and theologians.

Thomas Merton received in the mail at one time a child's drawing. From the child's drawing, he wrote a poem entitled "Grace's House." And as you listen to this poem, you are able to see the wisdom of the childhood drawing—indeed, the wisdom of the child in all of us.

Grace's House

On the summit: it stands on a fair summit
Prepared by winds: and solid smoke
Rolls from the chimney like a snow cloud.
Grace's house is secure.

No blade of grass is not counted,
No blade of grass forgotten on this hill.
Twelve flowers make a token garden.
There is no path to the summit—
No path drawn
To Grace's house.

All the curtains are arranged
Not for hiding but for seeing out.
In one window someone looks out and winks.
Two gnarled short
Fortified trees have knotholes
From which animals look out.
From behind a corner of Grace's house
Another creature peeks out.

Important: hidden in the foreground
Most carefully drawn
The dog smiles, his foreleg curled, his eye like an aster.
Nose and collar are made with great attention:
This dog is loved by Grace!

And there: the world!
Mailbox number 5
Is full of Valentines for Grace.
There is a name on the box, name of a family
Not yet ready to be written in language.

A spangled arrow there
Points from our Coney Island
To her green sun-hill.

Between our world and hers
Runs a sweet river:
(No, it is not the road,
It is the uncrossed crystal
Water between our ignorance and her truth.)

O paradise, O child's world!
Where all the grass lives
And all the animals are aware!
The huge sun, bigger than the house
Stands and streams with life in the east

While in the west a thunder cloud
Moves away forever.

No blade of grass is not blessed
On this archetypal, cosmic hill,
This womb of mysteries.

I must not omit to mention a rabbit
And two birds, bathing in the stream
Which is no road, because
Alas, there is no road to Grace's house!

It is All Saints' Day. My paper friend was two things for me. One, it was a reminder of my imperfect nature. No matter what my good intentions, there are always things left undone. A minor sin, perhaps, but that paper blown across my path was a nagging reality of my nature, my two-sided nature. The inability to rid myself of the paper led me to my second nature, and that is the child in me. That is innocence, naiveté. I must be that child in order to inherit the kingdom of heaven. Merton writes that between our world and Grace's runs a sweet river; it is the uncrossed crystal water between our ignorance and her truth.

On All Saints' Day, we remember all those saints, new and old and eternal, and on this day, we are going to make two new saints. To be baptized is to be sainted. We are going to baptize two babies today and make them saints, as all baptized persons are saints. In the water we are given new life which washes away ignorance and gives birth to truth. In baptism and in the Christ event that baptism rehearses, we are given not simply life everlasting, but eternal life. Life everlasting implies living as we now do. Eternal life implies living life as we are meant to do. Through each phase, we grow. We are baptized and spend the rest of our lives growing into our baptism. We are sainted, or sanctified, and sent on an eternal journey. The closest we can perceive what life looks like in its most natural form is the child. They brought children to Jesus that he might touch them, and the disciples forbade them. Jesus said, "Suffer the little children to come unto me, and forbid them not: for of such is the kingdom of God. Unless you become like a little child you cannot enter therein." And he took them up into his arms, and he blessed them. And people wonder why we Anglicans baptize babies.

On All Saints' Day, we remember all the saints through the halls of history. We make some new ones. We will celebrate the Eucharist, which is the summary of life, old and new. And in order to get to the table to receive your new life, you have to walk through the water first.

The font is the uncrossed crystal water between ignorance and truth. It takes a child to lead us. The child is grace. The child is the Grace in Merton's poem. In that font is the uncrossed crystal water between ignorance and truth, and today we will cross it. We are not bold enough, courageous enough, and are too ignorant to cross it on our own. We will allow the children to go through the water for us, and we will emerge with them as new as the babies who go through before us, because between our world and theirs runs a sweet river. It is the crystal water now crossed. Crossed by the cross of Christ, which makes us saints now and forever.

Amen.

1983

March 6, 1983
Exodus 3:1–15

Moses was a murderer. Moses was a runaway. Moses was a semi-skilled laborer working in his father-in-law's business.

I do love the scripture. I do love our holy lore. I love our sacred story because it is so honest and affirming about who we are and who God is. And here it is again.

The story of the burning bush. The miracle in this story is not the bush that burned and was not consumed. The miracle in the story is that God chose a murderer, a runaway, who was meandering in misery in the desert, looking very little like Charlton Heston. You see, the miracle in our holy lore, our sacred story, is that the Bible is a love story. The burning bush is a fiery example of the story of love between God and his people. Scripture is so honest about who God is and who we are. *The miracle is that God doesn't love us because of who we are, but because of who God is.*

Grace is not cheap, but it is like a cheap tune that, once heard, we can't get out of our heads. Holiness is not something hazy and elusive that we know apart from the earth, but something we can know only as it wells up out of the earth in people, places, and events in the human situation. That is the grace of God and is a tune that turns in my mind, and that miraculous melody is the motif of meaning in our holy love story. The beat goes on. And the tune turns once again in today's Moses melody.

The story is everywhere. Wasn't it odd, that God, should choose, the Jews? Abraham, Isaac, Jacob, Joseph, Moses. The Old and New Testaments play the tune in rapid revolutions: "Holiness is found in humans."

God chose to reveal himself through Moses, a miserable, meandering murderer. He sent him over Moses' own objections of inadequacy to free his people from bondage. God reveals himself to us, through us. In our own earth, in our own country, in our own people, in our own places, in our own events. Where else? Who else? It is a miraculous melody, and I can't remove the tune from my mind.

I am reminded of the Jacob narrative in the book of Genesis. In Isaac's old age, he had borne God's blessing well, and the time had come to pass it on. His twin sons, Jacob and Esau, were timeless expressions of the theory of opposites. In one view we could see Jacob and Esau as one child with twin personalities of opposites. Isaac was old and blind. Esau was in line for the symbolic paternal blessing, as he was born but moments before his twin, Jacob. Yet, spurred on by a neurotic mother complex, Jacob sought to cheat Esau from his birthright and blessing—and he did. This human event was, as always, the context for the holy event.

Holiness is not something hazy and elusive that we know apart from the human, but something that wells up from the human event. And the timeless tune plays on. Holiness wells up in people, even people as clay-footed as Jacob the Crook, and in places as elemental as the river Jabbok, where Jacob eventually wrestled with The Stranger, who was no stranger. Holiness wells up in events, even as seamy as the time Jacob cheated his half-blind father out of Esau's blessing. In that event, Isaac speaks for the holy. When Jacob came to Isaac dressed as his brother, even in spite of his negative nature, his father could smell the blessing. The tune plays on as Isaac says, "See the smell of my son is as the smell of a field which the Lord has blessed!" as Isaac lays his hands on him.

And *there it is!* All in a moment! Jacob betrays his brother, dupes his father, and all but chokes on his own mendacity. Yet, the smell of him is the smell of blessing, because God, no less than Isaac, has chosen to bless him. In spite of everything, Jacob reeks of holiness. His life is as dark, fertile, and holy as the earth itself; he is a bush that burns with everything both fair and foul—yet he is not consumed because God, out of his grace, will not consume him. And the tune plays on...

And the tune may just have a verse with your name. One had better look and listen. Your story is as important as Abraham, Isaac, Jacob, or Moses. Your feet of clay may be wings of truth for someone. You are no better and no worse than our heroes and heroines of holy lore.

God speaks to us, through us. God loves us and desires to use us. That remains a miracle: God doesn't love us because of who we are, but because of who God is. The miracle is that, even though we are apple eaters, we remain the apple of his eye.

Our lives are bushes that burn, yet are not consumed, because God will not extinguish his flame of love.

Holiness is not something elusive that we know apart from the earth, but something we can know only as it wells up out of the earth in people, places, and events in the human situation. That is the grace of God, and it is a tune that turns in my mind, and that miraculous melody will not be extinguished. And the beat goes on, and the tune turns once again in today's Moses melody.

Amen.

❖ ❖ ❖

March 13, 1983
Luke 15:11–32

In the beginning and from the beginning, animals have been analogues to affirm and define humans. By comparison and contrast in parable and fable, animals have been used as metaphor and simile to show the human predicament and alternative.

A popular Eastern fable of the tiger is a paradigm. A motherless tiger cub was adopted by goats and brought up as a goat. He was raised to speak their language, emulate their ways, eat their food, and in general, to believe he was a goat himself. And then, one day a King Tiger came along, and when all the goats scattered in fear, the young tiger was left alone to confront him, afraid and yet drawn to his fear. The King Tiger asked him what he meant by his unseemly masquerade, but all the young one could do in response was bleat nervously and continue nibbling at the grass. So the tiger carried him to a pool where he forced him to look at their two reflections, side by side, and draw his own conclusions. When this revelation was complete, the King Tiger offered the young one a piece of raw meat. As the young tiger began to taste the unfamiliar flesh, his own flesh tingled. He felt his blood warm and the flesh became word. Lashing his tail and digging his claws into the ground, the young beast finally raised his head high, and the jungle trembled at his exultant roar.

Whether in fable or parable, the point is the same: human beings as they usually exist in this world are not what they were created to be. We were created in the image of God; yet, like a mirror that has a crack down the middle, we give back an image that is badly distorted. Like Adam, we were created to love and serve God, and one another, but we re-create God in our own distorted image and choose instead to serve ourselves as God.

Today's Gospel is the Parable of the Prodigal Son. The preacher preaching this parable in Lent is a caricature. Shopworn, predictable, the famous parable, the infamous preacher moralizing how we have all spent our inheritance in riotous living with wine, women, and song—on that question, I will share my Lenten discipline: I have given up singing…

But in spite of the caricature, I do not believe that the parable is essentially about irresponsibility with finances, or strong drink, harlots, or music with ribald rhyme.

The Parable of the Prodigal Son is about God waiting patiently while we decide whether we are animals or persons. This famous parable has its reflection in fable and song. In 1944,

Johnny Burke wrote the words and James Van Heusen wrote the music to a song based on this parable. The song was introduced in the movie *Going My Way* and was sung by Bing Crosby.

You know the song, and I would sing it, but I have given up singing for Lent!

> Would you like to swing on a star?
> Carry moonbeams home in a jar?
> And be better off than you are!
> Or would you rather be a pig?
> A pig is an animal with dirt on his face.
> His shoes are a terrible disgrace.
> He's got no manners when he eats his food.
> He's fat and lazy and extremely rude!
> But if you don't care a feather or a fig
> You may grow up to be a pig!

That is the Parable of the Prodigal Son. God gave his children great wealth called humanity—a gift called grace. We may be graceful or disgraceful. We are free to choose—to be persons or pigs.

The animal analogue visits us always. We are drawn to be swingers on stars or have faces of dirt—mysterious grandeur or pompous dust.

Athletics fascinated me. I spend a great deal of my life in sport. It, too, is analogous to human personality. Sport may be persons at play or animal instinct. It may be skill of body and mind in human harmony of play, or it may be the Missouri Tigers fighting the Arkansas Pigs. Isn't it interesting to realize that most teams are named after animals? The downfall of college and professional athletics may be that people are paid to act like they are playing. The human predicament is played out everywhere. Al McGuire, former NCAA championship coach at Marquette University, says that professional coaches must be smart enough to understand the intricacies of the game, yet dumb enough to think it is important. We call athletes stars or animals.

Would you like to swing on a star? Or would you rather be a pig?

The prodigal son is every person. We take our wealth of grace and spend it on trying to be God and wind up empty, living like pigs.

And yet there remains in us a higher calling. The image of God is within us, and God waits patiently until we discover ourselves. And the son in the pigsty came to himself; he got up off his hands and knees and cried, "I'm a person, not a pig!" And God waits for us to discover him in ourselves. In a world that runs from God, I suspect that maybe God speaks to us most clearly through his silence—his patient, waiting absence—so that we know him best through our missing him. The choice is always ours: Would you like to swing on a star? Carry moonbeams home in a jar? And be better off than you are! Or would you rather be a pig?

Amen.

April 3, 1983
Easter Day
Luke 24:1–10

I love photographs. The walls of our house are lined with family photographs. Birthdays, beach scenes, ball games, sacred places, family faces, events, moments, instants. A photograph captures images of time, but a picture cannot capture time itself. But once a significant time is captured in an image, one can see all time as potentially significant. That image framed on the wall of a baby eating his first ice cream cone does not freeze time, but it does signal the significance of time. The picture is an image, and the image is a symbol, and the symbol points to the significance of the moment for all time. Because a moment is captured in memory by an image, that image can be seen in every instant.

Today we come to celebrate the Easter Instant. There was in history a moment when Jesus was dead, as dead as any living being who no longer lives. The essential ingredient that made the person was gone from the body that housed his personality.

Jesus was dead. And on the third day, all that was essential to the definition of Jesus was alive. The Jesus that lived, died, and what his friends recognized as Jesus the week before was dead, and on the third day the essential Jesus was recognized again after the resurrection. Jesus lived.

Sometime, somewhere between the death of Jesus and his post-resurrection appearances, was the Easter Instant…

We do not come here today to simply celebrate a past event. We do not gather as an Easter people to worship a memory. The images of the Easter Instant found in scripture, song, and symbol are not the objects of our worship. We came today because we know through our experience that the Easter Instant is now, always in the eternal Now.

Our liturgy, our gathered community, our drama, is in a sacred place with a family face. It is a photograph in time. But unless what is framed in this setting is seen in all time, in every place, then we freeze-frame the Easter Instant and it rests with relics of a time no more.

The Easter Instant cannot be captured by a Kodak Instamatic. Any picture of Easter is only an image; the true Easter is in every instant of our lives when we know new life. Easter is only Easter when it is seen in every instant of life. Every heart beat, every breath drawn is an Easter instant. Easter means that in the instant of Jesus' resurrection that all life was redeemed. In the Easter Instant, what is essential in every human being essentially lives. No matter what the situation or circumstance, there is God in Christ redeeming the moment and offering new life even to what apparently is dead. In all time, in each moment, the Easter Instant is present.

We present today a picture of Easter. Lilies and liturgy—community in communion, with one common experience—the Easter Instant. Which is known in the resurrection of Jesus, the living Christ. This picture is an image, and the image is a symbol, and the symbol points to the significance of this moment in every instance of our lives.

I have buried premature babies and feeble old folks. I have sat with shocked parents surviving the deaths of teenagers. I have held the bony hands of cancer patients dying in increments of time. And my experience is that in every tear, from every tragedy and trauma, is reflected the Easter Instant. No glib guarantee, no pietistic platitude on this day—just proclamation and witness of experience in the eternal Easter Instant.

Today is not the day to play the one-sided rationalization game of proving the resurrection. The "seeing is believing" theology is human, to wit: Doubting Thomas, whose doubt was his criterion for sainthood. Today is not the day to set about rational arguments with those who don't believe. We are here because we know that believing is seeing. We believe in the resurrection of Jesus. We are an Easter people. And our believing allows us to see Easter in every instant.

Birthdays, beach scenes, ball games, sacred places, family faces, events, moments—every instant is Easter. Not captured in any moment, but experienced in every moment. Once we believe it, we see it, and once we see it, we see it everywhere.

A priest friend of mine read the burial office for the teenager daughter of one of his best friends. He came to the passage in Romans which is read at most funerals in our community.

When he came to the twenty-eighth verse of the eighth chapter, he read, "We know that all things work together for good to them that love God…" and in his mind he paused. The words ricocheted in his mind like an antiphonal litany of truth. We know…we know…we know… In that traumatic scene, his tears reflected the Easter Instant.

And he read on, with words that every Easter person knows—that nothing separates us from the love of Christ. Neither death, nor life, nor angels, nor principalities, nor powers, nor things present, nor things to come, nor height, nor depth, nor any other creature shall be able to separate us from the Easter Instant.

Amen.

❈ ❈ ❈

April 17, 1983
Acts 9:1–19

One of my definitions of love is "that I like you more than I don't like you." In a similar vein, perhaps a definition of greatness is that one becomes great only when he gives himself to something greater.

I want to talk about Saul of Tarsus today. Better known as St. Paul, but for our purposes, Saul of Tarsus will do. Paul became a saint because of his ability to finally give himself to something more holy than his own ego—and it took something great to be greater than Saul's ego.

I like Paul more than I don't like him. The list of reasons to like Saul/Paul is manifold. The fact that he wrote or influenced over one-half of the New Testament writings makes him unavoidable in admiration. His definitive doctrines on grace, justification by faith, ecclesiology, and evangelism make him a cornerstone in God's revelation of what it means to be a Christian and what it means to be the Christian Church.

But...one of the things I don't like about Paul is his conversion experience. The first reason today is that famous—or, in my case, infamous—story of the Damascus Road conversion. Need we rehearse the story of the blinding flash, that noonday indictment when Saul was left in the dust out of which he had come? There he was, the silver-tongued lawyer from the Hebrew court, lying on the ground, laid out inanimate, with dust in his mouth and blind as a bat. Only moments before, so secure in his self-righteousness, with Stephen's blood on his hands and the law in his pocket—off to Damascus to drag Christians to kangaroo court and then throw a party for them—not telling them that it was a rock concert, and the Christians were the only ones getting stoned.

My problem with Saul's conversion is not the story, but how the story has been misunderstood and misused.

First: the misunderstanding. Paul was not converted *on* the road to Damascus. Saul was indicted in a flash of truth, in the voice of Christ. Indictment does not mean conversion. One can be conscious of his sin, and yet continue to sin.

Confession means saying, "I am sorry." Repentance means doing something to ensure it won't happen again. An alcoholic can be indicted by family, friends, and the law as an alcoholic and still be one. He can even confess that he is an alcoholic, yet until he quits drinking, he is not changed into health.

Paul was *confronted* with his evil on the road to Damascus. But, he was *converted* in the Christian community. After he was told the truth by God in Christ in an undeniable experience, he was then taken to a home, where Ananias held him in his hands and said, "Saul, God likes you more than he doesn't like you. Even though you've got young Stephen's blood on your haughty hands, God loves you just the way you are, but you've got a choice to make: are you going to continue to wallow in the dirt, or do you want to be whole? The Lord Jesus himself appeared to you and sent me to hold you in my hands. Your evil side is strong, but God's Holy Spirit is stronger. You've got a decision to make: is it dirt or spirit you want to be?" That's a rough translation. And now a literal translation: "Then [Paul] rose..." It doesn't say he was raised up by Ananias; it doesn't say God lifted him up. It says he, Paul, got up on his own.

"Then [Paul] rose and was baptized, and took food and became strong again." The truth of that story is that Paul was convicted by the Spirit and was converted by love. And he found that love in the community. The Church gave him a bath and a meal. Baptism and Eucharist. And perhaps most importantly, Paul had to get up on his own. God convicts, and in Christ, provides the strength to overcome evil, but one must respond. Paul, like each of us, was not a victim, but a participant. God provides the opportunity and strength for change, but we are free to reject it. Paul chose spirit over dirt, but there was no guarantee that he would, or that because he did that anyone else will. But if Paul can, anyone can.

Secondly, not only is this story misunderstood, it is often misused. Simply stated, this is the story of Paul's conviction and conversion. It is neither the norm nor the model of all Christian conversion experiences. Many are told, or feel, that unless one has a blinding flash on a dusty road, one is not truly converted. Each person has his own encounter with Christ. The only similarity between any conversion and Paul's is that each of us has to choose between dirt and spirit. And only you can choose, and you have to do more than say "I don't want to be dirty"; you have to get up and have a bath. God loves us dirty or clean, but he likes us better when our faces are clean because then he can recognize us the way he made us.

Don't worry if you haven't had a Damascus Road experience. All that means is that you aren't Paul. And you can thank God for that. But you must remember that Paul's greatness did not lie in his abilities. His greatness came in the fact that he gave himself to something greater than himself.

He found his life by giving it up. Convicted by God, converted by love, Saul chose what he was chosen to be—that is, Paul—and that is why we know him as a saint.

All said and done, I like the story of Paul's conversion more than I don't like it.

Amen.

May 1, 1983
Acts 13:44–52; John 13:31–35

Life is lived somewhere between revelation and reality. Without revelation, reality is unbearable. Without reality, revelation is irrelevant.

Today's Gospel is the revelation of a new truth: "A new commandment I give to you, that you love one another; even as I have loved you, that you also love one another. By this all men will know that you are my disciples…"

Today's first lesson from the Acts of the Apostles is reality: "[the disciples were rejected]… the devout women of high standing and the leading men of the city…stirred up persecution against Paul and Barnabas and drove them out of their district. But they shook off the dust from their feet against them, and went to Iconium."

The revelation is the warm wrapping of grace in the incarnate love of Christ: that we are loved by God in Christ, and we must love one another as we are first loved, and others will see Christ in us.

The reality is that sometimes, even for saints like Paul and Barnabas, love is rejected. Freedom is the ingredient that lives in both worlds. Freedom is revealed as the grace of God, which is the ingredient that makes us human. Yet, at the same time, freedom is the harsh reality that rejects the graceful ingredient. Freedom is that gift which makes us human and yet frees us to choose to be less than human. Freedom lives in the world of revelation *and* the world of reality…reception and rejection.

We live our lives somewhere between the warm revelation and the cold reality. I offer today examples of each from two opposite corners of contemporary literature: one from chilling writer Flannery O'Connor and the other from the warm puppy Snoopy.

Flannery O'Connor, recognized as one of America's great writers, died in 1964, and her popularity is now rising. Ten years ago, I was given a book of her short stories entitled *A Good Man Is Hard to Find*. In that collection, enigmatic as it is, I discovered, as have many others, that O'Connor wrote from a Christian point of view; however, her writing was far from pious or even obvious. Her stories are blunt, cold, and harsh. She wrote about reality. She wrote about people as she saw them—self-centered, misled, silly, sometimes brutal, often ignorant—but indeed, ordinary people. She wrote about the struggle between revelation and reality—of people offered grace who both accept it and refuse it. In *A Good Man Is Hard to Find*, the short story which titles the book, O'Connor gives us a misfit and a grandmother as lead characters. The grandmother leads her son and daughter-in-law on a wild goose chase down a deserted dirt road to find a house she thinks she remembers as a young girl. There, she and her family are confronted by an escaped murderer called The Misfit. While his pals systematically kill members of her family, the old woman talks to the killer about Jesus. The Misfit says he wishes he'd been there to see Jesus…if he'd seen it himself, things might have turned out differently. As he goes on, the old woman "saw the man's face twisted close to her own as if he were going to cry and she murmured, 'Why you're one of my babies. You're one of my own children!' She reached out and touched him on the shoulder. The Misfit sprang back as if a snake had bitten him and shot her three times through the chest. Then he put his gun down on the ground and took off his glasses and began to clean them."

Cold reality is Flannery O'Connor's contribution…the old woman offered the Misfit love, the underserved gift of God. "You're a child of God," she said to him, "one of my babies, one of my own children," and when she touched him, he perceived it as the bite of the snake of evil…of course he cleaned his glasses after he shot her. He couldn't see the grace of God revealed to him in the touch of love. Freedom means you are free to reject even God's love. That's the cold reality.

But Easter people see. And what we see is more than the cold reality. We see the warm revelation. And though we live somewhere between revelation and reality, it is the revelation that makes the reality bearable.

In *The Gospel According to Peanuts*, Snoopy, the warm puppy, dressed in a flannel bathrobe and slippers, is philosophizing on health care. "I think I have discovered something." (Snoopy looks woebegone and slightly under the weather.) "Why, when you wake up at night and your head hurts and your stomach feels funny…the first thing you do is put on your bathrobe, then you drink a glass of water and take some pills and sit by yourself in the dark until you're ready to go back to bed. But it's not the pills that make you feel better—it's the bathrobe!"

Life is lived somewhere between the cold reality and the warm revelation. Without reality, revelation is irrelevant. Without revelation, reality is unbearable.

The revelation of God in Christ is that no matter how bad life is or we are, he loves us—we are his babies, his children—we are free to see that revelation or reject it. And, no matter how cold the reality or how dark the night, we can sit warmed, wrapped in the bathrobe of grace.

Amen.

May 22, 1983
Pentecost

I am fascinated with the impersonal pronoun "it." The use of the pronoun betrays the religious nature of man, and also betrays the contemporary agnosticism found in modern man.

If there is any motto that sums up the religious need in this generation, it is to be found in the desire to be "with it." People are authenticated, judged worthy, justified and affirmed with the descriptive prepositional phrase "with it." One's authenticity is decided: "He's really with it!" One is judged worthy: "He finally got with it." One is justified and affirmed on the basis of whether or not one is "with it."

There is also a call to be with it. A prophetic call that beckons one forth to it. It is a judging word from on high—"get with it."

And finally, there is a prescription for how to "get with it" in order to "be with it," and that is to "go for it."

This is the religious nature of the human. There is something outside ourselves that authenticates, calls, judges, and affirms. We need "it" in order to be.

Advertisers know this unconscious, primordial need in humans. They guarantee that their products will make us have it in order to be with it. And of course, out of our need to be with it, we buy it—literally and figuratively. In *The Serial: A Year in the Life of Marin County*, Cyra McFadden writes about having and being:

> Kate went about her rounds. She stopped at Phillips for some Chemex filters and her own special blend of Madagascar, Senegalese, and caffeine-free French roast, picked up a copy of *Zen and the Art of Motorcycle Maintenance*. She wound up at the Mill Valley Market to pick up fresh veggies for her Cuisinart, some smashing new cleaner for her Brown Jordon patio furniture. The market was swarming with young mothers in tennis dresses… despite the fact that she and Harvey hadn't finalized the parameters of their own interface, mainly because they still didn't agree on just how open their marriage ought to be, they were just terrifically stable right now…
>
> Harvey didn't make the scene at home at all Friday night before Kate moved out, so she left a note propped between the Salton Peanut Butter Maker and the microwave, giving him her new address and reminding him to feed Kat Vonnegut, Jr., who, she said, was "into Meow Mix."

Kate and Harvey never quite got "with it"!

The "it" we desire is sold to us. If we buy certain things, be seen certain places, or do certain things that are with it—wherever it is—we will be too.

Judith Viorst, a few years ago, wrote a collection of poems entitled *It's Hard to Be Hip Over Thirty*. Her most recent book is *How Did I Get to Be 40 & Other Atrocities*. She writes:

> I've finished six pillows in Needlepoint,
> And I'm reading Jane Austen and Kant,
> And I'm up to the pork with black beans in Advanced Chinese Cooking.
> I don't have to struggle to find myself
> For I already know what I want.
> I want to be healthy and wise and extremely good-looking.
>
> I'm learning new glazes in Pottery Class,
> And I'm playing new chords in Guitar,
> And in Yoga I'm starting to master the lotus position.
> I don't have to ponder priorities
> For I already know what they are:
> To be good-looking, healthy, and wise.
> And adored in addition.
>
> I'm improving my serve with a tennis pro,
> And I'm practicing verb forms in Greek,
> And in Primal Scream Therapy all my frustrations are vented.
> I don't have to ask what I'm searching for

> Since I already know what I seek
> To be good-looking, healthy, and wise.
> And adored.
> And contented.
>
> I've bloomed in Organic Gardening,
> And in Dance I have tightened my thighs,
> And in Consciousness Raising there's no one around who can top me.
> And I'm working all day and I'm working all night
> To be good-looking, healthy, and wise.
> And adored.
> And contented.
> And brave.
> And well-read.
> And a marvelous hostess,
> Fantastic in bed,
> And bilingual,
> Athletic,
> Artistic…
> Won't somebody please stop me?

The nature of human beings is that we want something beyond ourselves to justify us. And there is a profit to be made by promising us—"it."

So the pronoun "it" tells us of our nature. That pronoun also tells us of our theology. For "it" does not refer to anything. The "it" is impersonal. "It" is an unknown God. Agnosticism cannot name a god.

Religion, most particularly the Christian religion, proclaims that it is God, the source of all, that creates, sustains, calls, and accepts humans. We refer to God with personal pronouns.

Today, appropriately on Pentecost, we are telling one another and a baby girl and her family that she is created, sustained, called into life, and accepted by God. We do not refer to this child as "it." We name her Lindsay Catherine Willeford. And we are here to tell her and remind ourselves that she is not an it, nor is she a child of it. She is a child of God.

As long as our theology is an "it" theology, we will wander from one god to another, trying to be with it. We will name these gods with names like power, success, eros, or material. We will love power and never know the power of love.

The "it" we want to be with is, and has always been, God, and his Holy Spirit. Pentecost is the day to remember this. When we love deeply or are deeply loved, we feel "with it"—and that is because a spirit enters us that is other than human and by definition is, therefore, holy. And so we say to Lindsay Catherine Willeford: Come on! Get with it! Go for it! And when we do, we know what we are talking about—and pray she will too.

Amen.

❖ ❖ ❖

June 12, 1983
Luke 7:36–50

    We all have suppressed desires. I would not be so bold as to share all of mine with you. But one I have, I think appropriate to share this morning. I have a Walter Mitty desire to be a movie director. I know very little about the motion picture art form or its technical side, but that's not the nature of my desire. My desire has revealed itself in an interesting way. When I read, I inevitably wind up staging the narrative in a mental movie. And, I am the director. As I read and studied today's Gospel from Luke, I found myself directing this story as if it were a movie. Perhaps it would be helpful if we looked at this story in just that way.

    Scene: Camera follows Pharisee. He is a large man who fills out his ample robe; his arm is around Jesus' shoulder in a paternal gesture as they walk toward the Pharisee's home. Jesus is smaller in stature. He stares at the ground as they walk. Camera pulls back to reveal the street scene. Several follow Jesus and his host. There is an assortment of people. Some seem to be outcasts. Others, curiosity seekers. Others walk closely with purpose, as if they are included in the party. Several seem in serious discussion. Others, who line the walk, stop what they are doing and watch the group as they proceed toward the Pharisee's house. Camera pans a wall, approximately five feet tall. The wall protects an interior dwelling. The wall is made of what at one time was mud brick, but now has weathered to a single dirty brown and blank surface. Camera now inside compound and catches Jesus and the Pharisee entering a small gate in the wall. They are followed by the group. They are all men, dressed as cultured citizens befitting rabbis or other Jewish hierarchy. The gate closes. The camera, now back outside the gate, pans an assortment of peasants and outcasts who strain to see in the gate or over the wall. The camera, now placed on the wall, pans the courtyard interior. There are large tiles in the center section, clean swept, but still stained by years of weather and wear. In one corner of the courtyard is a sleeping quarter; in another is the cooking area with a large open fire, smoke rising from it. There is a small grinding stone; several clay pots are scattered about. In the center of the courtyard, a shelter covers the eating area. A thatch roof is the covering, supported by four rough-hewn cedar posts. Under the covering is a long table with pallets on either side for those who recline at meal.

    As the guests assemble around the table, the camera catches Jesus talking with those preparing the meal, mostly embarrassed women and young girls. There are two or three dogs sleeping or walking about. A rooster and several hens have been scattered to one corner by the courtyard activity.

    The camera focuses on the host, who beckons all to be seated. Special attention is paid to Jesus as the host calls him to the place next to him at the head of the table. The camera comes in close on the face of the Pharisee, who has the look of a man with mixed motivations.

His face holds a benign smile, yet his eyes cut nervously at his guest. The host offers a blessing, and the remaining guests recline about the table on the pallets. The table is a scene of much animated talk and activity. The camera is now placed in the corner of the courtyard, revealing the table scene. The head of the table is between the camera and the courtyard gate; the gate is not visible to the host or Jesus. The camera catches a woman slipping in the gate. She wears around her neck a flask of alabaster. She moves silently in behind the two at the head of the table. She is dressed as a woman of the street. Her face is hard, with too much makeup. Her eyes have a contradictory look of shiftiness and humility. Her hair is long and uncovered, black, with a soiled ribbon loosely affixed, threatening to fall. She walks as if on a mission, with purpose, but quietly, as if fearful of premature discovery. The camera follows her as she takes her place behind Jesus. The host is startled, recognizing her as a local prostitute. The camera centers. He has a scandalized look on his face. The camera then pans the table as the guests whisper and point. Jesus' eyes are forward. His face does not change expression. The woman fumbles with the flask around her neck and begins to cry. It is as if she had planned to anoint Jesus' head, but she suddenly drops to her knees from behind him—he is reclining—and she wipes his feet with her hair. The ribbon that was loosely fixed now falls to the weathered tile. Her actions seem unconscious. She suddenly remembers her task and anoints Jesus' feet with the ointment. She remains in a humiliated position at the feet of Jesus. The camera then pulls back, showing the scene of the woman, Jesus, and the host. The host says aloud, as if presented with evidence in a court case, to no one but for everyone to hear, "If this man were a prophet, he would have known who and what sort of woman this is who is touching him, for she is a sinner." The camera shows the smug look of a lawyer on the host's face, as if he is summarizing an argument before the jury. There is a long pause. The camera focuses on Jesus as he looks up from the woman. He faces the host, tilts his head with a faint movement from side to side as if in frustration, and finally says, "Simon, I have something to say to you." His voice is direct but patient. The camera catches the Pharisee folding his arms, petting his chin, and answering impatiently, "And what is it, Teacher?" The camera moves around the table and Jesus speaks. "A certain creditor has two debtors: one owed five hundred denarii, and the other fifty. When they could not pay, he forgave them both. Now which of them will love him more?" The camera stops on the face of the Pharisee as he looks away from Jesus and grabs a cup of wine. He draws it to his mouth, and as he answers, he does so disinterestedly, "The one, I suppose, to whom he forgave more." He gulps the wine as he finishes his answer. Jesus' eyebrows lift and his eyes light. He raises his voice, saying, "You have judged rightly." Jesus stands quickly, then kneels with the woman, places his arm around her, and looks into her eyes while he speaks to the Pharisee. The camera focuses on the two kneeling figures while Jesus pleads, "Do you see the woman?" The camera cuts to the face of the host. His eyes dart to the guests and back to the two kneeling. Jesus continues. The camera captures host, woman, and Jesus, and moves, circling them. "Do you see this woman?" Jesus repeats. He then stands and continues, "I entered your house, but you gave me no water for my feet, but she has wet my feet with her tears and wiped them with her hair." The camera follows Jesus around the table as he speaks. "You gave me no kiss, but she kissed my feet. You didn't even anoint my head, but she has anointed my feet with ointment."

Jesus reaches the head of the table and speaks to all. "Therefore, I tell you, her sins, which are many, are forgiven." Camera focuses on the woman. "For she loved much." He speaks directly to the host now. "But he who is forgiven little, loves little." Jesus bends down, grasping the woman by both arms and pulling her up, and says quietly, "Your sins are forgiven." There is much murmuring and movement going on about the table. One yells out, "Who is this, who even forgives sins?" The camera moves back to Jesus, who continues to hold the woman up, and focuses on the two as Jesus says directly to the woman, "Your faith has saved you: go in peace." The woman gives Jesus a quick embrace, turns, and hurries out the gate. The scene ends with Jesus watching her exit, standing alone. The image fades to black.

Now that is the story through my mind's eye. Since we have encountered it in the particular, we can now generalize. So here is the sermon:

Jesus was not the Christ because of his teaching—there were other great teachers.

Jesus was not the Christ because of the faith of the apostles—that came later.

Jesus was the Christ because he could love people unconditionally as only God can do. Even the unlovable.

And Jesus was the Christ because he loved people with all his heart and with all his soul and with all his mind. He is the Christ for us when we love him in the same way.

Amen.

June 19, 1983
Luke 9:18–24

Anyone who has heard me preach for some time knows that I feel that today's Gospel is the essence of the existential faith. If one is to be bold enough to call himself Christian and to say "yes" to the contours of that claim, then he must live out the Gospel lesson for today. This lesson forces a focus on the question: "What is the essential ingredient in being Christian?" If Christianity has a litmus test of who is Christian and who is not, it will not be found in doctrine, dogma, discipline, creed, canon, or catechism; the test will be in the singular question of today's Gospel. And the answer will then confront one with a claim, the contours of which are also included in this essential question and statement.

The Gospel from Luke's portrait of Jesus begins, "Now it happened that as [Jesus] was praying..." I wish there were an exclamation mark after the first three words. The way it is punctuated begins the narrative as it should, as an incident. But what follows is not incidental. I wish it read: "*Now* it happened!" so that it would be clear that what follows is no incidental event, but the essential event of the Gospel.

"*Now* it happened! As Jesus was praying alone, the disciples were with him; and he asked them, 'Who do the people say that I am?' And they answered, 'John the Baptist; but others say, Elijah; and others, that one of the old prophets has risen!'" And then he faced them and narrowed the focus to one penetrating beam of essence with the essential question of all Christianity: "But who do *you* say that I am?"

One cannot be Christian unless he answers this question personally. The Bible, the creeds, the doctrines of faith tell us about Jesus. One cannot become Christian by knowing information about Jesus. If being Christian means knowing information about Jesus, then we are what Herb O'Driscoll calls "a planetary memorial society, carrying a yellowing picture of the past." To be Christian is not satisfied in knowing about Jesus. Being Christian does not mean knowing Jesus as the Christ. Being Christian means knowing Jesus as your Christ.

Who do y*ou* say that he is for you? This question is not very far in sound from the popular pietistic language of the Bible Belt boondocks of my youth. More than once I have encountered the judgmental tone of the question: "Do you know Jesus Christ as your personal Lord and Savior?" The implication being that if you do, you wear a white hat which will be the ticket to heaven when the sheep are separated from the goats. And if you answer "no," you are unclean, unredeemed, and wear a black hat which leads one to a hell of fire and worms, which is not at all what I am saying. I am saying that if you claim to be Christian, then you must see Jesus as your Christ. If you don't, all it means is that you aren't Christian. God will be the judge of those who aren't Christian—not I. And the older I get, the more confused I become about who I am, but the clearer it becomes that I am not God.

If, then, we are to know Jesus as our Christ, how are we to know him? We are not with him as Peter was. How do we know him personally, lo these nearly two thousand years later?

I would suggest that we know him in at least four ways:

1. We know him in Book.
2. We know him in Community.
3. We know him in Meal.
4. We know him in Spirit.

Book: The Bible is a love story between God and his people. The climax of the story is that God loved the human so much that he became one. There are four portraits of God in history. Portraits according to Matthew, Mark, Luke, and John. If you want to know if Jesus is the Christ for you, then you must know what he said, what he did, and what his friends and enemies said about him and did to him. The portraits suggest that he was either a megalomaniac or the Christ. More claim the latter than the former. One of the portraits claims the word became flesh. If you want to know that, you need to read the word in the flesh. This book lives because it proclaims life. This book is the Christian book because it proclaims Jesus as the Christ. If you want to know Jesus, you have to know the book.

Community: The word of the book is best spread by word of mouth. Sometimes that word of mouth is a kiss. The most common way one knows that God loves him is when someone tells him and shows him. An easy way to visualize community is to realize that when someone puts his hand out to you in the name of Christ, he is only doing for you what was done for him. And one hand reaches out, forming a communion of saints. One hand clasps another, and there is an unbroken chain that leads back to the hand at the beginning, and that hand has the print of nails in its palm. What we have in common is Christ, and he reveals himself in love. When the word is a kiss and a held hand in Jesus' name, he is known. In Christian community, that is not uncommon or unknown.

Meal: The Eucharist is a sacrament. A sacrament is a time machine. It literally kills time. The meal makes the Christ event happen again. The meal comes after the book is read in community, and the event is played out and it happens again—for some, for the first time—and there is no time in the Presence. He is known in the breaking of bread.

Spirit: The Spirit is the principle of continuity in time with the reality of Christ. Better said, the Holy Spirit is the wings on which the Word flies through history. The Spirit's wings turn the pages of the book. When one is in the community, the word of mouth in kiss and held hand, the fluttering felt is the winds of the Spirit. When one sees the event in the broken bread, it is a bird's-eye view from the dove of love—the essence of Christ in the experience of word, love, and sacrament.

I hope you know Jesus as your Christ. But let me end by reminding you that to know Jesus as the Christ places a claim on you, and the contours of that claim can be rough—as rough as the splintered wood of a cross. If you accept Jesus as your Christ, it will cost you your life. You will have to give up all other saviors with names like success, power, wealth, safety, and ego. John Cheever said that "the main emotion of the adult American who has all the advantages of wealth, education and culture is disappointment"—so maybe those saviors die eventually on their own. In return, you are given the promise of a word, the kiss of a community, a meal ticket, and a bird's-eye view of what abundance really means.

Who do the people say that he is?

Who do you say that he is?

Of that question be more careful than of anything…

Amen.

July 17, 1983
Genesis 18:1–14

Faith and laughter have so much in common. In today's lesson from Genesis, Abraham is sitting by his tent door getting some relief from the heat, when out of the oak grove appears the Lord's messengers in the shimmers of the desert heat. Abraham welcomes them and prepares a fine noonday meal. While eating under the tree, they ask about Sarah, and their knowing her first name is the clear clue that they represent God. Sarah has not been introduced to them and is not present. Abraham replies that she is in the tent, which, of course, means she is within hearing distance. The messengers tell Abraham that in the spring his ninety-year-old wife will have a son. Sarah hears this, and being a post-menopausal woman, she knows the facts of life, so she laughs. The Lord then says to Abraham, "Why did Sarah laugh...Is anything too hard for the Lord?"

Well, as you know, nine months later Sarah did bear a child. And, she and old Abe named their only child Isaac. The word "Isaac" in Hebrew means laughter. The name was an obvious attempt to keep the joke alive.

Voltaire once said, "God is a comedian playing to an audience afraid to laugh." If Voltaire is right, then we, the audience, ought by now to have learned to laugh. Sarah and Abraham saw the subtle humor. Maybe the best way to surmount our own exasperating foibles is with a smile and, when appropriate, a good belly laugh. Laughter is, of course, like any part of human nature: it is simply potential. Laughter has its healing quality and its dark side.

Several years ago, Norman Cousins, editor of the *Saturday Review*, became suddenly ill. His disease was diagnosed as a chronic, progressive disease inflaming the joints of the spine. He was told that his chances of recovery were about one in five hundred. Cousins recorded the events of his malady in a book, *Anatomy of an Illness*. As he discussed his case with his doctors, they agreed that it was probably caused by stress. He asked himself the question: if negative emotions could cause illness, is it possible that positive emotions could result in cure? Cousins began to talk with his physician about his theory. The doctor concurred with the theory and agreed to an experiment. Cousins moved out of the hospital to a hotel.

There, he set up a screen and a projector and watched relaxing and humorous films. Cartoons, old *Candid Camera* episodes, Laurel and Hardy, and the Marx Brothers movies were viewed by Cousins. When he tired of comedies, someone would read to him from joke books and from articles by humorists. After watching one of the films for only ten minutes, he was able to sleep for two hours without pain. After a week, he could move his fingers without pain and he was sleeping restfully. Within a few months, he had recovered sufficiently to return to work. His only medication was laughter and vitamin C. He laughed himself well.

The new medical discovery of endorphins may be a key. These pituitary secretions called endorphins are somehow related to laughter and its beneficial effects. Endorphins are chemically related to opiates, such as heroin and morphine, and act to reduce and replace pain with feelings of elation. Many joggers experience a state of euphoria that is related to the amount of beta-endorphins in their bloodstreams. The endorphins act to relieve pain and tension, and can relieve stress and promote healing. Laughter is healthy.

But laughter has its dark side also. Freud reflected that laughter may be an expression of bitterness and underlying anxiety. Others have seen laughter as masking insecurity and fear, hence so many jokes about sex, religion, and death. Psychologist Henri Bergson, in an essay on the meaning of laughter, saw hostility in laughter. Laughing can be a feeling of superiority to someone else. Many jokes are jokes on someone else, noting the number of jokes about mothers-in-law, drunks, minorities, etc.

Laughter's light and dark side are related, yet not quite to the point of Sarah's laughter in today's story. Today's story is confirming laughter's light side as being healing, but it is also saying something about the nature of faith.

In an earlier part of the Genesis story, God had called Abraham out of a secure home and made a covenant or contract with him that he would be Abraham's God and, in return, he promised Abraham a land and a people.

So Abraham and Sarah set off, following nothing but a promise. And here they were, almost a hundred years old, and no land and no child, so had God broken his promise? Had God let them down? They had given up everything to follow this God and had nothing to show for their faith. And then, finally, when everything seemed lost, in comes God, in the fourth quarter, and fulfills his promise. Sarah's laughter healed the pain of sacrifice, and yet, it was more than a narcotic. Her laughter was a response to the faithfulness of God. Her laughter was at her own human doubt. Her laughter was pure, unabashed joy. As there is no faith without doubt, there is no joy without laughter. Faith and laughter have much in common.

In 1971, a priest friend came to me with his life in shambles. His marriage had fallen apart. He had become involved with another woman. His wife was an emotional wreck, and he wanted me to counsel them as a last effort before divorce.

Both were bright, attractive, and capable. One of the great areas of disappointment in their lives had been her inability to conceive a child. They had traveled all over the country in search of answers to her infertility. This issue had become the focal point of a very complicated psychodrama they were living.

Through much time, effort, grace, and a consultation with a psychiatrist friend, they began to pick up the pieces of their lives. They learned that some basic personality differences had created tensions that resulted in mutual blame centered in their inability to have a child. Once the dark incompatibilities had come to light, they decided to accept their differences and incumbent insecurities and learn to live their lives in a new, less romantic, yet more mature and healthy commitment. They left in 1972 for him to take a position as university chaplain on the East Coast. I didn't hear from them for two years.

In 1974, I received a phone call from my priest friend. They had just birthed their first child. Their doubt about their relationship and ability, and the recommitment of faithfulness to one another, had given them a new life and the child was the result. I asked before we hung up the phone, "By the way, what did you name your new daughter?" The reply was, "We named her Joy." I laughed.

Amen.

✠ ✠ ✠

July 24, 1983
The Ordination of Diane Jost to the Deaconate
II Corinthians 4:1–6

Let's talk about hermeneutics! Since it is apparent that you have nothing to say about it, I'll go first!

We are here to ordain Diane Jost to the Sacred Order of Deacons. It is a pleasant—indeed, a holy—task to so do. We are pleased that Diane has chosen to be ordained here at Christ Church Cathedral. Being a graduate of our seminary in Austin, having trained as a resident in Clinical Pastoral Education at St. Luke's Hospital, and considering the fact that she will be the first female staff chaplain at St. Luke's, and further considering that the Cathedral has been her church for the past year, it is most appropriate that she be ordained here.

Further, it is a pleasure to have the Right Reverend Herbert Donovan, the bishop of Arkansas, here today. Diane is a candidate for Holy Orders from the Diocese of Arkansas, and this provides a warm reunion for me, as Bishop Donovan is a dear friend. And I'm sure it is a pleasure for Bishop Donovan to be here, as he ordinarily is the preacher at services at which he presides. And this provides a rare opportunity for him to hear some good preaching.

Gordon Swope is back in the Cathedral, presenting Mrs. Jost to the bishop. Gordon was her rector at St. Mark's parish in Little Rock. Gordon is a child of this diocese and now retired here. Of course, here he is known as Dorothy Swope's nephew. Don't worry, Gordon, in Houston I'm known as Dorothy Swope's priest.

Whether you realize it or not, we have been talking about hermeneutics. Hermeneutics is the theological discipline of interpretation. It usually refers to the interpretation of the Bible, its exegesis and application to life, but it can typically also refer to the reflections upon any other sacred text, e.g., creeds, liturgies, and doctorial definitions.

Ministry, and most particularly, the ordained ministry, is a living hermeneutical principle. Bishop Donovan, in his role as Overseer Episcopas, is a symbolic hermeneutic of the incarnation. Gordon Swope, as priest, is a part of the ministry of the bishop as specific location of the Episcopal ministry in a person and place. Diane Jost, as deacon, is called and ordained as a hermeneutical symbol as she assists bishops and priests, with a special responsibility as servant, who represents Christ to the poor, sick, suffering, helpless children of God.

All these three orders then enable the priesthood of *all* believers as that truth is interpreted in hermeneutical symbol known as the Sacrament of Ordination.

This idea first came to me in a late-night conversation with the Very Reverend Urban Holmes, late dean of our seminary at the University of the South. Before Terry Holmes' untimely death in August of 1981, he was one of the Church's great contemporary theologians. In our conversation at Camp Allen several years ago, Dean Holmes first introduced me to the concept of ministry as hermeneutical principle. I was pleased to see this written down in his book, *Spirituality for Ministry*, which was published posthumously last year.

Holmes reminds us that the word "hermeneutic" comes from the name of a Greek god, Hermes, who was the messenger between humans and the gods. There are some interesting things to learn about ministry from Hermes. First, Hermes was sometimes thought of as androgynous. Ordained ministry is now recognized to hold the integration of the masculine and feminine principles of creation. Paul says that in Christ there is no male and female. There is no distinction in the eyes of God in the quality of gender. Both principles of masculinity and femininity are integral parts of the gift of personhood. Each person, indeed, holds qualities of each. Modern science and analytical psychology alike point to the reality that each person, both in body and personality, holds masculine and feminine qualities. The goal of the journey of wholeness is not to simply be a man or woman, but to become a person. And a healthy personality is the integration of both principles.

Ordained ministry, then, is an interpretation of the sacred truth or personhood. The title "parson" is an ecclesiastical title derived from the word "person." The hermeneutical principle of ordination is the responsibility of the ordained one to be fully a person and to represent that truth as the word of God, incarnate in his symbolic messenger, the parson.

A second quality of Hermes was that he was a trickster. He was full of surprises and, at times, a bit irreverent. The hermeneutic found herein is that the ordained one, as interpreter of God, must subvert the presumptions of humankind. The ordained person never lets the world assume that things are as they appear to be. As I am fond of saying, the world tries to convince us that plastic is wood. The secular world places a veneer of superficiality on the issue of being human beings in relationship to God.

Paul Tillich wrote, and I have it framed in my office as a reminder to me: "I sometimes think it is my mission to bring faith to the faithless and doubt to the faithful." The ordained one must represent to the world that Christianity has turned the world upside down. As Ted Wedel wrote, the American dream is to go from the log cabin to the White House. The Christian story is going from the White House to a log cabin. Jesus' parables, when studied, have a hermeneutical interpretation to change a worldview. If you don't believe that, ask the older brother in the Parable of the Prodigal Son or the laborer who had worked all day and received only as much as those who came late in the day.

The ordained one must be a hermeneutical symbol of the richness in poverty, the health in sickness, and the freedom in service.

Hermes did not carry his own message. The ordained, as interpreter of God to humankind and humankind to God, is an instrument of knowing, not the source. Christ is the sacrament of God. In the Incarnation, the manifest humanity of Jesus is the mediation of God and Man. Ordained persons are not God or Christ, only symbolic representations of that. If it is true that the ordained person participates in the sacramentality of Christ, then far more is it true that the authority of her or his office is derived from God and he or she is called to be a messenger. In today's epistle, Paul writes to this very point in his second letter to Corinth, "For what we preach is not ourselves, but Jesus Christ, as Lord, with ourselves as your servants, for Jesus' sake."

Lastly, Hermes traveled a difficult road. According to Greek mythology, chaos is the land between the gods and humanity. To be ordained means to be willing to enter chaos with the messenger of God in Christ. The ordained one must be willing to go into dark places with other humans. The hermeneutic principle is the interpretation of God's love in the personal presence of the clergy person and to be a messenger of love, so that God's perfect love can cast out fear. The ordained one helps people make it through the night—the deep, dark journeys of the soul.

So now, Diane, I say to you: let's talk about hermeneutics. Hermes is not our model of ministry, but a convenient way to talk about how we must be messengers between God and his people.

Remember this, as a charge:
1. Don't simply be the first female chaplain at St. Luke's. Be a person for others. And use your femininity when appropriate. Be a parson.
2. Show people that the world is not always as it appears. Show them the richness in poverty, the health in sickness, and the freedom in service.
3. Always remember that you are not God, only a messenger. You may be a fool for Christ, but don't be fooled into thinking you are divine.
4. Don't be afraid of the dark. Let your light so shine before people that they may see your good works and give glory to your Father who is in heaven.

Amen.

✤ ✤ ✤

August 28, 1983
Luke 14:1, 7–14

Today's Gospel is not an etiquette parable about how to find your place at a wedding banquet. Rather, it is a story of humility and equality. I wish it were that simple—that is, simply a story of pre-Emily Post positioning at wedding feasts. But I don't believe that Jesus of Nazareth came in order to rectify sloppy banquet manners.

Jesus used the hierarchical system of his day to make a point. He told the parable using an established custom to speak about humility and equality. In his time, seating at such occasions involved an arrangement whereby guests reclined on couches or pallets in groups. The center grouping was considered a location of esteem and was awarded on the basis of office, wealth, or power. If a more eminent person came late—a practice not infrequent amongst the prominent—one might be asked to relinquish his place. If one began with the assumption that his position was a lowly one, then he might be called higher.

Now the point of the parable has some clarity in the sense that Jesus knew that if we start with the assumption that we are unworthy in God's eyes, because of our sinful nature, then that confession is the beginning of our growth into acceptance of a high calling—that as persons, children of God. If we start with the assumption that we are worthy of God's love, then we will have to go back to the first assumption of unworthiness in order to be made worthy. This is one of those nice ironies in the nature of human nature. I'll return to this irony in a moment.

The second point of the parable is related to the first. If we have a need to be worthy, as I believe we do, we are seduced into feeling that if we are worthy in the eyes of our peers, we will, de facto, be worthy in God's eyes. Not so, says Christianity. God looks at us all equally—regardless of office, power, status, or wealth. We are all unworthy, and by God's grace in Jesus Christ, we are made worthy. When we are in touch with our unworthiness, we are then called to a higher place of worth.

Now my mind loves this kind of convoluted logic and ironic conclusion. The problem is not understanding it. The problem is communicating it to those who don't understand it. That is why Jesus told it in a parable and why preachers who love to appear wise by hiding behind convoluted logic ought to leave the parables alone and let them speak for themselves. I think most of you can see what Jesus meant in the parable without my confusing it for you.

But understanding the parable doesn't mean we can do anything about it. Because our need to be worthy is so great, if we are told that we must be humble in order to be worthy, then we seek to be more humble than anyone else in order to be more worthy.

There is the story told of the Bishop of Rome, with his cadre of prelates, who, having finished his evening prayers, knelt before the high altar at St. Peter's and said, "Oh God, before you I am nothing." He was followed at the altar by the archbishop, who knelt before the same altar and repeated, "Oh God, before you I am nothing." The dean of the cathedral followed in order and knelt, saying, "Oh God, before you I am nothing." As the three humble ecclesiastical leaders stood silently in the ambulatory, they noticed an old charwoman who had evidently seen and heard their plaint before the high altar, and they watched as she, too, took her place and knelt, saying, "Oh God, before you I am nothing." Seeing this, the dean leaned over to the archbishop and said, "Look who thinks she's nothing!"

Human nature is such that it will seek almost anything in order to be worthy.

In his novel, *The Magic Mountain*, Thomas Mann describes the social world of a Swiss tuberculosis sanatorium. The hierarchy of importance in this institution had nothing to do with money, talent, occupation, age, or social status. The hierarchy of patient importance had to do with severity of illness. The patients who were near death were the most important; they were the aristocrats, while the milder cases were less important. The point of the system was to become sicker in order to become more important. The implications of Thomas Mann's story are overwhelming in terms of man's basic sickness.

We are created equally and created equal. Yet, our need for acceptance is so great that we continue sick societal games of trying to earn or prove our worthiness. And we do so by comparing our worthiness with one another. George Orwell makes a most telling observation that "in Communism, the classless society, all are equal, but some are more equal than others."

God must have a sense of humor to tolerate the games we human beings play with one another, trying to prove to him how worthy we are. When all he wants from us is our humble admission that we are imperfect and for us to accept our undeserved acceptance.

Perhaps the human games of hierarchical class and status systems will never end, but maybe we can occasionally have a graceful laugh at the games we do play.

One closing piece of wisdom. If you see a prominent ecclesiastical figure proclaim that he is unworthy, don't compete with him, simply agree with him!

Amen.

September 4, 1983
Deuteronomy 30:15–20; Luke 14:25–33

I title this sermon: The Day Jesus Thinned the Crowd. Today's Gospel is one of those "hard sayings" of Jesus. It occurs as a curiously startling statement from the Prince of Peace who loved, healed, and held small children in his lap. A great multitude was following Jesus, and he turned on them and called the bluff of the pedestrian faithful and curiosity seekers. That crowd must have been full of those seeking a magic messiah, a Pollyanna prince who would promise prosperity in kind for fanatical following. There must have been in that crowd that day those seeking easy answers and pietistic platitudes that would work as a verbal Valium to tranquilize the anxiety of living in the fear of life and dread of death.

And I suspect what Jesus told them that day thinned the crowd. After his statement that day, I don't imagine he needed an 8,000 seat sanctuary to accommodate his following. I suspect his chances of being elected bishop on the first ballot diminished like the crowd, hurt by truth and wounded by prophetic wisdom.

For what he told them was not what they wanted to hear. What he said to the great multitude was: "If you are going to follow me, you have to hate your father and mother, your spouse, your children, brothers and sisters." Now, if that wasn't enough, before they took another step, he said, "And, in addition, you have to hate yourself!"

This is not a social gathering or a political movement. This is not a march on Rome or a magic messianic renewal of the Church. This is a cross-carrying crowd, and if you aren't willing to carry your own cross, get out of line. Don't follow me if you are afraid of the truth, and don't follow me unless you are willing to put your faith in me and what I represent as a priority over any single feeling, thought, memory, imagination, person, place, or event in life.

I suspect that by the time Jesus finished his stroll, you could have put the multitude in an oxcart.

I don't like what Jesus said, but I believe it.

Monday morning, early, I left in the dark to travel to East Texas to be with my mother who was lying in a Tyler hospital bed. As I turned off of the interstate highway, I went back in time thirty years or so. Day was breaking, and the fog was still in the shallow valleys on the edge of East Texas. I drove through the town of Buffalo. It is a town of 1,500, or so the sign says. You know the "You are entering" sign which is placed in line with several others, each of which welcomes and brags: Rotary Club, Elks Club, churches, and Home of the 1979 Bi-District Champs!

As I drove up the incline on the other side of the three-block town of Buffalo, I slowed down in honor of a yellow flashing light, cautioning for a school zone. To my left was the schoolhouse. It was somewhere between 7:00 and 7:30 a.m. Sitting on the front steps of the schoolhouse was a little boy of seven or eight. He had an anachronistic burr haircut. In spite of the late August heat, he wore a long-sleeved flannel shirt. He had on new blue jeans, rolled in one roll, calf-high. The shoes were not new. My guess was that he wore the flannel shirt and new jeans because his momma had taken him to Palestine, twenty-nine miles away, to buy school clothes. And since it was the first day of school, he wore them. On his left was a #8 brown lunch sack, folded neatly at the top. On his right, beside him, was a brand-new, blue, canvas-covered, cardboard three-ring binder. He was early this first day of school. I suspect his daddy dropped him off early on his way to work somewhere in the oil fields of East Texas.

I knew that little boy. I wondered as I drove away why that naiveté and innocence has to end. I wondered if he could possibly know what awaits him. I wonder today if Jesus meant that he would have to hate the hands that packed his lunch and neatly folded his sack and rolled his jeans. I wonder if Jesus meant he would have to hate his daddy who kissed him before he drove away and ran his hand over his burr head and said, "Be a good boy." I wonder if Jesus meant that he would have to hate himself, sitting quietly, waiting on the front steps of the rest of his life.

I don't like it, but I believe it. For if this little boy worships his mother and daddy, they are going to disappoint him. If he worships his wife and marriage, he will fall before a clay-footed idol. If he worships his own selfish desires for power, wealth, and status, then if he doesn't achieve them, he will hate them, and if he does achieve them, hate them the more.

By the time Jesus had finished his journey, the crowd had thinned to nothing. The crowd that remained gathered to watch him, alone with his cross.

But on the third day, the crowd began to gather again. Because slowly, it dawned on them. They now understood. Following Jesus meant that we must die to all earthly gods, even our own life, in order to live. His resurrection, then, would dawn in every death. If we could see that parent and child would die in symbol and fact, and new life would come if we were faithful to our ultimate God. If we could see that marriages would come and go, but our marriage to Christ would never end. That our own cross would have to be carried, in our own night's dark, but would be empty in the light of our own dawn. I'm not sure I like all that, but I believe it.

I left my mother on Thursday evening, still sick, but surviving for now. I drove through Buffalo. The school steps were empty; it was dusk.

The next day I awoke at dawn. I was home.

Amen.

September 25, 1983

I am drawn to today's subject as a moth to a flame. There is a flickering light that I cannot avoid, and yet to enter the flame is to be burned and consumed. So I will risk a flighty reflection and venture ahead knowing the cost and promise of flight and flame.

I shall begin in a brief and questionable logic. Numerology is not a major emphasis of my theological system, and yet numbers have had symbolic power in the Judeo-Christian story. In analytical psychology, the number four is a numerical symbol of wholeness. It is a complete number. The square, as a four-sided figure, projects a pattern of wholeness. Thus, four is represented in significant and subtle ways throughout scripture. If four is whole, then ten times that number is symbolic of the holy. Forty days and nights of rain set up Noah for his life's vocation of preserving humankind. Forty years of wandering in the wilderness prepared the people of God for the promised land and forty days in the desert for our Lord was an internship with evil and ordained Jesus for his journey as Savior.

Four is the symbol of wholeness and ten times that is considered holy time. On Thursday last, that date being September 22, I was forty. Ten times four I have visited the four seasons. Ten times four I have traveled the four directions. Ten times four I have heard the hooves of the Four Horsemen of the Apocalypse.

Now, you know the moth and flame. I am drawn to the reflection of a life lived in the light and yet fear the flame which casts shadows and consumes those who venture too near. To avoid speaking of being forty is to deny the significance of life, and to reflect on my forty years in a public place is to expose myself to the shadow cast in reflected light. Self-serving sermons, where one presumes to "know" or stands in some superior light above those who sit below, are only to expose the dark side of wisdom. That silhouette is the picture of maniacal pomposity, of self-righteous vainglory couched in some pietistic platitude which is a shadow dance of ego and evil, where the former denies the latter and the evil takes the lead in a song where the music doesn't fit the words and all who watch are uncomfortable and embarrassed, for the only one whose toes are stepped on is the dancer.

So it is as I reflect upon my fortieth birthday. The subject of age is the flame and I am the moth. I can either say too much or too little, come too near the truth to be tolerable or be so self-serving that my ego blocks the light and the only thing seen is my embarrassing shadow.

I have been carrying an image that is like any analogy or metaphor. The image is inadequate, for it will fall if investigated thoroughly, yet may communicate if seen only as an image. I imagine a man who one day arrives home and half of his house is consumed in flames. What is his response and what is his reflection? He may panic and think of all that is gone and lost forever; he may try to put out the flame with some quick and easy solutions. He may rush back into the burning half and never recover what remains in that which is left. He may rush into that which remains and act as if nothing has happened and never know when he is overcome with the smoke of a denied fire. In this image, some questions occur. Is there anything in the burning half of his house for which he would risk his life? If not, the house is not worth saving. If so, then no matter when the house is consumed, it has served its function.

Image and conclusion #1.

A second image that I carry is that of a man who arrives home one day and realizes that his home is half built. The foundation is laid, the framing is in place, the structure is complete. He sees before him now the joy of the subtle finishes, with molding, doors, windows, and furnishings, colors, lamps, and pictures on the walls. The fundamentals are in place, and he has the rest of his life to complete the interior. In this image some questions occur. Will the interior ever be complete? Which is more essential—the exterior or interior? And, finally, why is a house built from the foundation up rather than from the attic down? This I know. Once an exterior is complete, the interior grows, and though it may never be finished, it will need redecorating. I don't know which is more important, that is, a house's exterior or interior. I suppose both are essential, but I do know one lives on the interior of a house, not the exterior. And, in order to complete a house, the last half is spent on the inside, and I pity the builder who tries to build an attic without a foundation.

Image and conclusion #2.

Both images describe a life at midpoint. There is a panic and a peace. If my house is on fire, there are people in it for whom I would give my life. There are people I love more than my own life. The flame teaches me that. So, no matter when the house is consumed, it has served its function.

If my house is half built, then I revel in the subtle touches of interior completion which I can enjoy in increments of decoration and redecoration.

My life is built on the foundation that I am a child of God at any and every age. And that my meaning and purpose are revealed in my Brother and Lord, Jesus. And he who dwells in love dwells in God, and God in him. That dwelling may burn but will not be consumed. That dwelling will never be complete, for it is complete in itself. Whatever the age one is, is the best age, for love knows no end. I willingly give up my life for love…and that, too, is where I've found it.

Amen.

❖ ❖ ❖

October 30, 1983
Luke 19:1–10

In spite of the length of my body as compared to motel beds, theatre seats, and automobile steering wheels, I know what it is like to feel small. To be or to feel small is a metaphorical description of one's internal feelings, not one's dimensions. I stand tall as a case study that large people can feel small.

It has been years since I climbed a tree. It is not so much that my desire has diminished. It is just that the opportunity presents itself so rarely anymore. And though I feel small from time to time, it requires a large tree in order to support my desire to be in one. Also, now that I have turned forty, my limbs are not as flexible as those of a green-willowed youth or of a vital, flexible tree, which seem more to be made for one another than a brittle oaken man and a burly barked tree trunk. Yet, there are still days and events therein when I find myself "up a tree."

Luke's Gospel today tells us a story of feeling small and being up a tree. Let us take a large look at the small sinner, Zaccheus. The story of Zaccheus is a great story about being small.

We can imagine that Zaccheus stood barely five feet tall with his sandals on. He was the least popular man in Jericho, the town where Joshua fit the battle and the walls came tumbling down. Zaccheus was the head tax collector for Rome in the district and had made such a killing out of it that he was not only the shortest man in town, but the richest. A nice scriptural irony to which a critical eye cannot remain closed. When word got around that Jesus would soon be passing through town, Old Zac, living out of his secular bag of golden rules, knew that he must see in order to believe. Being short on height, Zaccheus shinnied up a sycamore tree so he could see what other people believed. But, as ironic as his big bank account and small heart, something happened, as it always does when one gets involved with love for Christ's sake. Old Zac climbed the tree in order to see and, rather than seeing, he was seen and was like a man who sawed the limb on which he sat. This was one of the great see/saw events of human history.

Jesus spotted Zaccheus and saw that his life had put him up a tree. So Jesus said, "I'll not only get you out of the tree, but I'll stay with you." In other words, if you don't like being up a tree, invite me in, and if you won't invite me into your life, I'll invite myself.

Now, those looking on couldn't see what they believed and couldn't believe what they saw. Here was this legman for the IRS, this sawed-off shyster, perched in a sycamore tree. When Jesus opened his mouth to speak, all of Jericho held its breath in anticipation of Jesus giving its small, large sinner uncharted holy hell. They expected Jesus to yell, "Woe unto you! Repent! Wise up!" But in the ironic love story, what Jesus said was, "Come down on the double, I'm coming to your house." The mob believed Jesus would either not notice him or put him on notice. But once again, God had the last laugh.

It is not reported how Zaccheus got out of the tree, but the chances are good that he fell out. Once again, Jesus is there, saving us from the fall.

Now, the good news is clear and clearly in the simple little story of a sinful little man. God in Christ accepts us where we are. When we feel smallest and most up a tree, looking for a way out, when we are looking for Christ, he sees us. And he invites himself in. And when that happens, we become much larger in heart and arrive with our feet on the ground.

Zaccheus so reordered his life that he promised not only to turn over 50 percent of his goods to the poor, but to pay back fourfold all he had extorted. The little man did a bighearted thing, and by giving up his smallness, he became large himself.

God loves us all, each and every one. Next time you feel small about your life and that smallness puts you up a tree, and you are looking for something to get you out—remember old Zaccheus. Human beings have been in trees since Adam. And God keeps getting us out, time and time again.

The celebration of that was Jesus being present at Zac's house for a meal. What a celebration. Jesus present at one's house for a meal.

Holy Eucharist!

Amen.

❖ ❖ ❖

November 6, 1983
All Saints' Sunday

The capacity of the Creator can be best described as a circle whose center is everywhere and whose circumference is nowhere. Think of the capacity of God.

Capacity is the ability to contain and receive. It is also the character of position assigned to one, as in "function." The capacity of God to be inclusive, to contain and receive, is as a circle whose center is everywhere and its circumference is nowhere. The character or function of God's presence is to be as universal as a circle whose center is in each person and whose perimeter includes the even unimagined boundaries of all that we have been and all that we can become.

Today is All Saints' Sunday, and one of the great baptismal days in our Christian calendar. We stretch our minds to encompass, in one celebration, all those who have journeyed as Christians before us and to initiate new Christians who will journey behind us. God is as distant as the stellar lights in eternity and as close as to have himself in the center of each of these babies in our midst.

What, therefore, is the capacity of these baby Christians, and what is our capacity in baptizing them?

The best movie I have seen in years, I saw this fall. It was, for me, so good that I saw it twice. With such little discretionary time as I have, it is witness to how I valued the movie. I saw it twice. The movie is entitled *Tender Mercies*. The story line is neither complicated nor novel. Yet, it is the very simplicity and sententious nature of the story that is so profound.

An alcoholic country-and-western singer finds himself hungover and busted at a crossroads filling station in West Texas. The metaphor is inescapable. He is at a crossroads in his life; he is empty and wakes up at a filling station. There he meets a widow and her young son. The relationship that develops between and among them can only be described as authentic. He is empowered by the mother's child to fill his emptiness with love rather than alcohol and to settle into a responsible lifestyle. Temptations continue. His ex-wife, who is also a country-and-western singer, comes to Austin to perform. And with her comes his daughter. He hasn't seen her in years, and all of the guilt of his past is personified in a visit with his daughter. In that visit, the face of the actor, Robert Duvall, shows embarrassment and sadness. The acting is great, for what is seen in his face is authenticity: embarrassment at who he had been and sadness at what he could have been with his daughter. It is a poignant, wonderful scene.

She asks her daddy, "You remember when I was a baby, you used to sing me a song? I can't remember the song, but I remember it was about a dove."

That same look of embarrassment and sadness is upon his face and he says, "No, I can't remember."

The scene ends with her driving away from this crossroads filling station, her car amidst the dust of the road, and he looks out a window at her disappearing before him and begins to sing the song that she remembered. The lyrics are "On the wings of a snow-white dove, he sends his pure, sweet love." That song is a baptismal song, written and sung as a spiritual. "On the wings of a snow-white dove, he sends his pure, sweet love" is a story of the baptism of Jesus.

As the story line progresses, he marries the woman at the filling station and the time comes for his stepson to be baptized. And, as a surprise to all, on the day his stepson is to be baptized, the hero steps forward to be baptized also. And in one of the most wonderful scenes I have ever seen, in this West Texas rural church, Robert Duvall goes under the water and when he comes up, he has the most incredible look on his face. As he shakes the water from his head, he has exactly the same look that he had with his daughter, but with one change. It is the same look of embarrassment, but now the sadness is a look of joy. Embarrassment and sadness to embarrassment and joy.

The humanity about which we are all embarrassed is still personified in this face, yet the sadness has now been changed to joy.

As the three characters drive away from the church in a beat-up pickup truck, the stepson looks in the rearview mirror and says, "I don't look any different, do I?"

Duvall says, "No."

The little boy says, "You don't either. I don't feel different. Do you?"

Duvall pauses and says, shaking his head, "Not yet." But the rest of the story shows that he is different—that he becomes different. His daughter is tragically killed in a car accident, and after he returns from her funeral, in the ending scene of the movie, he is hoeing in the garden. Once again, the metaphor is inescapable. As he stands in the garden hoeing, his new wife—his new love, his new life—comes to be with him, and he says to her, "I never trusted happiness." And in the closing scene, he is picking up trash and putting it in a bag. He didn't trust happiness, but now he knows joy.

The baptismal story is the story of capacity. We continue to be embarrassed about our humanity. Even though we are baptized, we do make mistakes, we do create failures and tragedies. Catastrophes continue to be a part of the fabric of this creation. Yet we need not be sad about the loss of any life—including our own—for we are joyous, not simply happy. He learned you cannot trust happiness. You can, though, be empowered by joy, and the baptism is the symbol of that.

The capacity of the Creator can best be described as a circle whose center is everywhere and whose circumference is nowhere. What is the capacity of these baby Christians, and what is our capacity in baptizing them? We are saying to them that the capacity is unlimited, for they are of God. They can become, and become more, and that though they will be embarrassed by the struggle of being human, they will know the joy of an unlimited capacity as to what they can become.

Capacity is the ability to receive, the ability to contain, the ability to become more, for that is limitless.

Our capacity here is not simply to take up space, as a friend of mine describes his vocation in life. Our capacity here is to tell them that truth and to put the water upon them as a symbol that they will never be incapacitated.

God's name be praised.

Amen.

✣ ✣ ✣

November 13, 1983
Luke 21:5–19

Let me take control of my own destiny, lest there be any who might ever question my faithfulness to the strength and relevance of the Gospel of Jesus Christ. I believe in God as revealed in Christ Jesus in spite of today's Gospel. Yet, *in spite of* the irrelevance of Jesus' words to me, I believe in his truth. I am, of course, referring to the concluding section of today's Lukan Gospel where our Lord proclaims if we trust him "not one hair of our head will perish"!

I want you to know that I believe in spite of that statement. It is also an example of why those of us who are bald can never be literalists about scripture!

What I really want to talk about is the next line, and indeed, concluding line of today's Gospel. The preceding section of Jesus' teaching says essentially that remaining faithful is always going to be difficult, for there is much competition for faith. Jesus says you will not be left alone and finally utters that which is my text today, "By your endurance you will gain your lives."

This phrase from the lips of our Lord is the gate of human wisdom. "By your endurance you will gain your lives."

I see three levels of Jesus' teaching in today's word. First, he was preparing his disciples for the hard work they would have to endure in the world of their time. The Jews would reject them, and the Gentiles would seduce them. And they would only discover their call in the competition for it. Secondly, Jesus is speaking of the world not only in the first century, but in all ages, whereby death continues to compete with life, and one cannot live until he endures the possibility of death. And thirdly, Jesus' words describe the inscape of each internal life. Neurosis is inner cleavage. Competition or war within requires endurance in order to gain wholeness.

Life itself is a test of endurance. Jesus spoke of endurance, not as a passive victim. The kind of endurance about which Jesus spoke is not the kind of endurance of a fettered victim being whipped by life, but more like Paul's image of the runner who endures the competition and finishes the race and discovers himself in the process. The victory is not in simple competition with others to see who can be first with the most, but with the endurance of pain and temptation, one discovers his own self—the gold that remains when the impurities melt in the heat of life—and the essential self *endures.* "By your endurance you will gain your lives."

There is much about life that is just difficult. I don't like that fact, but it is only the fool who denies it. The difficulty must have purpose unless there is no God other than chance whose vestments are caprice. Difficulty, disappointments, pain, and crises may be those things which tell us who we are *not,* and the endurance of them tells us who we *are.*

Every disappointment is a door closed, which tells me that that direction is not my path. Each rejection is a message that that is not the person with whom I am to journey. When a beautiful little girl does not get to be a cheerleader, that is a message that she is called to be something else. And for that, she can ultimately be thankful, if she can endure the disappointment.

One of the greatest disappointments of the first half of my life was the discovery that I did not have the skill to become a professional athlete. The door of disappointment was closed in my immature face. Yet a new path was opened. I would not trade one hundred headlines, or one hundred thousand clapping hands, or one million dollars a year as a professional athlete for one moment as a priest celebrating the Eucharist at the altar of God. That is not to say that the priesthood is more important than professional athletics, but it is to say that I am more Pittman as priest than as professional player. "By your endurance you will gain your lives."

Life seeks to define us. The definition comes through the trial and error of experience and the reflection upon it. The joys confirm when we are what we are called to be, and the despair tells us we need to move in a new direction. If we only knew joy, we would never move or change. Joy confirms us when we are right, and despair informs us when we are wrong. The system is simple, the journey is difficult. But by endurance we gain our lives.

Two weeks ago, I was lecturing before the Analytical Society of Dallas. The scope of my lecture was the compatible and complementary relationships between psychology and religion. In that lecture, I spoke of the psyche and soul as synonyms. And further, that the psyche or soul had an eternal nature about it. After I delivered my paper, during the question and answer period, a woman asked, "What about the soul—or better, what about the psyche—survives or endures into eternity after death?"

I responded, "We cannot name that in general. That what remains or endures is the essential self—we can only name that in particular. What endures is 'Pittman.' What is meant when we say 'Pittman' is to name what endures eternally."

To which she responded, "I don't understand that term."

"What term?" I asked.

"Pittman, the term Pittman," she said.

I exclaimed, "Why, that is my name!"

And amidst laughter and joy, she finally said, "Oh, I thought your name was Dean."

That dialogue somehow summarizes my sermon. Life is full of joy and despair. The joy confirms when we are ourselves. Disappointment and despair tell us when we need to become more. What remains in the heat of life after the nonessentials have melted away is the pure gold of our essence—or essential self—and that is what endures eternally. "By your endurance you will gain your lives."

And don't forget, we will never lose anything that is essential to our being ourselves—not one hair of our head (so to speak)!

Amen.

✤ ✤ ✤

December 11, 1983
Advent III
Matthew 11:2–11

In a time gone by, an archbishop had heard of how clever the peasants were and asked for one to come to the cathedral to meet him. The peasants chose a simple sexton, who set out to meet the archbishop armed with only a flat piece of unleavened bread.

The archbishop and sexton had no common language, and so in the audience chamber, the archbishop held up one finger. The sexton responded by holding up two. The archbishop drew a small circle in the air; the sexton drew a large one. The archbishop took an apple and offered it to the sexton; the sexton took his unleavened bread and offered it to the archbishop. The audience between the archbishop and the sexton was at an end.

The archbishop then turned to his advisors and said, "Yes, he was quite brilliant. I said, 'There is but one true faith,' and he countered with, 'But you must acknowledge that there is more than one path to God.' I said, 'You know that God orders the world,' and he countered with, 'But what of the universe?' I said, 'Well, you must admit the world is round!' and he said, 'From where I stand, it looks flat.' I found him very clever."

The sexton returned home and told the leaders that he had had a surprising encounter. "The archbishop said, 'I will poke your eye out.' I replied, 'I will poke out both of yours.' Then he described his wife, so I described mine. Then we had lunch and I came home."

Is it not obvious that the archbishop and sexton did not hear and see the same thing? In today's Gospel, John was in a literal and figurative prison. He was in the jail of Herod, but also behind the bars of his own uncertainty. John, like all who draw breath from the human situation, wanted to know for certain that the one he had baptized and the one about whom he had heard great deeds, was indeed the Christ. So John sent his disciples to Jesus with the eternal question of the human quest: "Are you he who is to come, or shall we look for another?" And Jesus responded, "See for yourself."

A friend of mine was once in an airport waiting area. He looked up at the clock on the wall and it read two o'clock. He looked back a few minutes later and realized that the clock still read two o'clock. He realized that the clock had stopped. But, he realized something else. That clock on the wall was dead right twice a day. He looked at the watch on his wrist and realized that, as far as he knew, his watch was never exactly correct. In consideration of the two times, he concluded that he would take the living reality over the dead certainty!

There is an old Irish epigram: "An Irishman doesn't know what he wants, and he won't be content until he gets it." It is, after all, the epigram of us all. Advent III, in the four-part harmony of our journey to Bethlehem, raises the question for us all: is Jesus what we seek, and is what we seek the Christ?

It is clear we seek something. As we heard last week, one cannot hear the voice in the wilderness unless one listens. We see this week that the word we heard is in the flesh if we will look and see.

But when we talk of seeing the Word in the flesh, we had better be clear about what to look for, or we will be like the archbishop and sexton who make signs, have lunch, and go home.

God's incarnation was and is in Jesus, but not limited to that time and space. When John's disciples asked for proof of the Christhood, Jesus did not speak of himself, but of the change he made in people's lives. Where there is new creation, there is the Christ. What we seek is life, and we will not be content with signs of life, only life itself. Christ is the living reality.

Christmas reminds us of the possibilities. And the incarnation is not limited to one century or one city. The Christ is present in one time, in one place, in one face, in order to be seen at all times, in all places, by all faces. If we seek the Christ, we must look for the dynamic force, which is life itself.

This is the word that is in every flesh. When the flame of life seems extinguished and there is more smoke than fire, it is hard to see that the spark of all life is the Creator and that the Creator is eternally in every creature, and where creativity lives, there is the Christ. "Are you he who is to come, or shall we look for another?" "See for yourself." Look for The Life in lives, not signs of life, but Life itself, and therein will be the Christ.

No matter what the circumstance, that spark of the Christ will not disappear, for it is the source of life itself. "In him was life, and the life was the light of men." Look and you will see.

And the Christian witness is the answer to the question of Advent III—sung in four-part harmony—there is no darkness nor death stronger than the light and life of Jesus who is the Christ. John's question was answered in the living reality, which is more powerful than the dead certainty.

Amen.

※ ※ ※

December 24, 1983
Christmas Eve

I bid welcome to you who have come as pilgrims of possibility, seeking the mystery larger than mind, seeking the significant larger than symbol, seeking the terrible freedom which we fear is here. I bid you welcome, but let us come with caution to the cradle of freedom.

We are pilgrims of possibility, seeking the wild possibilities given by God, represented in Christ, and offered to every generation by the Spirit which is none other than Holy.

Tonight is the mysterious reminder, the symbolic representation, that the possibility for authentic human existence is offered once again and we have come to behold; for what is born is the fulfillment of the deepest human longing—the possibility that we are free.

And yet, it is a freedom we fear. It is a freedom we deny and a freedom we crucify. For if we accept what is born in Bethlehem, then we have no excuses for not becoming what we were created to be. God in Christ has given to us all we seek.

The freedom is a terrible freedom, for if we accept it, then there are no excuses. If we accept the baby in Bethlehem, we can no longer complain that life is too complex, for it is as simple as the birth of a baby and summed in the sentence "God is love."

The freedom is a terrible freedom, for if we accept the baby in Bethlehem, we can no longer complain of being victims of a birth we did not request and a grave we cannot escape. For your birth was requested by God, and the tomb of time is emptied into eternity, and what you were born to be, you will continue to *become* eternally.

The freedom is a terrible freedom, for if we accept the baby in Bethlehem, then we can no longer complain that our parents weren't perfect and our peers do not accept us. For God is our parent and Christ our brother, and we are loved and accepted in eternity by God and in history by God in flesh, whose name is Jesus.

The freedom is a terrible freedom, for if we accept the baby in Bethlehem, then we can no longer complain that we didn't know. For we now know all there is to know—the formula is revealed: "We shall love the Lord our God with all our hearts and souls and minds, and love our neighbors as ourselves." All decisions and responses are based on this knowledge—that "God is love, and he who dwells in love dwells in God and God in him."

It is a terrible freedom, for the power of God will not destroy our freedom. Human power can make one do what you want him to do, but as for making him be what you want him to be, without at the same time destroying his freedom—only love can make this happen. And love makes it happen not coercively, but by creating a situation in which, of our own free will, we want to be what love wants us to be. And because God's love treasures our freedom, God allows us to be free to refuse his love or refuse our freedom. We are free to resist it, deny it, or crucify it. This is our terrible freedom, which love refuses to overpower, so that the greatest of all powers, God's power, is itself as powerless as a newborn baby.

So, let history record that on December 24, 1983, several hundred pilgrims of possibility huddled together in this cathedral crucible. The Word was heard, the terrible truth was revealed, and freedom was born once again; and it was proclaimed that we need not fear the freedom.

"Fear not, for behold, I bring you good tidings of great joy, which shall be to all people. For unto you is born this day, in the City of David, a savior, which is Christ the Lord."

Let us come now, not with caution but with unabashed joy, to this cradle of freedom.

Amen.

1984

January 29, 1984
I Corinthians 1:18–26; Matthew 5:1–12

A friend of mine says she hates surprise parties. The reason, she contends, is "that it proves you can lie and get by with it!"

I would contend, with apologies toward glibness, that Christianity is a surprise party. Not, of course, in the sense that it is a lie. To the contrary, life is the lie, and Christianity is the ironic surprise. That is, I believe, the unconscious appeal of Christ and his teachings. Christ and his teachings, and a teacher of Christ, like St. Paul, offer a continuing, countercultural message that has made "foolishness of the wisdom of the world."

One does, from time to time, feel foolish trying to be Christian in this culture. For this is not a Christian culture. At least, the gods of this culture are not Christian. And they are seductive gods. And seductive gods are, after all, not gods; they are devils. For the one God is not seductive. Though he could seduce, he does not. He honors the freedom he gave us and does not force his will upon culture, which is a most loving act, ironic and surprising as it seems. It is foolishness to the world. For the world does not relate well to one who has power but does not use it. The world does not relate well to a power which respects freedom and proclaims that the only true power is love.

This sermon today could quickly become uncomfortable. The priest preaching a prophetic sermon of social commentary can make the hearer feel patronized. And a consistent reaction would be to look for the hypocritical inconsistency in the proclaimer. I am not preaching to or about *you* today. This text before me is a mirror. If you see yourself anywhere in this image, own what we have in common. If you do not see yourself, then pray for those of us who do.

I am speaking today of a real danger in this culture of theistic, materialistic consumerism—the current tempting god of our culture. I am speaking of my own temptation to be consumed by my desire to consume.

I have a T-shirt in my closet that friends brought to me from New York. The shirt is one of those now-popular message shirts. It is gray with simple black lettering across the chest that reads: "Whoever has the most things when he dies, wins." Is that not the wisdom of the world? Jesus' logo in today's Gospel lesson and the Beatitudes don't sell well today. "Blessed are the poor, the mourners, the meek, the hungry, the pure, the peacemakers, the persecuted." In Christianity, they are the winners. A surprising, ironic wisdom. The Christian surprise party is full of losers. Whoever has the most things when he dies, wins? Jesus, by the wisdom of the world, was a loser. Surprise! "Has not God made foolish the wisdom of the world?" Paul put that on the T-shirts of Corinth.

The place at which I see my reflection in all of this is that, of course, we can judge the desire in culture for more things, bigger and more powerful; but I referred to this culture god as a *theistic*, materialistic consumerism. In simple terms, the consumer believes in God and believes God wants to reward him with things. The reflection that is most haunting is that I see the church as a part of this seduction. Bigger churches, bigger buildings, bigger budgets, more success, more notoriety, and we here at the Cathedral, unless we are very careful, will enter the local competition to see who can accumulate the most and become dead winners.

The desire in humanity to possess things will probably never be eradicated. For it is deep in the animal nature of human beings. The real evil is not in the desire to consume things, it is in being ignorant of the temptation to make this desire our god. The second evil incumbent in materialistic consumerism is that once we are satiated on things, we then turn to one another. I used to have another T-shirt that read: "Love people and use things, don't love things and use people." The real danger is when we cease to consume things and begin to consume one another.

The most popular movie of the year may be a statement about this contemporary god of human consumption. The title of the movie tells the tale. The title is *Terms of Endearment*. Clearly, endearment on human terms always has its terms.

The lead consumer in the movie is named Aurora. (It is also the name of a pagan Roman goddess of a strong, consuming light.) In the movie, Aurora consumes every character in sight. She begins with her husband who never makes it into the plot. He dies before we meet him, and we know nothing about him except that he evidently left Aurora very comfortable, for she seems to have all the resources she needs. She does not work or struggle; things are available. She has the freedom to consume people. Next, she consumes her daughter, her son-in-law, her neighbor, and several weak, sycophantic men in her court. The difficult thing here is that she does it in such a charming, humorous, beguiling, and yet calculating way. Each character has his or her own flirtation with strength against Aurora, but she systematically consumes them all. The uncomfortable reality is that the setting is Houston—some say a consumer capital—and her neighborhood is mine. It is a mirror placed before us. Aurora's endearment has its terms: devotion and devouring. She loved and was lovable, but not without terms and conditions. Lest we be too hard on her character, she is only an extreme of the frailty of human love. We cannot love without conditions. Only God can do that. And, on rare occasion, we are able to love one another as God loves us.

Emma, the daughter, is consumed by cancer. On her deathbed, she offers the only love without terms. In the movie's most poignant scene, she calls her two little boys to her bed and to the older of the two, she offers love without terms. He is angry at her for dying and angry at her for her relationship with his father. She says to him, "I love you. I love you even though you may not love me now. The day may come when you feel guilty about how you feel about me now. But don't. I love you anyway. Don't ever feel guilty."

The one in the movie who is most powerless is the one who offers the redemptive love. Blessed are the poor, the pure, the meek, the merciful. Surprise! We humans consume things and one another. We always put terms on our endearment. We think he who finishes first with the most is the winner, but Christianity is a surprise.

Only God can love without terms. And occasionally, he so enters humans that that image is lifted up as a hope for us all. It is possible to love without conditions. God has done it. He loves each of us abundantly, whether we have any things or not. And maybe, just maybe, those without much find it easier to accept love than those who have much. That is surprising.

Two things in summary: Christianity will always run counter to the culture—that is one of its tasks. God's wisdom is foolish to the world.

Secondly, we wind up consuming ourselves when we make consumption our god. And yet, the God of love, revealed in Christ, invites us all to his unconditional love—it is a surprising party.

Amen.

❖ ❖ ❖

February 5, 1984
I Corinthians 2:1–11; Matthew 5:13–20

Paul decided to know nothing among us except Christ and him crucified. And then Paul spends an ocean of ink explaining what it is he doesn't know. I attended a funeral several years ago. The preacher began a lengthy sermon by saying, "At times like these, there is nothing to be said." And he took forty-five minutes to prove it.

In today's epistle, Paul betrays the difficulty in speaking about God. He apologizes by saying, "All I ultimately know is Christ and him crucified." He then states further, "Faith does not rest in the wisdom of men but in the power of God. Yet, among the mature we do impart wisdom, although it is not a wisdom of this age or of the rulers of this age, who are doomed to pass away."

And he goes on and on again, finishing with, "So also no one comprehends the thoughts of God, except the Spirit of God."

Sometimes when I read Paul, or even more so when I read theology, I feel like the young basketball player whose coach was upset with his play. The coach, at a time-out, screamed at him for his lack of understanding, saying, "Johnson, are you ignorant or apathetic?" The young player responded, "Coach, I don't know and I don't care."

It is not that the intellectual exercise is not of value in doing theology. Intellect is not only valuable, it is vital. We must love God with heart, soul, and *mind.* After all, I am a subscriber of *The Journal of Religion and Intellectual Life*! I write and teach in the field of Analytical Psychology, and can be as vague and esoteric as the best. I know it doesn't sound very humble, but I have written things that even intelligent people don't understand! Perhaps what separates the intelligent from others is that intelligent people are just more articulate than others about what it is that they don't understand.

My point is, as Paul's, when all is said and done, more is said than done. Christ said it and did it. That is perhaps why he was the Christ. "Christ and him crucified." Maybe that is all we need to know. The agony and ecstasy of all life in one life. Christ and him crucified. If we know that, we know enough to live without what we don't know. Christ taught love and obedience. Love God, love his children. Love yourself as a child of God. Be obedient. Be that which God calls you to be. Don't be animals. Don't be gods. Be persons. Human beings with names. Christ taught it, lived it, and died it. He practiced what he preached. And what he preached was life—life as if you knew that what you don't know is the mystery that makes ecstasy worth the agony. Christ and him crucified. King and cross. No cross, no crown. No Good Friday, no Easter. No guts, no glory! Christ and him crucified.

Jesus lived all he revealed, and his life was the revelation. Birth is a mystery. We are born in mystery. Life gives us a few things to know. Those few tracks of truth are islands that form archipelagos which give us enough footing and direction to follow the command to love and obey and step into darkness with faith enough to take tentative steps forward on a little land in the sea of mystery.

Jesus did not confound us with theological circular argument. Jesus taught things we can taste and see. Salt and light. Jesus said, "You are the salt of the earth; You are the light of the world." Spice and shine. Life is not dull and dark when you are loved and have purpose. It is salt and light, spice and shine, taste and see. Christ and him crucified. Love and obedience.

Christianity, the life revealed in Christ, has given me a sense of meaning, purpose, and belonging. I have a life to be fulfilled. This has given me an inner security and, although I could never prove it, it has proved itself to me. I can taste it—like salt. God in Christ has given me a direction to go and that is to become my name. That is a light, a beacon which beckons. Love and obedience. Spice and shine. When I love and when I am what I am called to be, nothing else matters. I am not alone. I am outside time. He who birthed me calls me to him. This is my most profound experience; on the one hand, a bloody struggle, and on the other hand, supreme ecstasy. Christ and him crucified.

At a time like this, there is so little to say. I have taken fifteen minutes to prove it. It is not out of ignorance or apathy that I say I don't truly understand, or care, for anything, save Christ and him crucified.

Amen.

❖ ❖ ❖

February 19, 1984
Matthew 5:38–48

Where I grew up, people didn't talk about Christian names. They described one's formal, legal name as his "given" name. One of my closest friends growing up was John Eubanks. John was his given name, but everyone called him "Cheezie." Oral history, dictated by Cheezie, related that when John Jr. was born, his father proclaimed his namesake to be the big cheese of the family. Thus, Junior became "Cheezie." I didn't like Cheezie's father. I never had the chance to get to know him apart from Cheezie. Mr. Eubanks ran an appliance store. He was a loud, backslapping man who was president of the local Lions Club. I didn't like him because one day, in the secret sanctuary of the boys' restroom, Cheezie showed me several long, red marks on his back where Mr. Eubanks had "taken his strap" to Cheezie. Whenever I saw Mr. Eubanks slapping one of his friends on the back, I never failed to think of Cheezie and his stripes, shared in the secret sanctuary of Washington Grade School's first-floor restroom. Cheezie was determined. He was what our basketball coach called "plucky." For four years running, from 1952 to 1956, years that carried me from age nine to thirteen, my friend Cheezie held The Annual Cheezie Eubanks Invitational Basketball Tournament. The first prize was a traveling trophy. It was a plastic loving cup five inches high. His sister had gotten it from her boyfriend on Valentine's Day. It held a small bottle of dime-store perfume. It smelled of plastic and perfume. Though it was a well-publicized invitational tournament, there was only one invitation ever offered and it was to me. The traveling trophy made one trip and that was to my bedroom shelf. When we started the tournament at age nine, I was two inches taller than Cheezie. By the fourth year, I was half a foot taller. But Cheezie was determined. Every year, he planned his strategy, issued his one invitation, decorated his backyard with crepe paper, and believed that that was his year to have the traveling trophy returned to its proper place. After four tournaments—each holding a five-game series—Cheezie's record was 0 wins and 20 losses. But, as Cheezie bragged, he never finished lower than second place. The first-place trophy remains, to this day, at my parents' house.

In my fourteenth year, my last year in that small Oklahoma town, and the last year I spent with Cheezie Eubanks, he arrived one day at school with a brand-new, baby blue, Cushman Eagle motor scooter. He was proud. Cheezie didn't have much about which to be proud. He struggled to get by in school. His athletic prowess, no matter how determined, was predetermined by his small body and large, pigeon-toed feet. And though his father had declared him The Big Cheese, Cheezie bore the scars of domination. When I saw him ride up on that teenage symbol of masculinity, I could feel psychological change. Deeper than consciousness was an inner enemy whose name was envy. This inner enemy of mine was more powerful than adolescent consciousness. This enemy named envy hijacked my psyche, took over my immature ego, and projected itself onto a short, pigeon-toed victim named Cheezie Eubanks.

After some critical sarcasm from me concerning the baby blue color of this masculine machine, the enemy who controlled my consciousness demanded to ride the Eagle. Cheezie looked miserably at his inward-pointed shoe tops and mumbled, "My father told me not to let anyone ride it." I now know the sound advice, even from a big cheese backslapper, but then the refusal was a spark that ignited the fuel of envy, and my inner enemy became me, and I was unbecoming.

I struck Cheezie with a glancing blow to his thin shoulder. It was absorbed primarily by his thick corduroy jacket. The pain, though, was in his eyes. He looked at me with surprise. Eyes of surprise reflected disbelief that one who had heard his confession in the restroom sanctuary, the holder of the traveling trophy, the one who had sat by him while he ate paste in the first grade, this one had become his enemy. Cheezie stared for a moment in disbelief, and then he tightened his lips and squinted his eyes and rode away. He did not ride away because he feared his father's anger more than mine; he did not ride away because of lack of courage, for he had fought me for four consecutive years in the dirt of his backyard basketball court. He rode away because he knew that that which had struck him could not be defeated by striking back. He must have known that whatever had come over me was not stronger than our experienced, though unexpressed, love.

Jesus said, "You have heard that it was said 'An eye for an eye and a tooth for a tooth.' But I say to you, Do not resist one who is evil…turn the other cheek." The Gospel is lived in small, undramatic stories. The truth of religious life is lived in common experiences. Personal stories are symbols of the universal story of love revealed in the written word called the Gospel. Names, faces, and places are the experiential revelations. I have learned that Jesus may have been talking about our own inner enemies as well as outer enemies. And may have been talking about loved ones who may also be enemies. I can pray for and accept the Russians as enemies more easily than I can accept my own evil side or the dark side of those I love. But there is no difference.

Revelation is not limited to blinding flashes or mountaintop experiences. Christ appears in the most unlikely places. My witness is that I have seen him in grade school restrooms, second-place finishers with funny names. I have seen him in the reflections of surprised eyes and felt his presence as he rides away, borne as on eagles' wings.

I have seen him in me as my own inner enemy has been defeated by "plucky" love. I have seen him as the defeated one who is the ultimate victor.

Amen.

❖ ❖ ❖

March 4, 1984
Exodus 24:12–18; Matthew 17:1–9

There are several invitations about which one must be cautious: "Have you got a minute?" or "Give me five minutes of your time." Translated, these invitations mean: the cost of this encounter won't be measured by time. Another invitation about which one ought to be cautious is: "It tastes just like chicken." Translated, it means: whatever it tastes like now is in order to cover up its original taste. Another invitation about which one ought to be cautious is: "Come up with me on the mountain." Ask Moses and St. Peter about their mountaintop experiences before you take even a tentative step to a higher plain.

In today's first reading, Moses was invited up on the mountain to receive the law and the commandment. In today's Gospel reading, Peter was taken with James and John up on the mountain to see the fulfillment of the law and prophets in Jesus, where God revealed himself in Jesus the Christ.

The invitation is a beguiling one. For it is an invitation to be in the presence of God. It is a holy invitation to see the truth amidst the clouds of life. It means, though, that one may never be satisfied with the broad meadow or the narrow valley once he has stood on the high holy ground. Moses, after the mountain, became the poles of mountain/valley humanity, from incarnate father of the tribe of God, to a mumbling sojourner wandering in the desert valley afflicted by the holy pain of truth. Peter wanted to stay on the high holy ground so badly that, in a later dark valley, he denied that he had ever been to the mountain at all.

Maybe we need to realize that the reason God reveals himself on the mountaintop experiences of our lives is in order that we might recognize him in the valley. The mountains are moments, fleeting moments, so powerful and so bright that an image is etched in memory and imagination. This image of God then dwells within us in order that we might call it to awareness when we can see nothing but darkness. The temptation, though, is to assume that God is only on the mountain. That is why one must be cautious about mountain invitations. They are designed to allow us to live in the valleys, where things grow, but may stunt our growth as we desire to stay high, where nothing finally grows. Allow me to take another tack. At Thanksgiving, we found a lonely, hungry, wounded little dog. We found him on Kirby Drive. We fed him, bound his wounds, gave him a bath and a name. He is named Kirby; like good people of the covenant, his name describes the event of his salvation. Ever since that mountaintop experience, Kirby has had a problem. He is not satisfied to be a dog. Ever since he was treated like a human being, he has not been satisfied to be what he is—a dog. He wants to eat at our table, sleep in our beds, bathe in our tub. Kirby is at his worst when he tries to be human. I suppose if I let him drive my car, he would imagine that as a mountaintop experience. Kirby is at his best when he is being a dog. He is at his worst when he tries to be me. I suppose there are days when he wishes he had never been treated like a human.

Every analogy is a three-legged stool. When it is given too much weight, it will topple. I am not simply saying that humans are to God as dogs are to humans, but analogous relationships can be lights in clouds.

We are poised today, awaiting a desert valley season called Lent. We begin it by remembering the mountains. The holy pain of being human is that we have the image of God etched within us. And yet, we will, on Wednesday, be reminded of our desert nature. The ashes of last year's triumphal entry will be imposed in the sign of the cross on our foreheads, the holy contradiction of our dust and divinity that define our humanity. We spend our lives longing for God, left on the mountain and looking for his image in our darkness. The hope is that the God who disappears when we draw near on the high holy ground is the God who appears in the anxiety of doubt in the dusty, dark, desert valley. Christ, whose sign is a cross, is present on mountain *and* in valley. The victim is the victor. The cross of death is the sign of life. Christianity is an invitation to that life lived on high mountains, on broad meadows, and in narrow valleys. But it is not an invitation to live only on the mountain. Be cautious of any religion that invites you to mountaintops alone. Moses knew life lived in its variety of contradictions. Peter knew life on mountains and in valleys and denied and then proclaimed.

And, with due apologies to my little dog Kirby, he does know his identity, even though the world tells him that his food tastes "just like chicken."

Amen.

March 11, 1984
Matthew 4:1–11

I would not be so bold as to try to pinpoint with any historic accuracy when it was that Jesus grew up. I can't do that from my own life, much less for the Savior of all life. But I do believe that there is something in today's Gospel story of Jesus wrestling with evil in the desert which is his university experience. It is the experience of the universe. When he had to deal with his own temptation to worship material goods, or to worship insulation from the slings and arrows of life by hiding in the safe wings of evil, or to worship power and authority, which God knows he had, I think Jesus grew up in those days in the desert. Growing up is hard to do. Growing up is the human vocation. If Jesus is truly the Christ, then it means that he was incarnate in this life and lives his life as you and I must live our lives. That means that he must have had to grow up. Growing up for me has not been easy, and I suspect that it hasn't been for you. But somehow, growing up means taking the dark inner partner and shaking his hand and integrating him into your own internal family. Growing up has so many dimensions of difficulty for all of us.

Sometimes I get so tired of growing up that I want to return to the womb room. Yet, the only womb that awaits is the grave cave. Sometimes I feel like Christopher Robin who wandered so far from home, and I just want to get back to the House at Pooh Corner. My questions take me so far away that I long for days with clear answers, when I wondered such things as how high is up, and what will I be when I grow up. Now, I am the answer. I long for days when there were special people set aside to meet my needs. Nurses or doctors or parents or teachers. Now I'm set apart to do that for others. I long for days when time could not be told. Do you remember the days when you couldn't tell time? Days went by when I saw clouds instead of clocks. I had no appointments, no place to be except but where I was. My only deadline was sleep, and that came easily. Tears came easy then, because crying didn't cost so much, and laughter came easier because I didn't need it so much. Trust was all I had because love was my only possession. Snow or rain or sun were gifts, not intrusions that messed up my life or made me late. Sleep doesn't come easily when you are late. Irresponsibility meant unmade beds and clothes on floors and unclosed doors. My big decisions were what I liked and didn't like and how to fix a broken bike. My fears were the dark and the big dog around the corner with a little bark. And the world was at my back door because my backyard was my world. But somewhere between then and now, then has become now. I long for those childhood days and would not return if I could.

Growing up was difficult for Jesus too. Old men and little boys cry longingly always for the quality of each other. Little boys are afraid of the dark, and old men are afraid of the light. The wisdom of innocence and the innocence of wisdom. Running to adulthood we strive, running away when we arrive. Jesus' story is our story: the reconciliation with our evil, which ultimately is that which seeks to destroy us into nothingness. That growing up rather than down is the human vocation. Jesus was a little boy who grew to be a man and maintained the best, the essential qualities of each—a radical maturity and the soft, innocent quality of youth.

He was light and he was dark for the little ones, and he softens the light for us all, and lightens our darkness. He spoke the truth to family and friends. He cried when his friends died. He became what he was called to be. He cried in his backyard garden. He made a man out of a little boy who brought him fish and loaves. He made little boys out of his disciples who were fishermen when they forbade the children to come to him. He got Zaccheus out of a tree and did the same for everybody from Adam and Eve to you and me, and he did so by climbing on the Tree of Life. Jesus is the Son of God. He frees us to be what we've been—our faith, and what we will become—our hope, and allows us to be what we are—his love. He teaches us the quality of the qualities of life, the ironic nature of nature. He teaches us that we have to grow up in order to grow, or we'll wind up growing down. That only the grown-up can see the quality of little children, and giving up childhood means that we can finally have it, and that in losing it, we find it. The answers have some tentative clarity: that Jesus is set aside to meet our needs. He comes to us in the form of our needs. He cries and makes our tears less salty, and the easier we cry, the easier the laughter comes. The only ultimate decision we have to make is: is Jesus our Christ? For if he is, his story is our story, and dying to childhood doesn't mean dying because, in Jesus' story, death doesn't mean dying…it means growing up.

Amen.

March 25, 1984
Exodus 17:1–7; John 4:5–26

Today's Old Testament and Gospel lessons are literally dripping with water symbols. The people of Israel, in their wilderness wanderings, were parched in their journey. They were at one of those common dry spots in their quest for God. And Jesus, in John's Gospel, saw in a promiscuous woman that she desired more from life than to have her thirst quenched.

Let us address ourselves to these two realities of life: dryness and thirst.

"All the congregation of the people of Israel moved on from the wilderness of Sin by stages…but there was no water for the people to drink." Thus says today's lesson from Exodus. The stage at which we find the people of Israel is the dry stage. I know it well. In every journey, whether one recognizes his journey as spiritual or his life as religious, every life has its dry places. And when one is in a dry time and place, he is apt to be like the Hebrews: in a time of projected blame, wherein he blames everyone and everything for why he is dry. Arid acrimony is the dry clack-clack of one who thirsts and tries to quench his dryness by blaming another. "Therefore the people found fault with Moses, and said...'Why did you bring us up out of Egypt, to kill us and our children and our cattle with thirst?'" What the people of Israel didn't realize, and I'm not sure we do yet, is that dryness is a part of the experience of living. In the same way that we would never ingurgitate water if we didn't thirst, we would never thirst for life unless we tasted the dryness of it. Every life has its drought. That is the time or times when there is nothing green or blue. All is brown and yellow. It is the stage in life when there is no God and no growth. All is stale, nothing blooms. All the containers are empty, nothing is clean or clear, all is dry. One cannot avoid this wasteland, for it is here that one truly begins to appreciate the taste, the true taste of holy, living water. When one is dry, it is a dangerous period, for he will drink anything. One must be very cautious not to drink of that which dominates, but to wait until he cannot live without it, and then he can drink from it. Any superficial savior which promises to quench your thirst when you are dry ought to be avoided.

Look at today's Gospel as to how the true Savior deals with the woman's true thirst, as our Lord encounters the woman at the well. Jesus, as tired as he was from his journey, sat down beside the well. There came a woman of Samaria to drink the water. Jesus said to her, recognizing her thirst, "Give me a drink." The Samaritan woman said to him, "How is it that you, a Jew, ask a drink of me, a woman of Samaria?" For Jews have no dealings with Samaritans. Jesus answered her, "If you know the gift of God, and who it is that is saying to you, 'Give me a drink,' you would have asked him, and he would have given you living water." The woman said to him, "Sir, you have nothing to draw with, and the well is deep; where do you get this living water? Are you greater than our father Jacob...?" Jesus said to her, "Every one who drinks of this water will thirst again, but whoever drinks of the water that I shall give will never thirst; the water that I shall give will become a spring of water welling up to eternal life." The woman said to him, "Sir, give me this water, that I may not thirst again."

The true savior is God as revealed in Christ. That for which we all thirst is ultimately the source of the mystery of the universe. Moses knew this. Moses did not take advantage of the thirst of his people by giving them pietistic platitudes, but he went directly to the source, knowing that he was not the source, but that he must represent the source to the people. So God quenched the thirst, the dry period in that stage of the Hebrew congregation's journey.

In the same way, Jesus encounters this woman who has been thirsting through her life. As the Gospel says, when Jesus asked about her husband, she said, "I have no husband." And he said, "You are right in saying you have no husband, for you have five husbands, and the one with whom you are living now is not your husband." He recognized in this woman that her lust was really a thirst, and lust is the craving of salt by one who is dying of thirst. And so, Jesus promised her not temporary holiness, but the ultimate gift of holiness that can only come through a living water which comes from the Source of all existence.

Water is a symbol. It is a symbol of the very essence of being, for out of the womb waters we come, and a mist moved over the earth and the creation of humankind. The waters that have been crossed through the Exodus and sought in the wilderness. The water of baptism, which is the re-creation. The water is a symbol of life, of death, and of new life, of cleansing, of sustenance, but the water here clearly points beyond itself to the Source of all life. What the Hebrews thirsted for, and what it is we thirst for in our dark, dry places, and what this woman at the well thirsted for, is none other than God himself. One has to be from time to time in an arid place in order to appreciate what it is that gives one a true quenching of one's thirst.

There was another contemporary woman at the well—not in the wondering, wandering wilderness, or at Jacob's well, but in a small town in Alabama, where she experienced the transforming nature of water. It is a story of transcendence—of what is needed—not simply what is desired. And what is needed if we are to know, is a lifetime of transforming experiences, similar to the one in the life of the young woman in Alabama. This young woman was deaf and blind. Helen Keller's breakthrough occurred on a hot summer day, when she first apprehended the meaning of a word, and established a connection with the world, and a possible means of relating to another human being.

At first glance, there may appear to be no evident connection between us and Helen Keller. Her experience seems so unique that it has nothing to do with those of us who are not blind, or not deaf, or not desirous of a link with another, or even with a source. But still, whether in symbol or in fact, whether the wandering people in the wilderness or the woman at the well or the little girl in Alabama, the problem of religious knowing is that we do not hear or see that which is obvious.

As a young child, Helen Keller was stricken by a disease which left her blind, deaf, and unable to speak. Until the age of seven, she existed much like an animal in terms of her limited ability to communicate with other people and to understand the nature of the world around her. In the spring of 1887, her father employed a special teacher and companion for her, Anne Mansfield Sullivan. Working with Helen Keller through that spring, Anne Sullivan taught Helen how to spell rudimentary words by making certain finger signs on her palm. But this was a halting, inadequate form of communication. The child still responded much like a small animal in dealing with people and the things about her. All of this changed, however, one day in the summer of 1887. The record of that day was later made by Helen Keller herself in the following passage from her autobiography. Helen writes:

> We walked down the path to the well-house, attracted by the fragrance of the honeysuckle with which it was covered. Someone was drawing water and my teacher placed my hand under the spout. As the cool stream gushed over one hand she spelled into the other, the word *water*, first slowly, then rapidly. I stood still, my whole attention fixed on the motions of her fingers. Suddenly I felt a misty consciousness as of something forgotten—a thrill of returning thought; and somehow the mystery of language was revealed to me. I knew then that "w-a-t-e-r" meant the wonderful cool something that was flowing over my hand. That living word awakened my soul, gave it light, hope, joy, set it free! There were barriers still, it is true, but barriers that could, in time, be swept away.
>
> I left the well-house eager to learn. Everything had a name, and each name gave birth to a new thought. As we returned to the house every object which I touched seemed to quiver with life. That was because I saw everything with the strange, new sight that had come to me.
>
> I learned a great many new words that day. I do not remember what they all were; but I do know that *mother, father, sister, teacher* were among them—words that were to make the world blossom for me, "like Aaron's rod with flowers." It would have been difficult to find a happier child than I was as I lay in my crib at the close of that eventful day and lived over the joys it had brought me, and for the first time longed for a new day to come.

Helen Keller's experience is that of a second birth in the world. The word "water" had been lost and it was found. It was found out of her mystic consciousness...the recovery of this term, a term she had known before her illness. She was given a sense of life no longer constricted totally by the confines of her physical disabilities. While no sight or hearing returned, she began to discover a universe in which she had a place and a connection. The word gave her power to know beyond herself. It was a breakthrough, a moment of insight—a conversion—a living water, a living word. It awakened her soul—gave it light, hope, joy. Set it free. There were still barriers, it is true, but barriers that could, in time, be swept away.

Dryness, periods of dark doubt, only enhance our thirst in order that we might drink of the living water.

Amen.

❖ ❖ ❖

April 1, 1984
John 9:1–13, 28–38

As Woody Allen has so profoundly stated, "More than any other time in history, mankind faces a crossroads. One path leads to despair and utter hopelessness. The other, to total extinction. Let us pray we have the wisdom to choose correctly."

I can think of no better way to begin a sermon on April Fools' Day than with that kind of absurdist humor. For humor—most particularly, the ability to laugh at ourselves—is a most graceful ingredient for health. We must laugh at our human predicament or succumb to the sickness which leads only to death. Life is so full of ironies. There are contradictions, the puzzles and paradoxes, that make life tense and anxious. These ironies and contradictions are psychological and spiritual racks on which the human psyche is stretched. In religion, we understand that this stretching is necessary for growth, but we are also aware of how this tension can break the spirit. Humor breaks the tension before the tension breaks the spirit.

I mentally create titles for books as statements of the human contradiction, and as tension breakers for stretched spirits. For instance, there must be a book titled: *Cute Places to Eat While Suffering from Existential Anxiety* or *What Is the Safest Car to Drive on the Way to a Mental Breakdown?* This is a biographical title: *He Was Killed on His Way to a Quit-Smoking Class.* Or, most appropriately, *If Christianity Is a Celebration, Why Don't They Laugh in Church?* And, finally, *Can't You See That It Is Illegal to Heal the Blind on Sunday?* Which leads us to today's Gospel.

I think today's Gospel is one of the funniest in all of scripture! Here we have a parody, a pathetic parody, of religious institutions. Jesus saw a blind man, a man who had been blind from birth and was of the lowest estate, that of a beggar. He does a most miraculous thing. He makes this opportunity a living, mysterious metaphor for all of life in the healing of this singular blind man.

The disciples asked Jesus why the man was blind—whose fault it was that he was blind. Jesus responded that we are all blind to God's purposes. Jesus then said that his life of suffering and celebration would shed all the light needed to live in earthly darkness.

And then Jesus reenacted the Genesis story. He took water and dust and made clay, then he put it on the man's dead eyes. And with his breath, he bid him to a new creation through a cleansing baptismal ritual. Jesus re-created sight and light in the world, in this one blind man. Can't you see the incredible power? Can't you see the intricate revelation, revealed in symbol and fact? Can't you see the dust, water, and spirit combined in representing creation, presenting re-creation? Can't you see the incredible, intricate, incremental revelation of all men being born blind and the true light of the world is Christ? Can't you see the simplicity of scripture that tells all of life's story in one life story? Can't you see? Can't you see?

The Pharisees could only see that Jesus had worked on Sunday. They were like someone worrying about what car to drive to a mental breakdown. They were the Church. They were the clergy. And they couldn't see. The blind man saw and the sighted men were blind. Puzzle, paradox, irony…racks to stretch us spiritually. But to break the tension, we have to laugh at them and ourselves. Can't you see that it is illegal to heal the blind on Sunday? What a great title for a book.

Now, lest there be any who walk away this morning wondering what this sermon was about, let me be as clear as a blind man can be.

The man was born blind because he was born blind. We can't know why some see and some don't. But we can know that seeing with the heart is more important than seeing with the eyes.

Next, Jesus as the Christ is the vehicle by which we can always be re-created. We can—with dust, water, and spirit, in symbol and in fact—be made new, if not physically, then psychologically and spiritually.

And lastly, life is full of ironies, contradictions, puzzles, and paradoxes. These make life tense and anxious. These are spiritual and psychological racks on which the human psyche and soul are stretched. In religion, we understand that this stretching is necessary for growth, but we are also aware of how the tension can break the spirit. Humor breaks the tension before the tension breaks the spirit.

More than any other time in history mankind faces a crossroads. One way leads to darkness, despair, and death. The other leads through those to the light. Let us pray we have the wisdom to choose correctly.

I end at the beginning by telling you the title of this sermon: "There Is More to Seeing Than Meets the Eye."

Amen.

✤ ✤ ✤

April 15, 1984
Matthew 27:1–54

Annie Dillard, in her book *Holy the Firm*, speaks of us today: "The higher Christian churches—where, if anywhere, I belong—come at God with an unwarranted air of professionalism, with authority and pomp, as though they knew what they were doing, as though people in themselves were an appropriate set of creatures to have dealings with God. I often think of the set pieces of liturgy as certain words which people have successfully addressed to God without their getting killed. In the high churches they saunter through the liturgy like Mohawks along a strand of scaffolding who have long since forgotten their danger."

We come today in pomp, with apparent authority and parade in pageantry. Pomp and palm branch are sign and symbol of the triumphal entry of Jesus at Jerusalem. It is appropriate that we lose the liturgical drama, rehearse the story, and keep it alive for another year. It is a sacred story. It is the holy story of the people of God and of God in Jesus within his people.

But, we must also realize that the drama can either reveal the truth or hide it.

There is a dimension of the liturgy which appropriately reminds us of the triumphal entry of our Lord, when throngs recognized him as the One who was to come, the God-Bearer, the Messiah, the Christ.

And yet, the pomp and pageantry can cloud the fact that this Palm Sunday parade is the preface to death.

The Christian temptation is to play a liturgical ring-around-the-rosy, and never know what it is that is being said in our ritualistic rehearsal of the sacred story.

Ring-Around-the-Rosy is an appropriate nursery rhyme to illustrate how ritualistic retelling can reveal and hide the truth. Ring-Around-the-Rosy came out of the 17th-century Great Plague of London. It was a ritualistic response of children toward the evil plague, a psychological coping mechanism. Ring-Around-the-Rosy is reference to the rosy rash that appeared as a symptom of the plague. Posy was a bouquet of herbs carried in a pocket to protect against the plague germ. The "ashes, ashes" is a mispronunciation of "ah-choo, ah-choo," the sneeze or cough associated with the plague. And the "all fall down" is the dead dropping all around London as victims of the killer plague. Do we play ring-around-the-rosy with our liturgy? Are we willing to hear the truth? The triumphal entry and palm pageantry tell us that the Christ is come. And since that realization, he is reigning as king. Yet, even so, the struggle is not over, it is just overcome. We must suffer the bloody sweat of the Garden of Gethsemane. (No rose garden or ring-around-the-rosy rhyme.) We must suffer betrayal and denial after the Last Supper. We must be crucified on hard wood and die a thousand deaths in a one-day lifetime.

Let us not lessen the drama; let us live it. Let us not "ride on in majesty" as if nothing happened, or as if we can watch as passive viewers. Let us not play liturgical ring-around-the-rosy and saunter through the liturgy, forgetting the danger signaled in the sacred story. And let us not come back at Easter, to watch the joy of the ultimate joyful victory, unless we have looked death in the face in its forms called: denial, betrayal, sweat, blood, cross, and crucifixion. And let us not make the sacred story child's play by laughing and dancing only…

The final tragedy would be if someone here today did not realize that if you claim to be Christian, then this Holy Week story of passion and suffering is your story. If you claim to be Christian, then Christ has claimed you to live with him through the experience of life, death, and new life. Unless you are willing to die, there will be no Easter—just an empty liturgy, a kind of liturgical ring-around-the-rosy.

But, if you are willing to own your life and claim the claim on you, then come back next Sunday. We will experience the first Easter ever.

Amen.

✤ ✤ ✤

April 29, 1984
John 20:19–31

Lewis Thomas, in a delightful little essay entitled "The Corner of the Eye," describes a physiological phenomenon which results in the fact that there are some things that human beings can see only out of the corner of their eye. The niftiest example of this gift is what he calls the "small stars." I call them "squiggles." They appear at the corner of the eye, and when you try to look straight at one, it disappears. The explanation of this phenomenon has to do with rods, cells, cones, and retinas.

But it also has to do with the way we look at life. It just may be that the "small stars," the "subtle squiggles" seen only out of the corner of the eye, are the messages too often missed. If one looks directly at life, sometimes one only sees the obvious, which is obviously not the only thing to be seen, for there are some things that can be seen only out of the corner of the eye.

Today's Gospel, concerning Doubting Thomas, is one of the great theological pieces in all of sacred literature. Herein, St. Thomas has given succeeding generations permission to doubt. Even St. Thomas the Apostle doubted. And Jesus leaves succeeding generations with permission to believe: "Jesus said [to Thomas], 'Have you believed because you have seen me? Blessed are those who have not seen and yet believe.'"

Now, surely what is seen is a Risen Lord, Jesus by name and fact, Christ by vocation, and God, indeed.

Yet, as I studied this scripture this week I saw something out of the corner of my eye. A subtle but significant star. I became fascinated with why it was that Thomas, when told that Jesus had appeared to them, said, "Unless I see in his hands the print of the nails, and place my finger in the mark of the nails, and place my hand in his side, I will not believe."

I think the not-so-obvious message in Thomas' need to see and touch the wounds has to do with Thomas' refusal to believe in a God that wasn't wounded. Thomas' saintly role is to show us the sacred scars of our Savior. The one that Thomas called his Lord and God was the Scarred Savior, the Wounded God.

I have oft stated before that one does not enter heaven on his medals, but by his scars. No one leaves this life without them. One of the natures of love is to show one another wounds and scars and not turn away. I think I see, out of the corner of my eye, Thomas stating, "I want to touch his scars, his holy sacred scars. I will not worship a god who claims to have become human and leaves this world unscathed." The Christian God is the one revealed in the Christ, and that God, the one true God, is a scarred God that has, through his own suffering with us, sanctified and made all scars sacred. Health and heaven come from the same root word. Heaven symbolizes the time when we will finally be healthy. All wounds will be healed. The one Thomas called Lord and God suffered pain before he was glorified and entered heaven scarred.

There is something about the process of growth toward wholeness that requires doubt and pain and the resulting scars on hearts and hands. But there is also something miraculous about wounds healing. No one truly knows what heals. Perhaps the closest we get consciously to what heals is holding the hand, the wounded hand, of another. That can bring about miraculous healing.

The word "miraculous" comes from the ancient root word "smei." It is the same root from which we get the word "smile." Miraculous and smile: one effects the other, for they come from the same mysterious source.

Before me, I see a complicated life, full of doubt and pain and scars as proof. And yet, out of the corner of my eye, I see a small star which may be Christianity in summary. It's Thomas and Jesus holding hands and smiling. The hands have scars. The sacred scars themselves are small stars—healing in heaven in an Easter's instant.

Amen.

✤ ✤ ✤

May 27, 1984
Acts 17:22–31; John 15:1–8

Arthur Rubinstein was asked several years ago how he felt when people called him the greatest pianist of this century. He responded: "I get very angry when I hear that, because it is absolute, sheer, horrible nonsense. There isn't such a thing as the greatest pianist of any time, or any one nor any thing…"

Competition is to human beings as kicking is to horses. It is natural. There are times when it is necessary. Yet someone is generally hurt or put down because of it.

I have been a competitor most of my life. I believe competition is productive and even entertaining. Most athletics are based on who can finish first with the most. Much of capitalism has competition woven appropriately into its fabric. On the horizontal level, competition may have function. And yet, there comes a point at which competition disappears, like the junction of earth and sky—the horizon, the historical symbol of that which represents history and eternity. In the integration of history into eternity, the growth is away from competition and into completion. That which is complete grows into eternity; those things which compete all turn, and return, to dust at death's dark end. Jesus tries to say, in today's Gospel, that he is the true vine and we, his disciples, are his branches. If we, as branch, do not bear fruit, we wither and die. We must bear fruit if we are to be disciples. In typically human fashion, there has crept into Christianity a sense of competition. In a very simple analysis of a very complicated history, much of the Protestant work ethic is based on production of fruits (fruits are called produce) in order that we might glorify the Father by proclaiming more fruits than anyone else. And, thereby, be more worthy and more holy because we have produced more. Yet, competition defeats—only love completes.

Jesus' teaching is the opposite of competition. He tells us that "the last shall be first; that the defeated will be victorious; that those who work one hour will be paid as much as those who worked all day; if you have done it unto the least, you have done it unto me; the greatest among you shall be servant; humbled shall be exalted; a child is the greatest in the kingdom of God; he who is least shall be greatest."

In God's eyes, there is no competition among his children for favor—we are all loved equally. Like Arthur Rubinstein, I believe competition for the greatest is absolute, sheer, horrible nonsense.

Christianity has not eradicated the competitive spirit in humankind. It has only put it in perspective. Christianity has taught us that success and failure are different on the horizontal level and the vertical level. Wisdom is when that dawns on us, when the sun rises vertically over the horizontal boundary and exposes us to the true fruits of a relationship with Christ.

The fruits of the competitive spirit are power, success, numbers, quantity, production—the world's fruits. They are available to those who are willing to fight hard enough and sacrifice for them.

And then there are the gifts that the world cannot give. Paul called them the fruit of the Spirit: love, joy, peace, long-suffering, kindness, goodness, faithfulness, gentleness, and self-control. These are gifts, true gifts; they cannot be won, bought, sold, earned, stolen, borrowed, built, or destroyed.

When Jesus said, "I am the vine, and you are the branches, and together we will produce fruit," he was not talking about creating a corporate Christianity which would market faith like tomatoes and Toyotas, but one which would—through love—eliminate competition as to who was loved, and complete us by love.

That which competes, defeats. That which loves, completes.

Power, success, and happiness, as the world knows them, are his who will fight, beg, borrow, or steal for them hard enough. But peace, joy, and love are gifts only from God. God is our Beloved Competitor, who, through love, does not compete but completes. It is he who gives us everything by demanding everything from us. He gives us life by demanding our lives—our selves, our wills, our treasures. The defeat is the victory. The world has not yet fully understood that. The world continues to ask, "Who is the greatest?" And the answer is: those who produce fruits—gifts the world cannot give!

Amen.

❖ ❖ ❖

June 3, 1984
Acts 1:1–8; John 17:1–11

"Men of Galilee, why do you stand looking into heaven?"

> The events in our lives happen in a sequence in time, but in their significance to ourselves they find their own order, a timetable not necessarily—perhaps not possibly—chronological. The time as we know it subjectively is often the chronology that stories and novels follow: it is the continuous thread of revelation.
> —Eudora Welty, *One Writer's Beginnings*

I agree with Eudora Welty that events are the continuous thread of revelation. If revelation comes to us, it visits us in events—tangible events. To be religious does not necessarily mean to memorize a religious vocabulary or to know the Bible backward and forward. No more so than one who memorizes baseball jargon and batting averages is a baseball player. To be religious, one must live a religious life, not stand staring at heaven quoting scripture. For me, living the religious life means opening one's eyes and ears in order to see and hear the continuous thread of revelation. That revelation runs through the events, people, places, names, and faces of our day-to-day experience. Reflection on experience, through memory and imagination, may be our first taste of eternity, for time and space are transcended and some thread of revelation comes in reflection.

For instance, I saw the Gospel for today in a most unlikely place. I had a revelation of John 17 in the basement of the municipal civil courts building in courtroom #7. I had been called to Caesar's Palace because of a radical sin of omission. On the hierarchy of mortal and venial sins, this sin ranked below murder and above jaywalking. I was called to courtroom #7 because I had not had my car inspected and my license tag was expired. I explained to the rookie cop who issued the ticket that I had sent in the money for the tag renewal, but it had not arrived in the return mail. The cop was snippy in stating that I'd have to explain that to the judge! It was lucky for that cop that I was a mature religious man or she would have had a real fight on her hands.

So, under threat of a $77 fine, I appeared on Thursday evening, May 31, at 6 p.m. in courtroom #7 in the basement of the municipal courts building. Therein, I found many other accused sardines packed in bureaucratic oil of lapsed driver's licenses, tags, and registration stickers. There we were, packed side by side, in courtroom can #7. And then there appeared a messenger from an absent and anonymous judge. The messenger declared to us that there were three pleas available to us, and we should line up according to our plea. The line on the left was for the plea of "Guilty," the line on the right was for those who wanted to plead "Not Guilty," and the center line was for those who wanted to plead "Guilty with Explanation."

And to my amazement, the entire human predicament and situation was revealed to me; this event was a thread of revelation. To the right, no one lined up. Not one sardine viewed himself "Not Guilty." To the left, no one lined up. Not one of us packed in courtroom can #7, preserved in bureaucratic oil, viewed himself as "Guilty." Everyone in the room was "Guilty with Explanation." Therein, all in a moment in time, the truth of human nature was revealed. Not one of us experiences ourselves to be perfect—none of us claims to be "not guilty" as human beings. But none of us is able to admit that finally, without rationalization or explanation, that we are just simply "Guilty." No, we are all a bit guilty, but we have a reason or explanation as to why!

When my time came, I simply stated that I had now received my sticker for my tag and showed proof that my car was duly and legally inspected. The one who represented the judge took the proof of my claim and dismissed my case.

As I emerged from the basement into the much-needed fresh air, I realized several things. First, the $77 fine in courtroom #7 showed the classical religious #7. The days of creation, the sabbatical, the Sabbath. And, that my boyhood hero, Mickey Mantle, wore #7. Next, I realized that knowing that #7 and Sabbath were the same does not make me any more religious than knowing Mickey Mantle's number makes me hit home runs.

And, lastly, I realized that no human being wants to admit that he is guilty. But no human being is able to claim that he is *not* guilty. We all line up to rationalize our guilt. The world understands this, and provides systems for trying to fit punishment to crime and awards for injured.

But, in the Gospel, the judge is present and named. The messenger is the judge himself, who leaves the bench and enters the crowded courtroom and stands in line for us, and takes the punishment and turns to us and says, "You are free—free to go." The judge is the Savior. Read John 17 carefully, and you'll see.

One more thing: this freedom is given eternally, and the only requirement for the freedom is to *know* the Savior/Judge as Father and Brother.

There is in life a continuous line of revelation found in the most unlikely places. Those who look and listen are religious, for the Gospel is not in a book, but in the world. Reading a book about baseball can't compare with playing the game.

Amen.

❖ ❖ ❖

June 10, 1984
Acts 2:1–11; John 20:19–23

In searching for our link with the people at Pentecost, it is not as clear as a chain; it is more like a rope, bleached by time and frizzled by wear, handled and held by history's hands until, at times, it sees us as a thread in time that links us to the people at Pentecost.

So much has happened in the history of the Church since its inception in Jerusalem some few decades short of two millennia ago. The historical Church, the institutional Church, is in so many ways different from that early apostolic Church. In some ways, perhaps better; in many ways, worse; and in all ways, more sophisticated and complicated. And yet, like the quest for fire, the flame begun at Pentecost has traveled through earthquake, storm, and flood, and that which was ignited at Pentecost remains alive today. And it will be passed to another generation represented in these babies who will be made members of the one, holy, catholic, and *apostolic* Church, the very same Church, in spirit, that was founded by the Holy Spirit, the flame in the wind, at Pentecost two thousand years ago.

We must remember, though, the Spirit does not exist in order to justify the Church; the Church is justified only as it represents the Spirit. Our link, therefore, is not as tangible as a chain, but more mysterious—like a spirit that ties us with the people at Pentecost. A spirit, a Holy Spirit, a spirit wholly one with God and the very same Spirit that is Christ, the Christ, the central symbol of all spiritual wholeness known in and named by no other name but Jesus.

So it is that, ultimately, our link is with the people at Pentecost through history, yes, but more so through the Spirit breathed into people by Jesus and released over and over again, just like today when we will breathe into these children the same spirit that was in the wind and fire at Pentecost, and the same spirit that was breathed into the disciples by Jesus. Let's look quickly at today's Gospel.

On the evening of Easter Day, the first day of the week, the doors being shut where the disciples were, for fear of the Jews, Jesus came and stood among them and said to them, "Peace be with you." When he had said this, he showed them his hands and his side. Then the disciples were glad when they saw the Lord. Jesus said to them again, "Peace be with you. As the Father has sent me, even so I send you." And when he had said this, he breathed on them, and said to them, "Receive the Holy Spirit. If you forgive the sins of any, they are forgiven; if you retain the sins of any, they are retained."

Jesus stood in their midst and said, "Peace be with you." Having said this, he showed both his hands and his side to them.

I spoke several weeks ago on the passage from John which follows, that is, the Doubting Thomas section of John. Therein, I concluded that the interest and emphasis is not only on proof that this identity of Jesus was the body which hung on the cross, but more so evidence that our God suffers and is wounded. The wounds of Christ are his credentials to the suffering world. As William Temple wrote: "Only a God in whose perfect being pain has its place can win and hold our worship; for, otherwise the creature would in fortitude surpass the Creator."

Next, Jesus said, "As the Father has sent me, even so send I you." And when he had said this, he breathed on them and said to them, "Receive the Holy Spirit."

Jesus' words told them to keep his presence alive in the world. The incarnation of God in history was begun in Christ, but continued by the Holy Spirit, which would be in those who wanted to receive it. And he breathed on them and they were sent into the world. That Spirit can be seen everywhere, for it is a truth of life found primarily in relational love of God for his children and them, one for another.

The Spirit is not limited only to the Church; it is only to the Church that it has been given to point to the Spirit's presence in the world. For instance, a movie like *The Natural* can witness to the human need for what the Church proclaims. *The Natural* is this summer's mythic and, for some critics, mesmerizing movie about the human journey set as a contemporary legend in American's national pastime, baseball.

Roy Hobbs is a "natural" at baseball. At twenty, he leaves his farm and heads to Chicago to try out with the Cubs. Before he can do so, he is seduced by a woman in black and shot by her silver bullet, leaving him deeply wounded.

Having left his sweetheart and home, he rode headlong into the real world by railroad. He is derailed and lost. Sixteen years later, he emerges as a rookie in his mid-thirties, trying to become what nature had given him to become and overcome what the world places in his path. He does just that. He becomes the greatest baseball player ever. The plot turns when he is reunited with his long-lost sweetheart, whose lost love inspires him and he, though still wounded, overcomes all adversity and lives happily ever after.

I must state, personally, that this movie was so heavy-handed that I felt full, like I had eaten an eight-course meal in symbols. Though beautifully photographed, I tired of light and dark, women in black and white, Robert Redford's face, and lightning flashes. It was a little heavy to have the antagonist called The Judge, who sat always in the dark. To have the sportswriter who held proof of the hero's guilt or innocence named Max Mercy! Judgment and mercy could have been introduced more subtly. Roy sees his long-lost sweetheart stand in a crowded grandstand dressed in white and he hits a home run that shatters a clock on a tower in center field. We now know that love is eternal and myths kill time. And, in the closing scenes, when his woundedness threatens to do the hero in, he begins to shed blood out of his side; luckily, it did not pour from spike holes in his hands and feet.

All heavy doses of symbols aside, I must say that the message of the movie is one with which the Church should be familiar. We are born gifted, yet none of us are gifted enough to make it on our own. We will be wounded, and yet love heals all wounds. And second chances, new lives, and new births are always possible. When I hear that story—that word—even in a popular movie, my throat is crowded by joy.

The Christian essence is found everywhere. People are persons because God is in history—our history, our very story—as a father looking for children to become what they cannot by nature become without love. In Jesus Christ, God has done his caring and coming, and he seeks so as to participate in our longing, suffering, and needing in such a way as to make sense out of it. In Christ Jesus, he not only demonstrates that our suffering belongs to sense and meaning, but he sews up the torn places and anoints the scars. Then he breathes on us a commission to do no less for one another.

We must see him and show him, recognize and identify him in our lives everywhere we breathe. Our response to him is to become willing to let life flow through us, to be learners, hearers, and bearers. We must be willing to keep the flame, the warm wind of the Spirit, alive. Our link with the Pentecost people is a gossamer through time, the historic Church, but more so a Spirit in eternity that is breathed in love from one human being to another in Christian love from generation to generation.

Bring me the babies, that we might bathe them in water and breathe the Spirit into them, and rest assured that the Pentecost flame will not be extinguished by this generation.

Amen.

September 2, 1984
Matthew 16:21–27

Some anonymous, perhaps apocryphal, voice lamented this dismal epitaph of life: "Life is hard and then you die." That statement would not pass for truth, but it survives on a thread of truth. Suffering and death are ingredients in the life process. Jesus told his friends and followers in today's Gospel: "It is time to suffer in the city and die." Peter cried, "Can't you leap the tall buildings in Jerusalem in a single bound? Can't you outrun the speeding arrows? Aren't you above pain and death?" Jesus said, "Nope. It is part of the process. Peter, when you try to make me a super man, you speak like Satan. If you are going to follow me, then you have to live the whole of life. Follow me. Quit worrying about yourself. You will find yourself by giving up yourself for me. If you lose your life for my sake, you'll come alive. What will it profit you if you gain the whole world and lose your life? Follow me and life will follow you."

Two points today. First, watch what god or gods you worship. Those who promise you to be superhuman are the gods who die. The one God who promises you will be fully human is the one who lives. Second, we Christians believe that death is not the end of life, but a part of life, spiritually and physically.

A great tendency is for human beings to worship themselves. When we do that, we play God and worship pride. When that happens, we take human ideals, make them idols, and the gods die. For instance, there has been for some time an ideal that has now died from treatment as an idol. To be a woman meant to be beautiful, graceful, and talented. This cult coming out of Atlantic City told us, "There she is, Miss America. There she goes, your ideal." It is at one level possible to see the Miss America pageant as merely an over-publicized prank foisted on us by the advertising industry. And, Miss America is the icon of consumer society. And yet, there is something more there. The idolizing and objectifying of women as only ideal when they are beautiful with perfect bodies—that god deserves to die an idol's death, which, if not dead, is now tarnished and deserving of new thought.

Another danger area I see currently—and I realize this is not going to be a popular point—is what I would call American hubris. Hubris is a psychological inflation that will eventually burst. With the Olympic victories, which I loved as much as any, and this summer's political conventions, we run the risk of making a god out of ourselves. Just a caution…but any god who promises to be superhuman dies. We must be proud of being American, yet not deny that we have illnesses and weaknesses that cannot be overlooked by pride. Whenever any person or people deny their humanity and act as if they are God, then pride will prophesy death. Carl Sandburg's painful poem, "Four Preludes on Playthings of the Wind," speaks of the danger:

1

The woman named To-morrow
sits with a hairpin in her teeth
and takes her time
and does her hair the way she wants it
and fastens at last the last braid and coil
and puts the hairpin where it belongs
and turns and drawls: Well, what of it?
My Grandmother, Yesterday, is gone.
What of it? Let the dead be dead.

2

The doors were cedar
and the panels strips of gold
and the girls were golden girls
and the panels read and the girls chanted:
    We are the greatest city,
    the greatest nation:
    nothing like us ever was.

The doors are twisted on broken hinges.
Sheets of rain swish through on the wind
    where the golden girls ran and the panels read:
    We are the greatest city,
    the greatest nation,
    nothing like us ever was.

3

It has happened before.
Strong men put up a city and got
  a nation together,
And paid singers to sing and women
  to warble: We are the greatest city,
    the greatest nation,
    nothing like us ever was.

And while the singers sang
and the strong men listened
and paid the singers well
and felt good about it all,
    there were rats and lizards who listened
    …and the only listeners left now
    …are…the rats…and the lizards.

And there are black crows
crying, "Caw, Caw,"
bringing mud and sticks
building a nest
over the words carved
on the doors where the panels were cedar
and the strips on the panels were gold
and the golden girls came singing:
    We are the greatest city,
    the greatest nation:
    nothing like us ever was.

The only singers now are crows crying, "Caw, caw,"
And the sheets of rain whine in the wind and doorways.
And the only listeners now are…the rats…and the lizards.

We must exercise caution anytime we speak of ourselves as gods. Death will come to those who worship themselves or one another. Life will come to those who worship the one God revealed in Christ, who said, "For whoever would save his life will lose it, and whoever loses his life for my sake will find it. For what will it profit a man if he gains the whole world and forfeits his life?" Christians believe, yes, it is our experience that death will come to everything human. But each death of the human is potential change to that which is eternal. In death, life is not ended…changed, but not ended.

If we insist on worshiping bodies and faces, or one another, or cities, or nations, then death will end that idol. But, if we invest in the living Christ, nothing can end that forever. Amen.

September 16, 1984
Matthew 18:21–35

A woman and wife, exhausted and exasperated, exclaimed, after her husband came home drunk for the four hundredth time, "Only ninety more!" A friend quizzed her about her numerical hope, to which she responded, "The Bible says I only have to forgive him four hundred and ninety times. You know, seventy times seven. Well, only ninety more!"

Like most literal interpretations of scripture, the letter is intact, but the spirit of the text is missed in the poor woman's legal limit on forgiveness. In today's Gospel, Peter asks Jesus, "How often shall we forgive our friends when they sin against us? As many as seven times?" Jesus answers, "I do not say seven times, but seventy times seven!" Jesus then goes on to tell a parable, which clears up the issue and makes a singular parabolic point: God *forgives* us without limit. That is the least we should do for one another.

As Canon Logan reminded us in Bible Study several weeks ago, the only unforgiven sin is the one for which forgiveness is not asked. God is the source of the mystery, and one of the great mysteries is the freedom of choice, coupled with confusion, about which choice is right. Even those who want to do the right thing can't because of confusion, more than they won't because of conviction. God knows how freedom will inevitably, eventually cause separation, for when we choose against God's will, we are separated or in sin. Yet, much of the time, since we aren't God, we don't know His will. And we choose freely through glasses darkly. The only limitation on God's forgiveness—for God does understand the mystery—is placed there by us.

The only sin not forgiven is the one for which forgiveness is not asked. If God is willing to do that for and with us, the implication should be clear in reference to our forgiveness of one another.

The issue for me has never been God's ability to forgive me, but rather my ability to forgive myself or others, or accept another's forgiveness. And yet, the implication for Jesus is that all forgiveness emanates from God and we simply recognize it in ourselves and one another. And, most importantly and simply, we must accept our acceptance. We tend to forgive in direct relationship to our awareness of our own forgiveness. Those who don't forgive tend to be those who don't recognize or accept their own forgiveness.

We each seek completeness. What we call sins are signs or symptoms of our incompleteness. In order to grow toward completion or wholeness, we must grow in increments, and our sins are signs of where growth is necessary. Words such as neurotic or psychotic are contemporary incompleteness. In the old days, a psychopathic homicide was murder. And a kleptomaniac was a thief. Killing and stealing have been sins, signs of incompleteness, since Adam and Eve wanted to become whole without any work. Growth—that is, growing up to our call to be human—requires time and effort in which we will experiment, abuse, lie, cheat, steal, and kill in one form or another. In order to have the energy and power to start over at these crucial periods, we need to know that it is okay to start over. Where there is original sin, there is original love. Love is energy and power to start over, given as gift—grace—gift given for us. Forgiveness. No matter what you have done or been, you can start again.

Forgiveness is the process of naming and claiming your incompleteness and taking the energy of God's love in order to grow into and through the problem. If we can accept our own humanity and God's forgiveness for our free choices, some of which are wrong, then it is amazing how forgivable others become. When I am forgiven, others become forgivable.

A lady in another place at another time came to me distraught and destroyed because her husband had confessed an affair and was seeking forgiveness. She related, "It is horrible. I can't forgive him for how he has hurt me!" I asked her what unforgiven sin in her was a barrier to her forgiving her husband. A premarital pregnancy and abortion for which she had never felt forgiven was not only a contributing factor to her husband's affair, but a barrier to her ability to forgive.

I told her the story of the monk who went to his abbot as the abbot lay on his deathbed. "Father Abbot," said the monk, "tomorrow you will be in heaven with our Christ. When you are in his presence, remind him of my deep act of sin in my youth. Ask him if I am forgiven of the terrible act, and if it is his will, return to me with his response."

The abbot died and in three days returned to the monk. "Brother, I have returned to reveal God's forgiveness."

The monk asked, "You have been with our Lord?"

"Yes," said the abbot.

"And did you ask him of my terrible sinful act?"

"Yes," replied Father Abbot. "Our Lord said he remembered you, but concerning your terrible act of sin, he said he didn't remember, for what you are is because of who you were. He remembers you. Your sin is forgotten."

We, as Christians, can esteem ourselves. Not pride, for we know who we are. We name and claim our sin, and when we see it in one another, we look to one another as God does. We are forgiven, loved, gifted, grace given, forgiven.

I think of the poor woman who forgave her drunk husband four hundred times. God surely forgave her for indulging that drunk for that long, and we must do the same.

Amen.

❖ ❖ ❖

October 28, 1984
Matthew 22:34–46

At some point in our development, each of us has felt like Charlie Brown in general, and in particular in the *Peanuts* comic strip, whereby Charles Schultz has Charlie Brown lamenting to his friend, Linus, about his chronic, lifelong sense of insecurity. "It goes all the way back to the beginning," he says. "The moment I was born and stepped on the stage of history, they took one look at me and said, 'Not right for the part.'"

Insecurity has two clear purposes: to make or break the human spirit. Security is not to be confused with safety. Safety means freedom from danger, risk, or injury. Security means being rooted in something that will allow you to survive danger, risk, and injury.

Jesus offers us security in the face of all our insecurities. He does not offer safety, but security. Hear what our Lord Jesus Christ says in today's Gospel: "You shall love the Lord your God with all your heart, and with all your soul, and with all your mind. This is the first and great commandment. And the second is like unto it: You shall love your neighbor as yourself. On these two commandments depend all of the law and prophets."

Love/Agape, the unconditional love of God, is that which roots us secure in spite of the fact that life is unsafe. To be loved by God does not mean we will be free from risk or danger, injury or death. To be loved by God means we need not be insecure in the face of the unsafe. We can risk and court danger, knowing that we eventually will be hurt and die, yet the love of God makes us secure in spite of all the evidence which causes one to feel insecure.

Charlie Brown felt wrong for the part. The stage of life and the mysterious script cause some insecurity. The basic insecurity which makes us wonder if we are right for the part can be that which *makes* us. The question of who we are called to be and who we are to become is only answered by taking risks and acting with limited knowledge. That existential anxiety, or fear of the unknown, makes one feel insecure. Each of us knows the sense of contradiction and confusion that renders us unable to act. That is the point whereby insecurity can make or break. It is a holy moment. Rudolf Otto has written:

> If in a mystic moment
> You feel something drawing you into the situation,
> Something powerful like a magnet,
> And if at the same time
> Something within you is afraid, resisting
> Wanting to move back…withdraw…
> If you feel yourself wanting to run toward
> And run away from the moment at once…
> You can be fairly sure
> You are standing on Holy Ground.

Insecurity can lead one into his or her next growth period. Insecurity can call forth regenerating change; or insecurity can begin disintegrating change, whereby one feels insecure, seeks safety, is afraid to move, takes no risks, courts no danger, and dies a death of psychic debilitation, weakened and lame from fear.

The Christian Good News is that God loves us without qualification or condition. Jesus reminds us therefore that if God loves us, the least we can do is love ourselves and others. Jesus' famous words, "Thou shalt love thy neighbor as thyself," are as much a statement of psychological fact as they are ethical imperative. The truth is: we *will* love our neighbors as we love ourselves! The pattern we develop of relating to that person close to us, namely ourselves, becomes the paradigm of the way we will relate to all people. We need to believe in solitary love; you might meet an interesting person that way.

If we believe God loves us and sees us as lovable, then we need not be afraid to take a risk to become our part. Love of God allows love of self, and love of self allows love of others. That is a rootedness in love, a security that fears nothing. Christians have nothing to fear but nothing itself, for without love, we are nothing.

We cannot as Christians claim safety. We can claim security and proclaim that we are loved and free to risk and be injured and even be free to die. Unsafe, but secure. Grace means we can make no mistakes.

Insecurity, then, has two clear purposes: to make or break the human spirit. The insecurity that is always calling to us to become more makes us more than we deserve if we are willing to see change as growth. Some fear change even when it is from worse to better. The fear comes because of the confusion between safety and insecurity. The insecurity that fears risk and danger and seeks safety will be the place at which evil begins to disintegrate into the grave of nothingness, empty, nonbeing—hell. Hell is safe. Heaven is secure. Insecurity may be the Holy Spirit calling you to become more and more, or insecurity may be a hobgoblin calling you to become less and less.

If you worry about the ground on which you must decide—whether the insecurity is from heaven's call or hell's fear—then remember that you are on holy ground. You need not be afraid. Insecurity can only make you. Because of the love of God in Christ, the making of you was found in the breaking of Christ on a cross at Calvary.

Make no mistake—you can in the eyes of God make no mistake. You may always start again, even if you play the wrong part. The reasons of God are unknown to reason, but for some reason, God loves us and wants us to love ourselves and others. For some reason, he has made life unsafe. We will be hurt and pained. But, in spite of the insecurity, we can rest secure in the love of God through Christ to each one of us and every other person—rooted in the love of God from which nothing can separate us. It is a peace that passes understanding. In that you can rest *secure*.

Amen.

1985

February 10, 1985
Mark 1:29–39

I would wish that we would recognize the Christ as well as evil does. And vice versa. In verse 34 of today's Gospel, we are told that "[Jesus] would not permit the demons to speak because they knew him." Of course they knew him. Where there is love attempting to unite, integrate, heal, and make whole, there is evil seeking to divide, disintegrate, make ill, and leave nothing.

One thing that must be learned about life's rules—applying even to Jesus, the King of Love—and that is: to light a candle is to cast a shadow. Wherever there is love attempting to work its mystery, there is evil attempting to work its magic. Wherever Jesus was, there was evil also. Wherever holy things are, evil will be found lurking in the shadows, waiting for the time when it can disguise itself and begin its task. Evil could not work its way in Jesus' presence. He did not deny it and therefore allow it to disguise itself. He recognized evil and therefore he could control, conquer, or cast it out. He hoped in the beginning that *we* would know him as well as he was known by evil. After his baptism, the first person to greet him was the evil one in the famous desert dialogue with the diabolical. There we were taught that where there is light, there is darkness; where there is love, there is apathy; where Christ is, there evil awaits, offering magic in the midst of mystery.

For Jesus, evil existed in its own right. One's love or growth comes primarily through consciousness of and in opposition of evil, not by its denial. It is only consciousness and love which allow us to not only overcome the power of evil, but to use its power for healing and wholeness. Evil stands in fundamental opposition to wholeness. We must recognize that where good is, evil is also. The Christ is the consciousness of this and the symbolic power by which evil is silenced. Jesus would not allow voice or vote from evil.

Two examples, one corporate and one individual. In corporate terms, when a community develops a virtuous good, evil will disguise itself as self-righteousness. Christianity continues to fall victim to this. We have a gospel of love so valuable that we want everyone to have it. "And if you won't accept our freedom, we will imprison you. Accept our love or we will kill you." Thus, the Crusades and the Inquisition. No bigotry is worse than religious bigotry. The Crusades and Inquisition should be over, but from time to time they raise their anachronistic evil heads and enter a community to eliminate vice with virtue. And the community is seduced into villainous in order to enforce virtue.

In individual love relationships, we seek a union through intimacy, and where wholeness is sought, evil will disguise itself as love and seek to destroy the very goal of its opposite. We always hurt the ones we love. Evil will attach itself to appetite and gratification and seek pleasure or expediency over substance and appropriateness. Where there is strong love seeking union, there will be strong evil seeking discord. Where God offers grace, there is evil seeking disgrace.

Paul writes that where sin abounds, grace abounds more. That is the good news. Christ taught it first. We must be more aware of evil than the unholy or the pagan. For evil is more attracted to the religious than the irreligious. This tension of opposites is the reality of God.

Tom Stoppard writes: "Atheism is the crutch of those who can't bear the reality of God." I would wish that we would recognize the Christ as well as evil does. And would that we would recognize evil as well as the Christ does.

The good news is this: that love is stronger than evil if one will be bold, steadfast, and unafraid of evil. For it has been overcome in Christ. Love is stronger if one will strive to be conscious—self-conscious of evil rather than self-righteous. One's true self is that part of one which has embraced evil, quieted its power, and turned it into a positive force. One must love one's shadow through the light of Christ. Christ is the light, and the dark hath comprehended it not!

Amen.

❖ ❖ ❖

March 24, 1985
Jeremiah 31:31–34; John 12:20–32

On Thursday morning of this week, I spent a significant hour and a half listening to author John Updike speak with students and faculty at the University of Houston's Department of

Creative Writing. He said many things of substance. One of the most substantial statements was under the rubric of advice to a young writer: "make a virtue of necessity."

That which is necessary to life is that which is most common. That which is common loses its value because it is available to all. Scarcity tends to dictate value. Availability tends to devalue. Breath, necessary as it is, is undervalued as long as it is available. The same is true of heartbeat. It is so necessary that each needs, but as long as each has, it is not virtuous to obtain another heartbeat or drawn breath.

We undervalue necessity. That which is necessary is at the same time mundane. Updike's advice carries universal application and theological acuity.

Speaking to visiting Greeks, Jesus shows the virtue of necessity in today's Gospel. "The time has come for [me] to be glorified. I have come to this hour for a specific purpose. Father, glorify…like grain which must die in order to bear fruit, I, too, must die."

Jesus spoke of his necessity as virtue. Death is a common act. The most mundane. Death is a necessity of life. Jesus saw it as a glorious event. He made a virtue of all necessity—by his death.

The young writer must learn the necessity of discipline, editing, rewriting, reading, study, submission, rejection, and resubmission. Like the adolescent who must learn to delay gratification, one cannot be mature until one learns that the necessary must be accomplished in order for the glory to come to the virtuoso of any discipline.

Why, then, do we as Christians suffer under the burden of necessity? God in creation has glorified life—all of life. It is good. It is very, very good. And we seek only that which gratifies the pleasure principle. And we reject that which is necessary, avoiding the purpose principle. Necessity is virtuous. The world is our necessity. We continually look for a savior who will remove us from the world and its necessities. We will worship anything that will deliver us from the mundane realities. We somehow have been taught that salvation means deliverance from the necessary. And yet, the Christian message is that we are saved in and for the world, not saved out of and from the world. Jesus' death made all death virtuous. Necessary, still, but valuable. We are always looking elsewhere for meaning and purpose, as if it is to be found at another time, in another place. We are created for this world and redeemed in this world. Our meaning, purpose, and being is in the mundane miracle between birth and death. And then beyond. The miracle in life is in life. We believe in life after birth.

John Claypool, our Lenten speaker this Wednesday at noon, reminds us in his new book, *Opening Blind Eyes*, of the old Zen image of a man riding on an ox, looking for an ox. That is what we do when we look for meaning elsewhere. We go through life looking for an ox while riding on one. We must open our eyes to see the glory that lies about us. Believing is seeing for Christians. Believing that creation is good and that we are saved for this world. Once we believe that, we can see that the miraculous is in the mundane, the extraordinary in the ordinary, the wonder in the world, the virtue in the necessity.

This is what Thomas Merton called "a breakthrough into the already." A Sufi story helps. In a small land, they allowed limited imports. A man left the country weekly and returned with a donkey. The man grew more and more wealthy. The border guards, convinced that he was a smuggler, searched him and his donkey weekly and yet in vain. The man became one of the wealthiest in the land. On his deathbed, he was asked the source of his wealth. He responded, "I smuggled donkeys." We must, as Jesus says, "have the eyes to see."

We have a covenant with God. Jeremiah reminds us that the New Covenant is written, not on tablets, but in hearts. God loves us and created the world for us. Our life and all its necessities are holy ground. Even the ultimate necessity, death, has been glorified by God in Christ. Even death has virtue as that which defines life and is the transition from history to eternity. We each seek God elsewhere. We fear or ignore the holy miracle of the mundane and the wonder of the world by looking for meaning only in the easy, pleasurable, or happy. God is not everywhere, but is wherever you are. God is not elsewhere.

Amen.

✤ ✤ ✤

March 31, 1985
Palm Sunday
Mark's Passion

The conclusion of Mark's passion leaves us as the curtain in the temple, torn in two from top to bottom. A broken body is breathing a last gasp. Jesus of Nazareth, suffering servant, hanging across a tree of torn dreams and physical torment, crying as one forsaken. Looking into the twofold contradiction of a cross—one piece pointing to eternity and the other to history—the centurion, caught in the middle, saw the analogue in the temple tapestry torn in two. In the midst of a man who is God, on a visible contradiction of a tree rooted in history and pointing to eternity, the soldier saw the truth in the contradiction, "and the curtain of the temple was torn in two, from top to bottom. And where the centurion, who stood facing him, saw that he thus breathed his last, he said, 'Truly this man was the Son of God.'" Palm Sunday is Passion Sunday. Passion is from the Latin *passio* and the Greek *pathos*, which mean "to suffer." Passion is any strong feeling that requires something from the feeler. We suffer the contradiction of the pleasure and pain when we feel deeply about another.

To love is to suffer. Love is, at times, another word for hurt. As I am fond of saying, there is no risk of pain in love. You will be hurt. This is the contradiction. This is the passionate paradox. This is the torn in two from top to bottom. Some truths are so large that they require their opposite in order to hold the entire truth. Love is the greatest pleasure and the greatest pain. Passion is paradox.

God so loved the world that he gave it fire and ice, light and dark, life and death. Each is necessary in order that each may find its identity in its opposite. Love is joy and despair. Each is necessary in order to be complete. Passion Sunday is the Sunday we stand staring at a cross. The passionate paradox of the life-giver's dying, the lover of the world, despised by his neighbors. The Prince of Peace, murdered. The father, forsaking.

Passionate, pathetic as it is, the suffering servant hangs in contradiction. The truth is so large that it requires both life giving and death dealing. The centurion is the watchman who stares into the contradiction of a life-giver dying. He watches the curtain in the temple, torn in two from top to bottom, standing, facing the passion of Christ after the last breath of Christ. In the first breath the guard takes, he is forced to utter the words, "Truly, this man was the Son of God."

Between now and Sunday, please watch. Watch your own life—its passionate paradoxes which threaten to tear you in two—and see the truth in the tension. Watch like a silent sentry the last gasp of a life which needs to die in order to live. Watch as a sentinel of growth at the torn parts of your life fabric; see if a new pattern needs to emerge. Be passionate about your life and compassionate with your loves. We are all torn in two, rent in twain, by life.

And yet, there is the deep breath of hope which follows the last gasp of life. Truly this contradiction on a cross, the passionate paradox, Jesus the Christ is the Godfather and God, Son, and God Spirit of us all.

Watch for the torn in two to be made one. It has. It is. It will be. I promise with all the passion possible. I know that which dies lives, and that which is torn in two becomes one again. I promise. I am the watchman. I have seen it with my own eyes. Watch with me as we keep the Easter vigil in this holy week. I promise that it will, it will be…

Amen.

April 7, 1985
Easter Day
Mark 16:1–8

The greatest source of light for human sight is the sun. Yet, if we stare into the giant star, we will be blinded.

Frederick Buechner tells of the night he stood on the bridge of a small British freighter somewhere near the middle of the Atlantic:

> I was talking to a young officer with red hair who told me something that is very useful to know. He had been looking around to see if he could spot the lights of any other ships on the horizon, and what he told me was this: "The way to see lights on the horizon is not to look at the horizon, but to look at the sky just above it." And I discovered that he was right. This is the way to do it. Since then I have learned that it is also the way to look at other things.

I am not sure we really want to take responsibility for the resurrection. To look at it directly would eradicate our excuses and disintegrate our dependencies. We would be free if we looked at the risen son. But that much light might blind us. So, sadly, we live in the dark for fear of blindness. Resurrection to humans is as life is to fetuses. No fetus has any consciousness that he can exist without that umbilical cord; so it is with us. The freedom of resurrection is not good news when one is dependent on some source of life other than the Source of Life. The air of life is inhaled naturally. And we fear any mystery that changes what is natural. Anthropologist and naturalist Loren Eiseley has written:

> I am sure now that life is not what it is purported to be and that nature, in the canny words of a Scotch theologue, "is not as natural as it looks." It is not as easy to say as we once did that life arose naturally out of matter.

Eiseley concludes his examination of the immense journey of life by stating:

> I would say that if "dead" matter has reared up this curious landscape of fiddling crickets, song sparrows, and wondering [people], it must be plain even to the most devoted materialist that the matter of which he speaks contains amazing, if not dreadful powers, and may not impossibly be, as Hardy has suggested, "but one mask of many worn by the Great Face behind."

Resurrection means staring into the great face, without mask of nature. The supernatural cannot be tolerated by the human eye, except in the sanctuary of the symbol. Today is Easter, Easter Sunday, the day we can risk taking a direct look into the freedom of eternity. We need not look out of the corner of our eye for the subtlety. We need not look at the sky above the sun. We can, just for a moment, open our fearful fluttering lids and look directly into the truth—we are free.

Christ has cut the cord to the natural world. We can inhale the mystery for ourselves. Today we need not sit in the darkness for fear of blindness. We can risk looking at the light. It need not be reflected or deflected, corrected or directed; we can stand this one moment and stare at the magnificent truth. Excuses are absolved, reasons are resolved, fears are dissolved, and we are set free for this one magnificent moment.

We need not be guilty, anxious, cautious; we need not explain, rationalize, or justify; we can be children of the mystery, laughing and playing joyfully in eternity today. Easter is the promise that though it is human to be in bonds, the time will come that knows no boundaries. Easter is the promise that though it is human to see limits, the time will come when we can fulfill unlimited dreams. Easter is the promise that though it is human to fear, the time will come when the perfect lover will cast out all fear. Easter is the promise that though it is human to sit in the darkness for risk of blindness, the time will come when eyes and tombs will be opened, and human boundary, limit, fear, and darkness will be illumined and illuminated.

Today is the only day, and this moment the only moment, in which we can look directly into the light at the horizon and not fear blindness by looking directly into the eastward brink, and whisper our "Ah!" at the risen sun.

Amen.

✤ ✤ ✤

April 21, 1985
Luke 24:36–48

Incarnational theology is a sophisticated term, but put very simply, it's an experience. We tend to teach incarnational theology at Christmastime when the Word becomes flesh and dwells among us, full of grace and truth. But I suspect the best time to do so is with the post-resurrectional appearances of Christ, where we begin to be taught and enabled and given permission to recognize Christ in the midst of the faithful, maybe even occasionally in the midst of a faithful person.

In the early spring of 1970, I had been a priest but three months. It was time to take Easter communion to the shut-ins. Margaret Perry, a communicant of St. Paul's parish in Kansas City, lived deep in its inner city. I had not yet been there a year, but I had met Margaret. She had been a patient at St. Mary's Hospital the previous winter, and I had called on her there in December, shortly before I was ordained priest in 1969. She followed the church personnel and programs through the bulletin. When I saw her in the ward at the hospital, she was so sick that she could hardly lift an eyelid, but one lid she did lift, and with a rolling focus, she centered on me and said, "You're the new young priest?" "Yes ma'am, I will be on the twenty-ninth." I responded. She said something else with a whistling sound that comes from a toothless attempt at talk. I said nothing, hoping her statement wasn't a question. She penetrated the silence with impatience, for I had not answered the question I had not heard. "Where's Jesus?" she all but shouted. That was the question to which she wanted an answer. Knowing she had pneumonia, and frightened by her question, I patted and patronized her with a condescending, "Do not try to talk, Miss Perry. Let me have a prayer with you." I prayed for her healing, she closed her eyes, and I moved out into the broad sterile hallway of that old hospital with an unanswered question echoing like my steps in that passage into the cold gray winter day.

It was spring. I was now a priest. Time was to take Easter communions to the shut-ins. Margaret Perry's house was a second-floor walk-up. The stairs were on the outside and cross-stitched across the front of the building. When I knocked on her door, she yelled for me to enter. She sat in a worn, overstuffed chair with stuffing hanging from the rolled arms. Her feet rested on a hassock. She wore blue felt house shoes (holey) and a housecoat buttoned up the front save the last one, revealing hose rolled below the knee. Still, she wore no teeth. Her hair was a nest hatching a pair of wire-rimmed glasses. Squinting, she recognized me and smiled an open smile, and with a twinkle, she quoted, "How like a winter hath my absence been from thee."

Miss Perry, amidst newspapers from the '50s, magazines from the '40s, and food from who knows when, sat and taught me simple but sophisticated incarnational theology. I never think of the post-resurrectional appearances of Jesus, as we have today in Luke's Gospel, that I don't think of Miss Perry and her question of me that winter's day before I was ordained. Where is Jesus? After a time, I reminded Margaret of her question to me from her hospital bed and wanted her answer. She replied, "Where is Jesus? He ain't in hell. For God's sake, he is in you, boy!"

Our resurrectional theology teaches us that Jesus lives now in each of us—even in our own hells—he lives in his spirit which is holy. The image of God begins us. It stays with us until we are complete. That holy word came to me from a theologian in holey house shoes. And, if we are bold enough to call ourselves Christian, then wherever we are, there is where Jesus is—from Jerusalem to Kansas City to Houston. Wherever two or three of us are, he is in the midst.

I buried Margaret Perry in the winter of '72. There were few there. I quoted Shakespeare: "How like a winter [will] my absence be from thee." It was not understood by the funeral director or the two grave diggers, but Margaret and I understood. And so did Jesus, for he was there, too.

Amen.

May 12, 1985
John 15:9–17; I John 4:7–21

Marc Chagall died this spring. God's graceful artist of play, fantasy, and mystery was described by Picasso in this way: "Chagall must have had an angel in his head." Floating angels, green fiddlers, smiling pigs were the creative genius's media for mystery—creation as seen through recreation—that continue to catch us off guard and surprise us with the joy of a moment of playful beauty.

Chagall's theology was symbolized in his art and verbalized by the artist: "In our life there is a single color as on an artist's palette, which provides the meaning of life and art. It is the color of love."

Jesus and, nonetheless, St. John the Divine, give foundation to Chagall's floating angel when they play before our ears their poetic thoughts on love.

Jesus first, as it should be, for John is but an echo of the truth spoken by the primary source of mystery. And Jesus said, "As the Father has loved me, so have I loved you; abide in my love. These things I have spoken to you, that my joy may be in you and that your joy may be full" (as a floating fiddler green as grass and a pink angel soaring past smiling pigs). "You did not choose me, but I chose you. This I command you, to love one another."

And John, picking up his artist's palette of words, chooses Jesus' same color—love—and echoes the revealed truth: "Beloved, let us love one another; for love is of God, and he who loves is born of God and knows God. If God so loved us, we ought to love one another. God is love, and he who abides in love abides in God, and God abides in him."

Chagall is correct. In our life, there is a single color—it is love. It colors everything we are or do.

We are not talking here about the love that takes—eros. We are talking about the love that gives—agape. Greater love hath no human than agape which gives up itself for another. Eros, the desire of a subject to possess an object, is a *need* love. The problem of eros, and its companion, sexual love, is not in its lack of beauty (for erotic love can be beautiful) or in its lack of propriety (for in context, it can be most appropriate), but in its confusion with agape.

Eros is the instinctual need to possess. It is likely to be linked with and grow to mean a highly romanticized, sentimental sort of enterprise that comes and goes like the haze it is.

What makes eros tragic is not its need that is filled, but the greater need that is left empty. Our society is filled with people for whom the sexual relationship is one where body meets body, but where person fails to meet person, where the immediate need for gratification is satisfied at the cost of the deeper need for knowing. Where deep friendship, or Christian love, known as giving love, is sacrificed for erotic love, or need love. The sexual gratification is satisfied, but the need for companionship and understanding is sacrificed. The result is that the relationship leads not to fulfillment, but to a half-conscious sense of incompleteness, of inner loneliness, which is the sickness of our time.

Eros, the love born of need, is blessed when coupled with commitment. At the heart of it, I believe that eros love has as its goal the same as agape—that is, the need and desire to know. That is what Jesus meant when he said, "Greater love has no one than when he gives up his life for another." By giving up, I not only give my life to my friend, but also find it for myself. Agape love works as great a miracle in the heart that gives it, as in the heart to which it is given. To become fully a person, I need to sacrifice myself in agape love no less than my friends need my sacrifice. In the words of Frederick Buechner, "Eros, the love that seeks to find; and agape, the love that seeks to give, spring finally, I think, from the same deep impulse of the human heart, which is the impulse to be one with each other, and within ourselves, and ultimately with God." He, like John, echoes Jesus, "When we love, God lives within."

And yet, finally, we must realize that human love has its human costs. Though we seek to love one another as we are first loved, we are imperfect. We will confuse eros with agape. We will disappoint, compete, and leave incomplete. And we will be separated from one another in every way—most particularly by death.

In 1944, Marc Chagall's beloved wife, Bella, died shortly after they had fled Nazi-dominated France. In 1947, he completed his famous tribute to her loss, entitled *The Falling Angel*. In it a beautiful, bloodred, female angel plummets to earth amidst an appalled Chagallian chorus: a purple rabbi, a yellow horse, a crucified Christ, and, most sadly, a fiddle without a fiddler.

Human love has its costs, but God's love covers all costs. The price is paid in God's own passion. And nothing ultimately separates us from God's agape. As the artist of *The Falling Angel* wrote, even after his wife's death: "In our life there is a single color as on an artist's palette, which provides the meaning of life and art. It is the color of love."

It makes fiddlers green, horses yellow, angels fly, and even pigs smile.

Amen.

September 22, 1985
Mark 9:30–37

The thirtieth anniversary of Disneyland coincided with the two hundredth anniversary of the General Convention of the Episcopal Church. Even more coincidental was that the General Convention was convened at a place convenient to the convention: across the street from Disneyland.

The marketing division of Disney enterprises had promoted Disneyland as the "Magic

Kingdom." Saturday night, one week after General Convention adjourned, I, with some fellow deputies, adjourned to the Magic Kingdom. The comparison of Disneyland with the Church was inevitable. The comparison of the two kingdoms was pleasant. The contrast of the two was a more somber reflection.

I speak of the comparison and contrast, not as a pedestrian visitor, but as a veteran employee. It is obvious that I am an employee of the Church, but what is not so obvious is that I am a former employee of Disneyland. In the summer of 1967, after my first year in seminary, I worked at Disneyland. I was, alternately, a keystone cop on Main Street, a sheriff in Adventureland, and a cavalry officer on Tom Sawyer's Island. Until last year, I wore a Mickey Mouse watch as a memorial of a magnificent summer in the Magic Kingdom. Many believed that the Mickey Mouse watch was a symbol of my theology. The watch died earlier this year. So, I speak with some expertise as an former hireling of the Magic Kingdom and a current employee of the Kingdom of God.

The comparisons: both the Church and Disneyland are communities of memory and imagination. The lands in the amusement park reveal this emphasis. In the park, one finds Main Street, a nostalgic view of American life at the turn of the century. Also, there is Adventureland and Frontierland, each of which memorializes former days of jungle and frontier adventure. Those lands are lands of memory. Fantasyland and Tomorrowland are lands of a future or "once upon a time." Compared with the Church, the Church, too, is a community of memory (scripture and tradition) and a community of imagination (sacramental and eternal). Disneyland functions as an environment of ritual and costume, of pageantry and tradition. So, too, these elements are present in the ecclesiastical community. These comparisons are pleasant and interesting, but end as quickly as the cotton candy at the Main Street Emporium. For the contrasts between the Magic Kingdom and the Church are more remarkable than the comparisons.

Disneyland is so constructed that, once inside, one can see nothing of the outside world but the Disneyland hotel marquee. The entire emphasis of the Magic Kingdom is to accentuate the positive, eliminate the negative, and don't mess with Mr. In-Between. Disneyland removes one from the world and amuses one with the memory of how things were or how they might be, but never tells one how things are. Disneyland does not allow for inconsistency, suffering, illness, poverty, filth, war, or wound. I do not argue that it should, but in contrast to the Church, the Church is not a place of escape from the world. The Church may remember where it has been and dream of where it is called, but only in order to be relevant to where it is. The Church, through its worship and education, takes one outside the normal context in order to relate to the environment, not in order to escape from it. The Kingdom of God is very different from the Magic Kingdom.

My fear is that many want the Church to be like the Magic Kingdom. Many, I believe, expect the Church to be a place of escape, entertainment, and amusement. The Church has no legitimate role unless all its efforts are directed at becoming the body of Christ in the world. Jesus speaks to his disciples in today's Gospel, saying, "If any one would be first, he must be last of all and servant of all." The Church is not a servant of pleasure alone, but a servant of pain in addition. The Church is not a servant of fantasy alone, but a servant of reality also.

The General Convention is no artificial world. The General Convention, in an effort to be the tangible expression of the Kingdom of God, sought, as it should, to address itself to those things about which we can celebrate as well as mourn, support as well as indict, applaud as well as decry.

The theological Church has as its earthen vessel the institutional Church. The two churches may be seen as circles. The cynic believes that the two circles of the spiritual Church and the institutional Church never touch. The optimist claims they are concentric. The realist says they occasionally overlap.

The Church as institution, gathered in convention, is very different from a magic kingdom. The General Convention is the real world seeking through memory and imagination to enable us to live in the world. Its resolutions sought not to resolve so much as to educate about and address the realities of pain, war, suffering, and injustice. It did so because these are issues which we must not deny in the name of Christ, but serve for Christ's sake.

Popularity is not the Church's goal. Disneyland would go out of existence if it didn't please its customers. The Church would not be the Church or serve the world if it sought only to please.

Having worked for both, I prefer the Kingdom of God to the Magic Kingdom. For whatever it is worth, I didn't buy a new watch. And yet, I realize that there is a place for the amusement park and the Church. Let's just not confuse the two.

Amen.

✤ ✤ ✤

September 29, 1985
Numbers 11:4–6, 10–16, 24–29

The flame of the quest will not be quelled by empty aphorism or simplistic sentiment. The fire and flame are but elementary symbols of the Spirit which sets the soul ablaze. The human story is a universal journal of each personal journey. That story is a quest for answers to the human questions of: Where did I come from? Who am I? Who are you? And where are we going? There is woven into the collective fabric of the human unconscious a sense that there was a time when we knew the answers to these questions and there was no quest, only a peaceful paradise. But now, we are called and christened with a promise, which is placed in the soul as a fire and will neither be extinguished by earthly banality, nor will it consume the soul, for it is its source of energy.

There was a rabble among the people of God who had been called from bondage in an exodus through the sanguine sea. The people of Israel were wandering through the wilderness, hungry for truth and fearful that their appetite for food would dominate their quest for truth. "O that we had meat to eat! We remember the fish we ate in Egypt for nothing, the cucumbers, the melons…Moses heard the people weeping…and the anger of the Lord blazed hotly…Moses cried to the Lord, 'Why have you burdened me with the quest? I cannot carry the burden alone.'" And God did not answer the question of why he had set his people on a quest, but he revealed to Moses and the people that it was a collective journey. The truth seems to be that it is an individual journey and quest, but no one has to go it alone.

The quest is reflected in all of literature. From the Arthurian legends to *Moby Dick*, or to a popular contemporary novel like Bobbie Ann Mason's new book, *In Country*. *In Country* is a story of a contemporary American quest.

Samantha Hughes is fresh out of high school. It is the summer of 1984. The scene is a small town in western Kentucky by the apt name, Hopewell. Samantha's father was killed in Vietnam shortly before she was born. By letter home, he instructed his young, pregnant wife to name the child Samuel if born a boy; Samantha if born a girl. "They are good Old Testament names," says he. Samantha is raised by her widowed mother and Uncle Emmett, himself a Vietnam vet who carries physical and psychological scars from that war. Samantha grows up known as "Sam." Sam wonders aloud, as would any critical ear, if her name has anything to do with America being named "Uncle Sam." Her quest is for answers to the questions: Where did I come from? Who was my father? Who am I, and where does all this lead? Her wanderings are symbolized in her journey to the Vietnam Memorial in Washington, that black polished stone which carries her father's memory and her quest for an identity. "In country" was the term used by GIs for service in Vietnam's jungles. In the novel, it comes to represent the emotional odyssey of Sam Hughes trying to make sense out of what appears to be senseless. The story's scenes give a piercing view to contemporary America, as seen through the eyes of television, franchise fast foods, retail stores, and popular music. She is enamored with another veteran named Tom, who looks like rock singer Bruce Springsteen, yet is left psychologically impotent by the modern American embarrassment.

In her sparse, undecorated prose, Mrs. Mason shows us the sparse, numb, undecorated lives of much of America today. Sam searches. She is a runner. The author, in an interview, confessed that it seems "some people are born to run and some aren't. The characters I'm probably most interested in are those who are born to run but can't get very far and are trapped by circumstances." Sam is a woman who runs—a not-too-opaque view of America's confused quest for an identity and clarity that will make the soul's fire a light to lead rather than a destructive, selfish passion that consumes and leaves only ashes.

Sam leaves for Washington and the Vietnam Memorial in a beat-up, old VW, with her father's mother, Mamaw, and her Uncle Emmett. The climactic moment of the pilgrimage *In Country* is the arrival of the threesome at the memorial site:

> "I don't see it," Mamaw says.
>
> "It's over yonder," Emmett says, pointing. "They say you come up on it sudden."
>
> "My legs are starting to hurt."
>
> Sam wants to run, but she doesn't know whether she wants to run toward the memorial or away from it. She just wants to run. She has the new record album with her, so it won't melt in the hot car. It's in a plastic bag with handles. Emmett is carrying the pot of geraniums. She is amazed by him, his impressive bulk, his secret suffering. She feels his anxiety. His heart must be racing, as if something intolerable is about to happen.
>
> Emmett holds Mamaw's arm protectively and steers her across the street. The pot of geraniums hugs his chest.
>
> "There it is," Sam says.
>
> It is massive, a black gash in a hillside, like a vein of coal exposed and then polished with polyurethane. A crowd is filing by slowly, staring at it solemnly.
>
> "Law," says Sam's grandmother quietly. "It's black as night."

Sam and her family then begin to look for her father's name. "The memorial cuts a V in the ground, like the wings of an abstract bird, huge and headless." Sam searches. She climbs a ladder to reach her father's name. When she is eye level with it, she touches it. She smiles for a picture while she cries. Sam climbs down and finds the directory with the names of all the fifty-eight thousand dead.

> Sam flips through the directory and finds "Hughes." She wants to see her father's name there too. She runs down the row of Hughes names. There were so many Hughes boys killed...His name is there, and she gazes at it for a moment. Then suddenly her own name leaps out at her.
>
> SAM ALAN HUGHES PFC AR 02 MAR
49 02 FEB 67 HOUSTON TX 14E 104
>
> Her heart pounding, she rushes to panel 14E, and after racing her eyes over the string of names for a moment, she locates her own name...She touches her own name.

The book ends as Mamaw says, "Coming up on this wall [all] of a sudden and seeing how black it was, it was so awful, but then I came down in it and saw that white carnation blooming out of that crack and it gave me hope. It made me know he's watching over us." Silently, Sam points to her Uncle Emmett. "He is sitting there cross-legged in front of the wall, and slowly his face bursts into a smile like flames."

The flame of the quest will not be quelled. The fire and flame are elementary symbols of the Holy Spirit dwelling in each soul.

Our journey is to find our own name and touch it. We are all from Hopewell, looking into the black, bearing a white flower. Legs like a cross, we await the promised time when the truth will burst our faces into a smile like flames.

Amen.

※ ※ ※

October 13, 1985
Mark 10:17–27

"But Jesus said to them again, 'How hard it will be for those who have riches to enter the kingdom of God!'" In the limited context of today's Gospel, it may appear that Jesus is speaking only of those who worship money.

To take such a statement of power and limit it would be to try to capture light in a bottle. Jesus may have been speaking about the rich man who came to him wanting to know how to enter the Kingdom of God, but that was only a tangible example of how difficult it is for humans to enter the kingdom. The mystery of wellness requires sickness. Humans want to gain everything without giving up anything. The code is not complicated, just costly—omelets require broken eggs.

There is something inscrutable about the Kingdom of God and all of its synonymous terms: health, whole, haven, heaven. A one-dimensional mind is not apt to fathom the enigmatic nature of eternity and its immortal mystery. Why? Why is it hard to enter the Kingdom of God? There is an illusion of eternal comfort in denying death's kiss as a requirement to the kingdom. Death in all its staging develops a pattern of necessity for growth toward health and heaven. In spite of sanctuary and sacrament, Bible and prayer book, the existential terrors remain, all dressed in darkness and dread, and will not be diminished by denial. Jesus taught and lived that without death, in some form—be it spiritual, psychological, or physical—there would be no new life. It is hard to enter a holy place, for it requires giving up that which keeps you from entering. The code is not complicated, just costly—resurrection requires death. I love resurrection, but I resent the company it keeps.

The external death mirrors the internal deaths, which are multiple reflections of movement from old to new, loss to gain, terminal to eternal. So it is. To experience resurrection means that we need to enter the place of death.

Five years ago this month, I sat on the second floor of Latham parish house. It was my first formal talk with a formidable figure in the contemporary history of Christ Church Cathedral. William Barnard was in his third decade as choirmaster and organist; having, by the hard way, survived three previous deans. I had just arrived to the office. Mr. Barnard's reputation was one of authority, dignity, pride, and controlled professional precision, in both practice and in performance. As one former colleague described him, "Bill doesn't care about the world coming to an end as long as it was done with proper Anglican dignity and order." When he entered my office for his entrance interview, he would not sit until I did. He sat on the edge of the chair for the exchange of pleasantries. His appearance was one of nervousness. His eyes flitted quickly from side to side, and I remember a now-familiar nervous habit with his hands, a kind of flicking of his fingers, as if they somehow must be ready at all times to touch or reach for some mysterious black and white keys.

And then I asked him, "What do you expect from me as the new dean?" His look somehow changed. He sat back in that cracked leather chair. His hands formed a small church with the steeple pointing under his chin. His eyes focused on mine and he said, "We need you to love us and lead us." And there it was, all in a moment, my agenda. But even more so, it was, even if unconscious, an invitation to an intimate relationship of love, which is our only leader.

That unwritten yet binding vow and covenant became the code for my time with Bill. A code which was not complicated—yet costly. The cost was as in any relationship of colleagues who love one another. All glass, though committed to the light, is uneven, imperfect, and vulnerable to small bubbles of shattering realities. The penultimate costs were in discussions and decisions from two who were very different in talents. Those differences somehow fade, particularly when sentimentality masks memory in an attempt at something tenderer than the harsh reality of loss. The small costs pale before the ultimate cost. The time came sooner than either could have planned—for Bill to enter the place of death, and for me to go with him.

Bill's death was an irony in its form. His disease was one which causes its victims to lose all control of motor functions. For one who needed so much to control, Bill surrendered all physical control. The irony was as it usually is in truth: by losing, he gained. As he lost control of his body—he could no longer search for the keys with flexed fingers—the keys came in surrender. He simply learned that in losing control, he gained control. The dignity became not only a death with dignity, but a faith statement from a true Christian. Bill Barnard showed the community that though he could not control his death, he could control his life of love. He loved to and through the end.

Jesus taught and lived that without death, no new life comes. It is hard to enter the Kingdom of God, for it requires giving up something. The code is not complicated, just costly—resurrection requires death. Last Tuesday morning, Annette Barnard called Canon Logan and me. We went into the death place, which is where we were called when we agreed to love. I held Bill's clay-like hand, no longer searching for keys. And I touched his ashen forehead, making the sign of the cross as a symbol that there is no resurrection without a death. Bill Barnard died then and there. His death I resent, for it is costly. My children, how hard it is to enter the Kingdom of God.

But, there is then the Easter hope. The Kingdom of God is available before, during, and after death. God planted himself in history and implanted himself in our very soul. I have seen him in love.

Jesus is the Christ because he asks no more of us than he himself has done. It is hard to enter the Kingdom of God. But Jesus loves us and leads us by example, in his own life and in the lives of the saints he sets before us.

Amen.

❖ ❖ ❖

November 10, 1985
Mark 12:38–44

It is not what you have earned that has made you worthy. It is what you have been given, which is your inherited worth. Each human being is inherently valuable and therefore seen by the ultimate evaluator as having ultimate value.

God is giver of gifts. God gave you to the world, the world to you, and himself to each. Life is gift. God is both gift and giver.

You are in his image. You are gift and therefore a giver. You only express your worth by being worthy. Give of your life, not of your possessions only, and, in giving your worth, you will become worthy.

So it is with the widow's penny. Mark records that wonderful story of Christ's inverted worldview. The rich, powerful, religious people who contribute a little of their outward possessions are to receive condemnation, and the poor widow who gives all she has, what Jesus calls "her whole living," it is she who is seen as worthy.

Self-esteem, the belief in one's own fundamental worth, may be humankind's fundamental problem. All of scripture, from alpha to omega, is intent on communicating the fact that human beings are loved by God, not in general, but by name. No human being is a biological accident. Our worth is in our birth. And yet, we live our lives apologizing for our inadequacies, imperfections, mistakes, failures. We live as if our life was a mistake, and we live our lives trying to avoid making any more.

I hold currently a haunting vision. It came to me in a daydream. In a day full of dread and fear, this vision floated before the screen behind my eyes as a gift, a technicolor truth, which made me laugh out loud for no one's benefit but my own.

I was dead. In a silver mist, unaware of whether I had a body or not, I became a cloud circling about a mountain (my only visual model would be the Matterhorn—the one in Disneyland, not the one on the Swiss/Italian border). The vision itself was a comedy. It was a paradox of celestial apparitions. Mist and smoke, floating freely, mountaintop, and the disembodied voice:

> "Pittman! You blew it. You missed life. You misunderstood it all along. You didn't waste it, you just lived it wrong. You lived your life afraid. I don't understand it; I gave you all those wonderful gifts and you didn't enjoy them for fear of losing them. All I wanted you to do was give them away.

> "I gave you a body and you were afraid of it. You always compared it to others. Too big, too much, not enough. It was yours! It was incomparable. I gave it to you to enjoy, and you spent most of your time either denying it, fearing it, or being ashamed of it. You never understood what an intricate, wonderful gift your body was.

> "And your soul—I was in you all the time, and you lived your life alone and lonely.

> "And your mind! You thought it was for figuring out life. It wasn't. It was for experiencing life in all its complexity, not for figuring out how to keep from making mistakes.

> "Your children. They were gifts to enjoy. They were sunrises. And you were afraid of them. Afraid that they wouldn't turn out right. What was right? You thought that I was worried about all of what your culture called 'sins'! The little cheatings, lies, mistakes, failures...those were imperfections. I made you lovely, not perfect. Your only sin was that you lived your life in fear, tight and taut, and you didn't enjoy it enough. There was no way to fail, nothing to fear, and nothing to lose. You just never lived. You aren't dead, 'cause you never lived! You can return and refuse to live, or you can live freely and enjoy your gifts by using them, not being ashamed, afraid, or embarrassed to be human. That is your gift. You are free to choose."

That haunting vision made me laugh out loud. The truth sets us free, and complete love casts out fear.

I refuse to be paralyzed by fear. I refuse to live my life in fear and dread. That is perhaps the greatest sin: to not see life as a gift.

Albert Camus says life's only decision is suicide. Walker Percy, in his enjoyable book *Lost in the Cosmos*, defines the difference between a non-suicide and an ex-suicide:

> The difference between a non-suicide and an ex-suicide leaving the house for work, at eight o'clock on an ordinary morning:
>
> The non-suicide is a little traveling suck of care, sucking care with him from the past and being sucked toward care in the future. His breath is high in his chest.
>
> The ex-suicide opens his front door, sits down on the steps, and laughs. Since he has the option of being dead, he has nothing to lose by being alive. It is good to be alive. He goes to work because he doesn't have to.

A non-suicide is one who has never decided to live; an ex-suicide is one who has chosen to live and lives with his choices.

The enjoyment about which we speak is not the neurotic need to be happy and free from pain and problem, but the surprising joy found in life's many gifts, usually found in those things that we dreaded or were afraid of. Robert Johnson, analyst and author, says, "For every step forward, I take three steps back, which is all right, because I was going the wrong direction in any case."

Surprising joy. Enjoying life. We have a choice. Our greatest sin may be in not accepting our gifts. God gave us life. He gave you to the world and the world to you and himself to each. He wants us to simply live our lives by freely living; not bound in the narrow grave of fear and dread, but to simply live!

I used to see the story of the widow's mite as a humble, gray-haired, cowed woman walking up in shame and embarrassment, offering the two copper coins as all she had. It might be that she hiked up her dress and ran across the courtyard and jumped into the sanctuary and smiled a toothless grin and held her two coins high and said, "Here I am, God. I may not be much, but I'm all I got!"

At least I'm not afraid to see it that way and enjoy the story…

Amen.

November 24, 1985
John 18:33–37

If you are linear only, or lateral only, or only literal, you will not understand the Kingdom of God. You may enter, but you will not know that into which you are entering. So it was with the problem of Pilate, asking Jesus about his kingship. Christ is a kaleidoscope: turned from one direction to another, we see another vocation. But, in order to understand his kingdom as king, we must come in the back door, or, if we are like Pilate, we will beat our heads against the door, trying to understand something that cannot be understood on one plane. Poor Pilate.

Anne Sexton's wonderful book, *The Awful Rowing Toward God,* has a most joyful poem entitled "the rowing endeth":

> I'm mooring my rowboat
> at the dock of the island called God.
> This dock is made in the shape of a fish
> and there are many boats moored
> at many different docks…
>
> "On with it!" He says and, thus
> we squat on the rocks by the sea
> and play—can it be true—
> a game of poker.
> He calls me.
> I win because I hold a royal straight flush.
> He wins because He holds five aces.
> A wild card had been announced
> but I had not heard it
> being in such a state of awe
> when He took out the cards and dealt.
> As He plunks down His five aces
> and I sit grinning at my royal flush,
> He starts to laugh,
> the laughter rolling like a hoop, out of His mouth
> and into mine,
> and such laughter that He doubles right over me
> laughing a Rejoice-Chorus at our two triumphs.
> Then I laugh, the fishy dock laughs
> the sea laughs. The Island laughs.
> The Absurd laughs.
>
> Dearest dealer.
> I with my royal straight flush,
> love you so for your wild card,
> that untamable, eternal, gut-driven *ha-ha*
> and, lucky love.

Play and humor are undervalued in this society of material and rationality. Anne Sexton sees life as a poker game where everyone wins, and the laughter rolls hoop-like when it is discovered that each hand is dealt a wild card, which is called love.

That kind of surprise is humor and demands laughter. The unexpected twist to a story. The human laughs always at another when he trips and falls, not just making an object out of the subject that has fallen, but because of the surprise. Walking along, and falling. It's funny. We all gasp at the shock that all fall down: Adam and Eve, Abbott and Costello, David and Bathsheba, Laurel and Hardy, Peter and Paul. All fall. We are all fallen characters, imperfect, and our hand holds a one-eyed jack, and all have seen the other side of his face. And when we see another's backside, so to speak, we laugh. We laugh at the truth that we all play games of pretense and pomposity, puffed up and yet inevitably punctured by being human. Life pulls chairs out from under the proud, and when they fall, we all laugh. For we have that experience in common: we have all fallen.

Have you heard the one about the people who, once upon a time, wanted a king? God gave them one, but he and all his descendents were human. And this kingdom ended. The people cried out, "No, send us a God king, a messiah who will turn the world upside down."

So God sent them a God king. He came into the kingdom in a backyard stable and rolled into the kingdom like a hoop riding on an ass. The people rejected him because he said that life's only power was love. He said that each one of God's creatures was loved equally. The last would be first. The poor would be rich. The sinners would be righteous, and only children would enter the Kingdom of God.

He claimed he was king, but not of this world. He proclaimed himself to be the King of Hearts. The people got so angry with him that they killed him. After he died, there was a stone that rolled like laughter, like a hoop through history, and the funniest thing happened…and we laugh still.

There is a wild card set loose by this King of Hearts. The wild card is love. Every one-eyed jack can look at himself straight in the mirror with both eyes. The poor can play, the sinners can rejoice, the proud can brush the dust off their pants and roll like laughter's hoop. It's a rolling stone that gathers no remorse.

Every human being has fallen and is lost. Every person who has ever drawn breath has failed the test of temptation. Every man and woman has felt that he or she was dealt a bad hand or was a loser. But those who know the King of Hearts know that there is always the incredible wild card of unconditional love which is played in the only game that counts—it's a floating poker game—it's the Kingdom of God.

And the king is a clown on a mule that deals to all his brothers and sisters equal hands: royal flushes.

Today the King of Hearts has become the divine joker. Once again, the wild card has been played. The leader of this game has dealt Vivien and Scott Caven a surprise—the one like whom we must become—a child: Hubbard Scott.

What a surprise, the most powerful person here is the weakest one. The wisest is the most innocent. The neediest one is most fulfilled. The smallest is the greatest. It's enough to make you laugh out loud.

Bring us Hubbard Scott so that we can hear once again the rejoice-chorus that makes even the absurd laugh and calls us to love the Divine Dealer for his wild card, "that untamable, eternal, gut driven *ha-ha* and, lucky love."

Amen.

✤ ✤ ✤

December 15, 1985
Advent III
Luke 3:7–18

It is in the fifteenth verse of today's Gospel that the Advent pearl is hidden. The line reads: "As the people were in expectation,…" Expectation could also be translated: "great hope." The people were holding great hope.

Into this hope and expectation came John, the wild John of wilderness fame. He came saying, "Get ready for something new." The people were so ready for the newness that some were willing to give up the old in order to be ready for the never before. Some were even willing to let John be the Christ. Thank God, he was only willing to represent the Christ and not exploit that hunger with his own need to feed. He was satisfied to be what he was called to be and that was John, and he never confused himself with trying to be Christ. He told the truth, and that bad news became good news. The bad news was: if you want the new life, then you must be willing to give up the old, without knowing what the new will be. He said, in essence, that dead people are the ones who know it all. The alive are those who follow a rope called hope into a land called promise. They know nothing but hope and promise. These are the pregnant pilgrims who know only that what lies ahead is the coming of a reality that does not yet exist and has never before.

There is no amniocentesis which can puncture the womb of promise and determine the future. The only puncture point is the poignant moment of announcement that something new is coming, something which has never been before and will never be again. A once-and-for-all happening, which will fill an emptiness. But you must empty yourself of what you think you know in order to be filled with what you do not yet know. (That was a rough translation of John's good news.)

"As the people were in expectation" also translated great hope. The people were holding great hope. They were hanging on to a rope called hope and following it into a land called promise. Hope as rope is more than a sophomore rhyme. There is a Hebrew word for hope, *gawah*, whose root means to twist, to twine; and it is a word which seems to fit our purpose well. Hope is a hundred strands of experiences woven with promise that make a rope of hope strong enough to pull us into the unknown. We hope not simply for what is possible, for we already know what that is. We hope for that which we don't know, for it has never been. But John promises that one will come who can unlock the future in the present.

Promise must be unpacked. A promise is twofold: it is a now on which we base an expectation. John promised the future was promising. In Latin, it means to send forth. Promises are commitments to a future. Promise is a future full of hope. Hope is a conviction based on experience. Experience is the counting through reflection of how each today's joy was yesterday's promise.

Hope is a weaving of strands together into a cable of strength that connects us to the future and allows us to hold secure in the present.

This is the Advent pearl. We have hope. We have promise. No matter how dark, the star of promise heralds the coming of something that is going to be totally new, something that doesn't yet exist. We are the people of expectation of great hope.

Christmas reminds us that something came that never was before. It was incomparable. It came based on a promise. That fulfillment is the next promise, for the baby born is the one who died and then was born again and promised to return. Christians, by definition, are those who are crazy enough to believe him. To sit in the dark places and watch for the star of promise and to weave a rope of hope is the Advent message. To know that we have a future that we can only imagine.

No wonder this is the season of wonder. No wonder this is the season of expectation, anticipation, and excitement. No matter who you are, you will become more; no matter what you have done, you will do something new; no matter where you are, you will be called into a new place; no matter what you have, you will be given what you need; no matter how sick, you will become well; no matter how burdened, you will be relieved; no matter how unhappy, you will be joyful; no matter how alone, you will belong.

These are the strands of the rope of hope woven together in this time of wonder. This is the star of promise. Watch your horizon, the time is coming.

And now is.

Amen.

December 22, 1985
Advent IV
Luke 1:39–49

One of the little-noted, profound highlights of this year's World Series was an interview with Bret Saberhagen, the brilliant young pitcher for the Kansas City Royals. He was the winner of the final game and the recipient of the most valuable player award.

"Tell me, Bret," said the enthusiastic interviewer, "wasn't this the greatest day of your life?" Without a pause, the young pitcher replied, "No, the greatest day of my life was two days ago when my little son, Drew, was born."

Any of us who have been called to parenthood and received that incomparable, costly, mysterious, enigmatic gift of a child knows what this young father meant.

Theology may not be a natural science, but the genius of the Christian story—most particularly, its genesis story at Christmas and the incumbent theological system—is that the transcendent is seen in the natural. The Advent/Christmas story is, on the one hand, the mysterious, cosmic revelation of the God of love; on the other hand, it is the story of the announcement and birth of a baby boy. The journey of Mary to visit her relative, Elizabeth, as rehearsed in Luke's Gospel, is the naming and placing of the transcendent Spirit into a natural event. In this simple story, we have a natural event, but because of its simplicity, it becomes supernatural. Therefore, a special language and a special ear are required to speak and hear. There is, within this story, the pedestrian in the poetic, the miraculous in the mundane, the extraordinary in the ordinary.

Therefore, for the next few days before Christmas and for the rest of your life, you must hear with two ears and see with both eyes the history and eternity, the heavens and the earth, the source of all mystery and truth, a baby and God.

Shakespeare writes in *A Midsummer Night's Dream*:

> The poet's eye, in a fine frenzy rolling
> Doth glance from heaven to earth, from earth to heaven;
> And, as imagination bodies forth
> The forms of things unknown, the poet's pen
> Turns them to shapes, and gives to airy nothing
> A local habitation and a name.

The Christian Christmas story is imagination bodying forth, giving transcendence a local habitation and a name: Bethlehem, Jesus.

The young pitcher for the Kansas City Royals held within his imagination as a small boy that the greatest thing that could happen would be to pitch the winning game of the World Series and be its most valuable player. But he learned a most valuable lesson: all the hopes and fears of all his years came before him in one week. The love of a father for a son and a son for a father is the greater eternal truth when compared to any historical world accomplishment. In the World Series, the world loses to the truth of love when a father beholds a baby. Birth gives a name and habitation to truth. This is the word made flesh, the cosmic story in history.

No wonder something leaps within when we realize that which seeks to live comes alive in a new birth. This romantic story births something new every time it is heard with two ears and seen with both eyes. Alan Jones writes: "Romance in a mature way is a means of keeping important things alive in us, things that would die without it." When Elizabeth heard that heaven and earth would be one; when she saw that all we desire would be given habitation and name, a babe leaped in her womb.

There remains a child in each of us at every age. This is the time when romantic story reigns as king over every cynical Scrooge. We are, first and finally, not simply of the world, but within it. Our birth therefore is never final but ever new, every time we hear of something being born. We, too, leap within our own womb when the divine poet doth glance from heaven to earth and makes the unknown known as the imagination bodies forth and gives airy nothing a local habitation and name.

Jesus at Bethlehem is every new birth within each of us. Christmas is the greatest day of our life. No world accomplishment can compare to the mystery of love seen in the miraculous, mundane birth of a baby boy. What is there this day leaping within you? What in your imagination is dying to be born, bodied forth and needing to be named and claimed as your own?

I bring you glad tidings of great joy. Soon there will be birthed from you something new, never before, never again, at a particular time, and at a particular place. Could it be that this Christmas will mark your birth?

What in the world are we waiting for?

Amen.

1986

January 5, 1986
Epiphany
Matthew 2:1–12

> It was no summer progress.
> A cold coming they had of it at this time of the year, just the worst time of the
>   year to take a journey, and especially a long journey in.
> The ways deep,
> The weather sharp,
> The days short,
> The sun farthest off…

So begins Sermon 15, "Of the Nativity," preached by Lancelot Andrewes before King James I, Christmas 1622. This is the leaven for the first five lines of T. S. Eliot's poem, "Journey of the Magi."

> A cold coming we had of it,
> Just the worst time of the year
> For a journey, and such a long journey:
> The ways deep and the weather sharp,
> The very dead of winter.

And, of course, the priest and poet each are dependent on the original word as revealed according to Matthew, read this day as the Epiphany Gospel: "Now when Jesus was born in Bethlehem of Judea in the days of Herod the King, wise men from the East came to Jerusalem, saying, 'Where is he that is born king of the Jews? For we have seen his star in the East and have come to worship him.'"

Here, there is agreement from Andrewes, Eliot, and God: the wise know that they are called out of the darkest, worst time of the year for a journey, a long journey inward.

Annie Dillard claims: "Time is eternity's pale interlinear, as the islands are the sea's." So, for us, there is, in this life, little time to respond. Epiphany sheds light on the truth that there is no perfect time to begin a journey except now, for now is our only moment, and we are called by a star to a journey. The ways deep, the weather sharp, and the days short.

I know you have a journey to make. I know that you have come today to hear the truth. You must begin today, even if it means to begin again. Though it is never too late, there is never a perfect time to leave, begin, quit, stay, stop, or start; for the wise, they knew it was just the worst time of the year to begin a journey, especially a journey toward a truth where the costs were great and the way was to be deep. But time is our interlinear, a small chain of islands, an archipelago with distinct increments: beginnings and ends. This begins a new year. It is Epiphany, a revelation, that the time has come for you to become what you were created to be. And today, you are called through me, a translucent subject through which the star shines, calling the wise to the wisdom that whatever it is that you are to start, stop, continue, or begin again, this epiphany means that you see the light—that it literally dawns upon you that there are no more excuses, no perfect time; and, like the magi of old: "a cold coming [they] had of it, just the worst time of the year for a journey, and such a long journey: the ways deep, the weather sharp, the days short."

Your New Year's resolution dwells deep within your eternal nature, and you must birth it in this island time, this place, this fragile archipelago. The only way to get through the journey is to go through it.

Though wearisome, troublesome, dangerous, and unseasonable, the wise came...and by the few, they still come. Only a few are courageous enough to journey toward the truth by the hard way. Are you one of the chosen few? If not, then why have you come? Why are you here? If you desire to claim to be Christian, then you have a claim on you to journey toward the truth, wrapped in a husk of time, in a husk of light shining this day and calling you out of your dark place into a place of new light. You are called this day, no less than Abraham or Lazarus, to step out of your dark or dead place and journey toward the light, a new life. God is calling you through the wisdom of the wisemen who journeyed before you. But offer them no excuses, for they followed even though it was the worst time of the year to take a journey. A cold coming they had of it—wise ones know the way is going to be deep, weather sharp, and days short.

For the one we are called to see is the Christ who did nothing if he didn't follow a call to a journey—cold, sharp, and short. So, you can refuse to journey to a new life, but offer no excuses. For the wise and the Christ know the cost. Each excuse is a "no." And there are a thousand ways to say "no," one way to say "yes," and no way to say anything else.

A cold coming [they] had of it,
Just the worst time of the year
For a journey, and such a long journey.

Amen.

✤ ✤ ✤

January 19, 1986
John 2:1–11

I don't know if you have heard or were concerned, but Ricky Nelson crashed and burned.

Sacred story is, as any collage, a mixed media, experienced at many levels, viewed over and over, and each time can surprise with something new. The water and wine, Cana in Galilee, wedding feast story is such a sacred collage. There is, of course, the wonderful byplay between Jesus and his mother over the timing of his ministry. It is an issue for John in his Gospel, where he records the seven signs of Jesus' significance. The miracle at the wedding was the first miracle he performed. These stories, like good symbols, point beyond themselves as particular reference to greater truths.

There have been countless sermons about Jesus' developmental stage in his apparent mother complex, the importance of the first miracle at a marriage feast, and the series of seven signs recorded by John. They have been and will be preached in other times and places. But I saw this week in St. John's jewel a new reflected light. My surprise was in the statement of the steward to the groom: "Every man serves the good wine first; and when men have drunk freely, then the poor wine; but you have kept the good wine until now." What a promise Christianity has given us: the best is yet to come. What a promise we have been given, no less than the promise placed before Abraham and all who came afterward. Christ and his teachings are clear that life gets better, and the good wine will not be served before its time. I believe this to be true as a theological premise and promise, as well as in my personal experience. The world wants to trick us into believing that "it doesn't get any better than this," but Christianity tells us that in our relationship to God, the best is yet to come, and if that is true in our relationship to God, it is true in our relationship with ourselves and with others. We know this in the journey from alpha to omega, from history to eternity, that each death is changed into a greater life. We know this from our own historical planes of experience and age. Noel Coward wrote: "The pleasures that once were heaven / Look silly at sixty-seven." We grow into greater wisdom, and the good wine remains as that which awaits us, for it will be better than we have known. John Berger, in a book on Picasso, reflects:

There is not, I think, a single example of a great painter—or sculptor—whose work has not gained in profundity and originality as he grew older. Bellini, Michelangelo, Titian, Tintoretto, Poussin, Rembrandt, Goya, Turner, Degas, Cezanne, Monet, Matisse, Braque, all produced some of their very greatest works when they were over sixty-five. It is as though a lifetime is needed to master the medium, and only when that mastery has been achieved can an artist be simply himself, revealing the true nature of his imagination.

So it is with life.

I don't know if you have heard or were concerned, but Ricky Nelson crashed and burned. There is a tragedy in worldly fame, particularly if it comes early. Some of you may not know who Ricky Nelson was, but I do. I have long had a love/hate relationship with Rick Nelson. He and I grew up together. He, on TV, and I, in small-town America. He came from a family of four and so did I. He was the younger of two brothers and I, too, by two years, as he, the younger. I always envied him because he was famous and he had such understanding and wise parents. The perfect family came before me in judgment each week. They were witty, urbane, casual, carefree, and every crisis was tied in a nice bow within thirty minutes. The comparison between us was a judgment. And then, when we were teenagers, he became even more famous as a rock star. My relationship grew more entwined when, at fifteen, I was told by a girl I liked that my flat top and crooked smile looked like Ricky Nelson's.

I don't know whether you have heard or were concerned, but Ricky Nelson crashed and burned. I am concerned because at midlife I now know about superficial fame and fictional family life. I choose the deep reality over the superficial lie. My hero died divorced, rumored to be addicted to drugs, chasing his past in an old plane in the dark of night. Something must be learned in this American culture and generation about the lie foisted on us by TV. Something must be learned in this generation about authenticity versus superficiality: that it's okay to be from a small town and an imperfect family; that it's okay to be liked by a girl for who you really are rather than who you wish you were; that models are important, but comparisons are odious.

My hero died. But my Lord lives, and I wish Ozzie's son could have heard that every stage just gets better for those who have a relationship to authentic truth. Would that he could have heard from the good steward that the world will make you inebriated with the early superficial stuff, but the good wine will be kept for now. And that even at our worst, the best is yet to come.

Amen.

❧ ❧ ❧

February 2, 1986
Hebrews 2:14–18; Luke 2:22–40

Is it not once again as clear as a ball of fire against a blue sky, that no matter how spiritual or religious we may become, or however much scientific dominance we acquire over nature, the human being remains embodied in the constraints of a natural law. There inevitably and unavoidably remains the fact of death. The fact that every human being reaches an end when consciousness is extinguished, life processes cease, and the organism disintegrates.

Michael Smith, Dick Scobee, Ronald McNair, Ellison Onizuka, Christa McAuliffe, Greg Jarvis, and Judy Resnik have taken a place in the collective consciousness of the world. The implications of the Space Shuttle *Challenger* tragedy are manifold and yet singular: death presents awesome contradictions.

On the one hand, it is the most certain event that will occur in anyone's biography. Death's prison has no escapees. This is an ineluctable fact of the human condition—so ineluctable that, no matter how it is prolonged, it is inevitably simply postponed. On the other hand, over against death's certainty stands death's uncertainty. It will happen, that is sure, but when, where, and how remain a capricious triumvirate. The *Challenger* explosion in chain reaction has detonated the certainty of death and its uncertain capricious nature.

Another contradiction of death's nature is the reality that each must die alone, and yet with each individual death, some collective loss is felt. One need not necessarily die lonely, but each must die alone. Only I can die for me. The individual seeks in a life journey to become a unique, separate person...which leads to an individuated life and an individual death. And yet, paired with that truth is its opposite, best articulated by the dean of St. Paul's, John Donne:

> Here the bells can scarce solemnize the funeral of any person, but that I knew him, or knew that he was my neighbor: we dwelt in houses near to one another before, but now he is gone into that house into which I must follow him...No man is an island, entire of itself; every man is a piece of the continent, a part of the main...Any man's death diminishes me, because I am involved in mankind; and therefore never send to know for whom the bell tolls; it tolls for thee.

This week, once again, as clearly as a ball of fire against a blue sky, death's inevitability is seared in our collective consciousness. Seared and seated is death's extreme and its extreme contradictions. And yet, our conviction remains, that at the core, we are courageous. We will not be paralyzed by the fear of death, but enabled by it. Death's power is not in its end, but in its call to live, grow, stretch, progress, evolve, journey, explore, and risk. Death is the challenger. The spacecraft *Challenger* is now a symbol that death challenges us to live now, not in the past or future, but in the eternal moment. Death enables us to truly live. That is why the line is already growing of those who will take the next trip. And, it is a figurative call for each of us to line up and take a risk toward our own exploration of inner space, a discovery mission to take our place in the universe amidst all of life's contradictions—even and including death.

We now know at life's crux is a Christ. Simeon, in his revealed wisdom, knew that God completes life. "And it had been revealed to him by the Holy Spirit that he should not see death before he had seen the Lord's Christ." Once he knew the Christ, he could say, not in abdication, but in courageous faith, "Lord, now lettest thou thy servant depart in peace, according to thy word; for mine eyes have seen thy salvation which thou hast prepared in the presence of all peoples…"

The life issue is not simply death, but whether we will see the Christ even in death. The Christ event, once seen, makes death no less real, but even so more meaningful. For nothing will separate us from our source. For the Christ is the resource for life's meaning even in the face of meaninglessness. Simeon saw, and through his eyes we see that if we know, as the author of Hebrews knew, "that Jesus likewise partook of the same nature as we, that through death he might destroy the power of death and deliver all those who through fear of death were subject to lifelong bondage."

We, this day, mourn the deaths of the space shuttle crew. Their deaths, though inevitable, were a capricious shock. Though they died individually, we all felt the shock and resonance of the death toll. And know how even more so it is for their loved ones.

And yet, this collective event is a challenger for each of us, to live now in the power of love, another name for Christ, seen of old by Simeon and new in this generation.

Let us so live in the presence of the Christ and in love with one another that, no matter when our bell tolls, we can sing the *Nunc Dimittis*, the Song of Simeon: "Lord, now lettest thou thy servant depart in peace, according to thy word; for mine eyes have seen thy salvation which thou has prepared in the presence of all…" as clearly as a ball of fire in a blue sky.

Amen.

February 16, 1986
Lent I
Deuteronomy 26:5–11; Luke 4:1–13

> The Waste Land
>
> What are the roots that clutch, what branches grow
> Out of this stony rubbish? Son of man,
> You cannot say, or guess, for you know only
> A heap of broken images, where the sun beats,
> And the dead tree gives no shelter, the cricket no relief,
> And the dry stone no sound of water…
> I will show you fear in a handful of dust.

In Lent, we enter the wasteland, a land well traveled by pilgrims through the ages, so aptly mapped by T. S. Eliot. I do not know why it is so, but so it is: we must leave the garden and enter the wasteland before we see the Promised Land.

It began so well. "In the beginning" God created all out of nothing and said it was very good. And the serpent crawled up out of a handful of dust and said, "If you eat what I offer, your eyes will be opened and you will be like God, knowing good and evil." And since then we have known. We know of the temporary nature of life's gardens. We know of the sojourners and, like them, we travel from beginnings, through deserts, forging rivers, until we reach an eternal piece of land.

This morning's first lesson from Deuteronomy is a beautiful corporate credo of who we are: "A wandering Aramean was my father; and he went down into Egypt and sojourned there, few in number; and there he became a nation, great, mighty, and populous. And the Egyptians treated us harshly, and afflicted us, and laid upon us hard bondage." We have left the garden and entered the desert with our eyes open to both good and evil. A story of the people of God, for we now know that we are no longer innocent.

The Gospel today is the individual story. We as a people must wander the wasteland between the garden and river, but each individual has to stand alone in the desert—the dry, desolate place, the place where things grow only by the hard way.

Jesus left the river of his baptism, haunted by the possibility of an inflated self-image. The spirit knew of the temptation of such a revelation and led him—no, drove him—to the desert, the place where things only grow by the hard way, a place of silence, waiting, and temptation; perhaps, given as possibility, a place of revelation, conversion, and transformation. So the Holy Spirit drives the individual to the wasteland to fight with fear found in a handful of dust.

The "no" said by Jesus was a "no" to the evil one, but also a "no" to himself. Each of us has a superficial self which wants everything now. Each of us also has an essential, deeper self, symbolized by Christ, which causes us to become more and yields fruitful decisions that are not dictated by appetite or instinct. Jesus not only said "no" to the evil one, he said "no" to a part of himself. It is far easier to say "no" to evil in general than it is to say "no" to evil in particular, especially when it is to yourself. Evil is everywhere good is. Many of us are so afraid of the evil that we never seek the good. We fear the roots that clutch, the broken images, the dead tree. Out of that fear, we do not reach for the good, for we know that evil will be there, too.

A simple example: A man is invited on a free trip to Paris. He knows that his plane might crash or his ship sink. So he stays home. For fear of the evil, he forsakes the good. Paralyzed by fear, he stays where he is. He never grows, or sees new revelations, or becomes more, for fear of the evil. Substitute relationships, vocations, decisions, or actions for the free trip. Substitute your own sense of worth for the graceful gift given with no strings attached. Substitute, if you will, your own name, your own essential identity, for the graceful, undeserved trip to a promised land. Substitute fear of death for evil and you will see how evil, evil is. When evil sees us give up out of fear, forsake the good for fear of the loss, then evil wins again.

Jesus' wisdom was simple though not easy. When the evil one offered him everything, Jesus realized he had everything already. So, too, all of those things that we seek have been given unto us. And we need not fear anything, save the loss of the relationship with the giver. Jesus overcame evil. He did not eliminate it. We must do so in our own lives, enabled by his model. But, we can only do so by entering the wasteland, by facing the fear in a handful of dust, and by being courageous. Courage without fear is ignorance. You've got to be afraid before you can be courageous. And you must enter that which you fear the most, knowing that those things cannot be taken from you.

Jesus has overcome death, and we have been promised everything. Evil cannot win, for it has no ultimate power. We need not fear, for we have nothing to lose. The Promised Land is a return to the garden through the wasteland. This Lent, remember, we are created pleasing to God. We are pleasing to God, and God takes incredible delight in the gifts that we are, except when we are paralyzed by fear and waste away in a land barren by fear, frozen on pallets, only inches from water. We are called to the wasteland. Our eyes were opened by Adam and Eve. We were created pleasing to God. We must face our own evil and say "no," for the book of Revelation tells us that from the alpha of the garden, even through the desert temptations, we have been promised our completion at omega.

"Then I saw a new heaven and a new earth; for the first heaven and the first earth had vanished, and there was no longer any sea. I saw the holy city, new Jerusalem, coming down out of heaven from God, made ready like a bride adorned for her husband. I heard a loud voice from the throne proclaiming, 'Now at last God has dwelling among his people...and God himself will be with them. He will wipe every tear from their eyes, and there shall be an end to death, to mourning, and to crying and pain; for the old order has passed away.'"

Be mindful as sojourners that we are on a great journey; the greatest, most incredible gift possible—the gift of a journey—has been given to us as a free trip. Don't refuse to journey for fear of the evil. Don't remain paralyzed for fear of death, for you have been delivered from death into life. Be aware that you will have to travel through a wasteland on your way to peace, where pain and crying are no more. But for now, we must journey to the desert, where we need not fear the handful of dust, for the breath of God hath blown it away.

Amen.

February 23, 1986
Lent II
Genesis 15:17–18; Luke 13:31–35

The Christian face is cross-eyed by the freedom of our destiny. Shall we say, we are condemned to mystery and sentenced to freedom.

We are all on our way to our Jerusalem; that is our destiny. And yet, how we go, when we go, with whom we go, and what we see when we arrive are freely ours. We are condemned to the mystery of what Jerusalem means and sentenced to the freedom to go there our own way.

What is this Jerusalem about which we speak? Lent is a journey to Jerusalem. Jesus says in today's Gospel, "Tell that fox, Herod, my time is not yet come, but I must go to Jerusalem, for it cannot be otherwise." O Jerusalem, Jerusalem…the destiny for all of us.

Jerusalem is a holy city for three of the world's great religions. For Jews and Christians, its holiness began with God's covenant with Abraham and the promise of a land. David, Israel's king, chose it as his capital. He also chose Jerusalem for the site of the temple which his son, Solomon, would later build. So in fact it was, and is, the holy city for the Hebrew nation. Jesus knew that Jerusalem was his death place, the place where the old covenant would end and the new covenant begin. When he left the Mount of Transfiguration, he set his face resolutely toward Jerusalem, and it remains for Christians the holy city of our Lord's life, death, and resurrection.

Promised Land, holy city, temple, and ultimate end are something of Jerusalem's fact. It is more—it is metaphor for many mysteries of faith. Jerusalem is our historical destiny—death—and at the same time, "a new heaven and a new earth…The holy city Jerusalem," the omega, the ultimate hope, our happy home.

We are all on our way to Jerusalem to find our life. We are all on a journey to Jerusalem to die. We are all on our way to Jerusalem to inherit the promise and hope given by our father

Abraham. This is the freedom of our destiny. This is the mystery to which we are condemned.

Something of the nature of this cross-eyed look of Lent is echoed in Will Campbell's book, *Brother to a Dragonfly*, where Campbell's brother, Joseph, explains to Will something of the nature of martyrdom:

1. You only go to Jerusalem once.
2. Jesus was older than you when he went.
3. You ain't Jesus.

And so it is; there is a Jerusalem for all of us and a Jerusalem for each of us. It is our freedom. It is our destiny. The cross we eye in Lent is our hope and our fear; our corporate and individual end and beginning. This Lent, I am encouraged to follow Jesus on his way to Jerusalem while searching out my own way.

Robertson Davies, in his novel *The Rebel Angels*, writes of the end we each seek, which is a longing for integrity and wholeness. His clerical hero, Simon Darcourt, muses over the mystery of condemnation and the sentence of freedom; of our collective and individual journeys to Jerusalem:

> Oh, endless task! One begins with no knowledge except that what one is doing is probably wrong, and that the right path is heavy with mist. When I was a hopeful youth I set myself to the Imitation of Christ, and like a fool I supposed that I must try to be like Christ in every possible detail, adjure people to do the right when I didn't really know what the right was, and to get myself spurned and scourged as frequently as possible. Crucifixion was not a modern method of social betterment, but at least I could push for psychological crucifixion, and I did, and hung on my cross until it began to dawn on me that I was a social nuisance, and not a bit like Christ... Gradually, it came to me that the Imitation of Christ might not be a road-company performance of Christ's Passion, with me as a pitifully badly cast actor in the principal role. Perhaps what was imitable about Christ was his firm acceptance of his destiny, and his adherence to it even when it led to a shameful death. It was the wholeness of Christ that had illuminated so many millions of lives, and it was my job to seek and make manifest the wholeness of Simon Darcourt.

Davies had read C. G. Jung, who writes: "It is a noble thing to model one's life on Christ, but it is increasingly more difficult for one to live his own life as authentically as Christ lived his." It is echoed by Martin Buber when he says: "When I die God won't say, 'Martin, why weren't you more like Moses?' he'll say, 'Martin, why weren't you more like Martin?'"

God, the Holy Spirit, has entered me. I am on my way to my Jerusalem. Through the wasteland of insecurity, doubt, mistake, failure, fatigue, and fear, I accept my destiny and the freedom to make it, not only my end, but my beginning. I will travel to Jerusalem with Jesus to discover who I am by his wholeness. My life is a commentary on how I journey to Jerusalem. I will journey with my Lord, as myself. Whenever and however I must face my cross, I will do so knowing that it is a gate to the mystery of a heavenly Jerusalem. The mystery to which we are condemned—the mystery by which we are freed. The mystery we have been given as promise.

O Jerusalem, Jerusalem... Our fearful, happy home.

Amen.

March 28, 1986
Good Friday

And who will tell the story this time? Death and suffering, the twin children of chaos, must be named and claimed or they will reign as the bastard infidels whose power serves the prince of darkness.

Who will bell the cat and tell the truth that this day of suffering and death is a good day? The collective consciousness of this culture would deny death. The generation of materialism has come to view death as the dissolution of material and therefore a failure of sorts. So we reject, deny, and project death as for another person, or for another time. When something is denied, it does not disappear; it simply has free rein and great power.

The Church, through its rehearsal of the passion narrative, takes its rightful place as the one, the appropriate one, to tell the story that death and suffering are part and parcel of creation and have purpose—not in general, but in particular—for each person. For even the creator died a public death.

And so, who will retell the story in this time to a generation that no longer lives in an intimate relationship with death? In former days, when whole families commonly lived in two or three rooms with two or three generations, everyone saw death frequently enough. Infant mortality was the norm, and old persons the exception, but everyone died at home. When death comes today, the dying one is shipped away to the hospital, sedated, hidden, denied, and rejected, left to drift away, usually alone. How many have held a dying hand or seen a human being die?

Today, even the death of edible animals is unfamiliar. I remember the day of beheading Sunday's fried chicken as a backyard Saturday ritual. The slaughtering of animals is now done in the factory and not by the family.

Life's most familiar experience is unfamiliar to many Americans. And so to take the time, to fill a place, to tell the story once again is the unique job of the Church and its priesthood.

But even more so, we must conclude that this limit and boundary *death* and its twin *suffering* either end all meaning or make it.

Each possibility must be raised, and at the intersection, one must choose. Jean-Paul Sartre, in his book entitled *Being and Nothingness*, declares that death "removes all meaning from life." One must respect his honesty while recoiling from the horror of that possibility. Having held dying hands and hugged screaming widows, supported broken widowers, and cradled crying children, I know why it is that Sartre raises his extreme. Death's meaning is not apparent in the dark veil of tears. We cannot do away with it, change it, control it, or annul it. And what does it mean? It is all around us, no matter how we shift our eyes or shuttle it away. It was in this room yesterday in its most horrible reality when we prayed for help in the midst of things we do not understand. Death and suffering have visited us all and wait in silence only to return again in an egalitarian banality which seems for many, many times over, as meaningless.

Who will tell the story this time? Not for those who did not hear, but for those who do not know. Jesus climbed the tree willingly. No, not as suicide; that is the logical response to meaninglessness. He climbed the tree to dignify death and to open the possibility of death, not as an end, but a radical change; not as a grave alone, but a gate. Before we rush beyond that fact to the hope, let us remember that God in Christ has not eradicated death, just given it meaning and possibility.

To tell the truth, we must not race around the cross to an empty tomb; that is our temptation. To deny, repress, or pretend that because of Christ we will never die is to be seduced by the Great Lie. We must know the truth of the silent hand that grasped the nail and fell across the tree. We must tell the truth—the blood-spattered truth that sets children crying and adults screaming—that death is real, unavoidable, horrible, and personal. Jesus of Nazareth, son of Mary and Joseph, dripped blood before the Holy Grail, beneath a wounded wing and tattered veil; his death was as real as our death and those we love. He cried out forsaken as anyone would, because in his own inner life, he was experiencing the loneliness, the anxiety, the desolation and sense of defeat which is the cross borne for all. For the mind of humankind. And for what?

The mystery of that mist leaves us only glimpses through the fog. Death is evidently that limited situation which gives definition to history. Either death removes all meaning from life, or it gives life its meaning. Christians, in rehearsing the Crucifixion, realize that history is not the only plane of existence. The paradise from which we come is the same one to which we will return. Even criminals are given that promise. If human beings had not a horizon to our horizontal existence, there would be no unifying pattern. Life in history would literally be one thing after another. What John Macquarrie calls "an endless concatenation of contingencies." Life without limit would be a sentence with no punctuation. Without death, life would be a one-act play with no curtain and therefore no unifying plot.

The Church stands proudly this day telling the tale that the song sung by the thorned bird is one that will not be denied, though it causes even truth to despair.

Death is a boundary, created by God, and defined by his own son's death in order that life in history be lived with intensity and expectation. In this Christian view of the "death gives life meaning" faith statement, it is life's intensity, not its extensiveness, that is important. One may contrast our modern evasion of death and concern for longevity as missing life's meaning. Are we to avoid death? Or to live life? A life lived indefinitely, consumed with trivialities, and huddled in shadowed corners from fear, is infinitely poorer than a life which has zest, intensity, and some meaningful pattern, however brief its duration.

Ultimately, we know that life's limit, named death, is not an end. But that story we will tell Sunday. That empty tomb story is easy to tell, for it is good news, but we must tell the bad news before the good news makes any sense. Jesus' suffering and death were as real as sweat, blood, wood, and nail. That is the truth! The end should teach us all to begin today to live, not for then, but now; to grab what life has been given to us as gift and to proclaim, by God, it is not only good, but very good; to take that end we surely face, as surely as Jesus did, and make it a beginning that we live now.

That is why we tell the story anew. Death must be seen as either that which robs life's meaning or makes life meaningful. The Christian tribe tells this story once again this year so that our generation will not deny death or life's meaning.

> Retell the story once again
>   not for those who did not hear,
>   but for those who never knew.
> How the silent hand grasped the nail
>   and fell across the tree.
> How the Eden vine was cut
>   and tore the tattered veil.
> How upon the Holy Grail
>   the wine was shed by drops.
> Pause beneath the wounded wing
>   and ring the broken pail.
>
> Who will thorn the bird
>   and scream the song as sung?
> Where's the warming fire this night
>   to burn denial's tongue?
> Grow the rose once more
>   and pull its petals bare.
> Climb up on the singletree
>   and tell of truth's despair.

Amen.

✤ ✤ ✤

April 6, 1986
John 20:19–31

British philosopher Ludwig Wittgenstein penned this cryptic aphorism: "Whereof one cannot speak, thereof one must be silent." This statement initially appears to be saying that we only can speak about those things we know. When, indeed, in John Dominic Crossan's book, *The Dark Interval*, he proves to my satisfaction that what the philosopher means is that what *truly matters* in life is precisely that about which we cannot speak. Therefore, silence may be truth's most profound sound.

Concerning the many attempts to prove the existence of God, Kierkegaard ironically wrote: "With what industrious zeal, with what sacrifice of time, diligence, and writing materials the theologians and philosophers in our time have spent to prove God's existence? Yet to the same degree that the excellence of these proofs increase certainty declines."

Which brings us to today's Gospel lesson of Thomas' apparent doubt concerning Jesus' post-resurrection appearance. I say "apparent doubt" because Thomas' doubt was not necessarily about the risen Lord as much as it was doubt about the human claims of his friends. Further, it seemed very important to the apostle to know if the risen Lord was the same one who was wounded. Thomas wanted to see and feel Christ's wounds. He wanted to run his own fingerprints on the nail prints to know that the risen God was a wounded God. Thus, we could believe that our own wounds and incumbent scars would be of eternal worth. I believe Thomas ought to be called "searching Thomas," not "doubting Thomas," for his search led us to Jesus' powerful statement concerning what may be the fundamental religious issue. How can we speak in physical language about metaphysical truth? Jesus said to Thomas, "Have you believed because you have seen me? Blessed are those who have not seen and yet believe." Herein is the wonderful difference in the knowledge of the world versus the belief in the Kingdom of God. I would paraphrase Jesus to have revealed, "In the worldview, seeing is believing. In the eternal view, believing is seeing. And the blessed are those who see through their belief, and lost are those who wait to believe until they can see."

God's ways are not our ways. Eternity is not ruled by the boundaries of history, and history's boundaries are not the rules in eternity. Life in the historical, horizontal level is ruled by its boundaries, with death being the ultimate rule, the final horizon for horizontal life in the plane called history. Limits define life. And yet, in the resurrection story, the post-resurrection appearances, when viewed as the ultimate parable derived from Jesus' parabolic teaching, we see that the rules have been changed, the boundaries eradicated, and reason and its language are left limited by their own bounds.

The reason of eternity is belief; the language of belief is symbol, metaphor, analogy, and finally silence. "Whereof one cannot speak, thereof one must be silent...Be still and know..." This is why Kierkegaard is correct. If we can prove God's existence, then we have reduced God to our limits, and who in the world will believe in such a limited God?

I believe in God. I love the mystery when my reason is exercised to exhaustion, and the objective miracles which flow forth as a special language, and the subjective ecstasy that comes in the simplicity of a conversation between two believers who say:

"Do you believe in God?"

"Yes."

"I, too."

And then they see a spirit present in one another and that spirit is holy. The same one blown into us at creation. The same one blown into the disciples before Thomas' searching in that evening of the first day.

"Do you believe in God?"

"Yes."

"I, too."

That belief leads them to see God in one another. And that spirit effects a subtle smile, miraculous and ecstatic.

And that is all there is to say. Then they remain silent. Words will no longer edify. "Whereof one cannot speak, thereof one must remain silent."

"Do you believe in God?"

"I, too."

What follows is silence. Which may be truth's most profound sound.

Amen.

May 25, 1986
Trinity Sunday
John 16:12–15

A pagan once asked the wise rabbi Joshua, "Why did God choose the humble thornbush as the place to reveal himself to Moses?" The teacher responded, "God chose the humble thornbush to teach you that there is no place on earth bereft of divine presence, not even a thornbush."

On this Trinity Sunday, we seek to celebrate the central experience of the people of God. We, as people of the way of Christ, worship and relate to a God of transcendence, immanence, and inspiration. In today's Gospel from John, Jesus speaks of the transcendent father, his immanent self, and the spirit of truth as one dynamic reality, summed in the statement that the selfsame source of truth, incarnate in Christ, will send the spirit of truth and "he will guide you into all truth." This truth is the same as from the Father and the Son, now known as the Holy Spirit.

Transcendence, immanence, and inspiration: the triune experience of our faith. Transcendence means to exist or rise beyond human limits. God as sovereign source reigns beyond the human horizons of time and space. And yet, God is as near as the immanent presence of the human Jesus. This transcendent God always reveals God's self in tangible ways. God does so in names, places, events, symbols, sacraments, even humble thornbushes. The fullest revelation is to the community raised up through a personal experience with the intimate and immanent Jesus of Nazareth. Our experience and reflection upon it is that God is the union of the opposites of transcendence and immanence. How can this be? Such mysteries are beyond definition, and all arguments flirt with sophistry—a logical, but ultimately fallacious, argument. And so we must look for metaphor or analogy rather than logic. Transcendence and immanence are opposites that imply one another. Try this analogy. Image a bent line, as in a bow—perhaps a rainbow—it is both convex and concave at the same time, depending on how one views it. And so it is with our God: beyond and below, without and within.

The third person of the trinity is the Spirit. I choose this day to describe this experience of God's personhood as inspiration. The word inspire means to "breathe life into." God dwells within us to bring us and lead us to a new life of continual transcendence. We are to transcend ourselves, our own immanent selves. Inspiration has no history. It is creative. It is a moment of newness that has never been before. Its purpose is to make life and lead to new life. This is the inspiration of the Holy Spirit. The Spirit is autonomous and leads us where we need to go, even if it is not where we want to go. For the Spirit always leads to the truth. Most of us ask the Holy Spirit to lead us where we want to go, the safe places. When we make our life plans or decisions, we ask the Spirit to guide us where it is we have decided we want to go. And we would never transcend what we now know, never be or become any more than we now are. But truly being guided by the Spirit is to follow the truth, come whence it will, cost what it may. The Spirit of truth guides us—yea, even leads or pushes us—not where we want to go, or thought we would go, or our parents told us we should go, but where we need to go: to the immanent and transcendent truth. To be inspired by the Holy Spirit is to follow the guide into all truth. For the Spirit is calling humans to transcend themselves, obey the transcendent call, and follow. Those who are inspired by the Holy Spirit are not more moral or holy, just more aspiring. To aspire means "to rise upward, to soar." To be inspired by the Holy Spirit means that you aspire for more than mediocrity and mundanity—that you will transcend that—you will aspire for more. The alternative to being inspired by the Holy Spirit and to aspire for transcendence is to expire. That is a choice you have been given. I will take the autonomous breath of God over no breath. I will aspire rather than expire. Christians are called to be as eagles and flirt with the boundaries of human definition. The inspirations may come from anywhere, anytime, in anything. In immanent realities are tangibles, such as thornbushes, crowns of thorns, crosses, empty tombs, poems, a score of music, a painting, a sacrament, another, or something as mundane as a carpenter from Nazareth. We must look at and listen to everything, for each experience has the possibility to keep us alive and bring us new life. One moment of inspiration can make all time inspired.

Trinity: transcendence, immanence, and inspiration; Father, Son, and Holy Spirit. Charles Hartshorne speaks of God in persons in this summary statement: "The higher forms of power are not those which inhibit the freedom of others, but rather those which inspire appropriate degrees and kinds of freedom in them, the power of artists, prophets, men of genius and true statesmen. God is the unsurpassable, inspiring genius of all freedom, not the all-determining coercive tyrant."

I aspire to worship and know a God who transcends me—a complex, mysterious God—and through thornbushes and crosses inspires me to transcend myself and to seek a truth beyond where even eagles can fly. This is our faith. This is our Trinitarian faith. This is our history. This is our destiny. We are a people of the Holy Trinity.

Amen.

June 1, 1986
Galatians 1:1–10

I have often felt that Paul's epistle to the Galatians could be subtitled, "The Gospel of Freedom." The issue Paul addresses in the introduction, which is today's epistle, is what Jean-Paul Sartre addressed in his aphorism: "To be free is to be condemned to be free."

Paul had previously been to the churches in the area known as Galatia, an area north of the Mediterranean in north central Asia Minor. There he had preached a gospel of freedom. The thesis of Paul's gospel was always the same—that God in Christ had set us free—free to live, free to die, free to be worthy and acceptable to God in spite of our sinful nature. Galatians is Paul's Declaration of Independence. It is the Magna Carta of the Christian faith. The question was: "How can humans, who are by nature sinful, win the favor of God who is holy?" Paul's answer was: "They cannot. The way to please God is to have a relationship with God, to accept his graceful love and to stop trying to acquire favor and salvation by obedience to human law. God's forgiving love through Christ is the sole justification and authentication of one's life. This is the free love of God as experienced in the advent of the Christ event."

Paul had preached to the Galatians that the bondage was over. "You are free in Christ." Faith is absolutely opposed to bondage to the law. "We are now free to be human," Paul preached. The gospel is a gospel of love, acceptance, and freedom. And now Paul writes back to the churches at Galatia: "I came and preached a gospel of freedom. I am astonished that you are so quickly deserting him who called you in the grace of Christ and turning to another gospel, a legalistic gospel from which you have been freed."

This appears to be the nature of humans and the reason why the freedom gospel is such a scandal. The word "scandal" means "a rock in the road over which one will trip," and so freedom has always been for humans something in our pathway over which we continue to fall. Human beings are called to freedom, but with a tension created between human freedom and all the given factors that belong equally to human existence and remain as barriers to freedom. We are summoned to go beyond whatever conditions we are given, to transcend the common denominators, and become more and more uncommonly free. But the limits, definitions, and boundaries continually remind us of freedom's other side. The responsibility to be as careful and loving with our freedom as the one who bequeaths it so gracefully. There is nothing we can do—absolutely nothing—that can separate us from God's love which sets us free. And the tension of that responsibility, the burden of freedom comes, as Sartre says so clearly, as a condemnation to be free.

There is a well-known passage in the writings of Kierkegaard in which he speaks of the anxiety attendant on freedom: "One may liken anxiety to dizziness. He whose eye chances to look down into the yawning abyss becomes dizzy... Thus anxiety is the dizziness of freedom which occurs when the spirit would posit the synthesis, and freedom then gazes down into its own possibility, grasping at finiteness to sustain itself." Kierkegaard's image suggests that much of the praise of freedom that one hears is far too superficial, for those who utter it are apparently unaware of the anxiety of freedom. One must decide. It is not written on some tablet, brought from some mountain, written clearly before you. You are responsible for your own life, decision making, and responses. When one becomes aware of this, one then understands

Sartre's aphorism: "To be free is to be condemned to be free." To be free is to have laid upon one human care to commitments and human responsibility to others. To be free means to no longer be as the unconscious, unthinking, irresponsible animals. Animals are not born free; they are born in bondage to instinct and appetite and are never for one moment delivered from the constraints of nature. The contrast between the demands of freedom and the apparently very meager resources which finite human beings have for meeting such demands is frightening.

Paul should not have been surprised, nor should we, that people would choose a religion of rules and laws over a gospel of freedom, where love is the only rule and the only justice. I'm afraid we have not progressed much from the Galatians. Much of the gospel I heard preached in my youth and continue to hear echoed today is one of worship of rules and bondage to laws. This is human nature. But nature is what we are put on earth to rise above. The gospel of freedom puts too much responsibility on the individual. So in the vertigo of freedom, he grabs a banister of finite rule and clings to the known, clings to the smaller certainty, out of fear and anxiety. It is, for most, far freer to be bound to external rules than to be condemned to the responsibility of freedom whose only rule is love.

Freedom needs the protection of law because, as Luther made clear, the human will is subject to selfishness, and in any human society, there are constant attempts by some members to take away the freedom of others. Laws are necessary between humans, but irrelevant in a relationship between God and his children.

My true freedom is therefore not a license to irresponsibility, but a gift of love by God in Christ. I am free to live and free to die and have been bequeathed a life of freedom, and in my relationship with God, I can exercise absolute, incredible imagination about my possibilities. There are no rules. Except love.

I am free to be me and free to love you in spite of our incompleteness and the attendant fears that come with imperfection. If I accept the unconditional love of God, the least I can do is to love you in the same way that I am loved. Free to be me, free to be you; inadequate, irresponsible, incomplete, afraid, and yet free to overcome all; to become courageous, authentic, responsible, whole—truly free.

This freedom is a call to become whole through the experiment and experience of life's boundaries, to take just an occasional taste or touch of the experience of true freedom in order to see what our boundaries are. It is our hope, it is our promise, that the boundaries will eventually disappear like a red dawn. Nikolai Berdyaev writes: "Freedom is not something which [we] demand of God, but that which God requires of us." Let us not be afraid to accept the gift of freedom, for God's sake. Let us step out with tentative steps, like astronauts who stand at the edge of finitude. We are tethered to something tangible, dizzy at the unlimited possibilities, and yet willing to take a trusting step toward wholeness. Our bodies are those cumbersome suits that somehow conflict with mobility and grace. Occasionally, we are called into space that knows fewer boundaries, and we stand at the hatch of a shuttle and look out to all of the freedom and possibility, even though we are yet in these cumbersome suits, tethered to something real. Some of us will stand at the hatch, bold, steadfast, dizzy, but unafraid, and when we do, we scream throughout the universe, "Sartre is wrong!"

Christians are not condemned to freedom, we are called to it. Freedom is not the end of life, but its beginning. And it can begin at any time. It begins for you when you accept God's unconditional acceptance. And the time will come when we pull off the space suit, unplug the tether, and step out to all the resources found in the unlimited mystery of freedom's eternal gift. And we will journey on, freewheeling into the cosmos, and be one with our call to become free at last.

Amen.

❊ ❊ ❊

June 8, 1986
Luke 7:11–17

In reflecting on his first year in seminary and introduction to biblical study, Frederick Buechner writes in his book, *Now & Then*:

> I think for the first time, that holiness is not something hazy and elusive that we know apart from the earth but something we can know only as it wells up out of the earth, out of people…
>
> What I began to see was that the Bible is not essentially, as I had always more or less supposed, a book of ethical principles, of moral exhortations, of cautionary tales about exemplary people, of uplifting thoughts…I saw it instead as a great, tattered compendium of writings, the underlying and unifying purpose of all of which is to show how God works through [people] to make himself known to the world and to draw the world back to himself.

Buechner so aptly recognizes that scripture may be one of those points where divine transcendence and human inspiration touch. For instance, in today's Gospel, after Jesus heals the son of the widow of Nain, the crowd cries out the incarnational kernel of the Christian gospel: "A great prophet has arisen among us!" and "God has visited his people!" There it is, in two exclamations. God makes himself known and draws the world to him. A prophet arises and God visits. That moment, if blown up in an imaginary photo, would show, in a sort of mental dot matrix, a point at which the human and divine touch. And that is a holy place, a holy moment, a holy event. Something in someone, at some time, in a particular place and particular set of circumstances, rises up, wells up out of the real earth, and real people; out of humus and human and meets the holy other; at some point and peak experience, of a moment of full time beyond clock time; a point, a turning point; a crisis, a change, a Christ. Christ is the once-and-for-all event of a person arising and God visiting, and once seen, can be seen again and again in this, the only life in which the human and divine can be seen.

Let's window-shop in this story of the widow of Nain and see what we need to take home. First, we see that the Old Testament story of Elijah healing a son of a woman is very similar to the Gospel healing story. And that Nain is the place of Elisha's miracle of resurrection. Luke, including this story, establishes Jesus as a prophet with power, at least as great as the great Old Testament prophets. Secondly, we see something of the great compassion of Jesus. "The only son of a mother and she, a widow." Jesus had a special and unusual (for his time) appreciation for and sensitivity toward women and children...a trait of *real* men.

And then this most repeatable set of twin exclamations—a holy one has risen, and the holy one has visited—and the one conclusion: this is a holy moment.

Holy moments happen all the time in all time. I believe that the greatest problem within the religious realm is unawareness. It is what my friend, John Claypool, calls "riding on an ox looking for an ox." We just don't have the eyes to see that the true miracle in this Gospel story is that it involves real people in real places and a *real* man cares about a widow and her baby boy. And what wells up out of the earth and people is what God visits. And where human love reaches the point of no conditions, God's love meets it unconditionally. And at that point is a holy moment, and behold, a new creation.

The great challenge of the Church lies not in persuading people to work for something they do not possess, but to open their eyes to behold what *does* exist. This is the graceful religion which sees human and holy as possible at some time, in some place, with someone.

Erich Heller tells the following story of enlightenment:

> The late Munich comedian, Karl Vallentin—one of the greatest of a rare race of metaphysical clowns—once enacted the following scene: the curtain goes up and reveals darkness; and in this darkness is a solitary circle of light thrown by a street-lamp. Vallentin, with his long-drawn and deeply worried face, walks round and round the circle of light, desperately looking for something. "What have you lost?" a policeman asks who has entered the scene. "The key to my house." Upon which the policeman joins him in his search; they find nothing; and after a while he inquires: "Are you sure you lost it here?" "No," says Vallentin, and pointing to a dark corner of the stage: "Over there." "Then why on earth are you looking for it here?" "There is no light over there," says Vallentin.

More often than not, we humans have lived under the dark illusion that the miraculous and holy were wherever we weren't. Christianity tells us that wherever we are, there is a possibility for the holy to happen at this point. We must be willing to let the holy one assume whatever form he will and come in whatever manner he chooses. This willingness is absolutely crucial, and it must be coupled with our trust that God wants to be known to us and will visit us here, where we are. And God will visit us in names, faces, and places we never assumed, were taught, or expected God to be. This is the way authentic experience with the biblical God occurs. We look for the key only in the light, but God may be found in the dark corner, in the widow and dead son. We must move into the darkness, into the humus and human, and see that holiness is not something hazy and elusive that we know apart from the earth, but rises up, and God visits and makes himself known in real places and people—the miraculous in the mundane, the extraordinary in the ordinary.

It is absolutely crucial and critical that from this point, we cease to search for God anywhere else, for he will come nowhere else except in the events of our lives, even in the dark corners. Please don't be afraid to look, for if you do not look, the only guarantee is that you will never see "that holiness rises up from among us and God visits his people."

Amen.

✤ ✤ ✤

June 15, 1986
II Samuel 11:26–12:15; Galatians 2:11–21; Luke 7:36–50

> Some day, the day will end
> And never appear again.
>
> It will be neither inert nor
> Empty, just over.
>
> Time will return to the void
> Out of which it came.
>
> Material will make one last chemical change
> And disappear like light behind a closing door.
>
> And what for some reason was,
> Will be, for no reason, anymore.

This is the end begun by evil. With a word wand, the magician moves with slight of style from poetry to prophecy. The three lessons read today are summed in the antiphonal refrain: "I acknowledged my sin to you, and you forgave me the guilt of my sin."

Evil is a reality in this world. Evil is the anti-life force that is a part of the nature of things—even human nature. Evil in general is known as sin in particular. The goal of evil, through sinful acts, is nothingness. That is, to disintegrate life, piece by piece, particle by particle, till it will someday end and never appear again. "Why does evil exist?" is as substantial a question as can be asked. Any answer is speculative theory, and one slight step above the question and answer of: "Why is there something rather than nothing?" "Because…!" "Because" is a good answer, for it means "by cause." The reason there is something or the reason there is evil, is by cause, but the reason is beyond reason.

What we do know is that there is a force and a power moving in life that seeks to end things—end relationship, end commitments, end joy, end life. The goal of evil is to disintegrate life into nothingness: neither inert nor empty, just over. The force of evil is, perhaps, a ventriloquist and uses a stained-glass voice to disintegrate us back into nothingness.

Sin is the estrangement or separation from the good. Good is something which serves the purpose for which it was created. Good has as its goal completion or wholeness. Its process is creation and integration. Sin is destructive. Good is creative. Our religion, based on the word and action of Jesus, seeks the good, through awareness of the evil, and proclaims that God's love is stronger than evil. For God's love is that which leads us to completion in complete union with God.

The key to overcoming evil and its state, sin, is awareness. The best example of such awareness I know is found in today's Old Testament lesson.

When Uriah's wife heard that her husband had died, she lamented and then David sent for her. In case you don't remember, Uriah's wife's name was Bathsheba. David had seen Bathsheba bathing and taken her for his own wife in order to grasp what he wanted. Evil seized his desire, and he sent Uriah into the battlefront knowing he would be killed. And so he was. The prophet Nathan came to David and told him a parable of a rich man who took a poor man's only lamb and gave it away. On hearing the parable, "David's anger was greatly kindled against the man; and he said to the prophet Nathan, 'As the Lord lives, the man who has done this deserves to die…'" And Nathan, in one of literature's greatest examples of prophetic awareness, said, "David, you are the man." Within the pain of awareness, David confessed, "I have sinned against the Lord." Nathan, speaking in the strength of God's love, said, "David, the Lord has put away your sin. You shall not die."

The cost was great—yea, even the death of the child emanating from his sin—yet even death is overcome in divine forgiveness.

In Luke's Gospel, we hear again such depths to which God descends to overcome evil. Jesus says to a woman of the streets, whose sins were numerous, "Your sins are forgiven. Your [awareness] has saved you."

The darkness of evil cannot stand the light of awareness. All sin. This is the nature of things. No one escapes the contamination of evil. If we deny evil, we allow it to grow in the darkness. Awareness, enlightened awareness, through the prophetic word of love, will cleanse and restore. The act of forgiving love, by God in Christ, is stronger than any sinful action by any human being. Confession is awareness. God's unconditional love is absolution. Repentance is the new life which comes when we turn away from the terror of evil's night and face the morning sun.

Evil's promise is that:

> Some day, the day will end
> And never appear again.
>
> It will be neither inert nor
> Empty, just over.
>
> Time will return to the void
> Out of which it came.
>
> Material will make one last chemical change
> And disappear like light behind a closing door.
>
> And what for some reason was,
> Will be, for no reason, anymore.

God's promise is that:

> Someday, the day will not end
> And never die again.
>
> It will be alive and full
> For the first time and now just begun.
>
> All that was, will now be
> Born delivered from the womb of time.
>
> All matter will change to love
>
> And what for no reason was,
> Will be, for some reason, evermore.

These two promises are set before us. We Christians choose life, for the source of life has chosen us. And the only thing which can separate us from God is being unaware that we have a choice: to accept our acceptance and live on, or simply sit in darkness and wait for the day that will end and never appear again. I set before you this day life and death and encourage you to choose life.

Amen.

June 22, 1986
Psalm 63:1–8; Luke 9:18–24

I have always been fascinated by fountains. The soothing sound of running water has a primordial peacefulness. It must come as the pleasant reminder of the time when I was womb-bound, connected in a primary paradise of water sounds. The word "fountain" means spring and "spring" means source, origin, or beginning. Water was from the beginning something out of which we have come: mist at creation, ocean in evolution, embryonic at birth.

Today we baptize a baby boy, a firstborn child. Font and fountain are one. Life is as mysterious as the one who bequeaths it. As the water flows from a fountain in the continuous rhyme and repetition, so it is with life, death, and new life: water sound, water symbol, font and fountain, spring, womb, and source.

The more years grace offers me, the less I know; but what I do know, I hold more closely, as close as breath and heartbeat. I know that God is a source beyond that which is revealed in tangible ways. And I know that I desire such resource as the poet of today's psalm writes:

> O God, you are my God; eagerly I seek you;
> My soul thirsts for you, my flesh faints for you,
> As in a barren and dry land where there is no water.

This source, seen in palpable ways as resource, is that which births and sustains. And that source is available to us if we look everywhere. If we believe it, we see it.

There was a famous monastery which had fallen on very hard times. Formerly, its many buildings were filled with young monks, and its big church resounded with the singing of the chant, but now it was deserted. People no longer came there to be nourished by prayer. A handful of old monks shuffled through the cloisters and praised their God with heavy hearts.

On the edge of the monastery woods, an old rabbi had built a little hut. He would come there from time to time to fast and pray. No one ever spoke with him, but whenever he appeared, the word would be passed from monk to monk: "The rabbi walks in the woods." And, for as long as he was there, the monks would feel sustained by his prayerful presence.

One day, the abbot decided to visit the rabbi and to open his heart to him. So, after the morning Eucharist, he set out through the woods. As he approached the hut, the abbot saw the rabbi standing in the doorway, his arms outstretched in welcome. It was as though he had been waiting there for some time. The two embraced like long-lost brothers. Then, they stepped back and just stood there, smiling at one another with smiles their faces could hardly contain.

After a while, the rabbi motioned for the abbot to enter. In the middle of the room was a wooden table with the scriptures open on it. They sat there for a moment in the presence of the book. Then the rabbi began to cry. The abbot could not contain himself. He covered his face with his hands and began to cry, too. For the first time in his life, he cried his heart out. The two men sat there like lost children, filling the hut with their sobs and wetting the wood of the table with their tears.

After the tears had ceased to flow and all was quiet again, the rabbi lifted his head. "You and your brothers are serving God with heavy hearts," he said. "You have come to ask a teaching of me. I will give you a teaching, but you can only repeat it once. After that, no one must ever say it aloud again." The rabbi looked straight at the abbot and said, "The messiah is among you." For a while, all was silent. Then the rabbi said, "Now you must go." The abbot left without a word and without ever looking back.

The next morning, the abbot called his monks together in the chapter room. He told them he had received a teaching from "the rabbi who walks in the woods" and that this teaching was never again to be spoken aloud. Then he looked at each of his brothers and said, "The rabbi said that one of us is the messiah."

The monks were startled by this. "What could it mean?" they asked themselves. "Is Brother John the messiah? Or Father Matthew? Or Brother Thomas? Am I the messiah? What could this mean?" They were all deeply puzzled by the rabbi's teaching. But no one ever mentioned it again.

As time went by, the monks began to treat one another with a very special reverence. There was a gentle, wholehearted, human quality about them now which was hard to describe but easy to notice. They lived with one another as men who had finally found something. But they prayed the scriptures together as men who were always looking for something. Occasional visitors found themselves deeply moved by the lives of these monks. Before long, people were coming from far and wide to be nourished by the prayer life of the monks, and young men were asking, once again, to become part of the community.

In those days, the rabbi no longer walked in the woods. His hut had fallen into ruins. But, somehow or other, the old monks who had taken his teaching to heart still felt sustained by his prayerful presence.

Jesus asked his disciples who others thought he was. And then he asked the crucial question: "Who do you say I am?" Peter answered, "The Christ of God." If Jesus is your Christ, then baptisms are the tangible, palpable way by which we "put on Christ," Paul writes in today's lesson to the Galatians.

This Hellmann-Sweeney family has come before us today in faith. Bringing us a new life, born out of the wellspring of creation, like water from a fountain. They are an Easter people claiming that, for them, Jesus is the Christ, the resource of God, and knowing that those who are baptized in Christ have put on Christ. The Messiah is among us. To be seen in baby boys, in bread and wine, in one another, in sunsets and rainbows, in stories, and in symbols. Today, Walter Richard Sweeney puts on Christ to tell us that the Messiah is among us. In water, life, death, new life, rhyme, rhythm, repetitions of water sounds, symbols, water stories, font, fountain, spring, source, and resource.

Bring us the new story that has never been told. Let us hear the Christ in the fresh sound of the spring waters. Bring us the baby boy.

Amen.

❊ ❊ ❊

July 6, 1986
Luke 10:1–12, 16–20

The first time I remember being conscious of the Statue of Liberty, I was in the second grade. On Mrs. Gooch's square box desk sat a bank. The bank was a small bronze replica with a slit in Lady Liberty's head into which, on various occasions, we slipped pennies. I saw the true statue for the first time seventeen years ago on my first trip to New York. Like many things first viewed in pictures, it looked different in reality. I was struck with how green the statue was. I knew something of oxidation from my high school chemistry. As I stood looking across the harbor, a word floated up to my consciousness from something read at some time and stored in my memory's warehouse until this moment when needed. Patina.

The word "patina" came to me. What a wonderful word and what a wonderful color. A mature, soft green, developed through years of harsh life.

"God is subtle," Einstein said, "but not malicious." Life lived costs us the smooth, perfect, unblemished look of birth and leaves us a resulting patina. The rough nurture of nature is to scar, corrode, wrinkle, bend, and break objects and subjects alike. The subtlety is that wisdom is attracted to the imperfect and innocence to the perfect. The process may be that imperfection ends innocence, wisdom awaits wholeness, wholeness restores innocence— when wise eyes see the smooth skin of a sapling, they blink in horror at the cost of season and storm that will develop a bark strong enough for survival.

And so it is with a plant, animal, person, or nation. John Gardner, in the turmoil of the '60s, remarked that America was caught in the brutal crossfire between "unloving critics and uncritical lovers." A loving critic and a critical lover will know another person or group and must make the critical observation as a part of the love response, for it is love's responsibility to be honest.

America has its own developing patina. We are not as pure and unblemished as we were in our first developing stages. We have seen in the short term of two decades a lost war and a near-racial war. We are noticeably maturing by our blemishes and scars and corrosion of years and seasons of conflict. The subtlety of evolution by the author of creation is that we must stand and fall, wound and heal, sow and reap, in order to be and become. The one-hundredth year of liberty's symbol, the statue of freedom, reminds us that we develop a patina with maturity and must, from time to time, repent or renew and count our history by scar and star, in order to face the next subtle nurture of the harsh teacher, nature. The Fourth of July is time to celebrate freedom and evaluate how free we are. This year, we celebrate one of our great national symbols—the one-hundredth birthday of the Statue of Liberty. Proud, and yet in need of renewal. Strong, yet at the cost of storm and season. The patina is also a symbol that no growth comes without change and change is counted by its costs.

So now, without so much as a condescending transition, the conclusion for each of us is that of the woman in the water. Life is full of growth and change. Harsh reality creates patina for body and soul. The nurture of nature is difficult.

Annie Dillard, in her book *Pilgrim at Tinker Creek*, writes:

> "In nature…, the emphasis is in what is rather than what ought to be." I learn this lesson in a new way every day. It must be, I think tonight, that in a certain sense only the newborn in this world are whole, that as adults we are expected to be, and necessarily, somewhat nibbled. It's par for the course. Physical wholeness is not something we have barring accident; it is itself accidental, an accident of infancy, like a baby's fontanel or the egg-tooth on a hatchling. Are the five-foot silver eels that migrate as adults across meadows by night actually scarred with the bill marks of herons, flayed by the sharp teeth of bass? I think of the beautiful sharks I saw from a shore, hefted and held aloft in a light-shot wave. Were those sharks sliced with scars, were there mites in their hides and worms in their hearts? Did the mockingbird that plunged from the rooftop, folding its wings, bear in its buoyant quills a host of sucking lice? Is our birthright and heritage to be, like Jacob's cattle on which the life of a nation was founded, "ring-streaked, specked, and spotted" not with the spangling marks of a grace like beauty rained down from eternity, but with the blotched assaults and quarryings of time? "We are all of us clocks," says Eddington, "whose faces tell the passing years." The young man proudly names his scars for his lover; the old man alone before a mirror erases his scars with his eyes and sees himself whole.

As individual or nation, God sees us as we were created to be. We become what we are created to be by the hard way, and yet there is no other way. The only way to get through is to go through. We have the promise that we enter eternity through our scars and not our perfections.

This Fourth of July weekend we see the Statue of Liberty as a symbol of our freedom and a symbol of celebration and renewal, and we realize that the true graceful beauty is in the subtle, but not malicious, soft green patina, the presence of which tells us that our ultimate nurture is beyond nature and within it.

Amen.

July 13, 1986
Luke 10:25–37

I was five years old before I realized that gum was sweet. My brother used to tell me that he would "soften up" the gum for me and then give it to me. For years, the only gum I chewed had all the sweet chewed out.

I thought of that this week when the Parable of the Good Samaritan rolled up on the lectionary. How many times has this parable been told, read, rehearsed, written about, and preached upon? I cannot even count the number of times that I have preached upon this text.

This is the nature of the parable. It never loses its flavor. It must be told over and over, for it is a collective story of our people. The parable has a life of its own, and our responsibility is to allow it to live by telling it or reading it. Each and every new generation hears it anew. And each person hears it at a new age. I hear it differently at middle age than I heard it as a child. When I was a seminarian, I was teaching a church school class of six-year-olds. I told them this parable. I described the man who had fallen among thieves as beaten, left in the hot sun, dirty, sweating, and bleeding to death. Then I asked the class, "What would you have done if you had come upon this poor man?" One little boy popped up and popped off, "I think I would have throwed up." We hear the story differently every time we hear it.

Let's look at the story today, allow it to live, and let me reflect on one issue that came to me this week in my study.

I want to begin by reading a verse from the fourth chapter of John's Gospel. "There came a woman of Samaria to draw water. Jesus said to her, 'Give me a drink.'…The Samaritan woman said to him, 'How is it that you, a Jew, ask a drink of me, a woman of Samaria?' For Jews have no dealings with Samaritans.'"

The parable is told to the ear of the Jew for whom the Samaritan was a heretical, unclean, despised enemy. Jesus is possibly telling the story in a Jerusalem setting, from the oblique reference to the robbed man as going down from Jerusalem to Jericho. The traveler is "one of us," in a location we can all imagine—as in a member of Christ Church Cathedral, on his way from Houston to Galveston, was robbed, beaten, and left beside the Gulf Freeway. Along comes the presiding bishop, Pope John Paul II, Mother Teresa, a dean of a cathedral. They each pass by. The person who performs the good act and helps the wounded man is a Samaritan, a socio-religious outcast. You can fill in your own blank: a pornographer, a communist, a person with AIDS, a Libyan, an Iranian—whoever it is with whom you would have no dealings, for as it is stated in John's Gospel, "Jews had no dealings with Samaritans." In this story, if it is only about encouraging help to one's neighbor in distress, or even one's enemy in need, would it not have been better to have a wounded Samaritan in the ditch and have a Jew stop to aid him? Parables have surprises. One flavor left in the story is to learn that the "good" act evilly and the "bad" act virtuously.

Judgment is ultimately God's. Good people or bad people, friends or enemies, all have the potential to be their opposite. This is a mature awareness and a loving faith posture to realize that good people may do bad things and bad people may do good things. And with even more awareness in one's judgment about one's self, we have within us neighbor parts and enemy parts.

Think of your own interior life. Think of your great gift or talent, virtue or quality. Then think of your darkest fear, memory, act, vice, or negative quality. Retell the parable and place your best part in jeopardy and your worst part as the savior of your best. Then, we have incredible new possibility for interior growth. Maybe by seeing your interior enemy as having value, this will pour oil and wine on your unbalanced, broken, estranged interior life. For the outcast, the beggar, the prostitute, the tax collector, the lepers are the ones who got Jesus' attention in his love and teachings. Put this parable alongside the prodigal son, the great supper, the rich man and Lazarus, the Pharisee and the publican, or Zaccheus, and you will see how it is that the rejected one is the one who holds the power of healing. For when the rejected one is seen as neighbor, healing begins.

Look at your own life as the journey from Jerusalem to Jericho. Look at your best as robbed and your worst as neighbor and see how a parable works as a healing story. And you'll know why it is that we tell them over and over and why they never lose their flavor.

Amen.

❖ ❖ ❖

September 14, 1986
Luke 15:1–32

Over the whole world theater in which the human drama is played out, the cross of the risen Christ broods. In today's Gospel lesson, we hear parables, stories, of Jesus' resurrectional brooding. Perhaps the final function of preaching is a brooding over the Easter implications in our human drama. "To brood" means literally to sit on eggs until they hatch. Christ broods over us until we emerge fully human.

In Luke's Gospel, chapter 15, Jesus tells three consecutive parables. The chapter begins, "Now the tax collectors and sinners were all drawing near to him. And the Pharisees and the scribes murmured, saying, 'This man receives sinners and eats with them.'" Then Jesus strings together three sequential parables in an esplanade of brooding, which occupies the entire fifteenth chapter. Two of the parables are before us today: the parables of the lost sheep and the lost coin. Verse 11 to the end of the chapter is the third consecutive parable, the prodigal son.

I have been struck by how Jesus, or some unknown editor (perhaps Random House or Holy Spirit Press), placed these three stories together. Each makes the same point, yet each has a different lost character: an object, an animal, and a person. The lady has lost a precious coin and seeks diligently until she finds it. A shepherd has lost a sheep and leaves the ninety-nine to find the one. And in the third, a father has lost a son and waits patiently until he returns. The differing predicaments come from the three different lost ones. The coin, an object, is lost, but doesn't know it. The animal is lost, knows it, but can't do anything about it. But the prodigal son, a person, is lost, knows it, and can do something about it.

And so, the message is in each and all of the three parables. God will go to any extreme, even to doing nothing, in order to find or be related to us. But we must know we are desired and have a conscious desire to turn or return to God. This is God's nature: to honor human nature. We are free to choose whether to remain lost or return home.

Now concerning the nature of God's brooding over our lostness, I am reminded of a wonderful story told to me by Father Abbot Timothy Sweeney, of St. Meinrad's Monastery in Indiana. He and I were leaders of a retreat in New Harmony, Indiana, in the spring of 1985. At coffee, he told of a trip he took to the Holy Land. One day, he decided to rent a car and travel outside Jerusalem's brown hills to see if he could find some shepherds at work. Sure enough, after some directed travel, he came upon a flock being tended by a shepherd and his dogs. And as luck, or revelation, would have it, as he drove up the hillside on a small, one-lane road, a sheep left the flock and ran across the trail in front of his car. And sure enough, soon after, here came the faithful shepherd. The abbot, viewing the scene, felt he was seeing the Parable of the Lost Sheep played out before his very eyes. About that time, his beatific vision was interrupted by a loud screaming, whereupon he saw the shepherd grab the lost sheep by two hands full of wool, turn him around, and drop-kick him back across the road toward home. The revelation was, as always, unexpected.

God, in Christ, broods over our lostness, but from time to time, at least for those who look and listen, gives us a nudge, or a kick, in the metaphorical pants, to direct us back home.

The Easter implication is that new life comes from all forms of death, from relational to physical. We humans are neither objects nor animals. We have wills, freedom to choose. God will nudge or kick us to bring our attention to the fact that resurrection is the brooding Christ over the world drama.

This week a friend sent me an article by Tom Bethell entitled "King David's Royal Family." It is a piece about a house in Greenwich Village, where Mother Teresa's Missionaries of

Charity run a home for AIDS patients. In the article, Bethell describes the baptism of a patient named Tom.

> Like the sisters and following the Indian custom, he was barefoot in the chapel. [The priest said to the candidate], "Do you renounce Satan and all his works?" "I do." Tom had become Thomas and he had chosen the additional name of Peter. "I baptize you in the name of the Father and of the Son and of the Holy Spirit…"
>
> Thomas Peter stood in a white plaster receptacle as the water was poured over his head—enough of it to streak his dark-colored work clothes. Then he went outside and returned, wearing white trousers and shirt. His wife, daughter, and especially his son hugged him emotionally.
>
> It was hard to tell what impression it all made on the other patients, most of whom sat impassively throughout the ceremony, but many received communion.
>
> Earlier I had talked to Tom alone in the chapel. He sat and talked with a completely relaxed candor and tranquility for an hour or more. He said he was completely free of drug addiction. He had received "hundreds" of blood transfusions while on kidney dialysis, he said. So maybe he got AIDS that way. "But with an IV drug record, they blame it on the drugs," he said.
>
> "I blame nothing. I don't think I would have ever come to God without this. They would have found me in the street. I used not to be able to talk about these things. There are people here who want what I have received. But it took all these years of pain and suffering to find it. I can get on my knees and pray now and feel refreshed. No better feeling in this world. And inside I want to tell the world."
>
> He said that some resolutely exclude the truth, "keeping up a front all the way to the grave. They do. They know what you are saying is true. But they despise it. I used to. Broke all Ten Commandments many times over." To others with the same illness, he would say: "Now is the time to give back something to God, even if only prayer. I imagine that each and every one needs reassurance to try to grasp Christ. But don't despair. Just think on it, because Christ is the only way out of this. And any miracle that comes will come through Christ. Even in sickness you can bear the pain, because you share the pain with Christ. I've had so many people go before me, who died. Some had longer tails than the devil. In the end they ask for Christ. They say, 'Oh God have mercy!', strange sounds from men who cursed and blasphemed. But in the end they grasped the peace."

Over the whole world theater in which the human drama is played out, the cross of the risen Christ broods. We are not objects or animals. We should not treat one another as such, for God doesn't. God treats us as children and loves us in spite of ourselves, with no conditions. Augustine wrote the ending to this brooding when he wrote: "You have made us for yourself, O Lord, and our hearts are restless until they rest in you." Finally, I believe, as

Jesus taught me in his brooding, that nothing is lost. Nothing.
Amen.

October 19, 1986
Genesis 32

If you don't know the story of Jacob at the Jabbok by now, it's time that you learned. This story is of such collective wisdom that it ought to be rehearsed by every family as surely as the nursery rhyme or the family history. This story from Genesis is a part of our genesis as the human family of the covenant.

When Isaac, of Abraham and Sarah, was old and his eyes were dim, he called his son Esau, the older of the twin boys, to receive his blessing. Now the tradition was that the oldest son would receive birthright and blessing from the father. This was the law by tradition. Isaac and Rebekah had had twins, Esau and Jacob. Esau was born first and Jacob second; Esau came forth red, all his body like a hairy mantle, and Jacob came forth holding his brother's heel, his first of several free rides at Esau's expense.

The fact of opposites in the world is set in this story. Esau was a man of the outdoors, a forager and hunter, rough-hewn and earthen. Jacob was a quiet, yet cunning, man who stayed home and dwelt in tents. One day, Esau came home famished from a day in the field. Esau was a man of nature; Jacob, a man of nurture. Jacob was cooking some red pottage. Esau asked for a bowl and Jacob said, "First, sell me your birthright." Esau said, "I am about to die, of what use is a birthright to me?" So, for a bit of pottage, Jacob obtained the birthright. Esau sold his inheritance in order to satiate his appetite. Herein the human condition is found. Are we to live our right to birth by appetite? And what of our nature in the Spirit? This is the tension and contradiction between what is natural and that which is supernatural. Was Jacob's exploitation of Esau appropriate to a higher calling?

And then again, when the twins' father, Isaac, was old and his eyes were dim, time had come to pass on the patriarchal blessing. God has blessed Abraham, and then Isaac, and now the blessing was to be passed on to Esau. Had not Rebekah intervened, we would worship the God of Abraham, Isaac, and Esau. But the maternal intuition knew that the blessing of God for the world would be better served by her sensitive son, Jacob, than by her sensual son, Esau. So she set up one of the greatest artifices in religious history. She sent Jacob in dressed as Esau, and he received the blessing from the blind Isaac. Here we see that calling may be a higher responsibility than tradition or law. Rebekah knew that Jacob was called to lead, not Esau. But the law stood between him and the truth. So, she assumed a situational ethic and created a righteous ruse and followed a truth higher than fact.

When Jacob appeared before his father, Isaac, the old man said, "Come near and kiss me, my son." So Jacob, in deceit and disguise, came to his blind father and kissed him. And Isaac smelled him and blessed him and uttered a poetic example of how God can instill insight that transcends eyesight, for Isaac proclaimed: "See, the smell of my son is as the smell of a freshly plowed field which the Lord has blessed." Even in the stench of Jacob's mendacity, old Isaac could smell the blessedness of irony, truth, destiny, and bliss. "The smell of my son is the smell of a blessed field." What a message concerning God's ability to transcend the predictable with the surprise; that holiness can emerge from human sin, and how truth and destiny can be sensed even in the midst of selfishness.

Jacob was born to a call that would be heeded in spite of all. Fleeing for his life under Esau's anger, Jacob then spent a long period of time having to bear the responsibility of his action. In so doing, he spent much of his life waiting and maturing. Through a series of tests and times, Jacob secured his wife Rachel, and through wise and cunning ways, he followed God's call to return home, to lead the people of God on toward their call to be a blessing to the world.

And now the scene for the story of Jacob at the Jabbok is set. Our Old Testament lesson can be told with possibilities for meaning as rich as a fruitful field. Jacob stopped by the water at the river Jabbok to rest before he crossed back into the land of his father. He feared his brother and dreaded the lonely responsibility of his calling to be a father of a nation. When he was alone, he prayed, "O God of my father Abraham and God of my father Isaac, O Lord, you called me back to my country and my people, and I will do you good. I am not worthy of your steadfast love and all the faithfulness which you have given me in your blessing."

And that very night, a man wrestled with him throughout the night until the sun rose and broke the day. When the man did not prevail against Jacob, he touched the hollow of his thigh. Jacob was wounded and limped the balance of his days. The wrestler of revelation was departing when Jacob cried, "I will not let you go unless you bless me." And the stranger said, "What is your name?" And he said, "Jacob." Then he said, "Your name shall no more be called Jacob, but Israel…" Jacob became his call. He knew through his wound who he was, but he could neither capture nor name the one from whom the ultimate blessing flowed. Jacob knew though that he had wrestled with God in order to enter his full life.

The story of Jacob at the Jabbok is so full of truth that to detail an enumeration would be to name grains of sand or stars.

Some sentences stay with me and inform my awareness, "fixing emblazoned zones and fiery poles" in the enchanting night of my life. Such as: the sensitive and sensual need one another as well as the fair and foul. How maternal nurture calls us to transcend nature and follow our call beyond the constraints of what used to be. The ironic surprise of God using sin to make saints and how truth can be sensed even in a lie, much as the smell of blessing in a field of dirt.

And what of the cost of a call and time to mature? How it is that we must wait to become whole? And then again, that when we wrestle with God, we are each scared and wounded, and wholeness only comes from what is rent in twain.

Jacob at the Jabbok will never live again unless the story is told. And truth will never die as long as the story is kept alive. Let it never be said that we did not seek the truth as surely as it has sought us in the mystery of the sacred story of human history: Jacob at the Jabbok.

Amen.

❊ ❊ ❊

October 26, 1986
Luke 18:9–14

A friend of mine who had lived a lot of life and distilled from it a magnum of wisdom from which he freely poured, once said, "Deliver me from religious people." The sage was a priest.

Pope-Hennessy's study on slave traders in America, *Sins of the Fathers*, reveals how respectable Englishman John Newton packed suffocating human beings, chained to one another, into the hold of his ship and then retired to his comfortable cabin to read the Bible and say his prayers. Good Lord, deliver us from religious people.

William Evarts composed a ditty on our pious pilgrim ancestors: "The pious ones of Plymouth who, reaching the Rock, first fell on their own knees and then upon the aborigines." From religious people, good Lord, deliver us.

In a dialogue between a religious scientist and an unreligious theologian, John Updike, in his book *Roger's Version*, speaks of religion's dark side. The young scientist, Dale, argues, "The Devil is doubt. He's what makes us reject the gifts God gives us. He makes us spurn the life we've been given…" "Funny," said [Roger] the professor, "I would have said, looking at recent history and, for that matter, at some of our present-day ayatollahs and Fuhrers, the opposite. The Devil is the absence of doubt. He's what pushes people into suicide bombing, into setting up extermination camps. Doubt may give your dinner a funny taste, but it's faith that goes out and kills." From religious people, good Lord deliver us.

Jesus told this parable to some who trusted in themselves that they were righteous and despised others:

Two men went into the cathedral to pray. One was a priest, a dean and rector. The other was an unsaved man. The dean stood up and prayed to himself: "O God, I thank you that I'm not like other people—greedy, mean, promiscuous, secular—and thank you that I am saved and on the inside circle of the 'more saved than others society.' I go to Eucharist three times per Sunday, I tithe my income, and would place my humility above anyone's..." But the unsaved secular man, standing as far from the altar as possible, wouldn't even lift up his eyes, but knelt down and cried, "O God have mercy on me, a sinner."

I'm promising you that the secular humanist sinner went home justified rather than the other. For everyone who places himself on a pedestal will get knocked off, and everyone who bends low enough to be humble will be placed high. From self-righteous religious people, we pray delivery, and Lord, have mercy upon us all.

If we believe that religion will protect us from sin, then we are not only self-righteous, but also self-deceiving. Only God, in Christ, can deliver us from sin. Not our behavior, not our social status, not our ecclesiastical status, not our denomination, not our liturgy, not the Bible, not our education, not our discipline, not our superiority. Only God, in Christ, can make us righteous.

The worst wars in the history of humankind have been the religious wars. The worst bigotry is religious bigotry. The worst hubris is religious self-righteousness. More sin has been wrought in the name of religion than in the name of evil. Evil loves to disguise itself in religious leaders, religious movements, and religious notions, such as "I was only doing it for his own good" or "Thank God we are not like them."

Jesus told the parable about the tax collector and then he acted it out. In Luke 18, he says the tax collector who was aware and repentant was justified, not the Pharisee who was self-justified. (The Pharisees were the priests of their day.) And then in the very next chapter, Jesus entered Jericho and saw a chief tax collector named Zaccheus. Here Jesus acted out his own parable and justified a tax collector.

Zaccheus was a sawed-off shyster perched in a sycamore tree. Jesus walked by and, as Frederick Buechner relates, Jesus said:

> "Get down out of there in a hurry. I'm spending tonight with *you*," whereupon all Jericho snickered up their sleeves to think he didn't have better sense than to invite himself to the house of a man that nobody else would touch with a ten-foot pole.
>
> But Jesus knew what he was doing. Zaccheus was taken so completely aback by the honor of the thing that, before Jesus had a chance to change his mind, Zaccheus promised not only to turn over 50 percent of his holdings to the poor, but to pay back, four to one, all the cash he'd extorted from everybody else. Jesus was absolutely delighted. "Today salvation has come to this house," he said, and since that was his specialty after all, you assume he was right.

Zaccheus makes a good example of what religion is truly about because he stands for all of us. Buechner continues:

He's a sawed-off little social disaster with a big bank account and a crooked job, but Jesus welcomes him aboard anyway, and that's why he reminds you of all the others, too.

There's Aaron whooping it up with the Golden Calf the moment his brother's back is turned, and there's Jacob conning everybody including his own father. There's Jael driving a tent peg through the head of an overnight guest, and Rahab, the first of the red-hot mamas. There's Nebuchadnezzar with his taste for roasting the opposition, and Paul holding the lynch mob's coats as they go to work on Stephen. There's Saul, the paranoid, and David the stud, and those mealy-mouthed friends of Job's who would probably have succeeded in boring him to death if Yahweh hadn't stepped in just in the nick of time. And then there are the ones who betrayed the people who loved them best such as Absalom and poor old Peter, such as Judas even.

All of them were like Zaccheus, all of them religious people. The characters of the Bible were sinners before they were saints, human before heroes and heroines. They were not born religious. They became religious not by judging others, but by being in touch through recognition of their own unrighteousness and joining a group of other sinners who trusted that you became righteous through your unrighteousness.

I think there is some wisdom in my saintly old sage of a priest friend. Deliver us from religious people! For God's sake, deliver us from those who have no sin or doubt, for they have no need for Christ—for Christ's sake, good Lord, deliver us. Have mercy on me, a sinner.

Amen.

❖ ❖ ❖

November 9, 1986
Luke 20:27, 34–38

For the sardonic cynic, who sees the worst human scenario being life everlasting, I have some good news. I had such a friend say to me, "Life everlasting? I can't think of anything worse." I say to him today: Well, look at it this way. There is one good thing about it: Jesus says, "In heaven, we neither marry nor are given in marriage." I think my cynical friend may not be convinced, but his wife would be pleased to hear the good news.

Today's Gospel presents to us once again the problem of post-grave existence and the incredible difference between resuscitation and resurrection. Not only is heaven a conceptual problem, it is a linguistic problem. For instance, the Sadducees, a Jewish legalistic sect, did not believe in the resurrection because, as fundamentalists, the doctrine was not in the first five books of the Torah, and therefore, they could not accept it. They only believed in the literal word of God and missed the revelation that came after the Pentateuch. Because their point of reference was legalistic and literal, they asked Jesus a literal, legal question about a woman who was inherited by her six brothers-in-law after her husband's death: "To whom will she be married after the resurrection?" Jesus answered, "You are putting earthly categories on heaven. In the resurrection, there will not be such a thing as marriage." (Good news for my friend's wife.) "All you need to know about life after death is that God is not a God of the dead, but of the living; all live to him." It's mystery—and mystery is not a problem to be solved.

The concept is difficult. That is to say, how can we conceive of an existence we haven't yet entered? And since language requires experience and reason, is it not reasonable that we have no experience on which to base a language or set of terms by which we can describe a place we have never been? We have only a promise and an intuition. For many, in this post-age of reason, that is not enough. So for them, I think there is evidence in this life that life doesn't end at death.

First, we know that our lives unfold in stage after stage. Womb life is a death and birth at the same time. So is childhood. In adolescence, we leave childhood as surely as we left the womb. No stage ends. We accumulate all our previous life to create our present life that includes all lives, deaths, and new life. No present or past stage has enough experience to understand a future stage. To speak of heaven to those on the history side of grave's gate is like a lawyer explaining to a child the corporate structure of Exxon. Or perhaps better, for the Kingdom of God, it is like a child explaining to a corporate lawyer that the only way to sanctify time is not to try to measure it.

The concept of eternity, though difficult, must be contrasted with the concept of life everlasting. Life everlasting means that life as we know it will continue after death. That was what my cynical friend said would be so awful. That is resuscitation, being brought back to life—not resurrection into new life. Jesus clears that up once and for all. In heaven, earthly categories such as marriage will be as irrelevant to us as umbilical cords are now.

Eternity does not begin at death; it begins at conception. Eternity is not endless time or the opposite of time. It is the essence of time. When we are with somebody we love, doing or being something we were created to be, then we have little, if any, sense of the passage of time—time flies or stands still; it is a good time. This is the nature of the sacraments—the sacraments kill time. They make all that has been, all that is, and all that will be, present all in a moment. Broken open.

And yet, I believe, since we are now in eternity, that there are experiences of eternity in this life. As human beings, we know occasions, experiences, when we stand outside the passing of events and glimpse their meaning. Some times are beyond time, and through these windows we catch a glimpse, a glimmering, of what life is about in general, of what our lives are about in particular, and this revelation, though now only a reflection, integrates not only the present, but the past and the future as well. These moments are the spirit's intuition of wholeness.

In her autobiography, *One Writer's Beginnings*, Eudora Welty writes of this eternal experience of eternity:

> When I made my first attempt at a novel, I entered its world—that of the mysterious Yazoo-Mississippi Delta—as a child riding there on a train: "From the warm window sill the endless fields glowed like a hearth in firelight, and Laura, looking out, leaning on her elbows with her head between her hands, felt what an arriver in a land feels—that slow hard pounding in the breast."
>
> The events in our lives happen in a sequence in time, but in their significance to ourselves they find their own order, a timetable not necessarily—perhaps not possibly—chronological. The time as we know it subjectively is often the chronology that stories and novels follow: it is the continuous thread of revelation.

Death is a fact. No doctrine of eternity denies this empirical reality. All that has been birthed, dies. Faith does not deny death.

Faith dignifies death. The Christian faith faces death, bluntly and biologically. Faith affirms that the apparent absurdity of death is, in this realm, absurd. Death, with its own experience, implies that there was something before, that there is something within, and therefore, something after. There is a haunting sense of incompleteness, a sense of the absurdity of why it ends before it is complete, and a sense of how the ending completes in its own way, except for those of us yet on this side. The sense of process is experienced by the fact that nothing we know is complete. Therefore, the faith is the conviction that completion will come, because we feel it coming in the eternity that breaks into time. Christ is the completion, one with the Father, revealed in this time and yet is the fullness of time. Christ promises that we, too, shall become complete, whole, at home—heaven.

Power to become comes from this faith in Christ. This is the urge to completeness. This is the gospel's urge. This urge to be one with oneself and with all that was, is, and will be is what death and its frustration, life and its limitations, stand opposed to. The urge to become more, full, essential, known in glimpse and glimmer of revelation, coupled with Jesus' promise that we will become complete, completes a statement opposed to death as an end.

Given the choice of death-ending life or life-ending death, I will choose, because of my experience of eternity, known in the essence of time, revealed in a thread of revelation throughout my life, that it will continue even through death. And I will exemplify my choice by respecting death, but not fearing it, for I believe in life after birth and that when compared to eternity, physical death has no power. It is an important transition because it is a transformation, and all of that completeness and lack thereof that we have experienced in this life will be offered. I have only the language of symbol by which I can communicate to you something of the foretaste of this sense of wholeness. I invite you today to a heavenly banquet in which time will stand still. Your essence and mine will be made whole: one, broken in Christ's death and resurrected as love, confrontation, communion, community. Now we are in eternity. You might say, married.

Amen.

✤ ✤ ✤

November 30, 1986
Advent I
Isaiah 2:1–5; Romans 13:8–14; Matthew 24:37–44

As I read Matthew's Gospel for today, I hear in it an Advent echo called preparation. Somehow I am not worried about the section where Jesus says, "When the son of man comes...then two men will be in the field; one is taken and one is left. Two women will be grinding at the mill; one is taken and one is left. Watch, therefore. You must be ready, for the Son of Man is coming at an hour you do not expect." I'm not worried, because if Jesus literally means that one man and one woman will be taken and one man and one woman will be left, then the criterion for being taken will be those who are ready to go. I'm not worried, because I'm ready. Also, I believe that the difference between those who are accepted and those who are doomed is the difference between those who want to go and those who don't.

For instance: a woman came to me several years ago and said that she had a problem. Her son had a friend and playmate who was Jewish. The little boy had asked his mother, "My friend, Isaac, is Jewish. Will Isaac go to heaven?" The anxious mother asked me, "What should I answer?" I said, "Tell your son to go back and ask Isaac if he wants to go to heaven. And then tell him that if he wants to go, he can."

In order to go wherever the mystery leads, it requires readiness and willingness. Freedom dictates that we don't have to go to heaven if we don't want. The choice is ours. Now, concerning readiness, this is the Advent theme of preparation. Advent is the waiting room in time and space for the mystery to enter and lead us on to our next phase. This may be a cataclysmic end in general or particular. It may be a history-bending birth, it may be a phylum of personal growth, it may be a promise come true. It may be a beginning or an end, and always both.

How do we wait? How do we prepare? How do we make ready? My favorite model of how not to wait is from Samuel Beckett's tragicomedy in two acts, *Waiting for Godot*. Two pathetic characters, Vladimir and Estragon, sit in banal, absurd, and disconnected conversation, waiting for a character named Godot. Godot is the French diminutive for little God. These two talk, and wait. The only two choices they seem to have are either to commit suicide or wait. And neither alternative appeals. At the first of the play, they discuss suicide:

Estragon:	What about hanging ourselves?
Vladimir:	Go ahead.
Estragon:	After you.
Vladimir:	No no, you first.
Estragon:	Why me?
Vladimir:	You're lighter than I am.
Estragon:	Just so!
Vladimir:	I don't understand.
Estragon:	This is how it is. The bough…the bough… Use your head, can't you?
Vladimir:	You're my only hope.
Estragon:	Gogo light—bough not break—Gogo dead. Didi heavy—bough break—Didi alone. Whereas—
Vladimir:	I hadn't thought of that. Well, what do we do?
Estragon:	Don't let's do anything. It's safer.

And there it is, the point of the play; the predicament of the characters. They are waiting for a small god to rescue them from the boring absurdity. They won't even consider suicide—it is safer to do nothing.

At the end of the play, Estragon loosens the cord that holds up his pants in order to finally hang himself because Godot has never come. When he does so, his pants fall to his ankles. Vladimir looks at him.

Vladimir:	We'll hang ourselves tomorrow. Unless Godot comes.
Estragon:	And if he comes?
Vladimir:	We'll be saved.
Estragon:	Well? Shall we go?
Vladimir:	Pull on your trousers.
Estragon:	What?
Vladimir:	Pull on your trousers.
Estragon:	You want me to pull off my trousers?
Vladimir:	Pull ON your trousers.
Estragon:	True.
Vladimir:	Well? Shall we go?
Estragon:	Yes, let's go.

The stage directions read: "They do not move. Curtain."

How shall we wait? How shall we prepare? Well, not like the characters in *Waiting for Godot*. We shall not sit in the boredom of banality and absurdity of either sitting or suicide.

I rather believe that we should wait by embracing the mystery and living this gift we have been given called life in the world. We wait by living fully into the life we have been given.

Dr. Douglas Adams, one of the leaders of the Christian Spirituality and the Visual Arts conference two weeks ago, quoting William Sloane Coffin, said:

> When we get to heaven, God is not going to be standing there with a clipboard with our life on it, checking off all of the things we've done wrong. When we get to heaven, God is going to say, "Show me your slides! Tell me about your life. Was it good? Did you enjoy it? I gave you colors, smells and stories. How about your body? Wasn't it great! You what? You were afraid? You sat? And waited? Because you were afraid? You didn't journey, you didn't grow! You didn't taste! You didn't smell! You didn't touch! You didn't see! You didn't hear! My God! You've already been to hell! Welcome!"

We wait by embracing it all and not sitting like some want to do, in fear that we won't be chosen. We've been chosen! Unless you don't want to go, and then you can stay in the field and work, or at the mill and grind. I'm going to take pictures!

Paul says, "We owe no one anything,"—I assume that includes God—"except to love one another." That is how we prepare for whatever is to come: by embracing the world and one another.

Advent means someone in some form at some time is coming. The one is Christ. When, where, and how is not to be known for now. If we want to be a part of what Christ is, we may. If we don't, we don't have to. In the meantime, the in-between time, we must prepare. How? By loving everything. Embracing it all: the dark and light, the dread and hope, the now and then, the joy and despair. And in so doing, we will be ready for whatever genesis or new covenant that is to come.

Or, we can sit and contemplate suicide and play it safe until we are atrophied in the wasteland of fear. We have a choice: to embrace grace or sit and wait for a lesser God. What will our stage directions read?

Amen.

❊ ❊ ❊

December 7, 1986
Advent II
Isaiah 11:1–10; Matthew 3:1–12

Washington Grade School sat on a hill in Drumright, Oklahoma. I attended elementary school there. Though it was not ten miles from my house by a walk in the snow, it was several blocks away. My father traveled; we had one car, so most mornings I walked behind my brother and his friends or rode my bike, a Hawthorne, ordered from Sears and Roebuck. Walking to and from school, I received more information of interest than in the hours seated in the wooden chair desks which still had inkwells. A major mentor on the path to school was Edgar Vice. He had opinions on every subject and value-rich area of American and human life. He was even older than my brother, so therefore he held the sagacity fitting such a sixth-grade sage. His information was more abundant than accurate—particularly, his facts and knowledge about girls, his favorite subject. Though his descriptions were imaginative, they later proved to be inaccurate. It was Edgar, along with Gerald Mullins, who held a religious debate on the nature of heaven and hell. Edgar's theology concluded that smoking and drinking would land you in hell. Gerald argued that Jesus was stronger than the devil and beat him up in the desert so we didn't have to worry about hell. Edgar countered, "Then how come Brother Bannister at the Free Will Baptist Church told my dad that?" Gerald had no answer. Though Edgar proclaimed that abstinence from tobacco and alcohol was necessary for salvation, it was Edgar Vice who gave me my first cigar, beside Dan Ard's barn on the way home from school. I have since mellowed on the judgmental aphorism that "one must practice what one preaches."

Hanging in the hallway of Washington Grade School was a print. In the picture was a young child with his arm around the mane of a lion and at his feet were animals: a lamb and a wolf, a leopard and a calf. Edgar Vice told me one day that that little boy with the lion was Jesus. Just that. No explanation, no interpretation. How strange it was that that picture was Jesus. It was out of context. All the pictures I had seen of Jesus as a child included either the holy family, or him on his mother's lap, or crèche scenes of one form or another. But here it was before me, this enigmatic little child with the animals around him in this tranquil, peaceful, promising scene.

I now know that the print was one of a painting by Edward Hicks, a nineteenth-century Quaker, who painted over sixty different versions of the *Peaceable Kingdom*, an important piece of American religious folk art. In these paintings, Edward Hicks is visualizing one of the greatest passages in Holy Scripture: Isaiah 11:1–10. Herein, the prophet first proclaims that a shoot will come from the "stump of Jesse." Jesse was the father of King David. What is predicted is that a new branch will grow from his family tree; that is, a new David. This new ruler is described surprisingly as a child, and his leadership will be peace: "The wolf shall dwell with the lamb, and the leopard shall lie down with the kid, and the calf and the lion and the fatling together, and a little child shall lead them."

The scene is part of my childhood—the unassuming child in the calming embrace of a lion. The prophetic message as to who the child was didn't come from Isaiah, or John the Baptist, but from Edgar Vice, the Free Will Baptist. I have, from that time, known that a peaceful kingdom exists in spite of information or evidence to the contrary.

In the first grade, Dio Daily fell from the retaining wall and cut his head; his white shirt became drenched with blood. I led him to Miss Weaver, our first-grade teacher. Beneath the picture, she held his head in her own full skirt until the bleeding stopped.

In the second grade, they told my friend, Michael Dourghty, that his mother had died.

They did so in the hallway with a picture of an unassuming child in the calming embrace of a lion.

In the winter of the third grade, Mary Jo Nash came back to school after having contracted polio the summer before. On her crutches and braces, she hobbled down the corridor past the *Peaceable Kingdom.*

Through the Korean War, a tornado, third-degree burns on half my body, my mother's stillborn baby, and a classmate killed by a drunk teenager in a car, I dwelt beneath that enigmatic child embracing a wild animal. And Edgar Vice told me, even before Isaiah, that it was Jesus.

The last time I saw that picture with my eyes was in the eighth grade, before we moved to Oklahoma City. But many times since, amidst the tragedy and trauma of the real world, that image lives within as a central promise. Advent means coming. Advent means preparation. Advent means pondering a child's view of the world. And that view integrates the past with a future that holds us in the present. Within us is the promised child who, in spite of the death and pain, embraces the savage animal and nothing shall destroy us. What a nice promise.

That child has come, and will come, whenever he is needed. And we have it on the highest authority: "It is Jesus." And here ends the lesson from Edgar Vice.

Amen.

1987

January 18, 1987
John 1:29–41

If you haven't already, then I politely suggest that you accept Jesus Christ as your personal Lord and Savior. I do so for obvious reasons. First, today's Gospel is the account of the conversion of Andrew. This is the first chapter of John where Jesus begins his ministry and does so by converting his disciples: Andrew, Peter, Philip, and Nathanael. I think everyone ought to be converted to Christ. My second reason, a bit more subtle, is to use Andrew's conversion as a model of what our relationship with Christ might be.

In the text today, there is a very important utterance from Andrew that I think can unlock a whole new understanding of conversion and faith. In verse 38 of John's first chapter, Jesus turns and sees Andrew and his friend following him, and he says to them, "What do you seek?" And they say to him, "Rabbi (which means teacher), where are you staying?" Jesus says to them, "Come and see." Now, what is important here is the word "rabbi." The parenthetical explanation is only half right. The word rabbi does mean teacher. But more accurately, the word "rab" or "reb" means teacher. The "bi" of rabbi means "my." So "rab" means teacher, and "rabbi" means my teacher. When Andrew spoke thusly to Jesus, he committed himself to Jesus. Jesus would become his "personal" teacher. Now, back to my opening line: if you haven't already, then I politely suggest that you accept Jesus Christ as your personal Lord and Savior. The advantage to this is that, if you do so, people won't keep asking you if you have accepted Jesus Christ as your personal Lord and Savior. And when they do, then you can say, "I have." Then, when they want to have you witness or tell them about your faith, you can say, "It's personal."

For it is. Each of us needs a conversion to a definite teacher, a rabbi, a personal set of values, and teaching that can enable us as we journey toward our completeness. This conversion is usually a response to a crisis, or a "being stuck" in the dark and void of decision, response, and responsibility. We become ourselves in the process of decisions, relationships, crises, and change. Selfhood has a radical historical, and radically personal, character. Our perceptions and conceptions are formed through historical events. Different moments in our lives are of unequal importance. Our lives consist of certain turning points—moments of deep awareness—around which other events arrange themselves. These peak moments are moments of revelation; they tie together loose ends; they give us fundamental orientation and meaning.

Such conversion moments, if we listen, will coincide with Jesus' teachings. The gospel is our story. And when *our* story touches *the* story, we are converted. Such moments are the cracking open of our world where God's word may touch us. But such moments are always personal. Not necessarily private, but they will be our story and not like anyone else's. Sharing can be revealing. When James Pike was chaplain at Columbia University, a young woman came to him and stated, "I can no longer believe in God." Pike responded, "Tell me of this God in whom you can no longer believe." When she finished, the priest responded, "I do not believe in that God either."

Our problem is that the doctrines are reflections on our experience. The doctrines, which are ways to express our faith, sometimes can become barriers to faith. We worship the God of experience. We do not worship the experience of God. People who want to coerce others by making them fit formulas or molds have created idols of doctrine.

Richard Selzer, in his essay "Diary of an Infidel," writes: "Long ago I accepted the notion that faith is something given to selected men and women, like perfect pitch. It cannot be sought after. No amount of yearning can produce it." Dr. Selzer's definition of faith is, unfortunately, too narrow. It implies some predetermined notion of faith as determined by someone else. Someone needs to give him permission to have his own faith, his own rabbi. Given such, he might realize that the yearning which cannot produce faith may be his faith. It is not the body of doctrine; it is the heart singing the truth.

Peter Marin, in an essay in *Harper's Magazine* this month, writes: "Pavlov, the Russian psychologist, once theorized that the two most fundamental reflexes in all animals, including humans, are those involving freedom and orientation. Grab any animal, he said, and it will immediately struggle to accomplish two things: to break free and to orient itself."

Our religion, Christianity, is about freedom and orientation. Seized by a life of complexity, darkness, crises, and tragedy, we seek to remain free to grow toward that for which we yearn—our own wholeness—only to realize that that for which we yearn is the source of our yearning. That yearning is the voice of God, and we need to pay more attention to the yearning itself than to the object of the yearning. We are free, and our freedom means that we are called, nudged, by one in the same spirit; the Spirit that calls us is the Spirit that moves us. In the midst of complexity, darkness, crises, and tragedy, as we seek to be free to become ourselves, we need some orientation, some direction. We will jerk loose from anything that grabs us, but we will seek something to call us. That is what the Christ does. The Christ grants us all freedom and then calls us in one direction. Jesus does this. He respects our freedom and calls us to follow. But, beware of any of his disciples who claim that you must orient yourself according to their rules. Let your rabbi be Jesus, not some insecure, egocentric demagogue who wants you to follow him. I think you ought to accept Jesus as your Lord—not the church or a book or a doctrine or a place or a person. Make Jesus your Christ.

A popular television evangelist said recently that if he didn't raise $4.5 million for his hospital that God told him he would end his life. If you don't believe in that God, I understand. I don't believe in that God either.

Amen.

❖ ❖ ❖

February 1, 1987
Matthew 5:1–12

Something changed when I read the Sermon on the Mount for myself. I don't have a turning point story of conversion. My turnaround is still in process and, I hope, in progress. One of the interesting things that happens in seminary is that one has to read the Bible. I had never done that before. Oh, I had started or tried. I always found Bible reading like exercise. Hard to start, but easy to stop. So, most of my biblical knowledge was gained through three sources. First, what I call cultural osmosis. That is to say, through clichés, characters, sayings, and the like. The problem with this was that I knew that Abraham, Isaac, Jacob, and Moses were characters from the Bible, but they were intimidating because of their power. Peter and Paul I thought for years were twins. The story of David and Goliath I associated with football because Bud Wilkinson used that as an analogy one year when Oklahoma upset someone in the Orange Bowl. Till I was a middler in seminary, I thought "a stitch in time saves nine" was from scripture.

My second source was Sunday school. There, I always had a feeling that God was either a cosmic cop who enforced or punished or a celestial bellhop who met your needs when you rang. I must admit, something got into me through Sunday school that made me feel like Jesus was on my side. Also, when they talked about God as Father, I felt like I did when I was in my daddy's lap. Maybe my biblical facts were not so accurate or clear, but not all my theology was bad.

My third source of biblical study was Hollywood and the likes of Cecil B. DeMille. Through *The Ten Commandments, The Robe, The Silver Chalice,* and *The Greatest Story Ever Told*, I learned that the Bible was an adventure full of bathrobes, gladiators, and buxom women. The good guys always won, even if they died. Once again, the facts were shallow, but the theology wasn't so bad. It must prove that God can use even kitsch to reveal himself.

The point is that in my junior or first year in seminary, when I heard the title "the Beatitudes," I knew that everyone there knew something I didn't know. For all I knew, the Beatitudes were teachings about bad attitudes. But soon, I discovered in a course on the synoptic gospels. (If you think beatitudes threw me, you should have seen me when I enrolled in a course that had synoptic in the title.) Anyway, in that course, we studied the Sermon on the Mount. And in Matthew's Gospel, I discovered in the fifth chapter, the Beatitudes. There began my turnaround. These are Jesus' teachings where he lists the blessings to be found in human doubt and pain. My first reaction was that this tone was so much different from the Ten Commandments, which are the shoulds and oughts and things for which one is punished. Here, his teaching is of acceptance, inclusion, and unconditional love. I read the Beatitudes like a lullaby and felt as if I were in my daddy's lap, rocking in a chair and being patted softly on the back. "Blessed are you, blessed are you, blessed are you…"

I even did some scholarly work. Every Greek student is given a dictionary and a cross-reference. Most seminarians do Greek exegesis like one orders from a menu in France with a traveler's lexicon. I looked up "blessed." In Greek, it is *makarios*. It doesn't just mean blessing, as in patting on the back or making holy. It means that, but more so; it means "to be blessed beyond expectation." It means to be surprised by the unexpected. For instance, "Blessed are the poor in spirit for theirs is the kingdom of heaven" is a surprising statement. Poor in spirit doesn't mean small amount of spirit, it means the opposite of spiritually arrogant. Those who are not self-righteous, those who know that they don't know, those who know their limits, those who are satisfied to be human—those have an unexpected surprise: the Kingdom of Heaven is entered by the humble, not the superior.

What joy! Even in mourning, even in human loss, we will be comforted. Comforted means strengthened. Through necessary losses, we will find new and unexpected strength. I read on like a hungry man at a free buffet.

"Blessed are the meek." In Greek, meek is *praus*, which is a horse, full of spirit like a racehorse, who will accept a bit—one who will control his pace, but doesn't have a broken spirit. "Meek" is not milquetoast, it is a strong one who knows his own strength without beating on others.

Scales fell from my eyes…

Surprised are those hungry for truth, surprised are those who offer mercy to inner and outer enemies, they receive what they give… And on and on I went.

The turnaround, which began then, is still in transit. Ever since reading the Beatitudes and, indeed, the Sermon on the Mount, I have felt that Jesus' job was acceptance. Later that year, I read *The Courage to Be* by Paul Tillich, in which he writes: "The courage to be is the courage to accept oneself as accepted in spite of being unacceptable." I knew what he meant; God had revealed that to me through the Bible. I have never been the same since.

A second thing that turned around was my fear of the Bible. Since then, I am not afraid to read, study, interpret, or even preach from the Bible—because it is just about you and me.

And, thirdly, I realized that even though Peter and Paul weren't twins, they, too, were blessed not by their holiness, but by their humanity.

And finally, I learned that God was going to reveal his truth even if it took bathrobes and buxom women. Blessed are both. And blessed are you.

I am like Karl Barth, the great German theologian, who is known as the founder of neo-orthodoxy. He is one of the finest theologians of our time. When he was asked, "Dr. Barth, if you summed up all of your biblical studies, what message would you give to the person struggling to understand the biblical truth?" Dr. Barth answered, "Jesus loves me, this I know, for the Bible tells me so."

Amen.

✤ ✤ ✤

March 8, 1987
Lent I
Genesis 2:4b–9, 15–17, 25–3:7; Romans 5:12–21; Matthew 4:1–11

From the beginning, God has demanded of human beings hard choices in order to allow us to grow toward God.

"And the Lord God commanded the man saying, 'You may freely eat of every tree of the garden; but of the tree of the knowledge of good and evil you shall not eat, for in the day that you eat of it you shall die.'…And the man and his wife were both naked, and were not ashamed. Now the serpent was more subtle than any other wild creature that the Lord God had made. He said to the woman, 'Did God say you shall not eat of any tree in the garden?' And the woman said to the serpent, 'We may eat from any tree except the one in the midst, neither shall we touch it lest we die.' But the serpent said to the woman, 'You will not die. For God knows that when you eat of it your eyes will be opened, and you will be like God, knowing good and evil.'"

And you know the rest of the story. Their eyes *were* opened, and they were ashamed of their nakedness.

Now, from the beginning, freedom has not been something which we demand from God, but that which God requires of us. Freedom means choice. And choice means experience, and reflection upon experience means wisdom the hard way. Choice, the ever-present existential choice, is the hallmark of human freedom. And our freedom and its use is the way by which we grow toward God. God's image within us is in the mystery of creativity found in the tension between our freedom and God's clouded will.

The problem with choice is not that we must choose between good and evil, but that we must discern which is good and which is evil—and even more creatively, we must, through choice, arrive at the wisdom that in good choices and evil choices, each has the other within it.

Adam and Eve made the evil choice, with resulting rejection and death. And yet, within the evil, they achieved the wisdom of awareness. They knew in an existential moment the cost and call of freedom—and we must never forget it.

Most of us want or expect of religion a deliverance from the ambiguity of life's contradictory choices. We want clarity of God's will and long for the choice without cost. Why is it that every decision is both life-giving and death-dealing? Why is it that every "yes" is a "no"? Why is it that the will of our own spirit and the will of God seem to be competitive and contradictory? Why? Why? Why?

This is the lament of Lent. Why must we always be so torn in the torment of the choices about our lives? Even if we give our life to obeying the will of God, why is it that that will hides beyond a dark glass and is always paired in a contradiction? "I would be willing to be obedient to the will of God if I only knew what it was!"

Parker Palmer, in his book *The Promise of Paradox*, writes: "The contradictions of life are not accidental. Nor do they result from inept living. They are inherent in human nature...We are, as the Psalmist says, 'little less than God' but also 'like the beasts that perish.'"

This is, of course, the human situation—yea, even the human predicament. I declare that this year, my Lenten discipline is to live the paradox and pray for the grace of God to allow me to do so.

Thomas Merton reflects this discipline:

> I have had to accept the fact that my life is almost totally paradoxical. I have also had to learn gradually to get along without apologizing for the fact, even to myself...It is in the paradox itself, the paradox which was and is still a source of insecurity, that I have come to find the greatest security. I have become convinced that the very contradictions in my life are in some ways signs of God's mercy to me; if only because someone so complicated and so prone to confusion and self-defeat could hardly survive for long without special mercy.

The mercy of God is found in the Gospel account today. God suffers the temptations and contradictions with us. The point of the evil one tempting Jesus in the desert is not to put us down because we don't make good choices in the same way Jesus did. We are not Jesus Christ. God knows how tempting freedom is. The point is to show us that God in Christ suffers the contradictions with us.

Are we, then, to continually live in the tensions of contradiction? No. Our Lenten journey is to travel with all our decisions about life toward the great contradiction of the cross. And to see that the liberation comes in the hard wood of the contradiction. We travel into the cross of contradiction aware that life in freedom brings death and death in grace brings life. If you push life to its extreme, you have death, and if you push death to its extreme, you have life. There is no contradiction; it is an integration. The cross stands as a symbol of the Christian journey. In the cross, God strips the false illusions of our world and leaves us as naked as Adam and Eve, because it is better to live naked in truth than clothed in false illusions that we know the difference between good and evil.

We need not always live in the belly of a paradox or in the tensions of contradiction. We can rest occasionally and eternally in the peace that where "sin abounds grace abounds more."

Because of God, we are called to the naked truth that we must choose. In Christ, we are clothed in the truth that nothing—no false choice, no broken mistake, no illusory image, no death—can separate us from the love of God.

The Lenten paradox is that we live in the cross-parched desert of contradiction and, at the same time, we live in the ocean of grace. We have the promise that one day we will know that the tension and anxiety we so hated were the wings of the spirit that carried us to the ecstatic oneness with the source of all. Whatever it is that we live without, we will be given; what we don't now understand, we will know; what is broken will be bound up; whatever is incomplete will be filled. Lent is working with awareness toward the time beyond time, when there is no contradiction, no paradox, only the clear, unambiguous, eternal presence of love. Between here and there, there is a desert and a cross. We cannot go any other way. The only way to get through the contradiction is to go through it. We are on our way. We are the people of the way.

Amen.

March 15, 1987
Lent II
Genesis 12:1–8; Romans 4:1–5, 13–17; John 3:1–17

The great twentieth-century theologian, Edgar Vice, who took his early training with me at Washington Grade School in Drumright, Oklahoma, friend of my older brother and champion of the colloquial aphorism, lay in my front yard one spring night and reflected, "Boy, them stars sure do make a fella feel little!"

It was not my first struggle with authority, nor was it my last repression of expression. I did not verbally disagree with Edgar. He was older, larger, and tended to enforce his logic with violence. So I simply disagreed in my own mind. The panorama of individual lights in the sky's dark abyss made me feel large and important, not little. Edgar made me feel little; the stars made me feel important. How was it that out of the vast expanse of interstellar space—galaxies, suns, planets in their courses—I could be conscious of them? Rather than "them stars making a fella feel little," they seemed to beckon me to a life that was more than I could even imagine. The stars were revelations of grandeur, placed there for little boys to follow, up and beyond the red dirt of their birth.

This is the message of our faith. This is the Lenten awareness. Given to Abraham in Ur of the Chaldees, spoken to Nicodemus at Jerusalem, this is the call of our God, to be born not of the insignificant flesh, but of the very spirit of the universal source. So we see in today's Old Testament lesson that God called Abraham out of his smaller country into a greater covenant. In chapter 15, we hear from God what Edgar Vice didn't yet know and I knew only by intuition: "And God brought Abraham outside and said, 'Look toward heaven, and number the stars, if you are able to number them.' Then God said to Abraham, 'See the stars…So numerous shall your descendants be.' And he believed the Lord; and he reckoned it to him as righteousness." Your descendants shall be as numerous as the stars. We are descendants of Abraham, called into a covenant of love as large as the universe and as specific as the earth and as personal as a little boy on a spring night lying back on a bed of grass.

Nicodemus didn't know what it meant to be born again. He knew that because of Adam and Eve's choice to reach for the forbidden fruit that God had said, "Dust you are, and to dust you shall return." But he had forgotten that the covenant meant that no matter what else happened in the world, God would look on us as favorably as stars and rainbows. Jesus reminded Nicodemus and, I hope, us that we are of the dust at birth, and yet, because of God's unconditional love, we are reborn of the unconquerable spirit.

I wish Edgar Vice were here to hear this. Edgar, you don't need to feel small or of little worth. You never again need to feel unimportant, unloved, or insignificant. Don't you know that God so loved the world that he gave his only Son, that whoever believes in him should not perish but have eternal life? Edgar, you need not be afraid of the world or yourself or of things present or things past or things to come. We need never feel as though our birth was accidental or our life inconsequential. We are as significant as Abraham, Isaac, or Jacob. As vital as Sarah, Rebekah, or Rachel. We are stars—we are blessed.

Edgar, I hope you never attempt to wall yourself from the world and treat it as evil. We must respond to our call and claim to take our place as sons of God. We are born of dust, and because of the signs in the stars, we are reborn of water and the spirit. Our lives unfold before us as mystery and gift. Hear the breeze? Feel its marvelous, mysterious presence? It blows our lives where it wills. We hear the sound of it, but we don't know whence it comes or whither it goes—so it is with those of us who are born of the spirit.

We must love the world, our lives, our past, our future. We must love our bodies, our minds, our memories, our imagination. We must love the world, for God so loved it that he entered it, heralded by a star in the eastern sky. God called us into the world by our birth and into eternity by our rebirth. We now have promises to keep; unlived life to know; unknown experiences to become. Remember, our life is from the same source as the stars. We are in the presence of God—"the [one] who gives life to the dead and calls into existence the things that do not exist." Jesus did not come into the world to condemn it or us, but that we might be made alive, saved by him; saved from emptiness, saved from fear, saved from mediocrity, saved from inferiority, saved from imperfection, saved from inadequacy, saved from triviality, saved from dust and death. How about that, Edgar? Still feel little?

Lent reminds us of our dust nature and of our spiritual nature. We need not fear ever again to be alive forever. We need not feel small or intimidated by the vastness of the universe and all its confusing complexities. And if Edgar Vice were here, I'd tell him to his face that I disagree with him. He isn't here…is he?

Amen.

✣ ✣ ✣

March 22, 1987
Lent III
Exodus 17:1–7; Romans 5:1–11; John 4:5–42

James Thurber once did a drawing of a man at his typewriter and all about his feet, on the floor, are crumpled pages of paper, and he is staring down at a blank page in discouragement. "What's the matter?" his wife is saying. "Has your pen gleaned your teeming brain?" Thurber's cartoon is about writer's block. The wife's statement is a quotation from Keats: "When I have fears that I may cease to be / Before my pen has glean'd my teeming brain."

As a preacher, I bear twin fears: the one of Keats', that I should die before I share all the glory and wonder of God's works; the other, more real, that my brain will cease to teem at all.

As I look at the three lessons today, I wonder how I can find another way to express the Christian conviction that God loves sinners in spite of their sin. In the Exodus lesson, "The congregation of Israel moved on from the wilderness of Sin by stages…" At their encampment, there was no water for them to drink. The people murmured against Moses and said, "Why did you bring us up out of Egypt, to kill us and our children and our cattle with thirst?" God then empowered Moses to strike a rock at Horeb that the people might drink.

In the Gospel, the adulteress at the well had had five husbands, and the one with whom she was currently living was not her husband. And yet, Jesus gave her real water, but more so, the living water of God's unconditional love.

And Paul writes in today's epistle to the Romans: "Why, one will hardly die for a righteous man—though perhaps for a good man one will dare even to die. But God shows his love for us in that while we were yet sinners Christ died for us."

My mind is steaming with this truth, but how, once more, can my pen glean my teeming brain?

How can we say again that human beings cannot save themselves by good behavior alone? It is only the unilateral, unconditional love and grace of God that we are given eternal life: now. Eternal life begins for us at baptism, not death. To live gracefully and graciously; we don't deserve it, but it has been given to us, to live now! Even though we are sinners, we are loved. How can we say again, in a new way, that even our most righteous acts of overcoming sin hold sinful self-righteousness within them?

> In the woods of the Far West there once lived a brown bear who could take it or let it alone. He would go into a bar where they sold mead, a fermented drink made of honey, and he would have just two drinks. Then he would put some money on the bar and say, "See what the bears in the back room will have," and he would go home. But finally, he took to drinking by himself most of the day. He would reel home at night, kick over the umbrella stand, knock down the bridge lamps, and ram his elbows through the windows. Then he would collapse on the floor and lie there until he went to sleep. His wife was greatly distressed and his children were very frightened.
>
> At length the bear saw the error of his ways and began to reform. In the end he became a famous teetotaler and a persistent temperance lecturer. He would tell everybody that came to his house about the awful effects of drink, and he would boast about how strong and well he had become since he gave up touching the stuff. To demonstrate this, he would stand on his head and on his hands and he would turn cartwheels in the house, kicking over the umbrella stand, knocking down the bridge lamps, and ramming his elbows through the windows. Then he would lie down on the floor, tired by his healthful exercise, and go to sleep. His wife was greatly distressed and his children were very frightened.

Thurber gleaned this sinful bear from his teeming brain. Even our most righteous acts are fraught with sin.

Human beings are not capable of leading religious lives without God. Even our most righteous motives hold self-righteousness within them. Even our most humble motives seek to be more humble than anyone else's. God doesn't love sinners more than others—because there are no others! God didn't love the prodigal son more than the older brother; he loved them equally. God in Christ didn't love the woman at the well more than those who have never committed a sin—there are no others. He who is without sin, Jesus challenges, pick up the first stone... And they all went home, for they lived in glass houses.

I know no other way to say it. Each human being is a sinner. We all do things for which we need forgiveness, about which we are ashamed, and even in our righteous acts, we fall on our faces like Thurber's sober, unbearable bear.

And yet, since we can't be justified by our behavior, and since we are justified by faith, we have peace with God through Jesus Christ. We rejoice in our hope. Moreover, we even rejoice in our sufferings, knowing that suffering produces endurance, and endurance produces character, and character produces hope, and hope does not disappoint us because God's love has been teemed into us.

That was gleaned from Paul's teeming mind—and poured from my pen—and forgive us both for assuming to speak for God, except that suffering produces characters, and as long as there are characters like Thurber, his bear, St. Paul, and you and me, there will be much gleaning from many pens, ceasing Keats' fears that we will cease before our pens have gleaned our teeming brains. We are sinners—glorious, graceful sinners—loved by the God who created us, who redeemed us and sustains us, unilaterally, without condition.

Amen.

❖ ❖ ❖

March 29, 1987
Lent IV
Ephesians 5:8–14; John 9:1–38

The first blind child I ever saw, I saw when I was a child. Neighbors on the corner moved in early in the summer next door to Dr. Neil. My mother and I walked to the store on a crisp June morning; the sky was huge, the sun had climbed to its mid-morning station, on the horizon were banks of clouds whipped in peaks of white. My mother told me that the new neighbors had a daughter my age who was blind. She would join them for the summer. During the winter months, she was away at a special school. My brother asked "how" and I asked "why." There always seemed to be more answers to "how" than "why." "The little girl had been born premature," said my mother, "and something happened in the incubator that caused her blindness." That answered "how," but to this day I don't know "why."

The Pharisees were concerned to explain how the man who was born blind was so born.

They equated sin as cause and blindness as effect. They asked Jesus and Jesus responded, "It was not that this man sinned, or his parents, but that the works of God might be made manifest in him." He then said, "As long as I am in the world, I am the light of the world."

Jesus didn't answer how the man was blind, but why.

In a re-creation of the Genesis story, Jesus made clay from dust and spittle and baptized the man's eyes with the clay. And the man's sight was restored. The Pharisees, not satisfied, wanted to know how it was that the man born blind could now see. The man gave them new insight to which they remained blind. "I was blind, and now I see." This was all the man knew, but it was all he needed to know.

We Christians, from a distance, might divine three insights from this story. First, truth depends only on itself. Truth will come in a variety of forms. The truth of this story is in the miracle, where reason is driven beyond itself. Eyesight may be a metaphor for insight. Our bodies carry us in history as tangible vessels for revelation. The blindness of this man gave truth a vessel. Jesus' healing of his eyes gave opportunity for a new insight, which is the second awareness.

For hundreds of years, the Old Testament shows, the Hebrew people dreaded seeing God. Such sight would result in immediate death. But to see Jesus Christ, knowingly and with faith, is to live. The man born blind had the sublime privilege which those who claimed to see had denied themselves. Through the man born blind, we now know that to see God in Christ is to live. We can now see something of God when we look at Jesus, and in looking at Jesus, we can see something of ourselves. Our lives are enabled by looking at Jesus, and through him we are given our meaning, our purpose, and our lives.

The third insight from the man born blind is that there are just some things that we cannot know. Why he was born blind and why Jesus healed him are within the realm of the mysteries. They are encased in the same source as good and evil, life and death. No matter how much we know, there are some things we will know only when knowledge ceases and we are one with our source. How peaceful it is when we can inhale breath and exhale spirit and know not where it comes from or where it goes, and be concerned only with the knowledge that we are alive. Those who have seen the Christ are trustful, hopeful, and peaceful. It is a peace, which passes understanding.

The afternoon after my mother told me of the blind girl on the corner, I rode my bike slowly past her house. The windows were open onto her front porch and the curtains blew just past the sills. From within her house, I heard a piano being played with a most peaceful rhythm. The tune was Brahms' "Lullaby." I knew the tune because it was the one I was trying to learn when I quit my piano lessons that winter. My talents lay elsewhere. The last song I learned was the one I heard coming from the open window of the blind girl's house. Whoever was playing that lullaby played it in a way that I knew I never could…

Amen.

April 17, 1987
Good Friday

There is within the human psyche some archetypal movement toward maturity. This interior driving force is no less powerful nor any less deniable than that unseen energy between moon and tide. Something substantial, inscrutable, and mysterious draws us out of innocence by the purifying heat of experience, as if some precious metal must be distilled by fire and flame. The impurities of immaturity will be burned away, and no resistance or ignorance will retard life's lunar tide when necessity pulls the sea past itself.

The Chinese elm in front of the house in which I grew up has always been a symbol of something primordial and eternal in its natural reality and symbolic presence. Like any tree, it was an axis mundi, around which the neighborhood turned. Its roots, gnarled and exposed, disappeared to the earth's epicenter into and out of the fecund womb of all creation. Its branches took their call upward seriously, in spite of their own weight of leaf. Rooted and tough of bark, yet adaptive and pliant; delicate and vulnerable, yet sturdy enough to hold its own limb weighted with a child.

How many of my own experiences were birthed about the branches of that tree. I learned who I was in messages from my parents whispered and yelled within its summer shade and raw winter bareness—the concurrent mixed messages of unconditional love and dissatisfaction with my desire to remain a child. That tree stood still in silent judgment and hope as I was pulled into maturity by love and judgment and my own ever-present existential choices. I learned to ride a bike balanced against its trunk. After a near-death experience at age six, I convalesced month after month staring from my bed at the world that continued to turn around that tree.

My innocence has left me in degrees. I suspect there is more to flee before it returns. One story is symbolic of my broken innocence. Before age ten, I was given the mixed blessing of a BB gun. The masculine symbol stirred such psychic energy that it became a catalyst for new instincts until then dormant. Being a younger son, my masculine mentors were my brother and his gang. They could conquer nature with their weapons—slingshots, bean shooters, rubber guns—all were instruments of power. My brother was particularly adept at shooting birds. His power and proficiency always judged my impotence and error. One late spring evening, before dusk, my brother was off throwing his paper route. My father was a traveling man, away to Pawhuska, or Broken Arrow, selling his company products. Mother was in the kitchen; the smell of fried meat and baked bread wafted through a rusted screen door. Alone with my androgynous instrument, a gun called Daisy, I looked for birds. In the top of the Chinese elm sat a small brown sparrow. Like a lunar tide, something within me overtook me. I took my gun and pressed its cheap metal against my cheek. Like Adam and Eve, I knew in a moment the choice I had and I had no choice. My mundane drama was the rehearsal of the human situation—powerful, primordial, natural, religious, historical, eternal—this frozen moment summarized my twin nature of creator and destroyer. I blinked as I pulled the trigger, and the weapon exhaled a puff of violence and the bird fell. This premeditated accident set off in me such a mixture of feelings that I could taste them in my mouth. Rushing to the broken sidewalk beneath the tree, I saw my own lost innocence, embodied in a brown sparrow, dead and no larger than my hand. All of the world's history of violence screamed in a stroll to a tree before the terrifying illumination of human nature. In that triumphant moment of defeat, it was no more than a glimpse, just a porthole vista, but clear enough to strike the end of my innocence.

No murderer, no rapist, no adulterer, no maniacal dictator exterminator held more potential for evil than I. Both the evil, and the violence, once in a system, are always there and powerful. The only issue is degree, not fact. Even then, as a boy, I knew I existed in a world outside and held a world within that I had not only now seen, but was an actor in. And that world included a dimension of uninhabitable sorrow.

Whatever the Good Friday message may be, it clearly states that there is a dimension of the world that holds horror in its corner. Teilhard de Chardin prophesied a chilling truth: "Whatever human beings are capable of, they will do." God in Christ rehearsed the symbol of the tree. In the garden, the tree was central, standing as a link between earth and above. "Leave the good and evil to me," states God's truth as penned by the Hebrew poet. The forbidden fruit is as ambrosia to those who seek it. And yet, when tasted by humans, its rancid, foul taste never leaves our mouth. But that story is ended. Evil has entered the world. How? Who in the world knows? All we can know, we now know: evil exists. Those who deny its existence are most under its spell.

The new story is told today. Another tree is planted in history. This cross is at the center of the world, which is no longer just a garden. And now God tastes the foul breath of death. Only the one who holds the key to creation can change its rules. And God in Christ has done so today. All our destructive tendencies are actualized in the innocent death of Christ and our own death of innocence. We now know our nature. At the new tree, we are given God's true nature. God hates nothing he has made, even if it betrays, denies, or crucifies him. This is the power of the unconditional love of God for his children.

Christianity does not turn on sentimental stories of picture-book Bibles, but on the horrible truth of birth and death. Once we know the horror of freedom and the power of evil as it affects our existential choices, and once we own our own dark side, then we can see that Christianity turns on an irony and the joy of its surprise. God takes the instrument of death and makes it a symbol of love.

Whatever we have done. Whoever we are. No matter how horrible we have been. No matter how horrendous our choices. No matter what…God has reconciled the world to himself in the death of Christ. We can now stare death in the face. The deaths we create and the one which re-creates us. Whatever else Christianity states, and in spite of all its subtlety and confusion, this day we clearly proclaim that God in Christ has overcome evil and death, yours and mine.

The call to maturity means the death of innocence. And once that has been experienced, then we can begin again and look for the barren tree of our maturity seen in the hardwood of the cross. We can look for that tree to bloom again. And then await the day when once again we can be as children and swing innocently in its branches.

Amen.

❖ ❖ ❖

May 3, 1987
Luke 24:13–35

Like all truth, the key to today's Gospel revelation is hidden. That is to say, after years of reading the story of the Road to Emmaus, I missed a most beautiful phrase and have a new insight. Isn't that nice? Isn't that a wonder, at midlife and mid-career, to still be a novice student delivered from cynical, mundane, professional smugness that pretends to know? I see something new.

> [On the first day of the week, two of Jesus' followers] were going to a village named Emmaus, about seven miles from Jerusalem, and talking with each other about all those things that had happened. While they were talking and discussing together, Jesus himself drew near and went with them. But their eyes were kept from recognizing him. And he said to them, "What is this conversation which you are holding with each other as you walk?" And they stood still, looking sad. Then one of them, named Cleopas, answered him, "Are you the only visitor to Jerusalem who does not know the things that have happened there in these days?" And he said to them, "What things?" And they said to him, "Concerning Jesus of Nazareth, who was a prophet mighty in deed and word before God and all the people, and how our chief priests and rulers delivered him up to be condemned to death, and crucified him. But we had hoped that he was the one to redeem Israel. Yes, and besides all this, it is now the third day since this happened. Moreover, some women of our company amazed us. They were at the tomb early in the morning and did not find his body; and they came back saying that they had even seen a vision of angels, who said that he was alive."

Here it is. In order to see the risen Christ, we must see him through a vision of angels. A vision of angels...isn't that nice?

And then Jesus taught them; and his teachings opened their eyes, and "he was known to them in the breaking of the bread."

Three parts. First, we must pray for the vision of angels. Second, we must open ourselves to his teaching. Third, once we are opened through the teaching, we may see him even in the most common element—even, shall we say, in our bread.

So much of our life is spent seeing things on a horizontal walk down our road journey called history, and we do not see the risen Christ even in our own dust. We will not see the truth of God only through our own eyes. We must pray for a vision of angels and live with God's holy word, most especially Jesus' teachings, in order to see the risen one wherever we are. Once we have seen him anywhere, we can see him everywhere.

Simply begin this Easter season to pray for the vision of angels. Begin now to read, study, and open yourself to the Word, and then prepare to be amazed that that which you seek will make itself known to you wherever you are. That which you see you will find when your time comes. Christ will reveal himself in the abiding and amazingly mundane places. In dust, in death, in trauma, or tragedy. In friend, event, relationship, or job—those who have the eyes will see—even in brokenness.

We must pray to see. We must make our life's dedication and vocation a prayer of openness...

> We must sleep with open eyes, we must dream with our hands,
> we must dream the dreams of a river seeking its course, of the sun dreaming its worlds,
> we must dream aloud, we must sing till the song puts forth roots, trunk, branches, birds, stars,
> we must sing till the dream engenders in the sleeper's flank the red wheat-ear of resurrection,
> the womanly water, the spring at which we may drink and recognize ourselves and recover,
> the spring that tells us we are men, the water that speaks alone in the night and calls us by name,
> the spring of words that say I, you, he, we, under the great tree, the living statue of the rain,
> where we pronounce the beautiful pronouns, knowing ourselves and keeping faith with our names,
> we must dream backwards, toward the source, we must row back up the centuries,
> beyond infancy, beyond the beginning, beyond the waters of baptism,
> we must break down the walls between man and man, reunite what has been sundered,

life and death are not opposite worlds, we are one stem with twin flowers,
we must find the lost word, dream inwardly and also outwardly,
decipher the night's tattooing and look face to face at the noonday and tear off its mask,
bathe in the light of the sun and eat the night's fruit and spell out the writings of stars and rivers,
and remember what the blood, the tides, the earth, and the body say, and return to the point of departure,
neither inside nor outside, neither up nor down, at the cross-roads where all roads begin,
for the light is singing with a sound of water, the water with a sound of leaves,
the dawn is heavy with fruit, the day and the night flow together in reconciliation like a calm river,
the day and the night caress each other like a man and a woman in love,
and the seasons and all mankind are flowing under the arches of the centuries like one endless river,
toward the living center of origin, beyond the end and the beginning.

Those words are from Octavio Paz's poem, "The Broken Waterjar."

We must pray for the vision of angels to allow us to see even the broken water jar as the source of life.

We must pray to see that the dust of our own feet may eventually, when it rises up to our eyes, reveal the risen Christ at our side. And our eyes up to that time have been kept from knowing, but our time has come.

We must pray to have our eyes opened to see the eternal new life found even in the breaking of our bread.

Amen.

❖ ❖ ❖

May 10, 1987
Acts 6:1–9, 7:2a, 51–60

There is a scene, unseen, that can only be sketched in one's own mind. It is of a stoning. Evidently, a stoning was hard work, and those who were called to the first line—the official stoners, as it were—would come stripped to the waist. It is difficult to throw a stone that is larger than your hand, and it is difficult to kill a human being with a single stone of that size. And so stones and bottles and pieces of whatever available, bones or other things, were thrown until the person was attested to be dead. The official Jewish court would send one of its younger clerks out to attest to the fact that the one accused, usually of blasphemy, was dead. In our imagination, we see all of the repressed, self-righteous behavior and the screaming, taunting words. Stones are thrown on a hot day. Men sweating, stripped to the waist—stone by stone, punishing, pounding, penetrating flesh.

The first lesson today is from the Acts of the Apostles. "Now in the days when the disciples were increasing in number, the Hellenists [Jews who spoke Greek] murmured against the Hebrews," those who were in leadership in a new movement called "The Way"—the ones who had taken the place of the president of the Eucharist, the presiding officer, the presbyter, the priest. (This, we might paraphrase, is the first example of the congregation complaining about their clergy, an ancient practice still found today in many congregations.)

They were complaining because the widows were neglected in the daily distribution. One of the ancient traditions of Judaism, carried into Christianity, was the care for those who could not care for themselves. The Jews who spoke Greek said, "Well, what about our people? Why aren't you helping us?" The clergy said, "Why, it is not right that we should give up the preaching and the studying to serve the tables. Therefore, brethren, pick out from among you seven men of good repute, full of spirit, and wisdom to whom we may appoint this duty. But we will devote ourselves to prayer and to the ministry of the word."

Thus we began, early on, what is known as clericalism, where there is a division: the embryonic beginning of a ministry called the Diaconate. *Diakonia* means to serve, and those who were appointed to serve were the first deacons. It was the beginning of a three-ordered ministry: the episcopacy, or bishops, which is those who oversee; the priests, those who are charged with keeping the tradition alive and sacrificing at altar; and the deacons, those who are called to serve. Not only was there an ordered ministry evolving, but also the separation between those who were ordained and those who weren't.

"So we will devote ourselves to prayer and to the ministry of the word." What they said pleased the whole multitude. And they chose Stephen, a man full of faith and the Holy Spirit. And they chose six others with long Greek names. They sat before the apostles and they prayed, and then they laid their hands upon them, which is an ancient tradition of touching and passing on authority. And Stephen, full of grace and power, did great wonders among the people. So Stephen, by tradition, was a deacon—one who was called and set apart to serve.

There are, within the Church, two expectations of people. One is, the Church is there to serve us. The other is, we are here to serve the Church. Now those who think that the Church was created to serve them are those who complain because the widows and orphans aren't getting their distribution. "Well, what about so-and-so, and why hasn't the Church ever...?" and "They didn't come to see me in the hospital!" And yet, they are the ones who call, complaining that they can't get the date for the wedding of their daughter. "The Church is there to serve us!" We should move heaven and hell in order for the Church to serve you. They have taken on a membership in a country club, and they will fire the manager if they do not get the service they want. If they pay their dues, less than one percent of their total income, they expect to be able to call on the clergy as their family chaplains. And then there are those who think that they are there to serve the Church. That they have been commissioned at baptism to take on a ministry, and rather than waiting for somebody to come and serve them (as the one lying before the pool at Bethesda for years, thinking somebody had to come and make him well), they decide that the way you get well is by giving yourself away. There are those who believe that service is perfect freedom.

And then there are those who integrate the two and really take on a patient-doctor relationship in a hospital for sinners. When they are sick, they take up a place and are served by those who are well. When they become well, they get up and give their bed to another, serving those who are sick. The Church is here to serve and to be served. An integrated reality is the posture that says, "I've been called into a ministry at my baptism. I take on the *diakonia*: when I need it, I ask for it; when I don't need it, I give it." To serve and to be served. Many say, "I am not worthy to serve. I am not trained. I'm not perfect."

Remember, the price of imperfection is relevance. It is relevant to serve the Church. But you will do so imperfectly; I know from experience. So, if you are waiting for perfection, the world will pass you by. If you are willing to go ahead and offer what you have, like that little boy in the feeding of the five thousand…all I've got is just a few fish…offer it up. It is amazing what God will do with it.

There is another point in this story about Stephen. The reason he is so effective, the reason he is a saint, the reason we remember him every December on his saint's day, and the reason he is recorded so prominently in the beginning of the Acts of the Apostles, is because Stephen lived. The only way you can live is to decide what you are willing to die for. You can never live, be fully and truly alive, until you decide what you are willing to give your life for. Is there anyone for whom you are willing to give your life? Are there those for whom, if they were suffering, that you would take on their suffering? Is there anything to which you are committed, for which you would give your very own life? Is there anything—person, organization, or image—that you love more than your own life? If you are not able to say that, then you have not yet lived. Stephen found something for which he could give his life. That God in Christ has destroyed death by his own dying, so that we might have nothing to fear. The world can take nothing away from us, not even our own life, for we have been given it eternally. Stephen knew that. He was willing to serve and be served, and he found something for which he would give his life and he lived.

There is an irony about all of this: God is not mischievous in his revelation. Just subtle. The irony is that if we will give ourselves away to Christ or to another, we will discover ourselves. If we will do that, then we will live. It is an irony. And if we do that—rather than bury our treasure in the ground, afraid to live, not knowing who we are—we know; we are children of God, called to love one another and serve one another. In so doing, we are saying that we are willing to give our lives for one who has given his life for us, and we discover that we are alive for the first time.

It is ironic. And that irony is woven into the fabric of every story that we rehearse from this lectern, through three-year cycles of biblical study. Those who have eyes to see and ears to hear, the irony is written in there. It is just an image we have, of one who discovers that he is alive by serving, who gives himself to another and discovers who he is, and believes that God in Christ has destroyed death. When we do that, it may be costly; it may be unattractive, traumatic; it may appear to be the worst thing that can happen to a human.

It is not a common sight to see a stoning, where men are stripped to the waist and you cannot throw a stone larger than your hand. At the stoning of Stephen, they stripped to the waist for the difficult task of killing a human being who claimed that Jesus was God. And then they began to rip off their garments and throw them at the feet of a young clerk who had been sent out by the Sanhedrin to witness the death and to attest that the first Christian martyr was dead. The subtle irony is his name was Saul. The beginning of Christianity is always through a death. The beginning of the rising tide of worth and meaning is at a death. And out of Stephen's death came the rising tide of Christianity through a young clerk named Saul, who took a ride to Damascus, was blinded by the revelation of God alive in Christ, and changed his name to Paul. Paul, the one who became a deacon, served his God, and gave himself away—because of them, we are here. Have you come to serve or to be served?

Amen.

June 7, 1987
Pentecost
Acts 2:1–11

This is the anniversary of the wedding of the world. Pentecost is more often referred to as the birthday of the Church and that it is; but more so, it is a wedding of the Spirit with humanity. Birth happened at Pentecost, and that birth, the birth of the Church, came about because of the marriage of God, the Holy Spirit, with the human community. In a real sense then, today is an anniversary. Today is a covenant renewal of God's promise to be unconditionally present as incarnation and as inspiration.

That kind of theological precision and metaphorical image may stimulate the mind, but how can that theology be translated into a message that will warm the heart?

Think of Bob Hope sauntering on stage swinging a golf club and singing, "Thanks for the Memory." For that is what we are about today. The theological terms are: *anamnesis* and *eucharistia*. In our anniversary of Pentecost, we celebrate the integration of extremes: creator and creation, God and human, eternity and time, life and death, holiness and sinfulness. All these come together in Christ, and the Spirit makes one community out of those who believe in the one Christ. *Anamnesis* is memory. *Eucharistia* is thanksgiving. Today we say thanks for the memories.

Memory as *anamnesis* means to make present through remembering. We affirm in the present experience that which happened before. In remembering, it occurs again. Today we will renew our baptismal vows. Pentecost is a day that the Prayer Book recommends for public baptisms. When there are no candidates, the renewal of baptismal vows may take the place of the Nicene Creed at the Eucharist. Following the sermon, we will collectively renew our baptismal vows. In so doing, we create the possibility of living in the present, and in the present, living more fully into what our baptism means. *Anamnesis* and *eucharistia*: thanks for the memories. Such memories in sacramental theology are not a past tense, but a present experience which calls us into the future.

The Spirit is not bound by time and space. The Pentecostal event integrates all that has been with all that will be and frees us to live joyfully in whatever present reality we have, even if it seems to be a place we don't want to be. The dynamic nature of baptism and Pentecost means that renewal and change are always happening, and those who are willing to wait and obey the call will enter a future where all will be well. That is called hope. And hope sings thanks for the memories.

Thanksgiving is Eucharist. Within the Eucharist is *anamnesis*; "This is my body, this is my blood, do this in remembrance of me." When we do this, Christ is present in *anamnesis*. The spiritual renewal then takes place like a new life in baptism. In Eucharist, we are baptized again and given our past forgiven, our present renewed, and our future whole.

A man came to me asking to be delivered from a horrible and traumatic memory. As we talked, it became clear that this near-death event in his life had been the life-giving symbol of his journey. Rather than ridding him of the memory, I asked him to enter into it more fully. Once he did that, in a painful series of discussions, I then asked him to make the memory present reality and to thank God for it. It was a baptismal event. It was a Pentecostal celebration. It was a "thanks for the memory." His past brought to the present made his wholeness a promise for the future.

This *anamnesis eucharistia* is no empty ritual or simplistic symbol, unless you see it as such. In Christianity, believing is seeing, and when we believe, we see. If you see it as functional and mysterious, and if you see it as present reality and transcendent hope, then today will be no less a birthday than Pentecost a wedding day.

For too long we have segmented religious life from real life. This Pentecostal renewal is not pietistic platitude; it is transforming power. It is relevant to past event, present reality, and any future dream or dread. This is real, palpable, experimental. It is in this moment.

I hope today will be for you a memorable event. One which will stimulate your mind and warm your heart, like Hope singing, "Thanks for the Memory."

I agree with Dag Hammarskjöld. This renewal proclaims: "For all that has been, we say 'thanks!' And for all that shall be, we say 'yes!'"

Amen.

June 14, 1987
Trinity Sunday
Genesis 1:1–2:3

Great inspirations of art, literature, and music are called into being by a trinity of needs: creation, redemption, and sanctification. Even in the unspoken, unsophisticated innocence of my childhood, I sat and stared at trees and unmowed meadows with two levels of lavender: thistle and clover. I would see summer mirages of primordial images. Confronted by the mystery of nature, I knew, in a part of me not bound by reason, that some source had created this passive pleasure, and through it, courted me in some seductive truth that all of this was gift—all of creation was gift, including me.

All of life was created by this source of mystery, called in our time, God. On this Trinity Sunday, we rehearse the triune experience of the Christian community of creator, redeemer, and sanctifier. The Genesis lesson reads: "And God saw everything that he had made, and behold, it was very good." And it was so.

The need of creation is built into each creature. Each of us has a spark of that source of the mystery within us. We know the creation in more ways than we can reason or explain, but like little boys seduced by unseen truth, we know at some invisible level that the stuff of source is in our very own substance. Why is it that we have such an instinct and urge to re-create and procreate? The creator is within us, as the artist in his art, the poet in his poem, and the composer in his tune. The doctrine of the Trinity comes to us today as a reminder that we are good, we are very good, and we are called to become more and more so, and with our lives contribute to the whole by our joyful response to the gift of life—that is to say, by living fully and creatively. Our responsibility to life is to live—not escape, not hide, not run, but live!

The redemptive need, in the second person of the Trinity, is the cost of freedom and its existential choice—the choice that Adam and Eve rehearsed for us and that each of us has to experience and relive in our own lives. Even as a child, I knew the confusion of choice. I knew my needs. I knew another's needs. When they were the same, it was creative. When they were different, it was competitive. When one of us lost, something was destroyed, broken, and needed redeeming. I knew how to tell the truth and to keep from hurting another, but I couldn't decide how to do both at the same time. When one of us lost, we all lost; all were in need of being put together again. I looked for the wise, healing Christ even before I knew His name was Jesus. The redemptive act is the graceful act. Grace means unconditional love and undeserved favor. It means that God looks at us and says, "You are good, you are very good!" We know of our need to be gracefully redeemed from our lack of ability to be perfect. To be creative means to express the source within by living creatively. To be redeemed means to live gracefully. And that means without fear—we have knowledge now that the healer redeemer is Jesus. And he has promised to redeem, once and for all, and for everyone, all failure and brokenness. And further, he has promised to be with us always.

The third person of the Trinity is the Holy Spirit, the sanctifier. To be sanctified means to be blessed by the Spirit as something special and inspired to become that special one. Each one of us has a spirit, this power of life in us, and like breath, it is not just something that is in us, but something that issues from us. The word "inspiring" has been so loosely used for so long that it no longer conveys very much, but again, in the original sense, the word means "filled with spirit, life breathing." To be inspired means to be charged by some invisible force that leaps through and from our lives like electricity. This Spirit is holy because it comes from the creator, dwells within the creature, and it is not bound by time or space. The Spirit for humans means that you can inspire me and empower me to become something I could not become alone, and that remains true whether we are ten feet apart or ten thousand miles apart, sixty or six years of age. There is a Spirit, loosed in creation, that has been woven into the fabric of the creature who is none other than a Spirit that is holy, that sanctifies, that blesses with words like "very good," sets apart for purpose, and inspires special vocation.

Most of the time we think of life and nature as a neutral kind of thing. And one has to admit that some evidence supports such a view. But Christianity, the community of the creative, renewed and set apart, contradicts life's neutrality.

To say that God is Spirit is to say that life does care and is dynamic, creative, renewing, and sustaining. Whether one calls it "life-giving source," "power of the Spirit," "Christ within," or "God," its most basic characteristic is that it seeks us and wishes us well, sees us as gift set apart for special purpose, and inspires us toward that end.

Heaven knows, there is terror and horror in life. It is not to be denied. The good die young and the wicked prosper, and in every family and life there is enough grief to make nature negative. But from deep within the hidden spring out of which life wells up, there bubbles into our lives, even in the dark or broken places—maybe even especially there—a power to light, heal, and breathe new life; inspiring, creative, and renewing. This is our blessing. Call this the Spirit or the Redeemer or the Creator—what we name it is not as important as the fact that we name it and that we have been named by it. And further, that we open ourselves to receive its creative, renewing, inspiring reality.

Christianity is a great inspiration called into being by a trinity of truth: Creator, Redeemer, and Sanctifier. All art, literature, and music are called into being by this need for creation, redemption, and sanctification.

And so are you. Did it ever occur to you, and therefore we, that we are the poem of God? That we are God's story? That we are God's tune? Think of that. It will fulfill a trinity of needs—creative, redeeming, sanctifying. It is good, it is very good.

Amen.

❖ ❖ ❖

June 21, 1987
Romans 5:15b–19

We are having a baptism today. One of the nice things about being in a place for a while is that you begin to get woven into the fabric of many lives. I'm pleased to say that I married her mother and father. I buried her great-grandparents, and her great-grandfather designed the Chapel of the Christ Child and redesigned the bell tower. We will welcome Caroline Staub to this place. And what is it of this place that we will tell her?

There are two images for you and for her about this place and the gospel within this place. Let's begin where we must begin for any truth, and that is with the Holy Word. Paul wrote to the struggling congregation of confused Christians at Rome: "And the free gift is not like the effect of that one man's sin. For the judgment following one trespass brought condemnation, but the free gift following many trespasses brings justification. If, because of one man's trespass, death reigned through that one man, much more will those who receive the abundance of grace and the free gift of righteousness reign in life through the one man Jesus Christ." In another place, Paul wrote: "Where sin abounds, grace abounds more."

We tell Caroline Staub today this is a world full of contradiction, confusion, and complexity, a world full of separation, but the free, unilateral, unconditional love of God welcomes, encourages, and includes you by name. Today. Jesus guarantees us, in the Gospel, that all of that darkness will come to light, that we have nothing to fear—for that which is covered will be revealed, that which is hidden will be known, and that which is told to us in the dark will be uttered in the light. What we hear whispered will be proclaimed from the housetops. And so we proclaim, clearly and without question or condition, that wherever sin is, grace abounds more.

I remember the first time I drove down Texas Avenue and up to Christ Church Cathedral. I was struck by two things. There was a startling contradiction: this glorious place in an urban context. It literally reeked of stability and longevity in the midst of superficiality, mirrored in glass plate and aluminum. At the same time, I saw a fence, a wrought-iron fence, with a sign saying "Keep Out." I was reminded in that moment of the poem by Carl Sandburg entitled "A Fence."

> Now the stone house on the lake front is finished and the workmen are beginning the fence.
> The palings are made of iron bars with steel points that can stab the life out of any man who falls on them.
> As a fence, it is a masterpiece, and will shut off the rabble and all vagabonds and hungry men and all wandering children looking for a place to play.
> Passing through the bars and over the steel points will go nothing except Death and the Rain and Tomorrow.

We are here to proclaim to this child of God that that fence is not a fence but a gate. It is open to the world—the Body of Christ is open to the entire world, given this piece of geography. All vagabonds are children of God. If there is one human being hungry, none of us can be self-satisfied. And the gate is open for the children to play. We proclaim that all human beings are welcome here. All are children of God. There is no requirement for coming to this place other than the desire for refreshment and truth and acceptance.

The logo of the Cathedral is not the fence, but the rood screen. It is a clear sense of definition of where we are and to what we are called. It is a symbol of openness and inclusiveness. Through its ample bays, the Word and sound of glory come. With its subtlety of architectural twist and turn, something of the complexity of life can be seen, but within it is the mandala of the shape of wholeness. It is a screen, to be sure, but that which is screened out is all that is perfect. In other words, if you are perfect, you can't come through here. If you are perfect, you have no need to enter the safety of this sanctuary. This, my friend Caroline Staub, is a place for all imperfect, broken, less than whole, struggling, pilgrim people. The gate is open to anybody to come in. The rood screen leads us to the symbol and emblem of pain and passion: the crucifix, the cross. Brokenness was not avoided even by our Lord, and the wholeness comes through the action of God in Christ.

In the beginning, the rood screen was known not as a screen, but as the gate of heaven. All of us pilgrims, the most recent one included, come to the gate. We come as beggars, being told that there is food available. We come and kneel, and as a matter of will, we rise up, seeking to become more, knowing that we must take our own steps, enabled by love, accepting an invitation to come forward. This is not a fence, but a gate—an open gate, a place through which the water will come, through which even death will be conquered, and a place that will bring tomorrow. The gospel is clear: it is available to the imperfect and the broken.

We will take this bit of dust, pour water over her and make clay, and then we will breathe the Spirit of God into her and animate her—*anima* is Latin for "soul." And we will make her more than instinct and appetite, more than nature; we will make her supernatural, a Child of God, right in the gate of heaven.

"Come unto me all ye that travail and are heavy laden, and I will refresh you."

Amen.

❖ ❖ ❖

September 6, 1987
Matthew 18:15–20

One of the undeniable and poignant realities of the great English cathedral is to see the integration of how things ought to be blended with the experience of how things are.

The grand majesty of space; the breadth, length, and height of what is possible; the subtlety of detail; the grandeur of vaulted ceiling, carved stone and wood; the sublime glass and its light play—all are architectural and artistic statements of the possibility of human greatness. And at the same time, the destruction, decay, and ruin of what has been. The continual erosion of what is temporal, transitory, and finite. Both are true of the grand cathedral and of the human being.

The human being has been described as a combination of mysterious grandeur and pompous dust. Always at one and the same time both. And, as in the grand nave, choir, and sanctuaries, with the human's greatest artistic achievements are always the gargoyles. In the midst of the pious expression of the holy sanctuary sit, as constant reminder, the grotesque figures, judging any human pretense, that each and all hold within something that is in contradiction to all that we show the world.

The punctured pretense of the gargoyles is the poignant reality of the human predicament. Even in the majestic statement of the religious edifice, we see crouched above, or hidden just out of sight, the monster or hag; the ugly, gruesome, blemished, teratoid creatures who remind us of how things should be *and* how they are.

This week, in some synchronistic wind of coincidence and fate, I have talked to three men who are each a part of my personal story. One I have known since high school, the other two were both fraternity brothers and teammates on a college basketball team—one a former roommate, the other my fraternity pledge dad.

The reason why we called one another was that each had a presenting practical need.

Each conversation lasted over an hour and has deeply influenced me. First, each man is a success in his field: insurance, securities, and banking. Each is a powerful person, a good, solid citizen. Each has produced goods and services for his community. Nine children among us, all will eventually take their place in creation and contribute. And yet, each holds within his story an honest attempt at living a life the way it ought to be lived and experiences of how real things are. Combining the conversations, there have been divorce, bankruptcy, alcohol problems, business failure, rebellious children, and generous moments of quiet desperation. No perfect life. No life without some scar, decay, or death of illusion.

In today's Gospel, Jesus is concerned about brothers and sisters being brothers and sisters. Using his motif from his Sermon on the Mount, he recognizes that all sin. And further, that even in the best of all possible worlds, there is an imp or monster that sits or hides, waiting to turn grandeur to dust. When your brother sins, be his brother. Within the personal bonds of love or within the symbolic community of the Church, be lovers, not judges. He says further that "when two or three are in loving relationship because of me, I am in the midst of them." What is not in today's Gospel is the next verse of Matthew's eighteenth chapter, where he tells the Parable of the Unforgiving Servant. The parable is about a king who forgave a servant and that forgiven servant refused to forgive those who owed him. The king said to him, "You are the true scoundrel; I remitted the whole of your debt when you appealed to me, were you not bound to show your fellow servant the same pity I showed to you?"

In every life, there is a gargoyle. One of the undeniable and poignant realities of the great cathedral is to see the integration of how things ought to be blended with the experience of how things truly are.

In my three conversations this week, there was no judgment, just love. Each man needed a brother who had known him when all things were possible and to love him now that things were real. I'm not sure that Christ's name necessarily needed to be mentioned, but I knew he was in our midst, for without exception, each man—powerful, successful—made the humble confession of love for a real brother. Grandeur and dust together. And without exception, all found a way to say that we love the other. Each needs to strive for all that is possible, and be loved for all that is real, and when that happens, Christ is in our midst.

Amen.

October 4, 1987
Matthew 21:33–43

Chelsea Nicole will be baptized today. She is God's chance. He has taken a chance in her creation that is God's choice. We need to tell her about life and death and commit to taking her through both, and in so doing, help ourselves.

One of my mother's favorite sayings was, "You can't have your cake and eat it too." In my child ego state, I used to wonder what that meant. Now, in my adult differentiated ego state, I know what that means, but I still wonder, "Why?"

"You've got to break eggs if you're gonna make an omelet," I heard my grandfather say. And hear another parable: "When the householder sent his son, the tenants saw him, and they said to themselves, 'This is the heir; come, let us kill him and have the inheritance,' and they took him and cast him out of the vineyard and killed him." In today's parable from Matthew, Jesus is prophetic about his own death. How did he know that he would die? And that his death would give new life? He must have known about cakes and eggs.

I'm not yet able to tell you why it is so, but I am old enough to echo sages from the halls of history. "Life is dependent upon death." God knows this too—and maybe God only knows why. God, too, died in order that creation might live. So it is. It is so. We can wonder why, or deny, but we cannot choose…for it is so.

The sooner we adjust our thinking to the reality that things end before new things begin and that things die in order that other things live, the sooner our expectations slide into place with the realities and the healthier our lives will become. We should know that, in the literal sense, things die in order that we live. Our life from food is dependent on death. Cows, fish, animals of many kinds, along with fruits and vegetables, all die in order that we might live. Life depends upon death. Living things die daily for our lives. At table grace, in addition to thanking God, we should thank the beans and Brussels sprouts.

When a baby is born, it is because he has died to the womb. The stages and phases of humanity are ends tapered into beginnings. Life is one continual relay race of batons being passed. We are runners, and each full of interior races ending when the tired phase passes its energy to a new stage. We are continually in a contradiction of mourning a loss and celebrating a gain. When the sixteen-year-old drives away on his first licensed drive, a child dies, and a young adult is born. The parents peer from drawn curtains and cry a mixed tear of loss and gain. The egg breaks; the omelet is born.

Looking for the inspiration to capture a "why" leaves me staring at a cake I want to keep and consume. This is the rhythm. We can either refuse to dance or join the chorus line—but we have no other choice.

A way to frame our wonder is to realize that the mystery has a source. And that that source participates in the dance. And the dance and the dancer are one. God made a choice when he created us. His choice was a chance. And so is life. Chance is God's choice and choice is God's chance. We choose in our freedom and refuse life when we choose to be more or less than human. To be human is to become human. That choice and chance mean change. Change means ends and beginnings. God's choice was a chance, and each chance is a choice and each choice is a change—but even so, there is so much over which we cannot choose. Therein God has chosen for us.

The Christ event is God's change. God entered history and chose to change the rules. He, too, died. And now, death means change, not end. In Genesis, our wrong choice ended life without death. God took a chance. In the gospel, God chooses to end all chance and make death, not an end, but a change. We don't have to like death any better, but we no longer need to see it as an end only, for it is now a beginning.

We have no choice about death's reality; we can only choose what it means.

Rabbi Harold Kushner was told when his firstborn, Aaron, was three that the boy had a rare disease which would produce rapid aging; that his firstborn son would be hairless, stunted in growth, look like a little old man, and die in his teens. On the death of his son, he wrote:

> I am a more sensitive person, a more effective pastor, a more sympathetic counselor because of Aaron's life and death than I would ever have been without it. And I would give up all of those gains in a second if I could have my son back. If I could choose, I would forego all of the spiritual growth and depth which has come my way because of our experiences, and be what I was fifteen years ago, an average rabbi, an indifferent counselor, helping some people and unable to help others, and the father of a bright, happy boy. But I cannot choose.

Perhaps the only choice we have is either to yield to pain and name it absurd or to acknowledge the pain and live at a new level of depth because of it.

Jess Trotter, the dean (now deceased) of the Virginia Seminary, upon the suicide of his son, addressed the seminary community by saying, "Ladies and gentlemen, I have been to the bottom and it is firm."

We may be empowered to do so because God chose to do so too—and that is, die that we might live. And further, to have new expectations that death means change, not end—that every grave is now a gate.

And that in heaven, cakes and eggs live forever—I'm not sure about Brussels sprouts. Amen.

October 11, 1987

One of my mother's favorite family stories revolves around the Church and money. One Sunday morning when I was three and my older brother five, my father gave us each a nickel to put in the collection plate at Sunday school. My mother tells the story: "You boys looked so cute. You had on seersucker shorts and starched white shirts. It was Mother's Day, and I pinned a rosebud on each of your collars. When Mrs. Plexico passed the little basket around, Jarrett put his nickel in the collection plate, but Pittman refused. The teacher beckoned by bouncing the coins with a few wrist flicks, but to no avail. Pittman's legs were so short and fat that they couldn't reach the floor, but he pushed himself against the back of the chair and held the nickel tightly in his chubby clenched fist. Jarrett crossed the circle of chairs and tried to pry the coin from his little brother's fat fingers. Pittman protested, 'My daddy gave me this nickel.' The teacher mediated. When we got in the car to drive home, Pittman sat in my lap and finally opened his hand and there remained the nickel, held so tightly that it had made a red ring in his palm and the coin was wet, having spent the entire morning in a chubby little clam-like hand."

Ah, nostalgia. Oh, how it hurts so good. Every story, of course, transcends itself or it dies. And so it is with humans. Unless we become more—we don't remain the same—we become less than we were created to be.

My three-year-old view was that what my daddy had given me was mine. I now know better. I can't hold my gifts. The nature of a gift is that it only becomes a gift, a good gift, when it is used for the purpose for which it was given. Though it is human nature to hold on to what we are given, it is the nature of the creative spirit to let go of possessions, lest they possess us.

Our very lives are gifts. If we refuse to live, we never complete the cycle. Within our lives are unique gifts of personality and skill. We receive them by using them; that is to say, by giving them to others. The nature of a good gift is that it is good only when used for the purpose that it was given.

That nickel came as a gift to be given away. It is a good story of bad stewardship. It is a cute story about a three-year-old, but a sad story if it is not transcended. What if I had held all my gifts for myself? I would still be sitting in a defensive posture, tight-fisted, and selling my soul for five cents.

Money is a symbol with intrinsic value. In Christian stewardship, money is very creative. When we give money for the good of others, we symbolize our maturity about possessions, while at the same time the symbol provides value and power to those who receive it.

We give away a percentage of our money to provide symbol and fact that we own nothing and are owned by nothing. Our Father has given us a gift. When we hold it, it possesses us. Money is passive-aggressive.

Another dimension of stewardship is the difference between offering and collecting. In our theology, the Church does not collect money, we offer it. We have an offering, not a collection. We see it as a response to the grace we've been given, the absolute, undeserved favor we have been given, that we offer thanksgiving. We don't collect thanksgivings. We receive them as offerings. We humans are gifted. We offer money as a symbol of thanksgiving for our gifts. Money has intrinsic value as symbol, for the Church then can give the money again for a greater good. Maybe if Mrs. Plexico could have pulled my well-intentioned brother off of me and kept him from trying to pry the money out of my hand, I might have given more willingly. I think even though the denominations that pry the money out get more money, the theology is poor. We Anglicans have rich theology and poor parishes!

Mrs. Plexico could have explained to me that my father gave me the money to give away. In thanksgiving for my father's gift, I should offer the gift rather than end it in my fleshly desire. I'm not sure that would have worked, but Mrs. Plexico would have been a better theologian.

If you haven't guessed by now, today is Every Member Canvass Loyalty Sunday. A time we tell the truth. You must give a percentage of your money away as the nature of gift, as symbol of freedom from being possessed by your possessions and as emblem of thanksgiving. In so doing, the church has money in order to complete the chain of the creative spirit. For the church will, in turn, give it away for the same reasons God gave and you give.

Or, if you choose, you can act like a child and say, "It's mine." But even if you act like a child, we are not going to strong-arm you and pry it away. I learned a long time ago that money held in a clenched fist leaves a deep impression which only disappears when we let go.

Amen.

❖ ❖ ❖

October 25, 1987
Matthew 22:34–46

> Buddha sits enthroned beneath the Bo-tree in the lotus position. His lips are faintly parted in the smile of one who has passed beyond every power in earth or heaven to touch him. "He who loves fifty has fifty woes, he who loves ten has ten woes, he who loves none has no woes," he has said. His eyes are closed.

Christ, on the other hand, stands in the garden of Gethsemane, angular, beleaguered. His face is lost in shadows so that you can't even see his lips, and before all the powers in earth or heaven he is powerless. "This is my commandment, that you love one another as I have loved you," he has said. His eyes are also closed.

The difference seems to me this. The suffering that Buddha's eyes close out is the suffering of the world that Christ's eyes close in and hallow.

—Frederick Buechner, *Now & Then*

The nature of Christian love is not a romantic, idealistic love, but is a suffering love. It is a purifying through pain of that which is essential in love, but also that which is the essence of the human being.

> The dove descending breaks the air
> With flame of incandescent terror
> Of which the tongues declare
> The one discharge from sin and error,
> The only hope, or else despair
>   Lies in the choice of pyre or pyre—
>   To be redeemed from fire by fire.
>
> Who then devised the torment? Love.
> Love is the unfamiliar Name
> Behind the hands that wove
> The intolerable shirt of flame
> Which human power cannot remove.
>   We only live, only suspire
>   Consumed by either fire or fire.

The fourth movement of the fourth poem of T. S. Eliot's *Four Quartets* is for today. Haunting, the "shirt of flame"—the suffering, intolerable shirt of flame—is a torment devised by love, and love is the unfamiliar name behind the hands that wove the intolerable shirt of flame.

We are to be redeemed from fire by fire.

All too poignant these words to me, for as a child, I wore a shirt of flames. Burned deeply in three degrees, I know the power of Eliot's metaphor. A shirt of flames which cannot be removed by human power. I know the pain of flame and the scar of life. Eliot confirms the pain of the human predicament: that the burning desire for love can only be redeemed by the fire of love.

We each seek a redemptive relationship that will soothe our deepest need. We each know that somewhere there are those to whom we are called, or are called to us, that appear out of shadows into lighted places—never expected—and that we are to know them and that they are to be significant. We are to love them. And we also, through these significant relationships, these purifying scars of life, know that to love is to hurt. Hurting love is the only remedy for the painful need for love. The only hope, or else despair, lies in the choice of pyre or pyre—to be redeemed from fire by fire.

"When the Pharisees heard that Jesus had silenced the Sadducees, they came together. And one of them, a lawyer, asked him a question, to test him: 'Teacher, which is the greatest commandment in the law?' And he said to them, 'You shall love the Lord your God with all your heart, and with all your soul, and with all your mind. This is the first and great commandment. And a second is like it. You shall love your neighbor as yourself. On these two commandments depend all the law and the prophets.'"

And there it is, all the words in a word. The secret of the kingdom holds no other key than the genesis of creation. A word that is the center and circumference of existence. A word that sets the heart longing and the word that satisfies the deepest urge. The word of simple summary of all need: love.

I am too far into life to be any longer satisfied by the romantic idealism of love. I know, even by a modicum of reflection, that all love has its costs and each love, its own unique pain. Even God's love, which knows no condition, is a scandal of embarrassment. For to be loved without condition leaves no excuse, no freedom from the painful journey to acceptance of our imperfection. The unconditional love of God leaves us no freedom from the reality that we must experience that love incarnate in another, and in ourselves. Life is a crucible of the purifying of the human soul through the flame of love, and the fire of its costs.

What a choice. To suffer the death of not knowing love, or to suffer the death of loving. But we are not alone.

Jesus loved the rich young ruler and he walked away. Jesus loved Lazarus and cried when he died. Jesus loved Judas who betrayed him. Jesus loved Peter who denied he ever knew him. Jesus loved the disciples who slept while he sweated blood. Jesus loved his life which was taken from him because of God's love for the world.

Love costs us our life, and we cannot live without it. We only love, only suspire, consumed by either fire or fire.

In a short life, we are given only a few relationships. And only a few of them are redemptive. When those few walk into our lives, they are holy moments. Of these few loves, we are more careful than of everything.

To love another is to know the process of life. To end and begin again and again. To grow through the pain, disappointment, and rejection. To know that some relationships will simply end. To become more because of the sharing, intimacy, and enthusiasm of knowing that another cares whether you live or die. To become whole as another completes your imperfection by compensation or acceptance. I am now not just talking about marriage. I am not just talking about parents with children, children with parents, or the significant others of life. I am talking about those people you know that have been given to you to love—even those that, because of love, the relationship had to end, or because of love, you could not possibly end the relationship.

We are commanded to make covenant and promise with a few, or even less, in order to live by the flame. For the flame that kills is the one which also warms, unites, and ignites.

To love others in the deepest sense is to allow them to be, by being themselves in relationship to one's self. That may mean devotion or silence, or both. That may mean presence or absence, or both. That may mean joining them or leaving them, or both. And each has its own pain and death.

The point is clear. Christians are called to die for love, rather than dying for fear of love's pain, for without love, we never live. Choose love's death; do not choose a death which comes when we refuse to love. Take the risk; for without love, we are nothing.

God's love is present when we love another and ourselves. The Spirit of life is in love. That Spirit is other than just human, that Spirit is holy. The Holy Spirit is a...

> Dove descending, break[ing] the air
> With flame of incandescent terror
> Of which the tongues declare
> The one discharge from sin and error,
> The only hope, or else despair
>   Lies in the choice of pyre or pyre—
>   To be redeemed from fire by fire.
>
> Who then devised the torment? Love.
> Love is the unfamiliar name
> Behind the hands that wove
> The intolerable shirt of flame
> Which human power cannot remove.
>   We only live, only suspire
>   Consumed by either fire or fire.

Which fire will consume you?

If you are Christian, you are commanded by Christ to die of love. For only in so doing will you live.

Redeemed from fire by fire. So:

> Buddha sits enthroned beneath the Bo-tree in the lotus position. His lips are faintly parted in the smile of one who has passed beyond every power in earth or heaven to touch him. "He who loves fifty has fifty woes, he who loves ten has ten woes, he who loves none has no woes," he has said. His eyes are closed.
>
> Christ, on the other hand, stands in the garden of Gethsemane, angular, beleaguered. His face is lost in shadows so that you can't even see his lips,

and before all the powers in earth or heaven he is powerless. "This is my commandment, that you love one another as I have loved you," he has said. His eyes are also closed.

The difference seems to me this. The suffering that Buddha's eyes close out is the suffering of the world that Christ's eyes close in and hallow.

Amen.

❖ ❖ ❖

November 1, 1987
All Saints' Sunday
Ecclesiasticus 44:1–10, 13–14

For some reason beyond reason, every All Saints' Day, I am reminded of Frederick Buechner's definition of a saint: "In his holy flirtation with the world, God occasionally drops a pocket handkerchief. These handkerchiefs are called saints." To his memorable metaphor I add, those are not lace handkerchiefs. The people who have been saints in my life are functional pieces of cloth, pulled from back pockets, rumpled, stained, and torn at the edges. Sainthood is imposed by experience, both for the saint and the one for whom the torn cloth symbolizes the holy.

To be a saint simply means to be sanctified. Baptism is the outward sign that each life is a sacred journey. Each life is a holy pilgrimage. "To sanctify" means "to set apart as holy." Baptism sets us apart to be a part of God's presence in history. We are all saints. Here and there, then and now, we are sanctified to be bearers of the holy for someone at some time. God dwells in each. And that Holy Spirit will percolate up through the imperfect pores of humanity in spite of activity or passivity, in spite of brilliance or ignorance, in spite of intent or chance. God has only humans through whom and to whom to reveal his love. Life is grace; the given-ness, the fathomless, the endless possibility is transparent in its extraordinary ability to reveal itself in the ordinary. Called or not called, God will appear—and that Word will be made flesh, your flesh and mine. Pink flesh of the baby's face or pallid skin of antiquity, any flesh can be the face of God for another.

To each of us baptized and to the pink, Word-made-flesh baby about to be sainted, I draw out an ancient word as an All Saints' Day charge: I charge you to be evangelists, sainted evangelists. The word "evangelist" is shopworn and carries the patina of too many overly zealous revivalists who only know conversion through fear and guilt. But it is a grand title. In the Greek, "evangelist" means "bearer of good news." If there is anything this world needs, it is some few who will bear some good news. It is the gospel truth—for that is what "gospel" means: good news.

Let us now praise the famous men and women of this generation who will give to one another some good news. Let us be saints for one another. In God's holy flirtation with the world, he has dropped us, as handkerchiefs, for one another. Not lily-white, hand-pressed doilies, but pieces of whole cloth. We will be saints when we offer ourselves to one another as bearers of a little good news.

The gospel is simple. It is not easy, but it is simple. We must remind one another in the midst of the bad news of contradiction, paradox, pain, tragedy, trauma, and catastrophe that there remains the Word in the flesh. That Word is that life is grace, even in its given-ness. And that our presence in the life of another is the presence of the grace and truth of the one who dwelt among us.

Be what others need. And allow others to be needed. Be as a handkerchief. Wipe a tear. Mop up a spill. Bind up a wound.

Be a bearer of a little good news. Be a saint. When the shadows of darkness have captured the heart of another—share with them the gospel. The gospel is word and action and not much of either. A hug or handhold—love and touch—that is the Word made flesh, full of grace and truth, that dwells among us. Where? Wherever one says "I love you" and gives a touch. And if there is a tear, don't fear, for it is the baptismal water, and can be easily absorbed by a rumpled handkerchief, stained from a world of experience, undramatically pulled from a back pocket, bearing a little good news. The Word has been made flesh and dwells among us, full of grace and truth. Love and touch.

Amen.

❖ ❖ ❖

December 13, 1987
Advent III
John 1:6–8, 19–28

The other night as I attempted to drift away from another day, I heard the incessant barking of a lonely dog. A lone sound in the dark, breaking the silence of sleep. It was a cry, an animal cry, out of the wilderness.

The dark night is not so bad, you know. For so long, and most recently, in my own vocabulary, the dark is a metaphor for a sad place of despair. A dark place conjures loneliness, oppression, and despondency. To be "in the dark" is to be unaware, unconscious, and out of control. Consider, though, that the dark holds its own worth, and the dark holds its own promise. Was it not out of the dark void that God birthed light? And so, too, therein are the beginnings of our own hungering journey? We were conceived in the dark and began our gestation in the darkness. The sperm and egg unite in the tenebrous tube, then womb, and grow into life before light. Our food is broken down into nourishment and rides our blood to its lightless destiny. Our organs play their own parts beneath a covering, shaded from light.

The dark is where things begin and appropriately where things need to end. The yapping dog barking at shadows and silhouettes the other night brought me closer to a new thought, an Advent image of why it is that this is a timorous time. The light bears its own dark side, and the dark holds its own light. The shrill and discordant yelping of that dog reminded me of the etymology of the word "cynic." A cynic is the one who sees every act of humankind rooted in selfishness. The cynic sees the worst in even the best of motives. The word cynic comes from the Latin which means "doglike." The currish tone of the cynic is like a yapping dog interrupting sleep on a peaceful night. The cynic's tone runs against hope like fingernails on a blackboard. The cynic looks on the dark side, even in the darkness. A cynical view of life sees life in a snarling statement of evil infecting every action. Religion is a convenient and popular target for the currish voice of cynicism. Advent is a time when the cynical side of life rises up to disclaim the Christmas story as fairy tale at best and exploitation by commercialism and materialism at worst. Cynicism is one voice we hear crying, like a dog baying in the night.

And then there is another voice. The voice of one crying in the wilderness. There was a man sent from God, whose name was John. He came for testimony, to bear witness out of the dark to the light…He said, "I am the voice of one crying in the wilderness, 'Make straight the way of the Lord'…" This voice is the voice of a prophet. Prophecy, I remind you, is not crystal-ball gazing. Prophecy is insight into the obvious which, for some reason, nobody else has seen. The prophet points out, with insight, the obvious. The prophet is not the opposite of the cynic, the Pollyanna optimist is. The cynic sees no good. The optimist sees no bad. The prophet sees both sides and the opposites within each side. This is the Advent prophecy of John. The good news is that the light is coming. The bad news is that the light will expose the darkness, all the frail pretense of the self-righteous, the unaware, and the pagan. Further, he sees that those who think of themselves as in the light are in darkness, and those in darkness will be revealed as chosen, as children of the light.

The Pharisees thought of themselves as children with brilliance in their exclusive law. John pointed out the darkness of their exclusive claim that God had chosen them only. He further claimed that those outside the pale of pharisaical Judaism were worthy of the light in spite of the fact that they sat in darkness. The darkness awaits the light; the light exposes the imperfect pretense of the self-righteous.

Advent is a mixed season of hope and dread. For each of us knows, at some level, we hold darkness and light. When John proclaims that he is bearing witness to the light of Christ, coming at Christmas, we are twisted in an anxiety of expectation and apprehension. You must fill in the blanks of your own story of what this light will expose. For some, or for some part of each, it will mean that something, as yet unknown, will emerge which will be at one and the same time both life-giving and death-dealing. For some, and for some part of each of us, the light of Christ will expose a long overdue change of life that will be as painful as birth itself, and the dread of such labor is now exposed. For some, and some part of each, the bearing witness to the new light will mean a gift of awareness that will make all the past worth each pang of labor just to have one glimpse given in the light. The Advent message is always so mixed—the hopes and fears of all the years are met on Christmas Night.

So it is with Christianity. We are not a people of denial that dream only of a white Christmas, but a people prepared by the Prophet John. So it is with Christianity. We are not a people of cynicism who sit alone and curse the dark like an incessant barking dog. But we are a people of prophetic hope who know that the darkness holds its own promise of light and that the light exposes the imperfection of what needs to die in order to be made whole.

We are now halfway through our Advent adventure. The dread is known and begins to blend with the appearing hope. John's voice of promise quiets the cynical and currish sound of despair. We still hear both, but we now know that the competing voices will ultimately be integrated. Those two voices—the animal sound of barking in the night and the voice crying of hope in the wilderness—will be integrated into one. Then we can anticipate a silent night, a holy night, where all will be calm, all will be bright, where we will finally sleep in heavenly peace, and sleep in heavenly peace.

Amen.

December 24, 1987
Christmas Eve

Yeats, in describing Shakespeare, commented, "I feel when I hear his plays that I am in the presence of a soul lingering on the storm-beaten threshold of sanctity." And here we are—bishop, priests, and pilgrims all—spiritual seekers, in from the dark with lingering souls, bowing now to hear the sacred story and kneeling at the border, the narrow and sacramental space, the threshold of sanctity, between the discarnate and incarnate worlds.

In spite of our vestment or garment, we hold at our center a spiritual seeker, searching for an integrated evening to hear the hope of the then, the now, and the when.

Who here has not a memory, either in fact or fantasy, of a child curled in a mother's lap hearing her read: "And it came to pass in those days…And so it was, that, while they were there…And she brought forth her first-born son, and wrapped him in swaddling clothes, and laid him in a manger…"?

Who here has not a memory of first hearing that sacred story in some small town or neighborhood church, or some great cathedral, maybe even this one? And so we long for the hope of then. And our longing for a hope of then takes us back to the even deeper memory of that night which was the holy night, when we were a part of the holy family hearing the firstborn of all creation, an infant's mortal and immortal cry. And even more so then, tumbling through time's tunnel, back to the hope of creation as it was first conceived even then, through the garden back to the moment when the mind of God created order from the chaos of nothing, when time was born from the womb of nowhere. This is the threshold of sanctity to which we have come, soul-lingering and storm-beaten, but we have come for the renewal of the origin of hope then, when peace preceded understanding.

We are spiritual seekers, searching for an integrated evening to hear the hope of then, now, and when. We remember the then and hope for the now. For now the peace must be within our understanding of the evil quality of the world. We must seek peace amidst the selfishness of egocentric appetites for power and dominance. We must seek peace in the midst of sickness, loss, trauma, and tragedy. Even now, as we bow toward the Sacred Story, we do so in the concentric and complex webs of human relations that leave us confused and conflicted as we seek to be whole in fragmented lives. Even now, as we bow toward the Incarnate Word, we do so with the fresh memory of a discarnate world where there appears to be no peace.

Storm-beaten, we come in from the dark—spiritual seekers, bishop, priests, pilgrims all—bowing to hear the sacred story and seeking an integrated evening of then, now, and when. The memory of then, integrated with the reality of now, brings us a fresh breath of hope for the when. For we know, even now, that the time will come for us, only now an amber image of the time, when we will be a new creation, reconceived by God and begun again; falling this time upward through time's tunnel like a baby born from an unsullied womb, delivered from the discarnate world into the arms of a future which will curl us in a loving lap to hear the story for the first time and know it is for us—that our time will have come.

Here we are. Then, now, and when, all integrated as we bow to hear the sacred story. "And it came to pass in those days…And so it was, that, while they were there…And she brought forth her first-born…"

Then, now, and when…all in a moment, peace preceding understanding, peace amidst understanding, and a peace that passeth all understanding.

It was. It is. It shall be.

And here we are—bishop, priests, pilgrims all—spiritual seekers, in from the dark with lingering souls, bowing to hear the sacred story and kneeling at the border, the narrow and sacramental space, the threshold of sanctity between the discarnate and incarnate worlds, seeing now that in Christ they are one. We are given the world anew as God has conceived it to be. And it was. And it is. And it will be. Born again. And again. And again.

Amen.

1988

January 17, 1988
John 1:43–51

My regrets I suspect are minimal. Not that I don't have them. It is just that I probably did the best I could with the burden of unlimited freedom of choice and very limited information. Today, it is not the regret that I didn't take one path over another, or one choice versus the other; it is more the wonder of how much of the mystery of God I have missed by my apathy toward the familiar or known.

After reading today's Gospel, I had the haunting words echoing in my memory: "Surely the Lord is in this place; and I knew it not." How sad those words. How tragic that phrase. If I regret, it is not my action or choice about which I sorrow, but my unawareness. How many times has God been in a place and I knew it not? Consider, if you will, how unaware of the mystery we have been by expecting the known not to hold the unknown, the familiar to be barren of new truth, the simple pleasure to be too obvious to hold the holy.

Today's Gospel bears such sorrow and wonder:

> The next day Jesus decided to go to Galilee. And he found Philip and said to him, "Follow me." Now Philip was from Bethsaida, the city of Andrew and Peter. Philip found Nathanael, and said to him, "We have found him of whom Moses in the law and also the prophets wrote, Jesus of Nazareth, the son of Joseph." Nathanael said to him, "Can anything good come out of Nazareth?" [How can anything new come out of the familiar?] Philip said to him, "Come and see." Jesus saw Nathanael coming to him, and said of him, "Behold, an Israelite indeed, in whom is no guile!" Nathanael said to him, "How do you know me?" Jesus answered him, "Before Philip called you, when you were under the fig tree, I saw you." Nathanael answered him, "Rabbi, you are the Son of God! You are the King of Israel!" Jesus answered him, "Because I said to you, I saw you

under the fig tree, do you believe? You shall see greater things than these." And he said to him, "Truly, truly, I say to you, you will see heaven opened, and the angels of God ascending and descending upon the Son of man."

Nathanael must have spent his entire life praising God for the gift of his friend, Philip, who helped him see what he would have otherwise missed by dismissing the son of Joseph from Nazareth. What good can come out of Nazareth? God was in that place and he knew it not.

Now are you closer to my regret? Not over my behavior so much as a wonder at what I have missed by an apathetic ignorance of the known, familiar, and simple while looking for the unknown, exotic, and spectacular…that God was in those places and I knew it not. If I have regrets it is over my unawareness, rather than my action or choice. It is all the places I have been, and God has been there, and I never saw God. I suspect it has been in the most simple, mundane, and ordinary places. Our theology tells us that God is in the midst of us. Do we look? And if we look, do we see?

How I pray now, no longer to be perfect. That desire has disappeared with the wisdom of age, the grace of God, and acceptance of evidence. My prayer now is to be able to see. To be aware through all my gifts of all the gifts in the one gift of life. It is now a matter of keeping my eyes open to the truth that God will reveal himself in tangible ways, in familiar faces, in known places. I pray to have the discipline to see, hear, touch, and taste the truth and meaning revealed in the son of Joseph from Nazareth.

Our theology tells us that God is in the midst of us. Do we look? Our tradition tells us God is in water, bread, and wine. Do we touch or taste? Our scripture tells us that God is within. Do we see God in one another? Or ourselves? Where must we go to see God? How many, many times God has been in a place and I knew him not?

Such a surprise God is in his appearing. In a baby, barn-born, of an unmarried young peasant couple. Such a surprise, God in his appearing in a desert bush aflame. Such a surprise, God appearing in the wind blown at a Pentecost pagan feast.

How surprised was Jacob. He had cheated, lied, and run away. Holding his brother's birthright blessing under his arm, he ran for his life as one of our faith's great liars and cheats. After he ran away, he slept on a stone pillow, alone in his mendacity, and he dreamed that there was a ladder with angels of God ascending and descending on it. And the Lord stood about it and said, "I am the God of Abraham and Isaac—and behold, I am with you—I will be with you and keep you wherever you go and will bring you back to this land"…and Jacob awoke and said, "Surely the Lord is in this place; and I did not know it." Maybe the Lord was in the lying; maybe the Lord was in the cheating; maybe the Lord was in the running away. Maybe we have looked in the wrong places. Maybe we have looked on the mountaintops and in the victories, and the pristine pure ideal. Maybe God is in places we've never thought to look, or have been afraid to see.

Jacob had gone to the lowest point of his life. He had stooped low enough to see God. God is a surprise. He will appear in the most unlikely people, places, events. He can just walk into your life. We must expect the Lord to be everywhere, for he may appear anywhere—most inexpertly in tragedy,

Sickness, mistake, or choice, as well as joy, celebration, and health; in nature or in the supernatural; in the unknown as near as the known.

How I pray now no longer to be perfect, but simply to be able to see. To be aware of the gifts given in all the gifts in the one gift of life. I pray to be able to see the heaven that lies about those of us who have been called to a clearer vision.

What good can come out of Nazareth? Come and see! You believe because I saw you under a fig tree? You shall see greater things than these…

My desire is no longer to be perfect. Experience, wisdom of age, grace of God, acceptance of evidence—all have taken away from me my desire to be perfect. My prayer is just to be able to see, to hear, to touch, and to taste God's presence…which may be as near as hands and feet.

What do we hear that is similar in the Jesus story and the Jacob story? In one story, we have a child of God running away from God; in the other story, the child of God is running toward us. In one story, we have one so involved in his own needs that he doesn't see the needs of others; in the other story, we have one who is so in touch with the needs of others that he meets his own needs by meeting theirs. In the second story, we learn that God will come out of the most surprising places and people—out of a barn-born baby of an unmarried peasant couple or out of Nazareth. We need to pay closer attention to those things from which we expect no good. Finally, we need to be aware that the angels will be ascending and descending in Christ and that may be anywhere, for since God has entered history in Christ, God can be anywhere.

I would remind you that in this religious world, we don't live by the theory that seeing is believing; rather, we hold the theory that believing is seeing. If you believe that God will be in a place, you will see him—even in the worst possible, lowest, hardest pillow points of your life. If you believe God is present, you will see him. Believing is seeing. Let those who have eyes, see.

Amen.

❖ ❖ ❖

January 24, 1988
I Corinthians 7:17–23; Mark 1:14–20

The romantic call of Christ to Andrew and Peter and the sons of Zebedee, James and John, is a call which elicits from us a joy to the brink of fear. "Follow me," says the wandering, enigmatic Christ.

The joy comes because we are all derelicts looking for a compass which leads through the complexity and confusion to a simple and clear direction that is our own. Joy comes at the possibility that to follow Jesus will at last or at first end our sense of abandonment and begin our clear call.

The joy, though, blends quickly, if not simultaneously, with fear. In First Corinthians, Paul writes a companion piece to Christ's call: "Let everyone lead a life which the Lord has assigned to him, and in which God has called him." The joy is that I have been called by Christ to follow him, as surely as Peter, Andrew, James, and John, but I must do so with my life; that haunting condition draws us to the brink of fear. "Let everyone lead a life which the Lord has assigned him and in which God has called him."

Today, the United Way and Houston Clergy Coalition for the Homeless have asked each parish in the Houston metropolitan area to take up a special offering for the homeless and to preach about the plight of the homeless in our midst. Estimates vary because of the difficulty in counting the homeless, but the estimates run that between two thousand and five thousand are without places to sleep on any given night in Houston.

The homeless present a literal and symbolic problem for those of us who have a home. The real problem is our Christian inheritance, whereby Christ has taught us that there is no peace for any of us until there is peace for all. And in terms of our responsibility, inasmuch as we have clothed, fed, or sheltered one of the least of these, we have done it unto Christ. From the beginning of our faith, we have been heirs of a claim for social justice for all of God's children. We have a claim on us to be our brother's brother and our sister's sister.

The great projected rationalization is a common one that occurs to each of us. These homeless are victims of their own lack of initiative, lazy, alcoholic, drug addicted, or simply victims of their own choice. The reason that such a rationalization continues is because in part it may be true. But a pause for a deeper thought and witness of reflective experience draws us to realize that generalizations do not heal or cure. Each case of a homeless person is unique. Did he or she choose to be abused as a child and inherit low self-esteem or dependency patterns? Did he or she choose a genetic disorder which resulted in low intelligence, inadequate coping skills, or mental disorders? Did he or she choose to be born to the poverty cycle that entrapped him or her as surely as the bonds of our own cycle of materialism have entrapped us? Those of us who are currently paying our Christmas bills are just as trapped in the insanity of the cycle of materialism. Did he or she choose to be born in the assignment that he or she has? How much choice did we make to be born to whom, when, or where we were born? Which of us chose either our heredity or environment which has so greatly determined where we sleep at night? Do we have warm beds because of the wisdom of our choices?

The real problem is that thousands of people do not have homes. The real reasons are a thousand causes. We cannot accurately answer the philosophical or psychological or theological question as to why. But those of us who have enough and more than enough can share. We give to the poor because they are poor, not because they are poor for good reasons. This is the literal problem. Thousands of people in Houston don't have a place to sleep at night. We can help by sharing money. The money for today's special offering will be given to some fifty agencies dealing with the homeless. Each agency is approved by the United Way. We do not seek to solve the problem, only address it. Make it conscious. Own it as real, rather than deny or repress or reject it as the rationalization that these people have chosen to be on the streets. We do not seek to end poverty, just simply to help people who are out in the cold to have a warm, dry bed. No idealism. No romance. Just reality.

The word "derelict" means an abandoned ship, a ship without a rudder. Our own compass program, headed by Kay White and assisted by Lizzy Hargrove, is our way of dealing with the endemic problems and the systems of why people are caught in the cycle of poverty and aimlessness. I commend this program as a direct way that you, through your resources to this Cathedral, through your patronage at our restaurant, have assisted the homeless, not just this day or a day in the future, but for seven years in this place. You are to be congratulated and thanked. But also, Kay White and Lizzy Hargrove are to be recognized and honored as people who go day after day into the depressing stench of poverty, aimlessness, depression, and oppression. We commend them and we offer our support and thanks to them and their great core of volunteers.

The deeper and symbolic problem of the poor and homeless is the subtle and often unconscious threat that these people pose to our own identity. For who among us does not fear facing the awareness that we each hold within a part of us that is abandoned, poor, and homeless. What joy that Christ would call us by name, and ask us, all of us, to come and be a part of his kingdom. What fear that we must be assigned a life and respond to the call. Who among us doesn't have within a rejected part of our own personality? Who among us does not see himself in the derelict who wanders endlessly without direction or resource? Who among us has a crystal-clear view of what our call is and what it is we are called to become? Which of us is not a candidate for the unconditional, unilateral grace of God, because we know in our own hearts the disgrace of decisions we have made, the lack of love and intimacy that we have experienced in our own spiritual journey? Who among us does not see himself in the derelict who is a mirror for our own fear?

Are the street people mirrors of our own great fears? Not only do we know that, but for the grace of God, there go we. But also, we know that on the interior we have assigned to our inner life a shadowy, haggard, rejected soul. The fright in us when we must encounter a beggar is the beggar in each of us who hungers and wanders aimlessly seeking love, affection, and acceptance.

The homeless *are* literal and symbolic problems for us. We have a claim to follow Christ. Where he leads is to compassion for those in need; we have a claim to follow Christ, and our fear is that we will not have sufficient resource to make the hard and narrow journey. When we see those who are so obviously lost, they mirror our own greatest fear that we, too, will wind up aimlessly lost, inadequate to the incredible call of Christ, the one who had no home.

Let us today declare that we are one with the poor and aimless. We know them externally and internally. Let us confess our fear that Christ is calling us to abandon the worship of material goods. Let us accept the joy of being called, but know we are called to the brink of fear that we may lose it all. Let us symbolize that mixed blessing with a symbol that has intrinsic value: money. But more so, let us recognize the fear constellated by the poor and move to the boundaries of joy by acknowledging that each of us is a child of God, and no matter what the external or internal reality, we each need to love and be loved. And that common need is so much more easily met with a night's sleep and quieted hunger.

Let us not be overcome by romantic idealism, nor seduced by cynicism. Let us love one another as we were first loved. It is for that that we each hunger, and only when we know that we are loved unconditionally, will we sleep in dreamless sleep, for we have been called. We have been assigned a task. A response is demanded. The way is narrow. Many are called, but few are chosen.

Amen.

❖ ❖ ❖

February 7, 1988
Mark 1:29–39

We were reminded last week by our guest preacher, Dr. Ernest Bel, of Mark's frenetic literary style. Mark uses the word "immediately" with great redundancy in his Gospel's first chapter.

> v 12: "The spirit *immediately* drove him out…"
> v 18: "And *immediately* they left their nets…"
> v 20: "And *immediately* he called him…"
> v 21: "And *immediately* he entered the synagogue…"
> v 23: "And *immediately* there was in their synagogue…"

Those were all in last week's lesson.

In today's lesson, the immediacy continues:

> v 29: "And *immediately* he left the synagogue…"

v 30: "And *immediately* they told him of her."

And later in the chapter:

v 42: "And *immediately* the leprosy left him…"

In one-fifth of the verses in the first chapter, Mark uses this word. Mark's literary style is one of activity; his favorite adverb is "straightway." Among his favorite verbs are: "arise," "shout," "run," and "amaze." In *The Literary Guide to the Bible*, John Drury writes: "[Mark's] shuttle moves fast through present moments, back and forth between precedents and effects. Events follow upon one another apparently helter-skelter. But they are linked by deliberately concealed significances."

It is one of the deliberately concealed significances that provides our meditation today. Amidst this frenetic activity of Jesus having to be the Christ, with calling, teaching, preaching, and healing, we find a simple but highly significant verse concealed between immediate events. Verse 35 reads: "And in the morning, a great while before day, he rose and went out to a lonely place, and there he prayed."

Even for Christ, even here in Mark's fast-moving shuttle, we see a need for withdrawal, aloneness, quiet time, and reflection. As I am fond of saying, most people, when asked how long it took God to create the world, will say six days, and on the seventh day he rested. That is of course incorrect. It took seven days, for the day of rest is the most important part of creativity. The time away, the time alone, the time of prayer and reflection.

And in the morning, a great while before the day, he rose and went out to a lonely place, and there he prayed.

Even Jesus Christ needed to get away.

There are three word-images about this universal need to have time alone to re-create: dark, aloneness, and prayer.

There is something about that image, "before the day," that establishes Jesus alone in the dark. The time before daybreak is a most creative time.

It is as Gerard Manley Hopkins writes in his most beautiful poem, "God's Grandeur":

> The world is charged with the grandeur of God.
>   It will flame out, like shining from shook foil;
>   It gathers to a greatness, like the ooze of oil
> Crushed. Why do men then now not reck his rod?
> Generations have trod, have trod, have trod;
>   And all is seared with trade; bleared, smeared with toil;
>   And wears man's smudge and shares man's smell; the soil
> Is bare now, nor can foot feel, being shod.
>
> And for all this, nature is never spent;
>   There lives the dearest freshness deep down things;
>   And though the last lights off the black West went

> Oh, morning, at the brown brink eastward, springs—
> Because the Holy Ghost over the bent
> World broods with warm breast and with ah! bright wings.

It is in the dark that we were conceived. It is in the dark that things grow quietly. It is in the dark that we become aware of how much we need the light. Nicodemus came to Jesus by night. Night, that last remnant of dark which is a fecund time where the great explosion of light gathers, pregnant and brown brink eastward, springs; where "lives the dearest freshness deep down things." The dark gives us permission to think thoughts not ordinarily thought, repressed by the day's demands; time to reflect without the need to react.

What a nice significance Mark has deliberately concealed within this Gospel: even the child of light needs time alone by night. Aloneness. The verse reads: "He went out to a lonely place." Lonely here does not necessarily mean forsaken. Though Jesus was to know a forsaken kind of loneliness. He cried out about such from the barren tree called a cross. The lonely here, I believe, implies a place where Christ could be alone. We need to be alone for at least two reasons. First, in order to be in touch with our inner darkness and the promised light which comes only when we are aware of the dark side of our life. The second nature of why we need to be alone is to realize that, for certain segments of our life and its choices, we are alone. There are certain decisions and actions that only we can make. In my own personal problem solving and shepherding others, I am inevitably drawn to the edge of how alone each of us is. Decisions are difficult because only individuals can make them.

Prayer. Prayer is many things, but at least one thing, conversation with God to which you listen. Prayer is best done in an alone place, at the brown brink of awareness, where unconscious thoughts blend with awareness. Whereby we know ourselves in new ways and God, too, in ways that are new. Prayer is a time to take our burdens, like heavy leather bags carried too long, that now may be unpacked. The dirty and musty along with the forgotten treasure are all opened and aired by a good talk with God and yourself.

Brown brink between dark and light, alone, talking with God.

Thank you, Mark, for your concealed significance in one small verse before the continuing shuttle: "And Simon and those who were with him pursued him, and they found him and said to him, 'Everyone is searching for you.' And he said to them, 'Let's go'…"

And so it is, even with saviors, and he left immediately.

Amen.

February 14, 1988
Mark 9:2–9

> A person spends years coming into his own, developing his talent, his unique gifts, perfecting his discriminations about the world, broadening and sharpening his appetite, learning to bear the disappointments of life, becoming mature, seasoned—finally a unique creature in nature, standing with some dignity and nobility and transcending the animal condition; no longer driven, no longer a complete reflex, not stamped out of any mold. And then the real tragedy…that it takes sixty years of incredible suffering and effort to make such an individual, and then he is good only for dying.

John Updike says, "If you scratch the surface of most ministers you'll find their views not so different from those of an agnostic." The beginning quotation concerning death is from Ernest Becker's seminal book, *The Denial of Death*. For many, most particularly for those of us who are priests, Updike's prophetic words hold some truth, particularly in light of Becker's confession of the fatalistic rise of the human, only to reach demise.

Death is my ultimate reality, and because of my professional life, I have constant penultimate reminders. Not only presiding over last rites of the elderly, but of those days- and month-olds and teenagers as well. I returned this week from my seminary with news of the deaths of two seminary classmates, men my age. Becker, in his fatalistic paragraph, captures something of the reality, and Updike, in his prophetic words of an agnostic—wanting to believe meaning between this birth we did not request and this grave we cannot escape, conveys that lingering sense of doubt: what does it all mean?

In studying today's Gospel lesson, the paradigmatic story of an epiphany, the Markan witness of the transfiguration, I was struck by another subtlety in this well-known story. We are aware of the tradition of Elijah and Moses being the symbols of law and prophets. Here on the mount is Jesus, with them integrating legalism and prophetic word, as the King of Love. We are aware that Moses and Elijah appear; they were believed by the Jews to have been taken up to heaven alive, and were expected to return before the Messiah. We are aware that the voice of God from the bright cloud tells the disciples that Jesus is the Son, the fulfillment of the Old Testament expectation, the one over whom these same words were spoken at the baptism: "This my beloved Son…" We are further aware of Peter's need to stay on the mountaintop and stem the tide of time by building three booths to perpetuate the high moment. And finally, we are aware that following this epiphany of transfiguration, which was to be the apogee of Jesus' journey, he went down from the mountain to Jerusalem to die.

But there is a subtlety, which is at midpoint with each of the previous points, on which the whole story pivots, and is the reason why both Becker's fatalism and Updike's agnosticism finally pale. The title of the story is "The Transfiguration." The Greek word from which we derive "transfigure" is the word *metemorphothe*. Another way to title the story is "The Metamorphosis."

What child has not entered the world of love, hope, and expectation in the natural discovery of metamorphosis? Mine was the Chinese elm in front of our house at 122 North Jones, Drumright, Oklahoma. Then, the words were limited: caterpillar, cocoon, and butterfly. Now I know egg, larva, pupa, and monarch, all of which total a proclamation of the mysterious process of metamorphosis—transfiguration.

How can we concur with Becker's fatalism that we live only to die, or how can we live in Updike's agnosticism of doubt when we have seen the epiphany in a Chinese elm? I have no trouble with the transfiguration; I have seen it in a tree in Drumright, Oklahoma. I will not deny death. I have seen it with my own eyes, held it in my own hands, heard its last rattle, smelled its gasping foulness. But I have also seen the disappearing bulb break ground. I have seen the barren branch with knuckled bud luxuriate a lush blossom. The transfiguration reminds us once again of the hope of change and its natural nature. Who among us does not pray for a metamorphosis, a transfiguration? Not to eliminate the old, but to take the Moses(es) and the Elijah(s) of the old covenant with us and bring them into an integrated whole with who we are and what we are called to be and to become.

Today is Valentine's Day, a day to remember those we love and love those we remember. Hearing this day the story of the metamorphosis reminds us of who it is that is the King of Love. And it reminds us that we are in covenant and promise with him and others that this love bears all things, believes all things, hopes all things, endures all things.

Jesus is the Christ. Such a fact is a fact as a caterpillar is a monarch. The King. The King of Love. Let us this day proclaim that death is never an end; in death life is changed, not ended. And that change is a transfiguration, a metamorphosis. Not only is it a metamorphosis for the one dying, but for those who go through a death with another. Their life, too, is changed, opened up to new and incredibly wild possibilities. Jesus' death was a metamorphosis of the world. Shall we say, in the deepest sense of faith, thank God Jesus died.

One concluding unscientific postscript. Between birth and death, the Christ is present, changing hearts. Where? Where there is love. "God is love, and those who dwell in love dwell in God and he in them." E. E. Cummings writes: "Be of love a little more careful than of anything." Where there is another who delights in you, there is a quickening of the heart, and that heart is a symbol of the life-giving source of love. If you have been given a heart, you have been given love. Love is life-changing, it changes caterpillars into kings. And when measured, death has never won a victory over the power of love. I have seen it in Oklahoma elm trees, in Jerusalem crosses, in a mountaintop metamorphosis, and in the quickening of my own heart, beating like the wings of a butterfly at the presence of love.

Amen.

❖ ❖ ❖

February 28, 1988
Lent II
Genesis 22:1–14; Romans 8:31–39; Mark 8:31–38

We are all looking, searching, and journeying. From Abraham and Isaac, to Little Bo Peep, and including you and me, we are all looking for the lamb.

Today's Old Testament lesson is such a seminal story of searching and being found. The metaphor for search today, and one of the symbols of the subject of our search, is the lamb.

Abraham and Sarah had waited so long for their promise. In their old age, God gave them their covenantal heir, Isaac. And then, the great God of surprise shocked his children by asking the proud father to sacrifice his long-awaited, only son. "And Abraham took the wood of the burnt offering, and laid it on Isaac his son; and he took in his hand the fire and the knife... And Isaac said to his father Abraham, 'My father!' And he said, 'Here am I, my son.' He said, 'Behold the fire and the wood; but where is the lamb...?'"

And so now another framing of the question. The universal question is a universal quest. Today, it is contained in the voice of a child, "Where is the lamb?" The human situation is one of a continuing search and journey seeking the elusive center of our life and the continuing shock that the search leads inevitably to the gate of death.

Jesus' message in today's Gospel is clear. "If any would come after me, let him deny himself and take up his cross...Whoever would save his life will lose it; and whoever loses his life for my sake and the good news will save it."

This Lenten message is the Lenten journey. In order to be found, we must seek; in order to find true life, we must enter some kind of death. In Lent, we make a conscious journey toward the cross...wondering, where is the lamb? Lent is an invitation to a journey, a strange and ironic journey; it is our voyage through life into the arms of death, into the deep, dark journey of the soul, the valley of the shadow.

All of life is a journey and all of our sacred literature is a journal, a commentary on the quest. Even so universal is the journey and so familiar the voice, that all of literature documents the pilgrim in pilgrimage: Homer's *Odyssey*, Dante's *Divine Comedy*, the legend of the Holy Grail, *The Lord of the Rings, Siddhartha.*

The three lessons today give us our one truth, which enables us to seek the truth come whence it will, cost what it may. That one truth is that the God who calls us into the search is the one for whom we search and our advocate as we search.

The Abraham-Isaac story is about at least three truths. One, God requires us to be willing to sacrifice all for a relationship. Two, that he will provide what is necessary. And three, in the end, he will give even himself in order that we might meet.

Paul promises us that as we search for that which will authenticate our lives, we can face any loss, because nothing will separate us from our source. Even if we must enter a spiritual or literal death, nothing separates us from the love of God. Though we must enter desert and valley with beast and shadow, we do so knowing that such tribulation, or disaster, or persecution, or famine, or nakedness, or peril, or sword—neither death, nor life, nor angels, nor principalities, nor things present, nor things to come, nor height, nor depth, nor anything else in creation—will be able to separate us from the love of God in Christ Jesus our Lord. We must be willing to sacrifice everything for the relationship. God will provide what is necessary, and in the end, will give of himself in order to meet us.

I have been asked to make a Lenten address in Florida in a few weeks. The rector has asked the Lenten speakers in his series to address the question: "What is the greatest danger facing the Church today?" As I have stewed over this question, I believe that the greatest threat to Christianity is apathy. For apathy is the opposite of love. It is that which in a benign, nonthreatening way disintegrates us. Apathy drains us of all of our creative energy and eventually begins to destroy us. Love is the energy force which moves us always forward in our quest to become whole humans. Apathy may be its opposite: no force in life. The hallmark of apathy is mediocrity. How can we ever be satisfied with the mediocrity of the known when we have such a clear call to seek the unknown? We are so satisfied to have the superficial comfort of safety when we must realize eventually that our only security is in the adventure toward the never before. The word "mediocre" means literally "halfway up the mountain." The great threat is to be satisfied to go halfway. The early Christians were called the people of the way—not the people of the halfway. They were willing to sacrifice anything in order to have a relationship with God. Those early Christians knew also that in an authentic relationship with another, they were dwelling in God and God in them. To go all the way means to risk losing everything to find the one thing. (In the Parable of the Lost Sheep, the lost sheep did not just get up and run off; he just slowly nibbled his way away, in one small, apathetic, mediocre munch after another.)

Risk is the reality. We live in a world where death, loss, and tragedy are the rules of our journey. There is no way we can avoid them, even if we camp halfway or refuse to move out of fear in an apathetic avoidance. The truth is that all of life depends on some death; each gain requires some loss. To be on this planet, there is no way to avoid such reality, even in the mediocrity of apathy. Yet death is not the only truth. Underneath these hard facts are mysterious gifts abiding and awaiting discovery for those who search. There is meaning and purpose, miracle and ecstasy. There is the deep but dazzling darkness of love. There is joy. The miracle of Christianity is precisely this: that in the face of tragedy, loss, exile, and death, there is new life; in spite of or within brokenness, there is the promise of wholeness.

This journey quest is no sentimental journey. It involves sacrifice, risk, and death, but only in order to open for us the gift of life, joy, and love.

So come now with the covenant of love and the promise of life. The lamb awaits us. Between here and there is a desert and a hard wood cross, but God will provide. Our freedom leaves us with a choice: we can build an apathetic camp and squat here in false security halfway, or we can wander on, going all the way.

For me, I will seek the Lamb, trusting that God will provide.

Amen.

❖ ❖ ❖

March 6, 1988
Lent III
Exodus 20:1–17; Romans 7:13–25

It is reported that Emily Dickinson, in a letter to a friend, wrote that "consider the lilies of the field" was the only commandment she never broke.

Today, as we walk through the three lessons, we can't help but reflect on the relationship between law and behavior. The Old Testament lesson is the giving of the Decalogue, the Ten Commandments. In Paul's epistle to the Romans, he confesses a war exists in him between the law of God and the personal desires in his own life. And in John's Gospel, we have Jesus in Jerusalem, in the temple. He has come to replace or fulfill the law, so he goes straight to the center of worship and legalism—the temple. There, he rewrites the law of sacrifice: he himself is the lamb, the ultimate sacrifice, which makes the old rules of sacrifice obsolete. He has changed the rules. He also turns the tables on the corruption and exploitation found in the legalism.

The law came into being in order to establish a relationship between us and God, and between one another. These principles for relatedness became rules, and the relationship then evolved between us and the rules rather than between God and us. The rules can become rulers.

Ruth Tiffany Barnhouse writes:

> Our religion is full of paradoxes. One which bears most pressingly on our
> morality is that Christians are urged to adhere to timeless principles ordained

> by God. But they are simultaneously urged to grow both personally and collectively, to "Sing a new song." The Bible is filled with admonitions to discard old and worn out childish habits in favor of a better way. Sometimes that better way is in direct violation of what was previously understood to be God's clear commandment. A famous example is Peter's dream, in which he is urged to eat of the animals hitherto forbidden as unclean...
>
> Few understand the fundamental difference between rules and principles. Principles are eternal and do not change. Rules do change, since they are only the cultural clothes worn by a principle to suit a particular time and place.

What Dr. Barnhouse is saying is important. Rules are essential for a society to function. But what is more important is to consider the underlying principles which create the rules. This was Jesus' message. "I have not come to do away with the law, but to fulfill it." The law is summarized in love. Jesus' new law is freeing, but like all freedom, it puts so much more responsibility on us. Love God and love your neighbor as yourself is a summary of the law.

But where are the rules? Paul expresses our anxiety. We have wants and needs that are sometimes in conflict with our principles. And we do the thing we hate and don't do the thing we want, and we don't understand our actions. At times, the principles of love are in conflict between what is best for me and what is best for another. Our choices sometimes are not simply between good and evil (given that choice, we would choose the good), but between two apparent goods or two evils. Sometimes we are caught in the anxiety of a greater good or a lesser evil. This is the human situation.

The summary of the law says that we should "Love God with all our heart, soul, and mind, and our neighbors as ourselves." Law is composed of rules of behavior, and yet the summary of the law does not mention rules. Jesus proclaimed that the absolute principle of behavior is love. St. Augustine knew and wrote that if we truly loved God with our whole being, it would be safe to do as we pleased, since we would not please to do anything which might disturb the harmony of God's divine plan for our species. This is true if we are able to love God perfectly, but we cannot. This is Paul's plaint? We are torn between self-gratification and growth and obedient call to God's will.

So herein is the human situation. Like most, I am better at framing the question than providing an answer. The best I can do is to remind us that we are in conflict always between the call to growth and change within eternal principles. And to realize that following rules, though important, may prove either impossible or the rules may become idols that keep us from growth and love. "I have obeyed all the rules from my youth, and yet I am unauthentic."

The good news is that all our actions, all of our thoughts, all of our considerations of the possibilities are ultimately redeemable. "Where sin abounds, grace abounds more." What God in Christ wants is for us to do the best we possibly can and live creatively within the tension of our call to grow in the principle of love. The admonition is that God just wants us to do the best we can, given the limit of our knowledge and the abundance of our freedom.

In order to do so, we must be as aware as possible and consider all the possibilities. How can we make good choices unless we know all the possibilities, and how can we know all the possibilities unless we are aware? When Jesus says that the greatest commandment of all is to love God and to love our neighbor, he is asking us to be as aware as we possibly can. We must act with the awareness of both the cost and promise of our decisions. Every decision is life-giving and death-dealing. The only decision that has resurrection is the one that is done with awareness. Such freedom, such responsibility; such grace and love.

About what Emily Dickinson wrote to her friend, we learn now what she means. Jesus taught that even considering the possibility of murder or adultery is committing the same in your heart. But we must consider the possibilities in order to choose. In the consideration of the possibility, we acknowledge consciously that we are capable of doing the very thing we hate. It is a mature person, says St. Paul, who can admit that he is capable of doing the thing he hates. The poet wrote that "consider the lilies of the field" was the only commandment she never broke. Perhaps, such awareness of such consideration is the essential confession, behavior, and hope of our religion.

Amen.

❊ ❊ ❊

March 27, 1988
Palm Sunday

Gustave Flaubert writes: "Human language is like a cracked kettle on which we beat out tunes for bears to dance to, when all the time we are longing to move the stars to pity."

This is the Sunday of the Passion: Palm Sunday. This day, we try to integrate the triumphal entry of the King of Kings and prepare for the week of Passion pointing to the cross. Flaubert is correct. What human language can express the historical story which is a primordial, archetypal, and universal story that transcends history and is a story of this moment and every moment? Our language is like a cracked kettle on which we beat out tunes that are never adequate to the event, moment, or message.

Some years ago I wrote a poem for a Good Friday meditation. David Ashley White has put that poem to music, and our Cathedral choir will debut the piece today as our anthem.

I have never respected a poet who would write a poem and explain it. The poem speaks for itself and has a life of its own that grows out of the poet, but outgrows the writer. The poem, though, helped me express the frustration of trying to put mystery into human language. This is Flaubert's frustration. And mine.

Telling the Passion story is like trying to ring a broken pail. Someone has to tell the story, the greatest story ever told, but no sermon, meditation, poem, or composition can capture the depth and breadth of the event and its innumerable implications. For each of the events of this Holy Week—the triumphal entry, the cleansing of the temple, the Maundy Thursday, the tears and blood of the Garden of Gethsemane, the inevitable Good Friday cross—each of those are tributaries to the one, rushing, inevitable river of destiny. God is never malicious in his mystery, just subtle. And each event is a subtle increment of Passion.

So how and by whom will the truth be told? The human ego always wants to deny threatening unpleasantries. And Jesus' death is not something that our consciousness wants to comprehend, even if it could. For there are three threads which make a knot that we can never untie, and that knot sits as a lump in our throat that we cannot express. When we tell the story once again—not just for those who haven't heard, but for those who have heard and have never made the story their own—these three threads are so threatening as to be like gossamers beyond our conscious ground. If we grab hold of them, then we must own them as our own. The threefold truth is that Jesus truly died as any human has or will. Additionally, we are responsible for his death as surely as the Jewish Sanhedrin or Roman procurator. And further, the cross, like a wooden pale, is planted in our own history and awaits us as our own personal death.

These existential realities are more than can be told or heard. Human language is beaten out on broken pails, but even so, the truth rings out: death is the ultimate reality.

I believe—yea, even know—at some level of unconscious depth, that we must integrate our death message as that which enlivens us. The Passion Week narrative is a truth, but it is a sanguine truth. Sanguine means blood colored. One who is of a sanguine personality has a humor of clear optimism, hope, and is passionate.

Here is our irony: truth and hope. The blood of Christ must make us passionate about life. Death's reality is the boundary which is a sanguine truth: his blood ought to make us live passionately. He and we are like the thorn bird, born to be impaled upon a thorn and sing a song beyond pain. And the song was in the egg before the bird was born, and the bird lives to sing the singular song that comes only through the pain of the thorn.

The vain despair is not in the death, but in the thought that one would die, having never lived. That's truth's despair. Jesus' death dignifies our own death, but more so, dignifies our life. We tell the story once again, not in order to be voyeurs of violence, but to see if this year someone will hear and begin to live. This death story is told in order that we won't wait another Lent before we begin to live.

Someone here this day is going to hear for the first time the message of truth's despair: that we were born to live as well as die. That we believe in life after birth. Even God in Christ dies, but through him we live, now. Will we wait another Lent before we choose to live? This Passion Sunday will, for some, mark a covenantal beginning to life through this passionate death.

The sanguine Christians are the ones who call the death day, Good Friday. Yes, Christ died. Yes, our blindness and fear killed him. Yes, we, too, will meet our own pallid death. But from now on, we will live passionately and compassionately, humorously, hopefully, joyfully, because this blood serves no purpose but to enliven us.

Human language is a broken pail, but by retelling the story, some will begin to dance, and the stars will be moved to pity.

This year, we begin our lives by telling the truth and then doing the truth. By telling the truth about death, and then beginning to live. It is, after all, a matter of life and death.

> Retell the story once again
>   not for those who did not hear,
>   but for those who never knew.
> How the silent hand grasped the nail
>   and fell across the tree.
> How the Eden vine was cut
>   and tore the tattered veil.
> How upon the Holy Grail
>   the wine was shed by drops.
> Pause beneath the wounded wing
>   and ring the broken pail.
>
> Who will thorn the bird
>   and scream the song as sung?
> Where's the warming fire this night
>   to burn denial's tongue?
> Grow the rose once more
>   and pull its petals bare.
> Climb up on the singletree
>   and tell of truth's despair.

Amen.

❊ ❊ ❊

April 1, 1988
Good Friday

Mary Anne Weaver, in the March 21 issue of *The New Yorker*, as "A Reporter At Large" writes of the horrendous civil strife in the obscure "lush teardrop of an island off the tip of India" called Sri Lanka.

In a line easily lost from that article, she quotes a Christian missionary named Brother Hillary. He speaks of the horror and devastation going on in that place:

> "Thirty soldiers went on a six-hour rampage, and a hundred and fifty Tamil civilians were killed. At Talari Junction, the soldiers stopped a government transport bus. The driver was a Muslim, the conductor a Sinhalese. The conductor told the soldiers, 'If you're going to shoot the passengers, shoot me first.' They shot him, then they shot thirty passengers. The wife of a village teacher in Parapangandal was breastfeeding her baby when the soldiers came. They killed her and, in a display of marksmanship, shot off the baby's toes. 'It took three days just to transport the bodies,' Brother Hillary said. 'There is no longer any petrol, no longer any movement. Life is dying here.'"

"Life is dying here." An obscure line from an unknown Brother in a little-known place sums up our Good Friday focus. Why the death? A question sung by Eve from east of Eden, a quick refrain heard from Abel beneath Cain's wrath when the voice of his brother's blood cried to him from the ground. Why to die?

And here we are, embarrassed by death and its ever-darkening cloud of threat, yet called to awareness by this Good Friday that:

> April is the cruelest month, breeding
> Lilacs out of the dead land, mixing
> Memory and desire, stirring
> Dull roots…
>
> What are the roots that clutch, what branches grow
> Out of this stony rubbish? Son of man,
> You cannot say, or guess, for you know only
> A heap of broken images, where the sun beats,
> And the dead tree gives no shelter…
>
> —T. S. Eliot, "The Waste Land"

The Church calls you this day to a new awareness that death's question is answered only by death. The horror of life must be faced and held in the forefront of our consciousness like a cross seared and sealed on our foreheads. For we cannot live without a reconciled death. And this day is the one day when life gains a devastating victory over death by becoming its opposite. Life is dying here. Today we enter that which we fear the most.

Here and now we enter the price of the paradox. God and human, life and death, heaven and earth, subject and object, mystery and reality, good and evil; all are held in contradiction. And the price of the contradiction is agony. Rent in twain, torn in two, we now must learn again that rebirth comes not after death but within it.

Born, from dying in a womb, nature teaches us of its rule that our daylight does not follow the dark, but emerges from within the dark. Our second birth does not follow our first death, but the new creation emerges from the drowning waters. Death is life's requirement. Our life is that which emerges from many deaths, each a tributary to the flow of life. Perhaps death's only virtue is its necessity, but so it is that always and everywhere life is dying here.

The Christian vision is a revelation. The God of creation answers the greatest human questions by becoming the answer. Jesus Christ is the creator's response to the questions of creation:

Where did we come from? Born of a woman, inspired by God is the Christ-answer.

Who are we? Children of God is the Christ-answer.

Why are we here? To live through our deaths and love with our lives is the Christ-answer.

Where are we going? On to the ecstasy through the agony comes the Christ-answer.

This Good Friday is the reconciliation of our contradictions. Today, we are restored in our freedom to a new life without fear of failures. We are free to fall, free to die, free to live. The image of God, blown into us at creation, is restored in Christ. Behold, there is a new creation, and the Kingdom of God is restored on earth as a possibility. It is now possible to live within the horror and the agony, because out of such, the ecstatic peace will emerge. "When" is only a possibility; "whether" is a promise.

After a recent lecture on healing, a young physician asked, "Where is the hope of wellness to one for whom, medically speaking, there is no hope?" My only answer came from my Good Friday theology. For some, maybe dying is the only way to get well. Jesus had to die. His death answered the question of why we die. Wellness emerges out of sickness; and new life out of death.

What a power we are given when the power of death is removed. We can only live when death's power is removed. The most powerful person in the world is the one from whom earthly powers can take nothing. The greatest powers of religious piety and Roman law tried to eliminate Jesus' life by removing it. And out of that death the power emerged.

Can the point be any clearer? We have nothing to fear. Our conversion experience is in converting our fear of death into power for living. Why are we so afraid to live? The killer has been killed. The victim holds the victory. If we refuse to live for fear of death, then death is our life. That which we fear the most is what we become. The death instrument, the cross, is our central symbol of Christian life. The death we fear has given us the life we crave. What powerful people Christians can be and become. We fear nothing. There is nothing that the world can take from us. We stand bold, steadfast, and unafraid in the presence of all the agony, for we know that even in the midst of it, and indeed at its end, is the ecstasy and the peace that passeth in all understanding. Can it be any clearer that we have nothing to fear?

"Life is dying here." We say, "Yes, we know." Evolution requires that awareness. But we are not satisfied to be slaves to reality, for we are in covenant with mystery. Mystery is reason driven beyond death's fact into the truth. Objectively, it is the miracle of life emerging from death; subjectively, it is ecstasy emerging from the agony.

Who, then, here today will be converted? Who here today will receive the power of life this death can give? Who here today will be reconciled to death's virtue? Who here today will begin for the first time to live? Whoever will do so will be born again, and live for the first time.

Eternity is now. It is not endless time or the opposite of time, but the essence of time. Today we have seen the essential human message. Life and death are not opposites, but in Christ are one. We are now in eternity, and nothing can take that away from us or us away from that dazzling dark mystery. We are a people of power, for the power of death has been removed. We are free—free to live, free to die. Nothing can be taken from us; therefore, we now hold everything.

Amen.

❖ ❖ ❖

April 2, 1988
Easter Even
Matthew 28:1–10

There is a curious Latin word that has worked its way into the vocabulary of psychology that properly belongs in the theological vocabulary of a resurrectional theology. The Latin word is *limen*. The word means "doorway" or "threshold." Entering a room or leaving it, one crosses a limen, and while there, in this borderline space, one is in liminality, if for only a heart's beat. Liminality is that gray line between consciousness and unconsciousness, between awareness and unawareness. The term "subliminal" refers to territory below the threshold of conscious awareness.

The Easter vigil is a symbolic and sacramental drama, whereby we open ourselves to allow Christ's resurrection to emerge from its subliminal influence through the threshold of awareness and become a conscious transformation of our very soul.

So here we are in the liminality, crossing barriers and boundaries; we are moving from darkness into light, traveling from silence into sound, going from death into life. The liminal threshold makes us dizzy with sight, sound, and life's quickening. Standing in the amber threshold of the wild possibilities that the dark and silence have kept from us in the wordless fear, we now feel the giddy gift of hope and promise, all shouted in the "He is risen" of our liturgy and "We are risen" of our experience.

The resurrection is something we know where deep down things grow. New life, doorways, windows, sunrises, tulips, and butterflies are all harbingers of the incredible, undeniable hope. Through God in Christ, and once a year in Christian liturgy, we become aware of the reality that no death is stronger than any love and every boundary and barrier is transcended, even our own dark doubt about our own future.

The liminality between dark and light is our Easter's golden glow announcing that Jesus' resurrection brings new life now. We are moving with every heartbeat and breath drawn toward that new light that moves us to embrace all the darkness for just this evening's glimpse of the risen sun. The subliminal hope is made known. The bright wings of the angel sit atop the rolling stone and reflect all our promises and proclaim them to be possible—yea, even predictable—for our time is come.

Worth is a human desire. Are we worthy? And, we wonder in the dark silence, is all the agony worthwhile? Here, in the total presence of an empty tomb, we know, even if it is a fleeting liminal knowledge, that all the dark agony of our human journey is worthwhile for just this glimpse of the emerging ecstasy of the never before in the just now.

These baptisms are the watering of the unconquerable souls of these human beings. We are making them Easter people. The subliminal hope is brought to awareness and can never be eliminated by life's dark doubt or death's shallow grave.

I proclaim in the name of God, and for the communion of Easter people, that all manner of things shall be well. Come now, knowing that through the threshold of new awareness, nothing we now know is worthy to be compared with the glory which is revealed. Let this evening of story, song, symbol, and sacrament be the once-and-for-all happening which will be the turning point of your journey through all your barriers and boundaries into the fullness of life. Let this Easter be your Easter. Allow this water to quench your dry doubt. Invite this Eucharist to quicken your heart and enter into the presence of a living Christ, and allow that presence to enter you.

Take this Easter with you, and when darkness and silence surround you again, recall the story, song, symbol, and sacrament, and move through the liminality into the awareness that all the agony will disappear in the ecstatic completion of the resurrection which is the essence of time and therefore available to you at any time.

The time has come and now is and will be forever. He is risen, and so are we.

Amen.

April 10, 1988
John 20:19–31

"The Gospels do not explain the resurrection; the resurrection explains the Gospels." So writes John S. Whale. The miracle of the resurrection lies not in the fact that a dead body was raised from the dead. The creator who fashioned the infinite complexity and magnificence of the cosmos and the cell certainly must hold such obvious creativity. The true miracle for those of us who are left here to interpret is the resurrection "in life" that Jesus' post-grave appearance brought to his disciples.

John writes of the dead in this life in the opening lines of today's Gospel. He describes a tomb in which the disciples have shut themselves: a room, dark and sealed, created out of fear and doubt. "On the evening of that day, the first day of the week…" Here John relates a wonderful contradiction of possibility. It is dark, and yet it is the first day. Will the living dead remain shut up in their fear and doubt of darkness, or will they consider this the first day? "On the evening of that day, the first day of the week, the doors being shut for fear of the Jews…" Shut doors, fashioned from fear. Of course, the disciples were afraid. Their fear of the Jews had an exterior reality. They had withdrawn from the threat to their own lives because they were followers of this blasphemous, messianic megalomaniac. But their fear had even more so an interior darkness which they had projected onto the Jews. Their agoraphobic fright had its true origin in their own mistrust of themselves. These, huddled together in fear, were the men of denial and betrayal. They were the ones who had slept through the garden of bloody sweat and at the Crucifixion had flown like pointed quail. Their dark fear had entombed them in the stench of their own guilt and insecurity.

The miracle of the resurrection is not only in Jesus being raised, but in how Jesus' appearance brought his friends back to life. The Gospel does not bother to explain the resurrection, for its "good news" is held in how the resurrection explains the Gospel.

When Jesus appeared to the disciples on the evening of that first day, he did not come with retribution, but with reconciliation. He did not shame those who had abandoned him. When he entered their tomb-like room, he did not say how disappointed he was in them. When he revealed himself, as in new existence, he did not enumerate their past sins or failures, but he said: "Shalom" (peace). For fearful, unworthy, and empty souls, there is no greater healing sound than for the victim to appear, well, breathing peace.

The ones to whom he returned were the ones who had failed him. For the point turns on this critical crises, that the Crucifixion occurred to end death before life as well as after the grave. What Jesus offers is reconciliation, not retribution. This is a great phylum in the evolutionary consciousness of religion. The reconciling love, this undying love which holds no condition, is our resurrectional theology.

Jesus' entire teaching had centered on the unconditional, reconciling, undying love of God. His parables were centered on the ironic surprise of God's acceptance of inadequate humanity. The new understanding is that God is an advocate, not an adversary. Jesus taught about the reconciling God; all of his parables were centered on this surprising, new understanding of God. Then, indeed, Christ became a parable. His death reconciles us to God. He became what he taught. His appearance brought a power and enthusiasm to his followers that has not yet ended. And in experiencing the story today, the peace reappears and the power is present once again.

"Jesus came and stood among them and said to them, 'Peace be with you.' When he had said this, he showed them his hands and his side. Then the disciples were glad when they saw the Lord. Jesus said to them again, 'Peace be with you. As the Father has sent me, even so I send you.' And when he had said this, he breathed on them, and said to them, 'Receive the Holy Spirit. If you forgive the sins of any, they are forgiven. If you retain the sins of any, they are retained.'"

Here, now, the empowerment. The forgiven must forgive. The blessed must bless. The role of the forgiven is not to lord it over the imperfect, but to offer peace to those in conflict. The role of the disciple who is sent is to bring not perfection, but completion. Jesus showed them his scarred body. A scar is a mark of healing. A wound is a mark of injury; a scar is a sign of healing. The scar is the sign of Christianity; it is the cross. The scar is the symbol of Christianity, not smooth perfection, but real completion. We are empowered to enter wounds and bring healing. That is the service of the sacred, scarred community of Christ. We have been empowered to forgive, bless, and make peace. We are to be peacemakers.

Finally, then, this reconciling resurrection must be encountered personally. Alan Jones writes:

> One of our problems is that very few of us have developed any distinctive personal life. Everything about us seems secondhand, even our emotions. In many cases we have to rely on secondhand information in order to function. I accept the word of a physician, a scientist, a farmer, on trust. I do not like this. I have to because they possess vital knowledge of living of which I am ignorant. Secondhand information concerning the state of my kidneys, the effects of cholesterol, and the raising of chickens, I can live with. But when it comes to questions of meaning, purpose, and death, secondhand information will not do. I cannot survive on a secondhand faith in a secondhand God. There has to be a personal word, a unique confrontation, if I am to come alive.

Here, then, is Thomas. He speaks for us all and is the point from which Alan Jones draws his conclusion. Thomas needed a personal encounter with the scarred, risen one in order to come alive. And he did. But where does that leave us, in generations after Christ has ascended? Recall Jesus' words: "As the Father has sent me, even so I send you." We must become Christ for one another. The incarnation and resurrection are about us and our relations with one another.

That room is like any room where any dwell who need the new life that only love can bring. Each of us waits for someone to walk into our lives and bring the miraculous good news that we are accepted without condition. And each of us has waited or is waiting for this unbelievable good news. But who among us will walk into another's room? Who among us will represent Christ to another? Who among us will bear his or her scars in the presence of another and breathe the peace of God? Christ has sent us to do that very thing. We are the wounded healers. We have experienced the wound and bear the scar, the sign of healing. We have been inspired and empowered to move out and walk into the dark places, not as Christ, but representing his healing love.

The Gospel does not need to explain the resurrection, for the resurrection explains the Gospel. When we love another without condition, without judgment, without expectation of perfection, that is the perfect love which casts out fear. Let us not remain here huddled in fear, for we have inhaled Christ's peace, and even as the Father sent him, so, too, he has sent us. Who knows where that sending will lead? All we know is that when we take on the responsibility of having been blessed and become a blessing for another, having been given peace and become peacemakers for others, having been forgiven and forgive others, then something of new life happens, and the resurrection explains the good news. All we know is that when we are bold enough to represent that new life for another, it will bring the quickening of new life to someone who has waited his or her entire life for us to come. Somewhere today, someone is waiting. So what are we waiting for?

Amen.

❖ ❖ ❖

April 17, 1988
Luke 24:36–48

We know about those who hold the weak symbols, praying that they will make us strong. The disciples then and now walk toward a future of uncertainty, holding death and life in unbalanced scales across weary shoulders. On the one side, the pain and cost of walking on pulls us into the dark abyss of doubt about the future. We have enough experience with death to know the costs of life. Every breath of new life has emerged out of some loss or brokenness that scars our memory, leaving an image of an imperfect past and uncertain future. The only certainty being that more brokenness and loss is as predictable as the return of hunger and exhaustion even after eating and sleeping.

On the other side, we have such a will to live, to grow, and to become what we imagine, that we walk on toward the dark, even for a glimpse of a new light. We move on because we know where deep down things grow that our life is not complete and that which will complete us is worth every conflict, contradiction, and loss, for there are fruits we have not tasted and feelings we have yet to know, and truth that knows no opposite, and life's joy that erases all doubt and cost.

So, we walk on, caught between scissors of life and death, like the two on the road to Emmaus who walked burdened with the unbearable weight of death and at the same time called on by the infallible hope of joy which awaits those who journey on the path of promise.

Of all my possessions—be they material, spiritual, or relational—the only one I pray I never lose is hope. For without hope, no thing, person, or dream will ever become what it was created to be. Beneath the burden of reality and its tearing conflict, if I ever relinquish hope, then the promise will die as if it never lived, and if the promise dies, all my life will account for no more than the empty and absurd exercise of preparing for nothing.

When Jesus appears after his death, his presence is the reaffirmation of hope and the once-and-for-all exclamation that all that is dreaded holds worth and all that is promised will come to those who journey on.

He spoke with them, and ate with them, and "he was known to them in the breaking of the bread." Out of the brokenness of their very human need, he appeared. "And they rose… and returned to Jerusalem and found the eleven gathered together and those who were with them who said, 'The Lord has risen indeed and has appeared to Simon!' Then they told what had happened on the road and how he was known to them in the breaking of bread."

> And then he appeared and stood among them and he said to them, "Why are you troubled and why do questions arise in your hearts? See my hands and feet, that it is I myself; handle me and see; for a spirit has not flesh and bones…" And while they disbelieved for joy and wondered, he said to them, "Have you anything to eat?" They gave him a piece of broiled fish, and he took it and ate before them.
>
> Then he said to them, "These are my words which I spoke to you, while I was still with you, that everything written about me…must be fulfilled." Then he opened their minds to understand the scriptures, and said to them, "Thus it is written, that the Christ should suffer and on the third day rise from the dead, and that repentance and forgiveness of sins should be preached in his name to all nations, beginning from Jerusalem. You are witnesses of these things."

When you are in the presence of one you love, you have very little, if any, sense of the passage of time or the boundaries of space. And, the opposite is true in the absence of love:

all you can consider is time and spatial limits. So it must have been for the disciples, and so holds the possibility for those who live in the presence of Christ and his promise that all will be forgiven and all will be given.

There is a wonderful saying that "to understand all things is to forgive all things." One of the things that Jesus did for the disciples was to open their minds to understand that all the conflict and death is necessary to the worth of the peace and quickening of the complete life. To understand all things is to forgive all things. Jesus opened their minds in order that they might understand, and then he said go and forgive! Understanding is so important to human relatedness—the awareness of who you are, who I am in Christ, and then to forgive, which is the act of giving. Such presence of love and such awareness of truth bring us the comfort of a holy hope that in spite of the pain, all things will be well. He showed them his hands and feet and said, "Specters don't have scars, people do." And the scars are the prints of experience which are healed by love and the pattern of wholeness in a life's tapestry. The scars are the proof that the person has journeyed, and they are the prints of a healing touch.

Christ's appearance revived hope. Hope is the breath of the spirit which keeps us moving when our mind is too aware of time and space and their limits. Hope is the transcendent spirit that knows more than knowledge and understands all things. When all possessions leave and disappear in the anxiety of doubt, hope is the last to leave. If hope leaves, then all we have left is nothingness.

In Christ, hope appears. And, in Christ, hope is not an apparition, but holds scars and opens understanding. I don't know if I would travel on under the unbalanced weight of life and death if it weren't for hope. And I don't know if I would have hope if it weren't for the promise as revealed in Christ

But I don't live on what I don't know. What I do know is that I have hope. A scarred hope, indeed, but with the knowledge that even God is scarred and reappears with a promise. "We know that all things work together for good to those who love God and are called according to his purpose."

The disciples walked on down the dusty roads and proclaimed that, in the essence of time, all things will be well. And we are heirs of that promise. So we, too, walk on, in faith and hope, and even now feel a quickening in our step.

Amen.

May 1, 1988
John 14:15–21

Jesus says, "If you love me…" The small word "if" is a large condition. The conditional "if," though, runs one way. Jesus promises an unconditional love. We are the conditional ones. This is the human condition: our inability to love without condition.

These Gospel words from Jesus, as recorded by John, are both the summary and statement of new law: obedience and love, and, at the same time, the promise of the Paraclete—the counselor, comforter, advocate, helper—the Holy Spirit. One of the things that we must hear when we hear the words of Jesus is that it is not like the words of the conditional love of the parent: "If you loved me, you would do what I say." Rather, it is the statement of the fulfillment of what is required by saying simply, "If you love me, you will have fulfilled my commandments." The only thing that Christ asks of us is to be related to him through love. "If you love me, you will follow my commandments." It is not the conditional love that we parents visit upon our children, or that we children have had visited upon us by our parents.

Jesus said to his disciples, "If you love me, you will keep my commandments." He says so, because his only commandments were to love. Love God with heart, soul, and mind, also neighbor and self. These are his commandments. But he doesn't leave us then alone, in that sort of desolation—that inability to love without condition on the human level. He goes on to say, "And I will pray the Father, and he will give you another Counselor, to be with you for ever, even the Spirit of truth, whom the world cannot receive, because it neither sees him nor knows him; you know him, for he dwells with you, and will be in you. I will not leave you desolate; I will come to you…because I live, you will live also." When I come to you as Spirit within, you will know that I am in my Father, and you are in me, and I am in you…

To love another human being is to know all the complexity of being human. It is to know both the quickening of the heart and the dread of loss. It is to know the fulfillment and the disappointment. It is to know the mystery and the dust.

And yet, we have a promise that in loving we will meet the Paraclete: God Incarnate within our own spirit. That if we will risk and if we will love, that we will receive love—for it is in giving love that we receive. If human beings attempt to do their best in loving one another, then there will be an element that transcends the two—which is a whole that is greater than the sum of the two parts. It will be the spirit of God dwelling in the midst of that; it will ultimately wipe out all conditions.

In Rollo May's work, *The Courage to Create*, he relates a story of discovery about the conditions of human love. As a graduate student doing research on a book which came to be called *The Meaning of Anxiety*, he interviewed two control groups: one of abused, abandoned teenagers; another of middle-class teens who had families and homes.

May's goal was to validate a hypothesis on anxiety generally accepted by psychology and psychoanalysis: that anxiety was in direct proportion to the degree in which a child had been rejected by his or her mother.

One of the women, named Helen, came from a family of twelve children; their mother, on the first day of summer, kicked all the children out of the house to go live with their father, a caretaker of a barge on the Hudson River. Helen was pregnant by her father, who had served time for rape. Like so many in her predicament, Helen would say to Rollo May, "We have our troubles, but we don't worry."

May was perplexed by what he found, until one day at an entrance to a subway in New York, the answer hit him "out of the blue." The young women with low anxiety, despite severe rejection, were all from the situation where the mothers rejected their children but "made no bones about doing so." There was no pretense of not rejecting them, and the children were aware of their rejection. Knowing this, they didn't expect what they wouldn't receive.

It was the middle-class young of the group who exhibited higher anxiety because they were lied to in their families about rejection. The words didn't quite fit the music. They were rejected by parents who "pretended they loved them, but actually did not."

May revised the theory by saying it was not maternal rejection in itself which caused the core of anxiety, but mixed messages of the mother who lied about her love, or set large conditions. May wrote: "Anxiety issued from not being able to know the world one was in, and therefore not being able to orient oneself in his or her own existence." It was a question of expectation. I do not mean to laud overt rejection or to scold unconscious mixed messages of sophisticated middle-class parents. It is to say that *every* aspect of human love has its own dark side—parental, spousal—any kind of love in which humans are involved will always have its dark side of rejection. Rejection is what we fear the most. St. Paul says, "I become that which I fear the most." This is the reality of all human love. Perhaps we should be more honest and say that rejection is a part of the process of love.

Jesus says, "I will not leave you desolate in your human love and your inability to love." Human love—that is, authentic love between human beings—is only authentic when the lovers accept God's unconditional love for each. Only then can they both love.

We see this pattern of darkness that rolls into a relationship even in nature. After a few days away this week near the lighthouse in Port Aransas, we went to the mainland to run on Friday. After a good hour's exercise, we sat to relax. The rumor came across the shoreline on boats from the Coast Guard radio that a squall was on its way, predicting winds up to fifty-five miles an hour, so we scurried back to the place where we were staying, a house on stilts by an old lighthouse. Sure enough, off the coastline rolled in the darkest squall clouds you've ever seen. A great sound-and-light show, ominous and black, unavoidably rolling in, and there came a feeling of high anxiety as the wind began to blow. As predicted, the wind did blow fifty to fifty-five miles an hour. Everything that was conditional was blown away. In the midst of this high anxiety of the dark side of nature, there was a sense that everything is temporary, and that each of us, in our own temporal side, longs for something eternal—some clear message—and if not the message, a symbol of promise and hope, because even in the respite, there rolls in the darkness. As soon as the squall had cleared our place, there came, as there always does as a result of the storm, an incredible calm, where the colors are greater than before, and so, the sounds. The gulls, reflecting this new bright sunlight, were like fireflies on the horizon. The water, even the brown water of that bay, seemed blue. And the sounds of the birds, and even the hush that came, were like the onomatopoetic breath of God. And then there appeared on the horizon—in a great panorama of promise—a giant double rainbow.

The storm and the rainbow are the realities of human relatedness. The storm comes with its dark, rolling clouds, as surely as we draw our own breath. But even in the midst of the storm, there are those of us who know—who have read, heard, and experienced that a bow has been set in the sky as a symbol of promise and hope. Jesus says today, "I will not leave you desolate." The Paraclete will come and be present in the midst of the storm.

I fear that my love for you will always be incomplete. I am incapable of loving without condition. And so I fear that my love will be imperfect. And yet, I have been given the promise and the hope that perfect love will cast out all fear. For we have been loved without condition. We can love as we are first loved. We have been given that hope and promise that God will never again abandon us. Our high anxiety emanates from our fear of loss, a disappointment, and rejection by another. If we accept the love of God and then reciprocate, we will have what we seek and can enjoy loving one another as we are first loved. Our love will always be imperfect, but perfect love casts out fear. It is the love we have been given by the completed one.

And so we are free now to love one another and experience all the complexity and simplicity, mysterious and mundane, joyful and sorrowful, the storm and the calm; to take a risk, continue a commitment. It will be well, for Christ proclaims: "I will not leave you desolate; I will come to you"—for God is love, and those who dwell in love dwell in God, and God in them.

Amen.

August 28, 1988
Mark 7:1–8, 14–15, 21–23

The late Urban T. Holmes tells a story common to many of us religious leaders. Following one of his sermons, Dean Holmes stood at the door with the familiar ritual greetings and handshakes. Following a litany of "Nice sermon, Father," a small, stormy lady scurried up to him. Looking straight at him, she announced without the slightest flinch, "If our Lord were around today and heard all of these new-fangled abominations in our Prayer Book, he would roll over in his grave!"

Jesus was confronted by the Pharisees and scribes. Some of his disciples did not observe the cleansing rituals of washing hands and vessels before they ate. The religious leaders asked him, "Why do your disciples not live according to the tradition of the elders, but eat with hands defiled?" And Jesus answered, "Well did Isaiah prophesy of you hypocrites, as it is written, 'This people honors me with their lips, but their heart is far from me; in vain do they worship me, teaching as doctrines the precepts of men.' You leave the commandment of God and hold fast the tradition of men."

Though I have often quoted the aphorism, "Tradition is the living faith of the dead, and traditionalism is the dead faith of the living," the issue hidden in Jesus' point is not to criticize tradition so much as to point out how such externalized religion leads to moral inferiority. I must quickly add, though, that the only threat greater to the Church than moral inferiority is moral superiority.

For one of the greatest theological errors is a misunderstanding of the central focus of Christianity. The center of Christianity is not the moral law, but the gospel. The good news is God in Christ has done for us what we cannot do for ourselves. The grace under which we exist allows us the freedom to search for our own inner moral vision in tension with the external moral law. Jesus' teaching about such came in his Sermon on the Mount, whereby he pointedly revealed what we each experience: that even though our outward lives may be moral, each of our motivations is mixed. Our hands and feet may be in the temple, but where are our hearts and minds? The opposite also holds true, wherein our behavior may not conform to the rules of our religion, and yet we may be obedient to a call greater than custom and conformity.

The moral inferiority comes when we presume that following laws and traditions gives us moral superiority. The truth remains that, even though our outward lives may appear to be in moral order, our interior life has its own blessed rage for order, and the tension between the two leaves most of us in a quiet desperation of unconscious disorder.

Jesus summarized all the law in his great commandment: love God and your neighbor as yourself. And, my experience is that even when I can differentiate these three loves, I don't have the skill to juggle them in symmetrical patterns, but at best keep only one or two in the air at any time.

Such confessional candor is not popular today, particularly from religious leaders. All about us today, we hear people lamenting the decline of morality in our time, old standards are being abandoned, behavior that once would have brought universal censure—even possible persecution—now goes unnoticed. Families are threatened; sexual behavior has undergone a revolution; deceit abounds in business; corruption flourishes in politics. Wherever you look, moral behavior seems to be deteriorating. This, of course, could have been said by the Pharisees in the first century.

At such a time, people look to the Church to assert moral leadership. Even people who are not themselves believers seem to expect the Church to safeguard the morals of society. To this expectation, Earl Brill, in his book *The Christian Moral Vision*, writes:

> The difficulty with this view is that people not only want the church to speak out, but most of them seem to have a very clear idea of what the church ought to say. Most people simply want the church to affirm or support their own moral position over against those other people who think and behave differently.
>
> Genuine moral leadership will visit that sort of demand. Rather than saying what is expected of it, a responsible church will explore its own moral resources and bring them to bear upon contemporary issues. If the church does this faithfully, the results may be quite different from what everyone expects…
>
> You may criticize this open-ended approach on the ground that it can be used by irresponsible people to justify nearly any kind of behavior. That is true, of course, but it is a risk we have to take. People who really want to do the wrong thing will do it without any help…people looking for convenient rationalizations can always find them. A faith grounded in a vision of human freedom and responsibility before God will always incur the risk of being misused.
>
> We are concerned primarily with our own behavior, not that of other people. Our question is: "What shall I do?" not what should another person do. The distinction is important because it is the difference between morality and moralism, which is the besetting sin of religious people.

This, then, is the point I believe Jesus is making. To take a position of moral superiority is to be seduced by one's own moral inferiority. He says, "You are hypocrites when you honor me with your lips and dishonor me by judging me and my friends about whether we wash our bowls before we eat."

Jesus told us that only God can ultimately love us and ultimately judge us. We are further told that, in fact, he judges us because he loves us. He has chosen to share with us his function of loving. We are called to love one another as he has loved us. But, he has reserved for himself the function of judging, possibly because he knows how much we love it and how poorly we manage to do it. Thus, along with the gospel of love, Jesus teaches: "Judge not, that you not be judged."

Of course we need moral standards by which we can learn from the experience of our mothers and fathers and have guidelines for civilized behavior. But, we must remember that the external law has evolved in order to recognize our freedom and responsibility as twins sustained by a system of love. We must be accountable both externally and internally, and when we cannot account for both, we thank God for grace and forgiveness.

Once again, the irony is that moralism is moral superiorly which masks morality and reveals moral inferiority.

Like the lady said, if Jesus could see the self-righteous, hypocritical judgment visited on people in his name, he would roll over in his grave.

For such judgment by one of his brothers or sisters for another of his Father's children would mean his life was in vain.

Amen.

❖ ❖ ❖

September 11, 1988
Mark 8:27–38

For a stretch of time, I have been enamored with a sententious saying about life's core decisions. I have used this pithy formula enough that many presume it originated with me. Let me assure you that, in preaching, the only thing original is sin. The aphorism is a challenge to conviction and asserts: "There are a thousand ways to say 'no,' one way to say 'yes,' and no way to say anything else."

I am struck this morning with wonderment about my life's turning points that have had as a hinge the times when I have said "no" by any other word and the times I have said "yes" with no other condition.

Today we hear rehearsed the fulcrum on which the entire Gospel of Mark balances. "And Jesus went on with his disciples, to the villages of Caesarea Philippi; and on the way he asked his disciples, 'Who do men say that I am?' And they told him, 'John the Baptist; and others say, Elijah; and others one of the prophets.' And he asked them, 'But who do you say that I am?' Peter answered him, 'You are the Christ.'"

Peter's confession was the world's first awareness and affirmation about who Jesus was and is. Peter's spontaneous word was the world's first "yes" to God's offer of unconditional love.

Many are wont to call this Petrine confession a conversion. And in many respects, it was. Peter was not converted to Christianity, but to God's love in Christ. Peter was not converted to purity or perfection. For in the next verses, after Jesus told them that this grace would come through suffering, rejection, and death, Peter rebuked Jesus. Jesus then rebuked Peter for speaking like Satan. Peter did not become perfect through his "yes" to Christ. For we know that when the suffering and death Jesus had predicted came to pass, Peter denied that he even knew who Jesus was. Peter's "yes" was a conversion to acceptance, forgiveness, and the grace that allows us to be human and loved at the same time.

In some way, Peter's confession was acceptance of his own acceptance. Paul Tillich writes: "The courage to be is the courage to accept oneself as accepted in spite of being unacceptable."

God made a covenant with Abraham. "I will be in relationship with you. I will be your God, and you will be my people." He further made a promise that, "This covenant would be eternal." The rainbow after the flood, the tears of God, is the sign of the eternal covenant. Jesus is the new covenant. This unconditional love is not only given in general, but capable of experience in particular, in person. When we say "yes" to Christ, we are saying yes to the scandal of unconditional love. It is scandalous, because it is unbelievable. For every human experience of affirmation is always attached by a string called "if." I will love you if; if you behave; if you perform; if you obey; if you are perfect, if you win. And the ultimate condition, "I will love you if you love me." We humans know little of unconditional love because, apart from God, we don't experience such undeserved favor.

"Who do you say that I am?" asked Jesus. "You are the unconditional lover," responded Peter. In so saying, Peter accepted Christ's unrestricted affection, affirmation, and acceptance. Forever after speaking evil and denying Christ, Christ's love remained, for Peter, the one who later said, "No, I don't know him," was the very one Jesus sent out to represent him. This love, this Christ, is some lover; he loves without condition. He keeps the covenant intact, just as promised.

When one says yes to the Christ, life does not become utopia. Suffering, pain, confusion, rejection, loss, and death remain. But if we accept our acceptance, these realities become irrelevant to the one sustaining word we need, for in Christ God has said "yes" to us. "And we know that all things work together for good for those who love God...Who shall separate us from the love of Christ? Shall tribulation, or distress, or persecution, or famine, or nakedness, or peril, or sword?...I am persuaded that neither death, nor life, nor angels, nor principalities, nor things present, nor things to come, nor powers, nor height, nor depth, nor anything else in all creation, will be able to separate us from the love of God in Christ Jesus our Lord."

Today's Gospel, and I pray, this sermon, will drive you into the corner of your limits and ask you: "What have you to say to this Christ?" Later? That's a no. Maybe? No, again. If? Negative. When? Refusal.

There are a thousand ways to say "no," one way to say "yes," and no way to say anything else. Just say "yes" and accept your acceptance, and all will be well. All manner of things will be well.

Amen.

❖ ❖ ❖

September 18, 1988
Mark 9:30–37

As I am fond of saying, "When someone explains something and I do not comprehend, I do not believe him to be of superior intelligence, I believe him to be inarticulate." So goes pride. Another rule of pride: when you intrude on my space, you are aggressive. When I step into your space, I am assertive. Pride rolls on…

Jesus speaks today of humility and servanthood. Both are threatening concepts for a humble parish priest. We servants of the Lord always run the risk of being overly proud of how humble we are. You remember the story of the bishop, the dean, and the sexton? The bishop and dean, following a high mass, knelt before the high altar. The bishop first confessed, "Lord, before thee I am nothing." The dean, in intimidated imitation, knelt before the high altar and prayed, "Lord, before thee I am nothing." The sexton watched these acts of contrite humility. After the humble prelates departed, he quietly entered the sanctuary and before the altar of God prayed, "Lord, before thee I am nothing." Overhearing the sexton's confession, the dean laughed to the bishop, "Look who thinks he is nothing!"

"And they came to Capernaum; and when he was in the house he asked them, 'What were you discussing on the way?' But they were silent; for on the way they had discussed with one another who was the greatest. And he sat down and called the twelve; and he said to them, 'If any one would be first, he must be last of all and servant of all.' And he took a child, and put him in the midst of them; and taking him in his arms, he said to them, 'Whoever receives one such child in my name receives me; and whoever receives me, receives not me but him who sent me.'"

Humility (an appropriate understanding of one's self), and servanthood (the following of your unique bliss or call) are two of the requirements for the call to discipleship. Humility means, in religious terms, complete resignation to our unconditional dependence on God.

Etymologically, humble comes from the Latin which means lowly or base, rooted further in the word "humus," which means soil. To be humble means to remember that we are dust and to dust we shall return. We did not create ourselves. And Jesus points out that the child is a symbol of humility and servanthood.

Jesus did not pick out the child as a symbol with some Victorian, romantic ideal that children are cute, unselfish, innocent, naive, and joyful. If that is true of children, my boys were never children. Jesus chose a child as a symbol because a child is absolutely dependent on a higher authority. And our dependence should be on no authority save the highest authority.

Should we not once again be aware of our humility? Hurricane Gilbert put us back in touch with our humanity and humility. How dependent we have become on lesser gods such as faucet water, electricity, telephones, air-conditioning, automobiles. We cannot control any ultimate, for God remains ultimately in control.

I don't know why we continue our addiction to perfection. We are so full of humus, earth, and dust that we must pay attention to our earthen quality or we will be no more than that. If we try to act like God, we always fall flat, like a little girl walking in her mother's high heels. Humans are full of humus. This awareness of our earthen quality makes us humble. It is okay to be human as long as you know your limits. We, as humans, are always arguing about who is the greatest or who is right. The fact is that the greatest is the one who knows who he isn't. We are all right, but we are each wrong.

Acceptance of the joy of being human is also the child at play. Play is the unabashed joy of knowing that our appetites and instincts are very human and wholesome as long as we don't make gods out of them. They are, though, ways by which God may come to us. Our hunger is our dependence on food, and God comes to us with his spirit in our food: sacramental and instinctual. That's why we say "grace" before we receive it.

Servanthood means putting yourself where you are called. That may mean in the way or out of the way. It may mean leading the way or following. But it always means getting ourselves and our selfish desires out of the way.

A powerful illustration of the point comes from Atlanta in the early seventies. A group of Christian leaders, committed to following the Sermon on the Mount as a way of life, not as an interim ethic before the eschaton, met in a large church to discuss God's will for how they might serve the poor more effectively. Among the group were Clarence Jordon, the founder of Koinonia Farm, and Millard Fuller, who would later become the founder of Habitat for Humanity.

During one of the sessions, the pastor of the church entered the room looking disturbed. Jordan asked him what was wrong. The pastor said he was glad the Lord had called the group to his church and hoped they could help him resolve his problem. It seems the board of deacons had repeatedly denied the pastor's request to raise the janitor's salary. Now, even though he loved his work at the church and saw it as a ministry, the janitor was preparing to quit to find a higher-paying job. The man had six children, lived across town in inadequate, cramped housing, and had to take an hour's bus ride each way since he could not afford a car. The pastor moaned and clasped his hands and lamented, "I guess there's nothing I can do."

Jordon looked at him and said, "Sure there is, that's easy to solve."

The pastor looked back, surprised but excited. "Yes, what's that?" he asked.

"How many children do you have?" Jordon asked.

"Two."

"Where do you live?"

"Oh, the church bought us a very nice house just down the street, four bedrooms."

"How much money do you make?"

"I...I guess a total package of about sixty-five thousand dollars."

"Well, there's your answer," Jordon said happily.

"What?" the pastor said, mystified.

"The janitor has six children. You have just two. All you need to do is switch houses. Then they will have more room and can live next to the church and eliminate the transportation problem. Then you can split your salary with the janitor, and he won't have to go elsewhere for work. You can live in his house on half a salary, and he can make it on his share of the salary in yours. You can forget the obstinate deacons, too. See, there's your answer."

I find Clarence Jordon's prophetic word so personally threatening that I can only end with it. Amen.

October 16, 1988
Mark 10:35–45; Hebrews 4:12–16

In an interesting way, Jesus' statement to the "Sons of Thunder" is not unlike his statement about breaking laws. The Sons of Thunder are James and John. In today's Gospel they told Jesus, "Teacher, we want you to do for us whatever we ask of you." And Jesus said to them, "What do you want me to do for you?" And they said to him, "Grant us to sit, one at your right hand and one at your left, in your glory." But Jesus said to them, "You do not know what you are asking!"

When Jesus was criticized for breaking the law by healing on the Sabbath, he taught, "The sabbath was made for man, not man for the sabbath." To James and John, Jesus says in essence, "The journey to heaven's wholeness was not created for you, but you were created for the journey." Between here and there, the way is difficult, the journey deep and dark.

Through the challenge of the cost of obedience to your call, you will enter the kingdom. The goal is not sitting on thrones in celestial palaces, but to find yourself by giving yourself away.

In today's epistle, the writer to the Hebrews states, "For the word of God is living and active, sharper than any two-edged sword, piercing to the division of soul and spirit, of joints and marrow, and discerning the thoughts and intentions of the heart."

I learned this lesson first from Miss Burnett after Byron Beckham moved to town. Miss Burnett was my grade school basketball coach. She was near six feet tall. She had played basketball herself, but that was long before the funding of women's athletics. So she sublimated her desire and talent by coaching grade school basketball in this little town in northern Oklahoma. Her style was somewhere between a dictator and a wise mistress of aphorism.

In the spring of my seventh grade year, Byron Beckham came to town. His dad was a roustabout in the oil fields and had come to town, like most, by an oil company transfer. I was the cock of the walk at Washington Grade School. I was larger than most, but with the gift of coordination. My basketball skills were like my body—head and shoulders above my twelve- and thirteen-year-old friends. That is, until Byron Beckham came to town.

Byron was one of those thirteen-year-olds who matured very early. He was my height, but his body carried muscular definition. His back rippled, his biceps bulged, and he could run like a deer and jump like a rabbit. The showdown between us loomed as inevitably as the sheriff and stranger at high noon in a Western movie. Like two strange dogs, we sniffed and stalked one another. The encounter came after the first basketball practice. Byron Beckham was good. I was more skillful, but he was stronger. My friend and prophet, Cheezie Eubanks, set the scene when he said to this pre-adolescent Tarzan, in defense of our friendship, "McGehee can kick your..." Cheezie didn't need to finish his prophecy. Byron rose to the challenge. "That beanpole!" snorted Beckham. With luck, the ensuing shoving match was quickly broken up by Miss Burnett. It was the first time I had heard the term "Sons of Thunder." She labeled us that, and with the wisdom of a mistress of adolescent psychology, she wed our competition by pointing out how much better mules pulled wagons when they went one direction rather than two. Byron and I became fast friends. We complemented one another in style and gift. On the rare occasions when I missed a shot, he was always there to rebound and put it back in the bucket.

We were undefeated. In the last regular-season game, before we entered the important post-season Sand Springs tournament, we lost a game to Oak Grove. That was a scrawny little team from a rural consolidated school near Cushing. Before the journey to the tournament, the Sons of Thunder were called into the presence of the wise teacher. Miss Burnett asked, "Do you guys think that basketball was invented so you guys could star? Well, let me tell you, you have a lot of blood, sweat, and tears ahead of you before you become stars. Plus, stardom isn't the goal." Like a wise teacher, she never told us what the goal was. And in some ways, I still wonder.

I love James and John, the Sons of Thunder, who wanted to become stars in heaven the easy way. Jesus said, "You don't know what you are asking." You don't know what is required to get from here to there. If heaven is our goal, we must remember that we enter through the narrow way, the eye of a needle.

In our culture, it is more difficult not to be Christian than to be Christian. Our discipleship is a cultural expectation. Therefore, the hard way is not risking our lives for Christ's sake, but living our lives for the sake of Christ. Our journey is an inward journey. Down through the law and rules of external culture to the rule of true heart, our call is to seek truth through the blood, sweat, and tears of living life at the center point. There is no easy way. The cost of discipleship separates; it is a two-edged sword that pierces the division of soul and spirit, joints and marrow, discerning the thoughts and intentions of the heart. We must ask the hard questions, take the road less traveled, follow our call—come whence it will, cost what it may.

We Americans journey on a luxury liner externally, but we must be prepared to give up all power and pretense if we are to obey our call. The cost of discipleship is the willingness to encounter the Christ even in the darkest, most desolate human being. To go the hard way means to give up all of those things which keep us separated from our brothers and sisters, to give up that which keeps us separated from ourselves, all of those things which we worship more than the living word. What are you willing to give up for Christ's sake? We Americans do not know much about the cost of discipleship because we are in chapels of ease. To those who have been given much, much will be required. Those who have been given many talents must make those talents prosper. You do so, not by burying them in the ground, but by risking them—by giving them up in order to discover who you are. The easy way is the road well traveled. The hard way is that dark way, the road less traveled. It makes all the difference. We are called to give up something or someone. That is the cost of discipleship. You must decide what the call means for you. First must become last. That which is the easy way must be given up, for the deep, dark journey of the bare soul is the only way to go.

Well, I guess you are anxious to know whether we won the Sand Springs tournament after the Sons of Thunder's self-centeredness lost the game to Oak Grove. Well, of course we did. But the real victory came because of the loss.

Once again, the Gospel isn't just in the Bible, but in the mundane events of ordinary experience and in real people like James, John, Miss Burnett, Byron Beckham, and a little boy out of Nazareth who became a star in heaven by the hard wood of a humiliating loss on a blood-, sweat-, and tear-stained cross.

A call to discipleship is not a call to sit on celestial thrones, but to give up everything; anything that will keep you from entering the narrow way, the eye of the needle, where joint is separated from marrow, spirit from soul. For weeks now we have been asked the question, "Are we ready?" The question won't go away.

Amen.

November 13, 1988
Mark 13:14–23

Today's Gospel is known as the "Little Apocalypse." The term "apocalypse" has come to mean the end of the world, when, in actuality, the Greek word *apokalupsis* means "an unveiling."

In this piece of scripture, Mark records Jesus as saying, "But when you see the desolating sacrilege set up where it ought not to be…then flee." Jesus then sets up a vision of a cosmic collapse that will accompany the future coming of the Son of Man. The remainder of the chapter is clearly apocalyptic. It ends with Jesus excluding all attempts to pinpoint the end, but solemnly enjoining all disciples to keep watch for it.

There are several things to keep in mind about the Second Coming. The first is to keep watch. In other words, our style of life ought to be of such heightened awareness that we don't miss Christ whenever or however he comes. When he came the first time, he came so unobtrusively that, except for Mary, Joseph, and a handful of shepherds, nobody much knew or cared.

Secondly, in spite of the quasi-professional predictions of when he will come, Jesus says himself, "But of that day or that hour no one knows, not even the angels of heaven, nor the Son, but only the Father." I am suspicious of anyone who seems to know more than the Son.

Another important consideration is that maybe the breaking in of the Son, as he says elsewhere, "like a thief in the night," might mean that the breaking in will be a breaking into our lives. It is conceivable that the Second Coming is an inward cosmic interruption rather than an external one.

Other random and thinly connected thoughts are appropriate as we speculate on this enigmatic prophecy. Perhaps we must hold both concepts consciously. That is to say, that the Second Coming will be both external and internal. The internal coming is the event and experience of discovering the Christ in ourselves or in another. We are asked in our baptismal covenant to "Seek and serve Christ in all persons, loving [our] neighbor as [our]self." If we should discover the Christ in another, it seems to me that the Christ will have come again, as surely as he came before. That would be a putting together of separate pieces and making them whole. What a sight to see; it might be like seeing the Christ. The Second Coming may be an internal event that comes when we seek and serve Christ in another human being. Surely, if and when that happens, there is a second birth for those who have the eyes to see. Remember, the word apocalypse means unveiling. On the external cosmic scope, contemporary science believes that the universe is expanding and all of Christian teaching rests in the hope of a final union with the source of the mystery. That time will come. That time will come when we see the Christ in ourselves or another, the great flower of creation has its last petal unfolded, and God by any other name will be unveiled.

No one can say just what will happen when that day comes, but that it will be a day of incomparable newness, and peace is assured by a covenant and promise wed deep in our relationship with the alpha who is also omega. There is nothing in this life that can be compared to the glory that will be revealed; there are great surprises in store for us.

My proclamation is sounded out of a deep intuition which I believe is a gift of revelation. The end will not be the Four Horsemen of the Apocalypse trampling history's imperfections underfoot, but the unveiling of completeness.

Jim Crane, in a little piece entitled "A Fable," hints at such:

> The end came very suddenly and in a way no one ever expected—not like revelation and not like the prophets of atomic holocaust had predicted. Nothing happened—resolutely nothing.
>
> At first everything seemed exactly as before, people got up in the morning and started about their business. It didn't even hit us at first that there was something wrong, terribly different. Each of us gradually realized that we could clearly see ourselves exactly as we were. We stood naked in the eyes of God!
>
> For the first time we really saw each other—we confronted each other fully and as persons. The inner person was suddenly visible for all to see, race had the power to see fully unhampered by his own limitations of vision. God had given us his vision, and we were judged.
>
> This was the last revolution. Governments fell, wars were ended, all of society was turned upside down. Many of the first were last, and some of the last became first. Not a drop of blood was shed.

What a terrible and wonderful image: all will be unveiled. That is in itself a judgment and a promise. Perhaps in the meantime, we just begin to be aware and look. For the unveiling may have begun and will not end until each looks for the Christ as the highest priority. And it may be that we need not look into the sky—but into the eye of another. Apocalypse means an unveiling. The unveiling will be a cosmic collapse of the curtain of imperfection that hides wholeness. The collapse will be the new genesis, the eighth day of creation, the Second Coming, and the universal beginning of complete love. In Christ such an end has already begun. Let those with eyes, see. It is available; it has been unveiled.

Amen.

November 20, 1988
John 18:33–37

For fact, our conscious concept of kings and kingdoms is dependent on history books, stories, movies, and a few remnant ceremonial royalties yet scattered throughout the world. But buried deep in our unconsciousness is an archetypal image of one who reigns as a benevolent and creative ruler. He is one who sits in a dreamy, unfocused kingdom who is at one and the same time protector of this world and yet bearer of some mysterious power from beyond anything available to common mortals.

Today is Christ the King Sunday. This is the last Sunday in the Christian year, as Advent comes to us next week. The final voice of the year is Christ's as he clarifies his vocation on earth before an earthly power, Pilate. It is as if Jesus leaves us with an image that fulfills our deepest longing for a power in our lives that comes from the mystery of beyond and yet dwells in the structures of human existence. For we experience ourselves as one in the radical reality of history and at the same time not bound by the spatiotemporal. Who among us has not wondered about the wonderful? Who among us has not longed from our depths for some truth, some revealing truth, that this is not all there is? We have longed to know that there is more to life than meets the eye. It is not so much that we wish to deny or reject the kingdom of the world, but more so that we hold deep within a dream, more substantial than the human fantasy, a dream of a kingdom where all incomplete curiosities, all incomplete understandings, all incomplete knowledge, will be finally satiated, like the disappearance of hunger, thirst, suffering, guilt, pain, and despair—all disappearing like fall smoke rising from fallen leaves. Such a deep hope, which constellates such a capacious dream, hears the voice of truth when Jesus says, "My kingship is not of this world; if my kingship were of this world, my servants would fight [for me]…but my kingship is not from the world." Pilate says in a rational voice, "So you are a king?" Jesus answers, "You say that I am a king. For this I was born, and for this I have come into the world, to bear witness to the truth. Every one who is of the truth hears my voice."

Did you hear? The truth is available. We now know that all our worldly desires will pale before the fulfillment of our deepest needs. This word can abet all our anxieties about our worldly conquests or defeats. Such a word from our King can raise our limited vision and give us a peaceful patience as we wait for the coming kingdom.

But moreover, we can inherit the kingdom now, for if we know that all the passion and pain will be integrated into a universal and personal truth, then we can live now and live abundantly, for we know that all will be worthwhile. Meanwhile, we do not wait until "kingdom come" but seek it here and now.

The King now dwells in the kingdom within. Such an internal emperor empowers, enlivens, and encourages us to live our lives abundantly. For our wellness is assured in a kingdom of paradox: then and now, internal and external, of this world and not of this world, heaven and earth, human and divine.

In this last Sunday of the year, the King establishes the nature of the kingdom. Next week we begin to rehearse again the coming of the King, his Advent. For now we rest in expectant hope, for we have heard the truth.

We are as those in ancient days who were called to move slowly to a new kingdom. They never asked what the weather was like in the new kingdom. They never asked what the land was like in the new kingdom. They never asked about the nature of the people in the new kingdom. Their only question was, "What is the nature of the King?" For if they knew the nature of the King, they knew the nature of the kingdom.

The Gospel has answered the only question we need know. He is Christ the King. We now know about the kingdom of love in which we live and to which we are called.

Amen.

✣ ✣ ✣

December 11, 1988
Advent III
Philippians 4:4–9; Luke 3:7–18

Did you know that the words "hope" and "hop" come from the same root? The modern English preserves the old sound connection. Hop means to "leap with expectation." To hop is the response to hope.

We continue with John the Baptist's preparation for the way of our Lord today in Luke's Gospel. John, whom we referred to last week as God's wild one, was the one who leaped in his mother's womb when Mary came into Elizabeth's presence. Hope and hop mean to leap with expectation. What was bred in the bone came out in the flesh. John became a prophet of hope, leaping through the wilderness crying out the advent of the long-awaited one. But if you remember, his cry was for action, not just passive, unresponsive irresponsibility. To the crowd that responded by coming to him to be baptized, he said, "Fruits are now more important than roots. You came from Abraham, but you must now become yourselves." And the crowd responded, "What shall we do?" The question posed by the crowd is more than an echo this day, for each new generation and every individual therein must ask the same question: "What shall we do?" John is very specific: Those who have two coats, share with those who have none; those who have food, do likewise. Tax collectors, collect no more than is your due. Soldiers, rob no one. John is not just preaching a social gospel of giving to the poor or an ethical business practice, though those results are important. Something more subtle is being spoken. John is penetrating a much-needed psychological neurosis. He is pointing out what keeps us from receiving the Christ when he comes. The Baptist hits us squarely with the cultural and individual narcissism whereby we are fixated on what we possess rather than being open to him who desires to possess us.

John, in simple terms, implies that we cannot receive the love we need until we are willing to give up whatever else possesses us. The obvious sermon to be preached today would be to scold this culture most of us live in, that is caught in the materialistic, narcissistic cycle of possessions and is acted out in conspicuous consumption at our secular Christmas celebrations and gift exchanges. Let that sermon stand in its own judgment. I choose, rather, to speak about the narcissistic fear that paralyzes us because we are afraid of losing our safe identities by giving ourselves away.

Esther Harding, in her book *The I and The Not I*, gives an unappealing, yet memorable metaphor that illustrates the point. She speaks of the "wood tick." Biologists who have studied the nature of consciousness in animals have discovered that each creature sees and hears only what concerns itself and is insensitive to all else. It is this self-contained, self-worship, self-concerned selfishness that keeps us from giving ourselves away and thereby discovering who we are. This is the kind of narcissism that keeps us away from the abundant life Christ brings. Each animal lives in a world of its own, bound by instinct and appetite, and whatever will satiate it. It does not perceive a greater world. Take, for instance, the wood tick. This organism needs the blood of a warm-blooded animal in order to reproduce. To accomplish this, a wood tick attaches itself to the bark of a tree and waits for some host to pass. Since there are many ticks in the forest and few warm-blooded animals, the wait has been known to be as long as seventeen years. During this time, the tick is only technically alive, but its worldview is totally self-centered and stuck in time.

The unappealing metaphor is more to the human advent theme. This is a time of waiting and expectation. But John proclaims that we must prepare for the coming Christ, not by passive sitting, being stuck like the wood tick to the known for fear of the unknown, oblivious to the world around us, but by giving ourselves to it. It is in giving that we are open enough to receive. Waiting is action. The mother knows the hard work of waiting in her pregnancy. The nest does not create itself. Waiting means preparation. What we prepare for is the life we were born to bear.

Hope, then, is the expectation for the coming of the life for which we were born. Advent is the reminder. Christmas is the rehearsal. This is the expectant moment that all the years up until now were preparing us for: the life that is now approaching.

Let us even now leap with expectation. Clear away the chaff of nonessentials. Let us cut away all the superficial. Let us see the roots of our past justified in the fruits of our future as we presently prepare for the new life in Christ. In the silence of our midwinter dusk, we hear our hearts beating time to the steps of this coming new life. The sounds of silence are the vibrations of the hope, hopping within, moving now, soon to be known. Let us concentrate just for these few Advent instances. For far off, and yet deep within, where wind and breath are one, we can feel the first and final moment of Christ's birth and ours. Do not remain frozen to the instinct of safety, but open yourself to the awesome approach of wonder.

"What then shall we do?" the multitude asked. Paul wrote in today's epistle: "Rejoice in the Lord always; again I will say, rejoice. Let all men know your forbearance. The Lord is at hand. Have no anxiety about anything...and the peace of God which passes all understanding will keep your hearts and minds in Christ Jesus...Finally, whatever is true, whatever is honorable, whatever is just, whatever is pure, whatever is lovely, whatever is gracious, if there be any excellence, if there is anything worthy of praise, think about these things...and the God of peace will be with you..."

God knows that we pray for that peace that passeth all understanding; that that is our hope. Our hope comes by the hard way, through labor and preparation of a life. We also know that the labor and preparation bring us to this point, the point for which we were born, to bear our own life. This is how to prepare and wait: leaping in expectant hope. The time is coming and now is. Be ye prepared.

Amen.

✤ ✤ ✤

December 18, 1988
Advent IV
Luke 1:39–56

However the mystery of new life is clouded in philosophical or theological language, the Christmas story clearly reveals that God does not birth God alone. We are now entering the final phase of the Advent season of labor. The Christmas story is the delivery of God into humanity, through a human. That human is a mother. Her name is Mary.

Today's Gospel is the combined story of the visitation and the Magnificat. I prefer to begin our final Advent thoughts with the verses preceding today's Gospel in the important words of the annunciation: In the sixth month the angel Gabriel was sent from God to a city of Galilee named Nazareth, to a virgin betrothed to a man whose name was Joseph, of the house of David; and the virgin's name was Mary. And he came to her and said, "Hail, O favored one, the Lord is with you!" But she was greatly troubled at the saying, and considered in her mind what sort of greeting this might be. And the angel said to her, "Do not be afraid, Mary, for you have found favor with God. And behold, you will conceive in your womb and bear a son, and you shall call his name Jesus." And Mary said, "Behold, I am the handmaid of the Lord; let it be to me according to your word." And the angel departed from her.

Mary then makes her visit to her cousin Elizabeth, who was pregnant with the wild one, John, hopping in her womb in expectation of the birth of God. And Mary sings the Magnificat.

Of all the myriad of implications about the incarnation, one subtle but significant revelation is that God does not birth God alone. When God enters history, he does so within the human context in tangible, palpable terms. And the entry is the open invitation echoed by Mary's unforgettable words: "Let it be to me according to your word."

This openness to the incarnation of God's presence entering our lives is an interesting and complicated part of the human nature. For to be open to new life means to be vulnerable to temptation. Ann Belford Ulanov writes of this part of the human psyche in her book, *The Wisdom of the Psyche*.

> Eve is the one who is open, curious, imaginative, wanting. She is the part of the primordial human in all of us that is desiring, interested, receiving and thus, temptable. The feminine she symbolizes has been held contemptible as a result. She is the feminine we fear because it can be so easily beguiled. Yet, Eve was in fact after wisdom, prudent practical wisdom, wasn't she? Mary took into her heart this God who had taken up residence in her. She housed what she saw and heard and she became the house, the church, for us all. In a womanly way she held the spirit in her heart, not fleeing, not solving, not denying, not simply affirming, but pondering it, looking upon it, making space for it…
>
> [When Jesus counsels,] "Be wise as serpents…" Don't we need the wisdom Eve was after to face the Devil's tricks? Isn't that the same imagination and intuition that is found in Mary, who takes the revelation and incarnation announced to her, all the way down inside herself and remains loyal to it, even though she must break conventions and face being made homeless as she gives her scandalous birth on the borders of human community, and must flee to a foreign country…

Dr. Ulanov strikes fear into the heart of the safe and predictable when she points out that openness to God's presence may be costly to convention. If it is true that God does not birth God's self alone, then he comes to and through the voice of one who says, "Let it be to me according to your word." This letting be is always a necessity for God to enter a human life. And when we allow God's Holy Spirit to enter our human context, human need for safety and acceptability may be shattered in the risk of what this letting be forces us to become. With this openness to where the spirit leads may come a painful break with a conventional past. In addition, with such openness, we may find other spirits entering in, which are not of God. The human predicament is in simple terms this: If we remain closed to the imaginative and unpredictable spirit of God, we may miss our call to be a handmaid for new life never before known; but if we open ourselves unconditionally to God's spirit, we will suffer the pain of change and may taste a forbidden fruit which causes darkness in this light of the new knowledge. We are caught between saying "no" because of the fear of pain and saying "yes," knowing that there will be pain.

The Christmas message seems to encourage taking the risk. For even if we break old patterns by accepting new life, the power of God's presence can heal and overcome whatever pain or death that results.

The fruit Eve ate brought new life in the light of awareness, but also brought darkness and death. But finally, the fruit of Eve became the fruit of Mary's womb. What Eve brought into the world by her "yes" necessitated the fruit Mary brought into the world in her "yes." Jesus overcame the power of sin and death. If sin entered the world through Eve, it was overcome through Mary.

If we are to err, it will be in our saying, "It will never be through me, for I fear the dark of doubt and the pain of change." If we succeed, it will be in saying, "Let it be to me according to your word." Mary's "yes" is a model for how it is that we are to respond when our call comes. Our fear is that our "yes" will allow pain, and death may make the womb a tomb from which no stone can ever be rolled away.

If there is one thing the human soul longs for, it is the glorious birth of new life. However the mystery of new life is clouded philosophically or theologically, the Christmas story clearly reveals that God does not birth himself alone. As we enter the final phase of the Advent labor, the angel Gabriel hovers above us, perhaps at your house, with the expectant murmur of his wings. Imagine that Bethlehem is outside your door, that the word is seeking to be made flesh, and that God will not birth God's self alone. The message comes to you, "Do not be afraid, you have found favor with God. And behold, will you conceive…"

And the world waits like a hovering angel, the only breath stirring is the beating murmur of the wings.

The word all creation waits to hear is through you the echo of Mary's innocent wisdom:
Let it be,
Let it be,
Let it be
Unto me
According to
Your word.
Let it be,
Let it be,
Let it be!
Amen.

1989

January 22, 1989
Luke 4:14–21

When John the Baptist was in prison, he knew that his journey was at its end. He sent word from his disciples to Jesus. His word was a question. The last word we hear from John is a question. In his imprisoned end, he speaks for all of humanity as he has his disciples ask Jesus, "Are you the one who is to come, or shall we look for another?" And Jesus answers, "Go and tell John these things that you hear and see: the blind receive their sight and the lame walk, the lepers are cleansed and the deaf hear, the dead are raised up and the poor have the gospel preached to them. And blessed is he, whosoever shall not be offended in me." His answer from Jesus is a paraphrase of Isaiah's prophecy about what things will come to pass when the Messiah appears.

In today's Gospel from Luke, Jesus was in Nazareth, where he grew up. He went to the synagogue, as was his custom on the Sabbath day. And he stood up to read. He read from the prophet Isaiah: "The Spirit of the Lord is upon me, because he has anointed me to preach good news to the poor. He has sent me to proclaim release to the captives and recovering of sight to the blind, to set at liberty those who are oppressed, to proclaim the acceptable year of the Lord." As he closed the book he said to them: "Today this scripture has been fulfilled in your hearing."

In two separate instances, Jesus used Isaiah's prophecy to two different hearers. First, to John, who was at the end of his journey. John was sitting imprisoned in his own doubt. He must have wondered if his vocation of being the preparer of the way was a foolish risk now exhausted in a prison cell. To him, the word from Jesus, that Jesus was the fulfillment of the prophecy, must have come as good news. John must have felt as Simeon did when Jesus was presented to him at the temple and Simeon sang, "Lord, now lettest thou thy servant depart in peace, according to thy word, for mine eyes have seen thy salvation."

But the hearers in the synagogue, when Jesus read Isaiah's prophecy and claimed that he had fulfilled the messianic hope, had a different reaction. To these words they said, "Jesus, the Messiah? Is not this Joseph's son?" The wise old man Simeon and the imprisoned John, both of whom held a cosmic consciousness, could depart in peace. But the living, who were imprisoned in a narrow worldview, were astonished that God would appear in history in a human being, from their own city, the son of their neighbors, Mary and Joseph.

Two implications emerge that hold relevance for our own worldview in this time and place. The first has to do with our own denial that God enters history in the common and ordinary. And second, the denial that our hopes could be fulfilled in our own lifetime.

Kierkegaard wrote in his journal: "The whole order of things fills me with a sense of anguish, from the gnat to the mysteries of the incarnation; all is entirely unintelligible to me, and particularly my own person. Great is my sorrow, without limits." Kierkegaard's torment was the direct result of seeing the world as it really was in relation to his situation as a creature. The prison of one's character is painstakingly built to deny one thing and one thing alone: one's creatureliness. The creatureliness of our existence is our great anxiety and embarrassment. The undeniable fact is that we are self-conscious animals, trapped in bodies, dominated by instinct and appetite, and all exist under this self-conscious dread of death. And here we hear our own voices echoed in those who wanted to deny that God would enter history as a creature who would simply live and die. God was from Nazareth, son of Mary and Joseph. The denial of Jesus by those in his own home is to deny that God would reveal himself in the common, ordinary people and events of our lives. We continue to look elsewhere for the fulfilling word. We cannot believe that our bodies, our instincts, our anxiety, our dread, or even our death might be the place where God reveals his nature. It must be someplace else. Is it possible that we still deny that God reveals his nature in human nature? I believe that if we are to transcend our animal nature, we must recognize that God has transcended his nature by revealing himself in our creatureliness. If God is to reveal himself at all, it must be in human nature. We accept our humanity when we realize that our humanity is acceptable to God. It must have been; God thought so much of human nature that he decided to become one himself. As Tillich writes: "The courage to be is the courage to accept oneself as accepted in spite of being unacceptable. In Christ you are made acceptable. Our vocation is to accept our acceptance. God became human, from Nazareth, born of a woman, in order that we could be free to be human, too. The denial of our humanity is to deny God. Is this not Joseph's son? Yes, born of a woman, at a particular time and place. If you deny that, then you deny that God will appear anywhere.

The second denial of Jesus as the fulfillment of the prophecy is to deny that we could find fulfillment in this life. We have tried to overcome our creatureliness by dreaming of a "sweet bye and bye." That time of fulfillment will come only after death. We do not truly believe that we can have the wholeness we seek as long as we have these troublesome bodies and this human nature. Perhaps that is true. But Jesus proclaimed that the Kingdom of God was at hand. He taught that heaven had entered history. He proclaimed his time as "the acceptable year of the Lord."

Our limited ego view of existence cannot hold the cosmic consciousness that we live in a paradox, that something can be two opposites at one and the same time. We dwell in the Kingdom of God now, and the kingdom is coming. But the Gospel is clear from Jesus' own answer to John's asking, "Are you he who is to come, or shall we look for another?" Jesus answers, "I am he."

I am convinced that the wholeness we seek we now hold within. We are just not yet conscious of the wholeness we are. My analogy is that the song the bird is born to sing is in the egg before it is born. The song is given at birth and the journey is toward the awareness of the song you are to sing. Both are true; the kingdom is present within, and we are journeying toward it. Both are true at the same time. Just as it is true that God exists in eternity and, at the same time, is born in Bethlehem to Mary and Joseph. How can this be true? Christians have to live in the anxiety or the enlivening of a scandal. God can be found in humanity, and that life can be fulfilled before death. How many believe that? It is easier to doubt it. Do you believe that your humanity is a place through which you can discover God? Do you believe that fulfillment in your life can come before death? That is the requirement of Christian belief. I doubt that there are many of us who do not have a doubt about that. The high-risk statement is for me to say, "I have my doubts." The evidence seems to be to the contrary. The evidence is that we try to cover our humanity by trying to act like gods; we seem to try to postpone our living because we cannot seem to get it all together in this life. Surely, Christianity is not about denying our humanity and waiting to live until we get to heaven.

Can we not catch even a fleeting glimpse that God is in our creatureliness and at the same time calling us beyond ourselves—not allowing us to be satisfied to be just creatures? Can we not hold, even for a moment, the revelation that God has come in our common humanity and calls us on to our uncommon existence through our experience of such? Or will we continue in the anxiety and dread of a whimpering humanity imprisoned in a narrow worldview that denies that God would visit us where we live? I don't want to wait at the temple until I die to begin to live. I love Simeon's song, "Now lettest thou thy servant depart in peace," but I want the Gospel song to be renewed and sing, "Now lettest thou thy servant begin to live, for mine eyes have seen my salvation." There are some things about which I have no doubt. Our lives have meaning in general, purpose in particular, and we belong to something greater than ourselves. If God is to be alive for us, God must be alive in our humanity. The singular screaming message of Christianity is that God so loved the human that he became one. Each of us is acceptable. Accept your acceptance. We are human and must not confuse our vocation with God's. Grace is undeserved favor. We are acceptable; we are called to become more and more so, not by denying our humanity but by fulfilling it.

This is the song that was in us before we were born and the song we were born to sing. About that I have no doubt.

Amen.

✤ ✤ ✤

January 29, 1989
Luke 4:21–32

"Unbelief is as much of a choice as belief is. What makes it in many ways more appealing is that whereas to believe in something requires some measure of understanding and effort, not to believe doesn't require much of anything at all." This quotation from Frederick Buechner frames our contemporary and timeless human situation vis-à-vis meaning and meaninglessness.

Today's Gospel from Luke is a continuation of last week's story of Jesus at his home parish, reading Isaiah's jubilee prophecy and claiming to be the Messiah. "Jesus began to say to them, 'Today in your hearing this scripture has been fulfilled'…and they said, 'Is not this Joseph's son?' And he said to them, 'Doubtless you will quote to me this proverb, "Physician heal yourself"…and he said, 'Truly I say to you, no prophet is acceptable in his own country.'"

Jesus then reminds them that when Elijah was rejected by his own, he went to the land of Sidon and shared a last meal with a pagan widow and her daughter. He further recalls that when Elisha was in Israel, many lepers existed, but he healed the Syrian, Naaman. In other words, if you reject me, I will shake the dust off my feet and bring new life to those who want abundant life, and those who want to cling to the past can live in the meager fear of the future. "When they heard this, all in the synagogue were filled with wrath. And they rose up and put him out of the city, and led him to the brow of the hill on which their city was built, that they might throw him down headlong." But then, he simply walked away.

In a certain way, I respect the good churchmen at Nazareth. I respect them because they got angry. If we could digress for just a moment, we will return to our contemporary rejection of Jesus and see how our rejection is worse than that of the Nazarenes. Anger is an emotion. There is a difference between feelings and emotions in spite of the fact that we use the words interchangeably. Feelings are the deep values we hold. Emotions are the expressions of feelings. Emotions are the smoke; feelings, the fire. In this case, the feeling was fear. The Hebrew people at Nazareth were afraid of Jesus' words because he was a threat to their security. In order to receive this abundant life, they had to give up their past superiority as the righteous, religious, chosen ones. They were afraid because that which would bring them new life had, one unexpected morning, just walked into their cathedral. They were afraid. Their fear was the beginning of an expression of their feeling. Anger was the emotion which expressed their feeling. When someone is angry, most often we can use the emotion to lead us to the feeling. Generally, the feeling will be either fear or pain, and often an indistinguishable combination of both. When others are angry with me, I can guess that I have hurt them or that they are afraid of me or threatened by me.

So it was with the Jews that day. Jesus was a threat to their old ways. They feared him and his word, so they expressed their feelings with the emotion of anger. Wisely, Jesus did not fight their emotion, but dealt with their feelings. Since he was such a threat, he just walked away. The worst thing to do with an angry person is to fight or argue. The wise thing is to remove the pain and fear. The wise healer knew this.

Now, back to my respect for the Nazarene Jews. I respect them because they held something valuable to which Jesus was a threat. When Jesus told them he was the expected Messiah, he insulted a deeply held belief. Today, so many of us wouldn't recognize a new Messiah if she came, because we have so little invested in our own belief system. My fear is not that we will kill Jesus when he returns, but that he will die of apathy.

Buechner writes that unbelief is so much easier, because it doesn't require much of anything. In a variation on a theme, Archbishop William Temple is reported to have said, "When people cease to believe in God I do not fear that they will believe in nothing, but I fear they will believe in anything." Contemporary Americans, because of the luxury of affluence, seem self-satisfied to live in the superficiality of consumption, and yet at some deep level, hunger for an existence that is more authentic than a car phone or a VCR in every room. Authenticity as individuals and intimacy in relationships are the two most common pleas I hear from those who are seeking an abundant life in the midst of material abundance. My concern is that if Jesus walked into our cathedral, we would not be as angry as we would be unaware.

We tend to follow the most recent popular self-help formula. That doesn't cost much thought or energy, no matter what price tag it holds. We are not very vulnerable to a promise of abundant life that costs us a deep investment in giving up our old lives for such new life.

Jesus does return to us again and again. Today's malaise is a lack of self-worth. Anytime we are offered the worth and abundance of an authentic relationship, we are offered an experience of Christ's presence. So many of us, and so much of each of us, is so satiated with external abundance that we are internally empty and unaware. This leaves us feeling invalid, and we live our spiritual lives as invalids. We don't rise up in anger when Jesus comes to us, we just don't recognize him.

Who among us is not lying on his pallet like the poor paralyzed invalid at the pool at Bethsaida? How many times have we been so consumed with consumption that we missed the life-giving love offered by one who is among us?

We are called upon to surrender to love, and through such surrender, we are given life. Christ is love and dwells within those who risk in love. In order to risk, we must give up the security of old patterns and, perhaps, even old values. Fear of pain keeps us as *in-valid* invalids. It is fear that we might have to give up something we value. Yet, that which gives us worth we so *de-value*, i.e., love. Do we have anything that Christ threatens? Are we afraid and therefore angry? I hope so. I hope that Jesus Christ is so threatening to you that he stirs the deepest values within you. That which you fear the most is that which you must enter. I guarantee you that Christ will walk into every life. When you find yourself drawn to or repelled by something or someone, stop, look, and listen closely. Something has grabbed your attention for some reason. It might lead you to the Christ within. We are asked to surrender to this call; this is the only way life is given to us. Christ is love and dwells within those who risk in love. In order to risk, we must give up that which we thought held great value for us; we must know the fear of pain. Gerald May writes:

> Willingness implies a surrendering of one's self-separateness, an entering into, an immersion in the deepest processes of life itself...it is mastery yielding to mystery...more simply, willingness to say "yes" to the mystery of being alive with another human being in each moment. Willfulness is saying "no," or perhaps more commonly, "yes, but..."

Abundance and abundant life are very different. One of them may leave us empty and invalids, the other won't. Christ has come to give us life more abundantly. The difficult way is to say "yes." The easy way is to say "no," or more popularly, "yes, but."

Perhaps it is more honest to reject love than to ignore it. The opposite of love is not this anger of the Hebrews, it is apathy. Perhaps it is more honest to be afraid and threatened. The reality that we come to Christ by the hard way is at the heart of the gospel. It seems to be at the heart of the gospel that we have free choice: we are free to love or not to love. But, if we don't love, we won't have anything to fear, because we will be nothing.

Amen.

February 2, 1989
140th Diocesan Council – Daughters of the King
Luke 2:22–40

Even from the tormented voice of the poet Anne Sexton, we hear of the human passionate yearnings for love and our deepest fears of evil and death. In her book of poetry entitled *The Awful Rowing Toward God*, she speaks in a slightly sardonic and yet cheerful tone about God's unfailing love:

> the rowing endeth
>
> I'm mooring my rowboat
> at the dock of the island called God.
> This dock is made in the shape of a fish
> and there are many boats moored
> at many different docks.
> "It's okay," I say to myself,
> with blisters that broke and healed
> and broke and healed—
> saving themselves over and over.
> And salt sticking to my face and arms like
> a glue-skin pocked with grains of tapioca.
> I empty myself from my wooden boat
> and onto the flesh of The Island.
>
> "On with it!" He says and thus
> we squat on the rocks by the sea
> and play—can it be true—
> a game of poker.
> He calls me.
> I win because I hold a royal straight flush.
> He wins because He holds five aces.
> A wild card had been announced
> but I had not heard it
> being in such a state of awe
> when He took out the cards and dealt.
> As He plunks down His five aces
> and I sit grinning at my royal flush,
> He starts to laugh,
> the laughter rolling like a hoop, out of His mouth
> and into mine,
> and such laughter that He doubles right over me
> laughing a Rejoice-Chorus at our two triumphs.
> Then I laugh, the fishy dock laughs
> the sea laughs. The Island laughs.
> The Absurd laughs.

> Dearest dealer,
> I with my royal straight flush,
> love you so for your wild card,
> that untamable, eternal, gut-driven *ha-ha*
> and, lucky love.

Though Ms. Sexton did not use classical theological terminology to describe God's unending love, her confession is memorable: "I love you so for your wild card, that untamable, eternal, gut-driven *ha-ha* and lucky love."

Today, on our Christian calendar is the presentation of our Lord in the temple. Luke's Gospel lesson rehearses the traditional Jewish custom of bringing the child to the temple for blessing and sacrifice. In this context emerges Simeon, symbolizing the nation of the people of God who had awaited the expected one who would redeem the people of God. And Simeon sings his song, the *Nunc Dimittis*: "Lord, now lettest thou thy servant depart in peace, according to thy word; for mine eyes have seen thy salvation which thou hast prepared in the presence of all peoples, a light for revelation to the Gentiles, and for glory to thy people Israel." And with his song, he speaks to Mary, "Behold, this child is set for the fall and rising of many in Israel, and for a sign that is spoken against (and a sword will pierce through your own soul also), that thoughts out of many hearts may be revealed."

This divine, unilateral, unconditional love of God which is incarnate in Christ is so easily robbed of its power by sentimentality that we never hear Simeon's prophecy that "a sword will pierce [our] soul." Alan Jones described it as "a kind of passion—even a kind of pain—for which we are starved."

Human beings tend to confuse love and approval. What most of us seek is approval, and we adapt our behavior to the call of parental or peer acceptance rather than to the call of God. Jesus did not pass the test of approval, and Mary's heart bore the scar. God's love comes to us in the pain of disconnecting ourselves from all the transitory temptations that promise happiness at the cost of meaning. The disciples were called on the premise that they must give up everything in order to follow God's wild card of love.

Here is the confusion. God is the only source of love. God is love. God, as source, comes to us in a graceful variety of resources. We, in our spiritual immaturity, confuse the resource with the source. Our temptation and tendency is to equate the resource with the source. We make gods out of everything which or everyone who is a bearer of God's love. We make idols out of symbols. We worship mothers, fathers, spouses, children, prayer books, churches, and sacraments. We even worship love as we reverse the metaphor that God is love and make love god. The pain comes through the realization that we must outgrow every transitory revelation as we grow toward the only love that never ends or fails. The Bible reveals again and again that we must not place our ultimate faith in any human creature or human creation.

Every time the people of God have confused themselves or their institutions with God, God has clarified the confusion with a truth that hurts.

Jorge Luis Borges penned the painful truth of spiritual growth in this poem:

Comes the Dawn

After a while you learn the subtle difference
Between holding a hand and chaining a soul,
And you learn that love doesn't mean leaning
And company doesn't mean security.
And you begin to learn that kisses aren't contracts
And presents aren't promises,
And you begin to accept your defeats
With your head up and your eyes open
With the grace of a woman, not the grief of a child,
And you learn to build all your roads on today
Because tomorrow's ground is too uncertain for plans,
And futures have a way of falling down in mid-flight.
After a while you learn
That even sunshine burns if you get too much.
So you plant your own garden and decorate your own soul,
Instead of waiting for someone to bring you flowers.
And you learn you really can endure…
That you really are strong,
And you really do have worth.
And you learn and learn…
With every goodbye you learn.

But such a surprise is God's love. It comes out of such surprising places as Nazareth, in Mary's son, in the pain of separation, in the hurt of growing up, in the trauma of disappointment, in the torment of disapproval, in the hard wood of the cross. What a surprise is God's love. And when it comes, it is a joy—such a joy. Such an Easter joy!

Jesus is God's surprise. As Anne Sexton reminds us, "A wild card [has] been announced," and it is God's unconditional love in Christ. The cosmic card has been played. And when all other things pass away, God's love in Christ always wins, for love never ends.

Amen.

February 8, 1989
Ash Wednesday
Matthew 6:1–6, 16–21

The German poet Rilke once wrote: "If my devils are to leave me, I am afraid my angels will take flight as well."

Today we begin another Lent. This season is a time to begin again to lift our awareness another increment. Awareness is like an aperture for the soul, whereby we can see ourselves as we are and exorcize the demon of denial. Denial is the demon that represses our awareness. It works through fear. For the human ego fears anything that threatens its image of itself. That is why we place the dust of ashes on our foreheads, to bring to our awareness and that of others, that we are human and human nature has always been vulnerable to the demonic.

The demonic is any natural function in the individual that has the power of taking over the whole person. Sex, eros, anger, rage, and the craving for power are examples of natural instincts that can move from angels to demons if we are unaware. As Jesus so clearly points out in our Gospel lesson, even the best motivation can become demonic. Giving alms, praying, or fasting can become self-serving and captured by hubris if we are unaware.

There is a remnant of Gnosticism in most of us. Gnosticism, meaning the denial of the world, flesh, instincts. We seek to deny our human nature. And when we do so, the demonic is free to reign, for the demonic is any natural function that is controlling the whole system rather than contributing its part to the whole. Any cell that ceases to function in its proper role and begins to seek to take over the functions of another cell is a cancer and will, if unchecked, destroy the whole. Denial is the enemy of health and becomes a demon in the system. Lent is not a time to deny our nature, but a time to become more aware of our nature.

Our opening collect is a prayerful permission for awareness: "Almighty and everlasting God, you hate nothing you have made and forgive the sins of all who are penitent: Create and make in us new and contrite hearts, that we, worthily lamenting our sins and acknowledging our wretchedness, may obtain of you, the God of all mercy, perfect remission and forgiveness;…"

God does not hate us because we are human. What God fears is that when we deny our humanity, then our nature may seek to try to be God. When we acknowledge that our nature is vulnerable to the demonic, we exorcize the demon of denial and take that natural urge and see it as an angel.

Let us therefore begin our Lenten journey by acknowledging that we are neither animals, of instinct alone, nor are we Gods, without any instinctual needs.

Either is demonic, to act as animals or to play God. Let us be aware of our human nature and realize that our instincts can either lead us away from God or into a relationship with God. The grace of God is that he hates nothing that he has made and will redeem any natural function that is out of balance. His gift that turns demons into angels is awareness. The theological term for awareness is "confession." Through confession, we bring to awareness our nature that has separated us from God. Absolution is re-creation. We are made new. God's love is stronger than any sin. "Where sin abounds, grace abounds more." God can turn dead ashes into sparks of new life. That is why we prepare for Good Friday's reality and Easter's mystery.

If we deny our demons, Rilke is correct, our angels depart also. If we acknowledge, through confession's awareness, that our nature can cause us to die, then our demons become angels that fly up out of ashes like sparks of new life.

So it is that we pray, "Create and make in us new and contrite hearts, that we, worthily lamenting our sins and acknowledging our [demons], may obtain of you, the God of all mercy, perfect remission and forgiveness; through Jesus Christ our Lord, who lives and reigns with you and the Holy Spirit, one God, for ever and ever."

Amen.

※ ※ ※

February 12, 1989
Lent I
Luke 4:1–13

From ashes to Easter is the Lenten journey. This lengthening of time is our annual metaphorical journey of evaluating our own life in our own time. We do so in a family tradition of meditating on our own sacred story. Today we begin with the rehearsal of the first temptation of Christ. Our lectionary annually begins our Lenten lessons with one of the synoptic Gospel's accounts of Jesus' dialogue with Satan in the desert. Having meditated on this story for two decades, I conclude that what the lord of lies offers Jesus is what our egocentric nature desires the most, and is that which is most destructive to human growth toward wholeness, symbolized in the journey from ashes to Easter. What Satan offers Jesus is the easy way. Is this not what the controlling center of our consciousness desires the most? The shortcut to meaning and gratification is the most tempting way. But what the Christ calls us to is the way of the cross. The way of the cross is the way of life for Christians. How tempting it is to be offered unending physical nurture in bread; to be offered unlimited power over self and others; to be offered physical safety against injury or pain. Most of our temptations which steal substance, rob quality, and retard maturity are those which offer instant solution, instant gratification, or immediate safety from the pain or crises which are the primary ingredients of growth.

Anyone who has had a natural gift or talent which comes easily knows how such an asset can become a liability to excellence. The gifted one has a greater responsibility to discipline, hard work, and practice, for what comes easily can retard growth. The greatest temptation is the easy way.

Life is no different. Religion is a particular set of stories and symbols that informs consciousness of the cosmic truth which each person seeks to repress. The cosmic truth about life is that difficulty, pain, loss, patience, discipline, waiting, anxiety, even death are not only necessary, but are the primary ingredients for growth. Joy, peace, pleasure, meaning, and love are also ingredients for growth, but they depend upon their opposites in order to appear. Stars are always available to us, but we can see them only in the dark.

Our calling is to experience life openly, with all its shades of opposition, and to grow through such experience. The temptation is to seek the shortcut to happiness by avoiding its costly companion of despair. Joseph Campbell, in his book *The Hero with a Thousand Faces*, writes: "It is only those who know neither an inner call nor an outer doctrine whose plight truly is desperate." Christianity, as focused on Lent, reminds us of our need to listen to our inner call and to obey the voice in an outward journey within appropriate boundaries. The truly desperate and tragic human is one without any call and no direction.

Our call is to become that unique person we were created to be. Our direction is to seek such identity within a community of pilgrims who are committed to loving and supporting one another in the journey by following the way enabled by the cross of Christ. The way is the hard way—that is to say, the full way. Jesus doesn't offer the easy life of emptiness, but the difficult life of abundance. The evil one offers a full stomach and an empty life. Christ offers a full life, empty of easy or quick solutions.

Several years ago in another parish, I was working with a young man who was seeking Holy Orders. As I listened to him, it became clearer and clearer that his inner call was to something from which he could hide by becoming a priest. For him, the religious life was a place to hide from the pain of life. In the course of the conversation, I asked him, "Of all the things in your life that you have ever done, which one would you most like to undo?" As he described in great, tearful detail the experience, I asked him a question to which by intuition I knew the answer. I asked, "What event in your life has brought you the most meaning and growth?" He sat, stunned. He knew for the first time life's incredible paradox. If he could undo his most painful experience, he would lose his most meaningful experience. The way of the cross is the way of life. The young man thought—like so many of us have thought—that the religious way is the easy way. This is what the evil one tempts us with, and in the most insidiously evil way, he does so within religion. Offering religion as an anesthetic against the experience of living is a great temptation.

Our call is to a religious life, but not in order to hide from the world. Our call is an inner call to experience ourselves in our lives. In Christian tradition, obedience means both an inner call and outward boundaries. To observe God's commandments as we seek to become ourselves is the tension of discipline. The commandments can be considered outer codification of universal laws governing the inner world. The teachings of Jesus and our own evolution, experience, and confession inform us that we, in our humanity, cannot keep the commandments. A hundred times a day, in large and small and in known and unknown ways, we break and fall short of the law. These outer commandments for the religious journey become a prescription for struggle, a measure of our imperfection, a revelation of how much we need God's grace. If it were not for the commandments, we might think we were perfect. They inform us of our struggle toward wholeness by working against the tension of boundaries so that we can become aware of the unbounded grace of God. This is the hard way. We become aware of our imperfection. We see our dust nature in the sign of the cross drawn on our foreheads Ash Wednesday. This dust cross reminds us of our own imperfections of which we become aware as we push ourselves, testing ourselves against the law.

The pain of breaking the law may be a necessity for experiencing the joy of God's unconditional grace. Rather than being a prescription for breaking the law, this brings an awareness of how one functions in one's life. It is an appropriate principle that we gain strength by pushing against something that is stable. As we do this, we begin to experience our own stability. Breaking the law is the nature of being human; unbounded grace for lawbreakers is the nature of God. At some point, these two truths cross. This is the way of the cross. In baptism, by the grace of God and in revelation in Christ, we are given the end of the story as it begins. In baptism, "we know that all things work together for good for those who love God and are called according to his purpose." We know that although things will not always be all right, they will eventually be well. So it is with the story of the cross and our Lenten journey toward the mystery of Easter. We know how it will end: in the end, it will be joy. Even now we must remember. Frederick Buechner writes:

> To hear yourself try to answer [life's deep] questions…is to begin to hear something not only of who you are but of both what you are becoming and what you are failing to become. It can be a pretty depressing business all in all, but if sackcloth and ashes are at the start of it, something like Easter may be at the end.

There is not an easy way. But we are on our way, the way of the cross, from ashes to Easter. We begin with the reality that life is real and so are we. God has become even more real than we by experiencing all of the pain, the loss, and the rejection in order to reestablish one law—the law of unbounded, unilateral, unconditional love. Thank God that we know the end of the story before we begin. It is through the grace of God that we take the first step. We begin by taking that first step, bold, steadfast and unafraid; we are journeying from ashes to Easter.

Amen.

❖ ❖ ❖

March 5, 1989
Lent IV
Luke 15:11–32

Jesus said, "There was a man who had two sons..." To the collective consciousness of the Christian family, those lines are a mantra of special words which allow ordinary awareness to heighten. For we know that the parable which follows will take us to a new awareness if we allow it. These sacred words are an ether to the ego. This simple story has the capacity to carry us to regions of inner space beyond our ordinary atmosphere, to the clear, unpolluted soul where truth dwells and exquisite, impalpable, spiritual knowledge abounds.

The parable has traditionally been called the Parable of the Prodigal Son. So named, but like any polyvalent story, it is beyond naming. It could be called the Parable of the Patient Father, or the Parable of the Older Brother, or the Parable of the Love Feast. The wonder of this kaleidoscopic story is that each turn of the telling gives another view and thus another name. For twenty years I have viewed and reviewed this sacred story, and each time I have seen some new truth—simple, subtle, and always sublime. Today, I will name the story the Parable of the Brothers: one who couldn't just say "yes" and the other who couldn't just say "no."

How interesting our stories become when, in reflection, we look at the corners turned or unturned by times when we said just "yes" or "no." Human freedom can be summed in our God-given ability to say "yes" or "no." How our life is tracked by our responses. Frost's two roads always loom before us in our human travel. Jesus said, "There was a man who had two sons..." The younger one was in that adolescent ego state where it is next to impossible to delay gratification—without a broad expanse of experience every impulse is for the now, and responsibility to others pales before the instinctual urge for experimentation and discovery of new worlds beyond parental and family boundaries. He demanded his inheritance and tested his limits, only to discover that his inability to "just say no" led him into worlds greater than his resources could serve.

The older brother took the safe and traveled road, stayed within family boundaries, and kept his resources within his control. He played his instincts on the safe field within the rules, and though he lost neither trust nor approval, he gained no more than what he was given. His younger brother lost the approving trust of his authorities, but gained a knowledge never to be found in the safe hallways of his home. How hard this lesson for each, and how unavoidable for everyone, the existential choice: yes or no.

The whiff of ether that sends us deeper into the story and into ourselves is to imagine that the brothers are two sides of one personality. The "yes" and "no" brothers dwell within the personality of each person. In our free will, we have a will toward the un-abandoned sense of freedom and experimentation that discovers limits by breaking them. And at the same level of free will, we have a will to seek the way which will avoid the pain that comes from breaking boundaries. Much of the time, we fall short of the unlimited joy of discovery by stopping at artificial limits and never know the possibilities that dwell beyond our fear.

These "yes" and "no" voices within appear to be at opposites and create a war of anxiety that can only be won by one side dominating the other. For most of us, most of the time, it is true. It is a shouting match between "yes!" and "no!" And the truth is that we are unbalanced, being dominated from time to time by one will or the other and living our lives in the dizziness of freedom on a teeter-totter of free will. The other option is as unappealing. That is to be stuck in a habitual pattern of irresponsible, devastating experimentation that respects no boundaries, or being stuck in a fearful lack of risk-taking that allows boundaries to bind us up into a bondage of fear that leaves a life of living death.

I do not have the answer as to which brother is the better in every case. If I did, life's mystery would be revealed, leaving life a predetermined path with as much freedom and meaning as a rat in a maze. The parable tells the cost and promise of each brother. And the choice is left where it inevitably is, and where it ought to be. The choice is always ours.

Another view is to see the brothers, not as ultimate opposites which are at war, but as complementary gifts of grace, whereby we grow through the creative urges of each. Drawn to each extreme of risk and safety, we are given both. And with a whiff of the ethereal possibility, we may see that we can discover safety in risk and risk in safety. For the integrating principle is the father who stands at the center. The home is where each will belongs. The one who stays home is home. The one who leaves home returns. The end is the same. The unconditional love of the father is that he accepts and welcomes each and allows each his own choice.

Now, before we lose the awareness that each brother is a part of each of us, let's take one more whiff of ether. The father is also within each of us. Our opposites are related by birth, for they are birthed by our own soul. The soul is the self we were created by and created to be. The father ultimately integrates the opposites into one family, indivisible, as in an individual.

We don't have to be either brother, for we need both. There is, at the center of us, a soul which accepts both and loves them equally, for they are each a part of the whole.

The good news is that if you are stuck in the dead safety of fear, in the hallways of an anachronistic home, you may need to leave by saying "yes" to a new life. If you are estranged and alone, out there all by yourself, you may just say "no" and come back home. For most, it is a rhythm of both until we develop a walk, a step, a pace, a path that is our own.

The good news is that at the center is the creative urge and the ultimate end. The father doesn't say "yes" or "no"; the father loves. And such a love is beyond "yes" or "no," for it sees both as necessary to the other and knows no boundaries other than unbounded love.

Take the story home. Read it for yourself. Take the story home, and it will lead you where you need to go.

Amen.

❊ ❊ ❊

March 12, 1989
Lent V
Sesquicentennial Sunday
Isaiah 43:16–21; Luke 20:9–19

The fear and hope of the Christian Church are expressed in two words with similar sounds but discordant meanings: opalescence and obsolescence.

Hear the reality of the fear:

> The major cause of attrition, however, has been the virtual demise of the church as a pillar of the urban community in the Twentieth Century…The reason was in part ethnic and in part socio-economic. As industry and commerce lured workers to the inner city, over-crowding and unemployment resulted, leading, in turn, to increased crime and a decrease in the standard of living. The middle class—the cornerstone of the neighborhood church and synagogue—fled to the suburbs. In most instances the church was given no choice but to uproot itself and follow its flock…or lose them. Where the churches stayed put, they were overwhelmed by the problem of how to keep operating, as congregations declined, buildings aged and maintenance costs rose.

That analysis, interestingly enough, does not come from either a historian or a sociologist, but from Alastair Duncan in his book on Tiffany windows.

Here and now at Christ Church Cathedral, we are surviving the fear of obsolescence. Today we celebrate the one hundred and fiftieth year of our founding on March 16, 1839. We do so beneath the opalescence of our famous Tiffany window. We chose this window as the focal point of our Sesquicentennial Celebration and Visions Campaign, whereby we have raised over seven million dollars to purchase the remainder of this block and build a new, and renovate an old, building. This window is a symbol of stability and longevity, and it is such a symbol because of its artistic uniqueness and its Christian name: "Charity."

Duncan, in his book about Louis Comfort Tiffany and his art, writes of Tiffany's unique contribution to the world of glass art:

> Tiffany was an accomplished painter known essentially as a colorist. The quality of glass was greatly improved upon. Rich, flowing colors were developed in varying degrees of translucency, often blended together in whiplash patterns which swept across each sheet. Soon afterward came the invention of "opalescent" glass—a variety not, in fact, totally opaque, but semi-translucent. It remains a quintessential American phenomenon, one that today still distinguishes American windows from those made elsewhere.

Obsolescence is our fear, opalescence is our hope. For if we do not continue to reflect the love of God in Christ as an opalescent community, we will become an opaque relic, a museum, and no longer serve the end for which we were created. The founders of Christ Church were the lights of their generation who, in spite of their humanity, knew that their community must have at its center a church which would reflect the love of God in Christ or the human community, known as Houston, would not prosper. For without such a symbol of love, no community will be continually aware of its common bond of equality in God's unbounded, unconditional love of each of his children.

As we remember today the lights of several generations that have kept God's presence alive in this church, we must be brought into a new awareness by Isaiah's prophecy in today's Old Testament lesson: "Remember not the former things, nor consider the things of old. Behold, I am doing a new thing..." Such is the rhythm of God's revelation. Always and everywhere, God is re-creating the old: building and renovating by transforming such into a new creation. Individuals are made new; creatures and communities are made into new creations. But the new creation comes through those who are continually open to the call to represent God in their time and place being, at one and the same time, appropriate to their heritage, yet understandable to their generation. Only when we are consciously willing to be the opalescent vehicles for God's love; only then will the light so shine before others that they may see our good works and give glory to God our Father who is in heaven. We must never rest on the simple remembrance of the past, but use it as an encouragement in the present to seek our vocation in this location: to represent Christ's revelation of God's love. We must always remember that our founder is Christ. In today's Gospel lesson, after telling the Parable of the Wicked Tenants, Jesus reminds us in such a prophetic way for this celebration today: "The very stone which the builders rejected has become the head of the corner."

If we ever forget that central truth, then we will not behold that God is doing a new thing. Knowing Christ as the cornerstone, we then can use these buildings to house and inspire God's love. If we ever forget, then we deserve to be broken as only brick and mortar and to fall upon that stone.

The opalescence of God's presence defeats obsolescence. We have, and we will, reflect God's love in this place. The name of our Tiffany window is "Charity." The word is from the Latin *caritas* which means love. We are here to reflect that charity of love. God uses opaque humanity, when it is willing, to be the revelation of His love.

Our call is echoed In a beautiful, untitled poem by Gerard Manley Hopkins. Listen carefully for the incarnational word of how it is that God reveals God's self in the several generations. For this occasion I will name his poem "Opalescence":

> As kingfishers catch fire, dragonflies draw flame;
> As tumbled over rim in roundy wells
> Stones ring; like each tucked string tells, each hung bell's
> Bow swung finds tongue to fling out broad its name;
> Each mortal thing does one thing and the same:
> Deals out that being indoors each one dwells;
> Selves—goes itself; *myself* it speaks and spells,
> Crying *What I do is me: for that I came.*
>
> I say more: the just man justices;
> Keeps grace: that keeps all his goings graces;
> Acts in God's eye what in God's eye he is—
> Christ—for Christ plays in ten thousand places,
> Lovely in limbs, and lovely in eyes not his
> To the Father through the features of men's faces.

In spite of appearances to the contrary, we in the Episcopal Church do have altar calls. Today, after the prayer of consecration, the bishop of Texas will call you to the altar to receive the "gifts of God for the people of God."

Do not come forward unless you are willing to be made new.

Do not come forward unless you are willing to enter a renewal of your baptismal covenant.

Do not come forward unless you are willing to continue in the Apostles' teaching and fellowship, in the breaking of bread, and in the prayers.

Do not come forward unless you will persevere in resisting evil, and, whenever you fall into sin, repent and return to the Lord.

Do not come to the altar unless you will proclaim by word and example the Good News of God in Christ.

Do not come unless you will seek and serve Christ in all persons, loving your neighbor as yourself.

Do not come forward unless you will strive for justice and peace among all people, and respect the dignity of every human being.

By coming forward, we will make a public covenant renewal to be the people of God in this place: Christ Church Cathedral. We will make a new covenant to be the opalescent body of Christ and give ourselves to this city for another generation. This is God's dwelling place, for God is love, and those who dwell in love dwell in God and God in them.

Amen.

March 19, 1989
Palm Sunday
Luke 22, 23

"Reason is God's gift, but so are the passions," writes Cardinal Newman. Today is the triumphal entry known as Palm Sunday, but it is also the rehearsal of the passion narrative. First, the joyful palm procession and acclamation of Jesus as king. Then follows the long, passionate account of Jesus' arrest, trial, and death. Such a contrast. It has been said that the gospel's true nature is irony. And nowhere is that more true than the unreasonable incongruity of the king riding on an ass, and the Savior hanging on a cross. Today is a sacred moment in the midst of ordinary time. A sacred space to ponder the unreasonable passion that is such a predominate portion of our religion nature.

"Passion" in this religious context means "suffering love." Passion is any powerful feeling—love, hate, joy, or greed—but the root is the Greek word *pathos*. The implied meaning is a strong feeling that carries a cost. The cost may come from expressing or not expressing the feeling, or the cost may come from not following the passion, but there will be a cost incumbent in the passion. The feeling is love, the cost is suffering.

The whole story of the Christ event is this suffering love. Unreasonable are the passions. Passions will carry us beyond reason and break boundaries, overthrow systems, quicken the living dead. But always with the cost of brokenness and change, even at the gift of new life. How can we rehearse the story of Palm Sunday through Holy Week, even to the cross and empty tomb, without seeing that story reflected in our own unreasonable, passionate fear of death and passionate will to live? Who among us is so calloused by the demands of ordinary time that we cannot be captured, for even a moment, by our own passion to be truly alive as we hear the story of Christ's life and death? Surely this man who died lived an authentic life. And surely within this story is some truth about all life. The source of life's mystery is breathing new life into those who will hear the ironic good news that life depends on those who are willing to live their lives as authentically as Christ lived his. And that his authentic life and death give us permission to do the same.

The Christian story is a call to the curious. If you have no curiosity, then all you know now is all you will ever know. The Christian story is for those who wonder about life and what it means to be alive. The Christian story is for those who want to participate in life rather than observe. Christianity is a call to the curious to come and live life abundantly. In order to do so, one must see reason as God's gift, but know also that there is something about life so incredibly unreasonable, that there is no feeling or will other than that irrational passion that can carry you to the abundance of life at its deepest and most expressive and wondrous and miraculous level. Give permission to put reason on neutral and be carried past in this irrational desire of Holy Week, for reason is a gift of God but so are the passions.

The driving will which breaks custom in order to know, by experience, life's deepest abundance is the Christian call. For why would Jesus have died such a passionate death if he had wanted us to live a passionless life? The vanity of Jesus' death and promise of eternal life is for his followers to remain and count and calculate the fears in life. If you come today to this sacred moment and do not hear the call to abundant life, then we are all in a line, counting our fears as we await the only end we know.

The curious, the ones who are called to wonder, are called to an unreasonable, passionate response to the Holy Week story. That response is to live abundantly because of Jesus' passionate, suffering love. And further, to live in the irony that those who cling to life out of fear of death are already dead, and those who are free to die are truly alive.

Listen to the whimsical yet deeply wise poem by Alastair Reid, which sums up the Christian call. The poem is entitled "Curiosity."

> Curiosity
> may have killed the cat; more likely
> the cat was just unlucky, or else curious
> to see what death was like, having no cause
> to go on licking paws, or fathering
> litter on litter of kittens, predictably.
>
> Nevertheless, to be curious
> is dangerous enough. To distrust
> what is already said, what seems
> to ask odd questions, interfere in dreams,
> leave home, smell rats, have hunches
> do not endear cats to those doggy circles
> where well-smelt baskets, suitable wives, good lunches
> are the order of things, and where prevails
> much wagging of incurious heads and tails.

Face it. Curiosity
will not cause us to die—
only lack of it will.
Never to want to see
the other side of the hill
or that improbable country
where living is an idyll
(although a probable hell)
would kill us all.
Only the curious
have, if they live, a tale
worth telling at all.

Dogs say cats love too much, are irresponsible,
are changeable, marry too many wives,
desert their children, chill all dinner tables
with tales of their nine lives.
Well, they are lucky. Let them be
nine-lived and contradictory,
curious enough to change, prepared to pay
the cat price, which is to die
and die again and again,
each time with no less pain.
A cat minority of one
is all that can be counted on
to tell the truth. And what cats have to tell
on each return from hell
is this: that dying is what the living do,
that dying is what the loving do,
and that dead dogs are those who do not know
that dying is what, to live, each has to do.

This is the Christian story. "Dying is what, to live, each has to do." What is unreasonable is to come to this week of passion and refuse to become passionately involved in life. Christ died in order to eliminate the fear of death. The dead are those who fear death. The gospel irony rings true, you cannot live until you are reconciled to death. In Christ, God reconciled the world to himself. The reckoning was a passionate act of unbounded, unconditional, suffering love. Some continue to live dead to life. And some will die to the fear of death and begin to live.

The curiosity is to wonder who, and Christians are the wonderful. The curious will live. "Face it. Curiosity will not cause us to die—only lack of it will." Come, behold this curious, unreasonable, irrational, passionate week, "only the curious have, if they live, a tale worth telling at all." This week, in this place, the story will be told.

Amen.

March 24, 1989
Good Friday
John 19:1–37

Instead of seeking a cosmic theology, a religious tradition, and an existential faith, we Americans continue our culture of denial by drinking, drugging, or eating ourselves out of awareness, or we spend our time working, shopping, and consuming, which are more acceptable forms of denial. And what is it that we deny by anesthetic consumption?

Ernest Becker, in *Escape from Evil*, frames the human dread:

> And this brings us to the unique paradox of the human condition: that man wants to persevere as does any animal or primitive organism; he is driven by the same craving to consume, to convert energy, and to enjoy continued experience. But man is cursed with a burden no animal has to bear: he is conscious that his own end is inevitable, that his stomach will die.

Perhaps more prosaically and more memorably, Erich Fried writes:

> A dog
> that dies
> and that knows
> that it dies
> like a dog
> and that can say
> that it knows
> that it dies
> like a dog
> is a man.

So it is, and no new insight can assuage our dread, and no denial can erase our archetypal consciousness that death is a reality inescapable, inseparable from our life. We thus carry within us twin and opposite urges. One is a will toward death and another a will away by projecting our fear of death onto another by killing him.

Dag Hammarskjöld writes in *Markings*:

> He will come out
> Between two warders,
> Lean and sunburnt,
> A little bent,
> As if apologizing

For his strength,
His features tense,
But looking quite calm.

He will take off his jacket
And, with shirt torn open,
Stand up against the wall
To be executed.

He has not betrayed us.
He will meet his end
Without weakness.
When I feel anxious,
It is not for him.
Do I fear a compulsion in me
To be so destroyed?
Or is there someone
In the depths of my being,
Waiting for permission
To pull the trigger?

So it is that we come today, this Friday, Good Friday. We stare at a cross on a bare altar and see there in our own fear and our own deceptive projection of our deepest dread that our repressed rage killed an innocent man.

Before we lapse into the comfortable guilt of the literal, our killing began at our choice to be human. The tree in that primary paradise was the beginning of our crucifying nature. Yes, we became aware by Eve's open eyes and her inevitable "yes" to the tempting call to know what God knows. But in our knowledge came our end. This tree, now a cross, has its roots in the mind's darkness.

To be human means to be seekers of God's knowledge. We have a will so strong as to cross all boundaries to find the subject in whose image we are a creature. And the ultimate barrier is that inescapable grave that we seek and deny in our twin and opposite wills, which finally kills what stands in our way.

In Christ, at the cross, God has set himself as the final barrier, and then first dark and light of our awareness. In Christ's death, we are robbed of all light, and in Christ's death, we are given our new enlightenment. This time, God is not barrier but one who empowers. God has died that we might see our death as a means to a beginning. Such an act of shocking insight means that we now need not wait until after our death to begin to live. We have been given eternal life, now. God has removed the ultimate barrier and has begun creation again. This time he, too, tastes human nature and dies for us, with us. What we cannot bear to know, he acknowledges and takes it unto himself. Because of our humanity, God acknowledges and becomes our darkness. We seek a cosmic theology to put together the scattered, fragmented pieces of our consciousness. We seek a religious story which we can see as our family story. Yet, we seek an existential faith that might make some difference to us this day.

Having finished a daily Eucharist in another parish at another time, I left the sacristy, having completed what is, by now, nearly two decades of rehearsing the ritual of re-creation known as the Holy Eucharist. What even by then was thousands of celebrations whereby I, as celebrant, had held aloft and high in hands of outstretched arms, a host of circular symmetry and I, as officiant, had broken that host in reenactment of Good Friday's cross purpose. Having finished a daily priest craft function, I turned into a vacant hallway. A woman in her mid-forties stood alone. She had been one of the faithful few who had received the mystery of life through the reenactment of Christ's death. She had been one of five who kept the feast that day. As we met, it was not an event to be portrayed by a novel or movie scene, and much the more religious for its lack of drama. She simply came to me and put her head on my shoulder and said, "The cancer has come back." I held her in silence. The two of us were one, for her news was my news. Her rebellious cells that had begun again to hasten her end were there for everyone who ever had drawn breath. Her death which came within months of that moment was a reminder that no denial and no projection onto another can satiate the sad reality that each will meet in some empty hallway the news that knows no stranger. That bell tolls for all humanity. She broke the silence. Her tears were the waters of her baptism, the water given to her at genesis, from the womb of her mother. She asked, "Did Christ really die for me?" The words were wired into my mind: "All glory be to thee, Almighty God, our heavenly Father, for that thou, of thy tender mercy, didst give thine only Son Jesus Christ to suffer death upon the cross for our redemption; who made there, by his one oblation of himself once offered, a full, perfect, and sufficient sacrifice, oblation, and satisfaction, for the sins of the whole world…"

The whole world history was all portrayed in that moment. "Did Christ really die for me?" What sense is there if our death is not God's death? What absurd, arbitrary, random whim of chaos is life if it is only to end in a corridor with two people clinging to a tentative question? Is there any way to affirm forty years of empty expectation to a watering woman if indeed death is the only thing we can finally say about life?

"Did Christ really die for me?" My answer was the simple affirmation. I said what Eve and Mary had said when they knew that to say "no" meant nothing new would grow. I just said, "Yes, yes, it is true." And that affirmation gave me a simple revelation which I shared: "And because of that, this is the most important time of your life." And it was. When I officiated at her funeral, we celebrated the Eucharist. I remembered her with those words wired into my own circuitry: Our heavenly Father, for that thou, of thy tender mercy, didst give thine only Son Jesus Christ to suffer death upon the cross for…this woman, for this person, for this human being, this singular solitary soul, for this friend, this mother of children, wife of husband, sister of brother, daughter of parents, friend of mine. Yes, Almighty God, our heavenly Father, for that thou, of thy tender mercy, didst give thine only son for this one moment. "Yes," I answered her question in a cosmic theology, in a religious tradition, in an existential faith that put at peace her rebellious cells. I broke the host, and knew in that moment…yes, yes, it's really true.

With all the sophisticated theology and psychology, whereby we diagnose the denial of death and the guilt of projected death onto others; whereby we understand human nature and fabricate a divine drama of reconciliation in the atonement of the cross—even so, our deepest fear and final word comes in the question held by two holding one another. Is it true, and does it make any difference to me? Does it make any sense? Does Christ's death make any difference to me? Did Christ really die for me? Yes. All our doctrine, ritual, and rite begin at some macrocosmic level and then work themselves through our own experience as we live our lives. We live a story, a liturgy, a rehearsal of our experimentation against all of the boundaries that we can push and transcend to the limit that finally funnels into one fundamental question: Does it make any difference? There are a thousand ways to say "no," there is one way to say "yes," and there is no way to say anything else. This people, be it this day—yea, a remnant people—have stood since that day, that Good Friday, whispering down through every hallway in history "yes!" All our doctrine, ritual, and rite make a singular sound, and that sound is a celebration that rings louder than death's tolling bell: "yes."

If we have anything to say that we can say…we are the Easter people of God, who hold one another in an affirmation of faith…yes. Yes. Yes. Let it be known that, in spite of all denial, a remnant is held together for this moment keeping the truth alive…yes. Yes.

Let it be so. I say…

Amen.

❖ ❖ ❖

March 26, 1989
Easter Day
Luke 24:1–10

Some time ago, I read an essay by Robert Fulghum about a man named Larry Walters. Walters, a thirty-three-year-old truck driver from Los Angeles, for as long as he could remember had wanted to fly. The time, money, education, and opportunity to be a pilot were not his. Hang gliding was too expensive, and a good place was too far away. So he spent a lot of summer afternoons sitting in his backyard in his ordinary old, aluminum lawn chair—the kind with rivets and plastic webbing that are ubiquitous in suburbia—and there he sat, day after day, dreaming of flying.

Within his limitations, Walters finally did what he could about his bliss. He hooked forty-five helium-filled surplus weather balloons to his aluminum lawn chair. He put on a parachute, grabbed a CB radio, a six-pack of beer, a few peanut butter and jelly sandwiches, and a BB gun to pop some of the balloons when he was ready to come down. Instead of drifting up a couple of hundred feet, this man in the flying chair shot up eleven thousand feet, right through the approach corridor of Los Angeles International Airport.

Walters, a taciturn man, when interviewed by the press as to why he did it, said, "You can't just sit there." When asked if he was scared, he answered, "Wonderfully so." Asked if he would do it again, he said, "Nope." And asked if he was glad he did it, he grinned from ear to ear and said, "Oh, yes."

Ever since I read about that man, I haven't been able to get him out of my mind. There is something so exhilarating and, at the same time, so sad about this man floating up in his lawn chair. The exhilaration comes from his indomitable will to fly and his ingenuity in finding a way to do so within his limitations. I am enlivened by that part of the human spirit and will that seeks to be carried up out of the mediocre and transcend boundaries and limits. But I am so sad that after all—after he had exhausted his physical limits, transcended as they were, and after he had run out of peanut butter and beer—he had to pop his balloons with a BB gun and come down to earth again.

I believe that the human spirit seeking to transcend itself and become more experienced, more aware, more whole, is none other than God's Holy Spirit "bearing witness with our spirit." But at the same time, let us be clear, that without God, human transcendence is always doomed to limited heights and to a natural law which reads: what goes up must come down.

Easter is not about human transcendence, but about resurrection. There are two concepts that the human ego confuses with resurrection. They are transcendence and resuscitation. Transcendence, for humans, means the ability to cross human limits. But human transcendence has one limit it cannot cross by itself and that is being human. No matter how much or how many times we humans transcend ourselves, we cannot, perhaps even should not, cease to be human. Resurrection is not to be viewed as, or confused with, human transcendence, though one can be seen in the other. We will return to that point.

The second confusion is that resurrection means being brought back to life. Resurrection means being raised to a new life. Lazarus was resuscitated. The exhilaration was in Christ's power over death in his raising of Lazarus. It was a precursor to resurrection, but poor Lazarus had to die again. Eventually, he was resurrected. So much of what we confuse is a desire to go back to another life. That is not the Easter power. The Easter power is in being raised to a new life which integrates all that is past into something wholly new.

Jesus was resurrected into a living presence, wholly new and wholly eternal. Knowing that powerful Easter presence means that new life can be experienced in this life. Having established the difference between transcendence, resuscitation, and resurrection, then we can begin to see the resurrectional power within human transcendence and new life within life before and after the grave.

Easter proclaims that all power for re-creation is God's creative power. That creative power is present whenever any creature is enlivened with the quickening of new life. Easter proclaims that the new thing and the final thing belong to God, the Lord of life. God is love, and this love is ultimate. Nothing separates us from this renewing, re-creative, resurrectional love. It means that cancer and AIDS and divorce, and hungry children, and the Pan Am Flight 103 and its victims, and any form of death are only penultimate when held under the arms of Easter's risen Christ. There is only one resurrection and that is Christ's resurrection, and within that power, we are all raised up out of whatever death we will ever know.

Mr. Walters' lawn chair flight was not a resurrection. But whatever it was that got him up out of his backyard mediocrity was a transcendent power that no peanut butter or beer can sustain. And that spirit is more powerful than any BB gun can burst. I'm sure the lawn chair flier doesn't confuse his flight with resurrection, but for a few moments, he knew the Easter hope, and he will never be the same again. Perhaps Easter means just that. Because of God's re-creative love in Christ's resurrection, none of us will ever be the same again. Never will we be any less, but always so much more, until ultimately we will transcend even our own humanity and become one with him who has given us our life. And when we reach that ultimate end, it will be an ultimate beginning of an awareness of a life where never again will we need a parachute, a CB, beer, peanut butter, or BB guns. There, we will finally be what, up to now, we have been becoming. If interviewed about our life on earth, when asked if we were scared, we will answer, "Wonderfully so." Asked if we would return to earth, we will say, "Nope." And if asked if we were glad we did it, we will grin from ear to ear and answer, "Oh, yes. Oh, yes!" This is the Easter faith. The Lord has risen. He has risen, indeed.

Amen.

April 2, 1989
John 20:19–31

Last week's *The New Yorker* carried a John Updike short story entitled "Short Easter." It is funny and, as always with Updike, it is well written and enigmatic in ending. There are two lines worth excavating, for they lead to deeper thoughts about Easter's mystery. The character in the story takes an afternoon nap on Easter day. He sleeps in his grown son's old room. When he awakes from his nap, Updike writes: "though the dream world tried to cling to his warm body, amid that unnatural ache of resurrection—the weight, the atrocious weight of coming again to life!…Everything seemed still in place, yet something was immensely missing."

In today's Gospel, the disciples awake from the nightmare of denial and betrayal and the horrifying death of their Savior. Huddled together in their fear, they stir in circles of despair and the unnatural ache of beginning again. Everything seems still there, yet something is immensely missing. Into that circle of fear appears their Lord in a shimmering silence and breathes the word "peace."

For years I have beheld that scene and exhaled relief that the resurrection means we can begin again. The disciples, desperate because of the death of their dream, awake to the promise of peace and purpose "to tell the world about the unconditional love of God that you have experienced in me, ye betrayers and deniers!" The ones who had slept through the bloody sweat of Gethsemane were now the ones sent out to proclaim the Good News, that all is forgiven. Even Thomas' doubt was satiated by Jesus' scars. (Do we get into heaven by our good marks or by our scars?) Such grace, mediated by that story, becomes available to each of us as we review our own lives in relationship to the truth, or the Christ, or the Good News. If, on an Easter day, most of us evaluated our own sense of peace because of Jesus in our midst, or even our sense of purpose by saying it was our responsibility to proclaim the Good News, who wouldn't go to sleep? We, too, are promised peace and purpose and the grace to awaken to a new life.

But so reading the story, I sense a residual sadness, for missing from the story—from the renewed body of the Risen One and the renewed apostles sent out to preach forgiveness and peace—is Judas.

Judas, chosen originally as one of the twelve, was evidently able and enthusiastic. He handled the treasury for the twelve. Judas' motives in betraying Jesus were, as any human motives, severely mixed. Can we not assume that Judas thought he was doing the right thing? Perhaps Judas wanted to please. He did what his church taught him. He turned in one who claimed to be God—an ultimate blasphemy. Perhaps he held a heavy mother complex and continued to seek the approval that nature and nurture withheld. Maybe he was subject and object of evil and was as much a victim as Christ. His alliance with Caiaphas was the logical choice over this rabbi without credentials who claimed to be the Messiah. Was he more culpable than Peter, who had denied knowing Jesus? Was Judas any more evil in his actions than the others in their passivity? Whatever Judas' motives or guilt, he could not bear the responsibility of his actions. Suicide seemed to be the only act which would deliver him from his despair. The black mood which came over Judas when he had to face the fact that his actions had crucified one who loved him, such a mood was too heavy to tolerate. So Judas did to himself as he had done to Jesus. He betrayed himself.

Judas could not bear the ache of beginning again. He could not bear the atrocious weight of coming again to life. Human sin is not an option. Sin is our nature. But in redemptive opposition to our nature, it is the nature of God to offer unconditional love. The wise teacher was seen by his student, bending near a bush. A scorpion was caught in a rock under the bush by his front claws. As the wise teacher tried to get the scorpion loose, the scorpion stung him again and again. The student asked the teacher, "Why do you hold your hand so that it is continually stung by the scorpion?" The teacher said, "It is the nature of the scorpion to sting; it is the nature of the teacher to release." Human sin is our nature. It is the nature of God to offer, continually and without condition, unbounded love. Judas could not handle the scandal of such unbounded love. He could not accept his own humanity. This is the terrible weight of new life. In order to be resurrected into peace and purpose, we must accept the death of our illusion that we can be perfect. The atrocious weight of coming again to life is the acceptance, consciously, of our own Judas nature. I know Judas. He is in all those I fear and hate. I know Judas. He comes to my office and cries over his imperfection. I know Judas, for he eats at my table and sleeps in my bed. I know Judas, for he is the dark figure in my nightmares. I know Judas. I am he.

Until I admit and confess my Judas nature, the weight of despair is so great that, at times, only a desperate act will deliver my despair. My friend and mentor, Robert Johnson, says that when one of his patients calls him and threatens suicide, he responds, "You are right, something in you needs to die. This is an internal story, don't externalize it!"

We each know the despair of discovering our dark side. We each know the tempting act of self-betrayal. We each know how heavy is the weight of beginning again. But let us rehearse the sad irony of Judas. Had Judas carried his despair one day longer, Jesus would have appeared to him as he did to Peter and Thomas and given him peace—just one more day.

Such a lesson of the resurrection. If in the radical darkness of despair we will wait just one day longer, the unconditional love may break in and breathe the peace that passeth understanding. The resurrection means that whatever our despair, even if we have through our own dark side created our own despair, we need not be desperate. Given three days and someone to love us, we will wake up and bear the weight of coming again to life. And when we awake, everything will seem still here, yet something will be immensely missing. What will be missing is whatever has been keeping us from living. What will be in its place is a new life, no less, but oh, so much more. Peter waited one more day—and he was sainted. So, too, Thomas. Poor Judas. Poor Judas.

But if you wonder where Judas is, my faith says he is with all the saints where sorrow and pain are no more, neither sighing, but peace and new life and the unnatural joy of God's unbounded grace.

If Judas isn't in heaven, I wonder who is.

Amen.

❧ ❧ ❧

April 30, 1989
John 14:23–29

Dr. Elvin Semrad, longtime clinical director of the Massachusetts Mental Health Center and professor of psychiatry at Harvard Medical School, had a sign on the door of his office which read:

> When door is ajar come in,
> When closed, I am busy,
> If emergency, please knock.

The sign was a facilitator for clarity about accessibility and limits. That is very important for the kind of counselor that a psychiatrist or a priest is, but not for the kind of counselor that the Holy Spirit is. In today's Gospel, Jesus says, "These things I have spoken to you, while I am still with you. But the Counselor, the Holy Spirit, whom the Father will send in my name, he will teach you all things, and bring to your remembrance all that I have said to you." Then he says a most hopeful, gentle, and graceful thing: "Peace I leave with you; my peace I give to you; not as the world gives do I give to you." The gifts that the world gives do not finally scratch the existential itch.

There is something in my experience about this Counselor that is not as clear as Dr. Semrad's sign. The Counselor that God sends is God's own Spirit. This is the spirit that Jesus refers to in the third chapter of this Gospel in this familiar way: "The wind blows where it wills, and you hear the sound of it, but you do not know whence it comes or whither it goes; so it is with every one who is born of the Spirit."

So, what is the nature of this Counselor that is so unpredictable that we don't know where or when it will come, blowing into or out of our lives, who is such a disorienting Counselor, who is unclear about limits and accessibility? How can Jesus promise us peace when what we feel about this Counselor is anxiety?

There are two clues given to us about the Holy Spirit's nature. Both are given by Jesus in this teaching today. In verse 22, Judas (not Iscariot) asks Jesus, "Lord, how is it that you will manifest yourself to us, and not to the world?" Jesus answers him, "If a man loves me, he will keep my word, and my Father will love him and we will come to him and make our home with him." We will move in with you. We will be as close to you as your own home—you do not have to go to an office in a tower for a consultation; he will come to you. This Spirit/Counselor's nature is as close as your own home. The Holy Spirit is one with the Father and Son and will dwell or make a home with one who loves God. The second clue about the nature of this Spirit/Counselor is that the peace given will not be the peace of the world. We seek the gifts the world cannot give, and the gifts are given by this Spirit.

Somewhere in the depths of our common experience, we know of that vague and elusive Spirit about which Jesus speaks. The Holy Spirit is the teacher of our life's journey. The Spirit initiates our journey, leads and directs our journey, and is the journey's end. Paul writes, in the epistle to the Romans, a clearer vision of the Spirit's vocation as Counselor: "But you are not in the flesh, you are in the Spirit, if in fact the Spirit of God [really] dwells in you…But if Christ is in you, although your bodies are dead because of sin, your spirits are alive…For all who are led by the Spirit of God are [children] of God…it is the Spirit himself bearing witness with our spirit that we are children of God, and if children, then heirs, heirs of God and fellow heirs with Christ, provided we suffer with him in order that we may also be glorified with him."

The Holy Spirit, as Counselor, is not the kind of counselor that dwells in an office outside of us that we can call on when we need him. The Divine Counselor dwells within us and calls on us to grow, stretch, and become. A convenient and popular misunderstanding of the Holy Spirit is that this Counselor is a kind of a cosmic bellhop that we call on when we need him to get us out of danger, suffering, or problem. But the nature of the Holy Spirit is that the spirit may call on us to enter danger, suffering, or problem in order that we might truly know the God within. So be it that we suffer with Christ so that we might be glorified. The only way to know this Spirit within may be to enter into those things we want the Spirit to deliver us from. Some Spirit! Some Holy Spirit! Some Counselor that dwells within!

The Holy Spirit is the Spirit of God who gives us an inward call to adventure. We do not call on the Spirit in need, but the Spirit calls us into need in order to discover the glory of life which can only be known in a commitment to journey wherever the Spirit leads us.

The Counselor is a comforter, not like a down blanket that warms us and protects us, but a comforter who makes us anxious and calls us to pick up our beds and walk. The Christian commitment is to love God. Love's invitation will invite God to take up residence in one's life. The Spirit will bear witness with our spirit and lead us into truth.

The popular PBS series by Bill Moyers, *The Power of Myth,* has a conversation between Joseph Campbell and Moyers on a point of internal truth that is very much akin to what I have tried to say:

> Campbell: I came back from Europe as a student in 1929, just three weeks before the Wall Street crash, so I didn't have a job for five years. There just wasn't a job. That was a great time for me.
>
> Moyers: A great time? The depth of the Depression? What was wonderful about it?

Campbell: I didn't feel poor, I just felt that I didn't have any money. People were so good to each other at that time...

There was a wonderful old man up in Woodstock, New York, who had a piece of property with these little chicken coop places he would rent out for twenty dollars a year or so to any young person he thought might have a future in the arts. There was no running water, only here and there a well and a pump. He declared he wouldn't install running water because he didn't like the class of people it attracted. This is where I did most of my basic reading and work. It was great. I was following my bliss.

Now, I came to this idea of bliss because in Sanskrit, which is the great spiritual language of the world, there are three terms that represent the brink, the jumping-off place to the ocean of transcendence: *Sat, Chit, Ananda*. The word *"sat"* means being. *"Chit"* means consciousness. *"Ananda"* means bliss or rapture. I thought, "I don't know whether my consciousness is proper consciousness or not; I don't know whether what I know of my being is my proper being or not; but I do know where my rapture is. So let me hang on to rapture, and that will bring me both my consciousness and my being." I think it worked.

Moyers: Do we ever know the truth? Do we ever find it?

Campbell: Each person can have his own depth, experience, and some conviction of being in touch with his own *sat-chit-ananda*, his own being through consciousness and bliss. The religious people tell us we really won't experience bliss until we die and go to heaven. But I believe in having as much as you can of this experience while you are still alive.

Moyers: Bliss is now.

Campbell: In heaven you will be having such a marvelous time looking at God that you won't get your own experience at all. That is not the place to have the experience—here is the place to have it.

Moyers: Do you ever have the sense when you are following your bliss, as I have at moments, of being helped by hidden hands?

Campbell: All the time. It is miraculous. I even have a superstition that has grown on me as the result of invisible hands coming all the time—namely, that if you do follow your bliss you put yourself on a kind of track that has been there all the while, waiting for you, and that life that you ought to be living is the one you are living. When you can see that, you begin to meet people who are in the field of your bliss, and they open the doors to you. I say, follow your bliss, and don't be afraid, and doors will open where you didn't know they were going to be.

Moyers: Have you ever had sympathy for the man who has no invisible means of support?

Campbell: Who has no *in*visible means? Yes, he is the one that evokes compassion, the poor chap. To see him stumbling around when all the waters of life are right there really evokes one's pity.

Moyers: The waters of eternal life are right there? Where?

Campbell: Wherever you are—if you are following your bliss, you are enjoying that refreshment, that life within you that has been there all the time.

In due respect to Joseph Campbell, and in agreement with him, I conclude that to follow the lead of the Holy Spirit is to follow your bliss. God moves in and leads us into all the openings we have ever desired. It may be through the deep, dark journey of the soul, but we need not be afraid, for the opening awaits us, no less than this angel of the Lord harkening through. Ah! Bright wings—those wonderful, colorful, enamoring, ecstatic, beautiful, pink, purple, then red wings, beckoning us to follow our bliss, come whence it will, cost what it may. This is our doctrine of the Holy Spirit.

Amen.

❈ ❈ ❈

May 28, 1989
Luke 6:39–49

If being blind is just a handicap, then why do we close our eyes when we pray? Jesus asks us today in his parable, "Can a blind man lead a blind man? Will they not both fall into a pit?" Jesus is, of course, speaking in a comic metaphor. Our Lord is not exploiting handicapped people by laughing at the unsighted, but to the ironic contrary, he is scolding those who had so much knowledge with very little understanding. The religious leaders were blind to the truth and were so concerned about the specks in others' eyes that they were blind to the log in their own.

The first blind person I remember meeting was a little girl in my neighborhood. A new family moved in next door to Dr. Neil on the corner of Broadway and Jones. My mother invited our new neighbor for coffee. I was nine or ten. Mrs. Meadows told me, "I have a daughter about your age. When she comes home for summer break, you must meet her." In the bashful discomfort of my age, I agreed that that would be nice. The truth behind my uneasiness, of course, had to do with a ten-year-old boy's dislike for girls in general and suspicious curiosity about anyone who went away to school.

When the new neighbor departed, my mother patiently explained to me that the little Meadows girl was away at the Oklahoma School for the Blind. Even then, maybe even most particularly then, I felt a sympathetic pain of fear. Blind. Who among us has not wondered what our world would be like without light. Colors, shapes, subtleties. No orange or purple, no decorating of a room, no sight of stained glass, let alone the fact of ambulation and navigation.

Our little town had an alley. Walking to Felt's Grocery took me by the Meadows' backyard. An early summer day, I walked past a little girl standing by the fence as her mother hung wet, wrinkled sheets to dry on the clothesline. "Good morning," said Mrs. Meadows, "I'd like for you to meet Marilyn." My first glance saw her head search for the sound of my voice. When she looked at me, her eyes rolled in that classic unfocused stare of the unsighted. My glance was the only time I looked directly at her. She asked me two questions. "Do you play baseball?" I said, "Yes." "Do you play the piano?" The truth was I had quit lessons after six laborious months and had in my repertoire two pieces, Brahms' "Lullaby" and the "Marines' Hymn." But I said, "Yes." Her mother suggested, "Perhaps soon you, your mother, Marilyn, and I could go to the park for a swim and a picnic." A day or so later the invitation came. My mother besought, I fought. My brother teased—and we went. I would like to tell you a romantic story of a wonderful afternoon of discovery. It wasn't until now. Then, I remember only intimidation and discomfort. Three things I remember. First, she could swim like a fish. Two, she had as much curiosity about the park as I had about the first European cathedral I entered as an adult. And third, she could play the piano better than anyone my age that I had ever seen.

Each human being suffers from a handicap. Some are more obvious than others. Nature is not perfect and neither are we. Nature makes mistakes and so do we. When we are the victims of mistakes, nature's or our own or those of others, we suffer a crisis of betrayal. Why me? The facts are that each of us will be both heir and victim of imperfection.

Providence bequeaths to each of us a palpable fault. It is a measure of our humanity. Such darkness causes us to seek illumination. Such illumination is insight.

Jesus calls us to seek illumination and insight. To focus on faults, mistakes, or handicaps is to see the speck and be blinded by the log. The true leader is the one who knows his own darkness and has entered it and through it seeks illumination and insight. The saints focus on God, not religion. Saints seek truth, not perfection. Saints seek an uncluttered appreciation of existence, a state of awareness that is wide awake and free from all preoccupation, judgment, preconception, and fallacious, superficial interpretation. Saints love. They love truth and human beings. That is why saints close their eyes when they pray. They seek insight. For those of us who are sighted, often the light of illumination is harder to bear than the dark.

Can a blind man lead a blind man? Metaphorically, the answer is no, but in a simple life reflected, a blind little girl can show a sighted little boy that she can outswim and outplay, and offer a curiosity that seeks the extraordinary in the ordinary.

The illumination and insight of Jesus' parables allow us to see life's parables and that each affirms the other. This is the nature of the revealed word in the sacred story. We wonder today who is handicapped and who isn't. Perhaps those who think they know all the answers and have discovered all there is to discover are the ones who are blind. Watch where they lead you; perhaps you might be best led by one who sits quietly with you, closes his eyes, and prays.

Amen.

❖ ❖ ❖

August 20, 1989
Luke 12:49–56

Three against two. Two against three. Father against son. Son against father. Mother against daughter. Daughter against mother. The division even spills over to include in-laws. This is hardly a picture of a mom and pop and two kids sitting in the pew, clean and fresh-faced, looking as together and undisturbed as a Norman Rockwell portrait.

These words from Jesus are difficult words, piercing words, that are the kind of such high frequency that shatter all crystal consciousness of assumptions of middle-class values about families. The great tendency, and I believe the incredible error, about this lesson is to take our current middle-class values about families and project them back into the first century, and become so upset and disappointed that Jesus has taught something about setting father against son, spouse against spouse, and in-law against in-law.

H. King Oehmig writes: "Jesus' view of human community was not a first century version of *Ozzie and Harriet*." In his book, *Summer of '49*, David Halberstam writes about the playoffs between the Boston Red Sox and the New York Yankees in 1949, but more than that, he strives to capture that fleeting bubble of post-war innocence in American life, or what Curt Gowdy, the sportscaster, called "the last innocent days of America." The symbol of the kind of innocence that became idealized during this post-war era was the great DiMaggio. His contemporary and friend, Ernest Hemingway, immortalized DiMaggio in *The Old Man and the Sea*, a favorite story of mine. The old man, Santiago, arose every morning and read the newspapers to see how the Yankees were doing and to see how the great DiMaggio was hitting. Those were idealized and romanticized days—we were home from the victory over the world, babies were booming, and all was well. So began what I believe was an ultimately diabolic view of the American family: *Father Knows Best* and *Ozzie and Harriet*.

Still, those of us who grew up in that era had some reality to test against it. A definition of religion is to struggle against all costs into reality. The reality of our own experience was that we did not exist in perfect families, and our family father did not know best, and he didn't hang around the kitchen visiting with mom all day—he went out and worked. The problems were not always tied in neat bows on packages at the end of shows. This incredible addiction to perfection in American family life began, the nature of which was that when we measured our own reality against *Ozzie and Harriet*, we felt inferior. There was something wrong with us or our family.

What Jesus does with these teachings was somewhat like the story of Alice in Lewis Carroll's *Through the Looking Glass*. At the outset of the story, Alice is comfortable in the parlor playing with her cat. Suddenly, it seems to her that the mirror over the mantel has become opaque, soft like gauze. Alice climbs up to investigate and falls unexpectedly through the looking glass into another world, where, as she claims, "it is rather hard to understand."

The scripture for us is that. It is another way to look at things. It is an introduction, an invitation, into another world where perfection is not required; imperfection is the requirement. In order to get into the Kingdom of God, the holy family, one must be imperfect. If one was perfect, one would not need the kingdom or a holy family. Jesus uses his words today ("I will set father against son, son against father, daughter against mother, two against three in a five member household, and three against two...") as a way to differentiate, to separate the idealized from the real. We each are baptized by fire, into the reality of human imperfection in families—where else? It brings us to the place we must transcend which is inadequate as we grow in our consciousness, and as we struggle to become whole and more. We know from the beginning, at the baptismal ritual, that we transcend that family of biological origin as we belong to a holy family—the people of God. Rather than having that dark view of ourselves as being inadequate and inferior because of imperfection, we begin to realize that our true family of origin is the holy family of Abraham, Isaac, and Jacob, of Sarah, Rebekah, and Rachel, of Peter and Paul, of Martha and Mary—of the family of God who have not been addicted to perfection, but who have professed imperfection as a means toward being acceptable one to another as they accept their unconditional acceptance from their father and mother in the holy family.

John Keating, the teacher played by Robin Williams in *Dead Poets Society*, says, "Just when you think you know something, you have to look at it in another way." Jesus' words today teach us, as Keating taught his students, to look from the side at an oblique angle, to come in the back door, to look down on things or up at things. Moreover, in this story, we see an opposite caricature of the *Father Knows Best* American family—an overbearing father tries to have his son fulfill his own emptiness, and an absent mother acquiesces to the tyrant father. This caricature of the American family is as inaccurate as that of *Ozzie and Harriet*.

What we find is that we are being squeezed, as it were, by the word of God, out of the cocoon of romanticism and idealism about what family life is supposed to be. We project onto the Kingdom of God the worldly values of the middle-class family, which is the 2.2 children, going to fine schools, everybody loving one another and sitting around the table, holding hands. That image has been destructive to the American collective psyche. Where we work out our humanity is in families! Where we exhibit most intimately our imperfections is within families. When we look at one another and conclude that father is not perfect, nor is son, we begin to outgrow the idealism that leads to the perfection and to accept one another as human beings. Because of the shattering gospel, there is no nuclear family—just God's family. That sounds inclusively sweet and cozy, but look again. You have, in baptism, been given up from your family of origin for adoption, and since God has no grandchildren—only children—you are now to see your spouse and children as brothers and sisters in Christ. As Oehmig writes: "Henry or Henrietta, and Henry Junior and little Henrietta, are not just a nuclear family seeking perfection, but they are brother-son, sister-daughter, of God. The perfect Christian household does not exist on earth, but in the kingdom of God."

The next step in our journey away from romanticism and idealism toward reality is to realize that perfection is not a requirement, but imperfection is, and the place that we experience that most intimately is with those with whom we are most intimate, and to erase through the hard words of Jesus, the addiction of co-dependency upon one another to fulfill every need. He finally sets father against son and mother against daughter in order that they might outgrow one another as the incarnation of perfection, and accept one another as brothers and sisters in the common humanity of the family of God. If we are able to do that, then the scandal of the gospel is that not only is that daughter or son at my family table, a brother and sister in the holy family with me, but also that poor, unmarried woman living in a tenement with ten children or that poor person dying by the inch of that insidious disease known as AIDS are my brothers and sisters in the holy family also. And I have as much responsibility for them as I do for my own family. This is the scandal of the gospel. We are separated from our dependency on one another as projections of our own imperfection, but also, we are determined in our responsibility that the world is a family, and that we dwell with brothers and sisters. The song I was taught in Sunday school goes: "Red and yellow, black and white, they are precious in his sight, Jesus loves the little children of the world." If we listen to these words of Christ, we learn that our worldview must be expanded—we live in a global family, not just a nuclear family. Suddenly the warm glow of the gospel burns with intensity; it is a torch that brings awareness; it is a fire that burns away all the impurities and leaves us a central gold: to start to act now with impartiality, respecting the dignity of every human being and accepting the imperfection of every human being. By the light of this flame, we will begin to see that others may not be perfect, but they may be for us the incarnation of God; that they may be, from time to time, something of the cool nurture of love in the immense heat of the world.

Don't misunderstand me—Jesus was not anti-family. But it is clear that he understood the human community as being larger than just the family into which you were born. All of God's children are our brothers and sisters. Of course, I would take it to another level and say that your own family within—every part of your personality—is acceptable to God, and that we must differentiate those in order to make a whole family of personality. So no matter how we look through the glass, we will get another view. When we look through that looking glass, we will see through in strange ways that help us keep from getting stuck in any familiar way. The Word of God comes to us today because once we thought we knew what families were, we had to learn it all over again. It is the nature of growth, awareness, and the kingdom that is to come.

I conclude by saying that Jesus' view of community was not a first-century version of *Ozzie and Harriet*, but a call into the reality of human beings living with human beings, being baptized by fire, again and again, into the reality that there is no perfection short of the kingdom. As surely as we experience the imperfection, we are called into the wholeness of the family of God where there is a place for each of us. "In my Father's house there are many rooms; if it were not so, would I have told you…" You have your own room. There is a place for you in the holy family—a place where, finally, you will never, ever again fear rejection or imperfection, the place that you know deep down and have dreamed of since the time you were born—the final, safe place. We don't have to wait until we die to begin to dwell therein, but we have to understand that our parents and children aren't perfect—just brothers and sisters on the way. That makes us much more patient with being alive.

Amen.

August 27, 1989
Luke 13:22–30

Etymology, that branch of linguistics that studies the derivation of words, has helped me to become more tolerant, if not accepting, of the jolting phrase, ubiquitous on roadside signs, barns, and bumper stickers: "Jesus saves."

Etymologically understood, the Greek word *sozo* means "to heal, to make safe, "to make whole." Therefore, when I see a sign or sticker with the proper noun "Jesus" and the verb "saves," I am *able* to translate: the historical incarnation of God in Christ is fact and symbol of the enabling power of love to be the primary source and ultimate resource for the constellation of wholeness for the human being. Were that on a sign or sticker, it would not fit, and would it fit, it would be ignored. So therefore, I am more patient with the admonition because I know what it means to me, and further, it would waste much metal, paper, and wood to write out the more detailed definition.

Though more patient, my lingering inability to accept the simple statement is because what I think its author may mean is that there is a kind of God that I do not worship…a kind of God who punishes us for being imperfect and brings us to him through fear and the threat of hell with graphic terms like burning therein. I do not believe in that kind of God. So here we are, back again to impatience.

In today's Gospel, Jesus is "journeying toward Jerusalem." (He is always journeying toward Jerusalem.) "Someone said to him, 'Lord, will those who are saved be few?' And he said to them, 'Strive to enter by the narrow door; for many, I tell you, will seek to enter and will not be able.'" This is another one of those hard sayings of Jesus.

Now, just a bit more etymology. The question asked of our Lord was, "How many will become whole?" Jesus, never answering a question directly, responded that numbers are not important in the Kingdom of God. "Strive to enter by the narrow door." In other words, don't worry about others. I call you to strive to enter wholeness. But I warn you, the entry is a struggle. Strive to enter. The Greek word used here that is translated "strive" is the word *agonizomai*. That word suggests strenuous exercise of muscle and energy. From this Greek word, we derive the English word "agonize," which means to suffer anguish.

The mental picture I have of this process is a man stripped to his waist, lubricated by his own sweat and blood, in a sinewy struggle to enter a narrow opening. This is, of course, the description of a baby being born. One more image that makes Jesus' words seem more authentic for striving to be whole is the agony of a man stripped, lubricated by his own sweat and blood, entering wholeness, struggling in the agony of being crucified on a cross as he enters the narrow grave (a synonym for "grave" is "gate."). Our image is of a child being born or the child of God dying.

Salvation, then, is not a saunter to the front of an auditorium to "get saved" as another verse of "Just As I Am" is sung; salvation is the struggle, the striving, the agony of becoming whole.

We already know this. Jesus' words are reminders. Like sacraments, they make known to us what is already true. We know that birth is always painful and messy. But this striving is not something we are to dread, for we have already begun. This striving is not something to fear, just a reality to expect. Our experience already tells us that "no guts, no glory" are the rules for growth. "No pain, no gain" ought to be tattooed next to every "Jesus saves" sign. These are the rules of the universe—no one escapes them, most particularly, God.

Though it may seem that Jesus' words, and my exegesis of them, tend to accentuate the negative, the opposite may be true. Gregory of Nazianzus wrote: "A soul in trouble is near unto God." For imperfect people like us, it comes as good news to realize that all our pain, agony, and striving are not judgments from God for being imperfect, but ways by which we struggle into God's kingdom. So forget this victim posture of "Why did this happen to me?" or "Why is God punishing me?" or "Why am I struggling?" It is because you are a human being. It is not a punishment for imperfection; it is the way by which that stone which is your soul is polished through the gristmill of reality. No one gets off the hook, including and most particularly, God.

John Sanford, in his classic *The Kingdom Within*, states in regard to entering the kingdom:

> It is those who have recognized that they have been injured or hurt in some way in life who are most apt to come into the kingdom. There is no virtue in our weakness or injury as such,...But only a person who has recognized his or her own need, even despair, is ready for the kingdom; those who feel they are self-sufficient, those whom life has upheld in their one-sided orientation, remain caught in their egocentricity.

Jesus taught us *by his own life* that we enter heaven or wholeness by our scars, not our medals. You will remember that Thomas' doubt was not about Jesus' presence, but about whether Jesus was still scarred. Thomas' question was, "Do we worship a scarred God?" Jesus' answer was, "Look at my hands, look at my side. I have entered heaven by the narrow grave—a gate through the scars." He showed Thomas that in the upper room to quell any doubts about the function of strife. We worship a wounded God, and that God does not wound us unmercifully, but calls us through this experience into a kingdom that now we cannot even imagine. Is this not good news for us, a scarred humanity struggling to become whole?

Perhaps the positive and enabling analogy, or even more so the experiential corollary, is the event of birth. The fetus strives to enter a new kingdom through a narrow door. The agonizing organism struggling to become a human has outgrown the small world of the womb. The potential person is stuck in a life that he or she has been called to leave. Studies indicate that the urge to leave the womb is not initiated by the mother, but is initiated from within the deep instincts of the fetus. The striving therefore is placed by God into the very nature of the human from the beginning. The human that does not agonize is not human. Agony is a part of the human process by which we grow from birth to birth. The fetus then struggles against the limited world, and through the labor pain, lubricated by his own blood, the fetus enters the new kingdom by the narrow door, into a world unimagined, a world capacious with possibility, a world full of light and dark and smells and sound, a world that appears to that infant as an incredible kingdom.

The greatest pain and joy ever experienced are the agony and ecstasy of birth. This is the first and last truth. So why are we surprised by Jesus' words, "Strive to enter the narrow way"? We know about that—we've known about that from the very beginning. We have known it every time we took a step. Think about your pain and agony now in a new way. Think about your scars, not as ends, but as signs of beginnings. Each of us carries a scar of birth in the center of our body. The scar in our center is the sign that we cut the cord keeping us in an old, inadequate existence. We enter life scarred, but the scar is a sign of birth—that we finally, because of our own initiative from within, left the narrow grave of the womb through the narrow gate to life. We entered life scarred, but now that sign is a sign of joy that we are alive.

So, in summary, in spite of analytical psychology, systematic theology, and linguistic etymology, perhaps all we need to know and say is that Jesus saves, and you must be born again. When you listen to that, however, listen to it through the halls of history and through the experience of your own journey, because there is an echo, if you hear it correctly: Jesus saves, and you must be born again, and again, and again, and again, and again.

Amen.

❈ ❈ ❈

September 3, 1989
Luke 14:1, 7–14

"For every one who exalts himself will be humbled, and he who humbles himself will be exalted." This is today's wisdom from our rabbi Jesus. Our great teacher places this illumination in the enlightening Parable of the Marriage Feast. "When you are invited by any one to a marriage feast, do not sit down in a place of honor, lest a more eminent man than you be invited by him; and he who invited you both will come and say to you, 'Give place to this man,' and then you will begin with shame to take the lowest place. But when you are invited, go and sit in the lowest place, so when your host comes he may say to you, 'Friend, go up higher'; then you will be honored in the presence of all who sit at table with you. For every one who exalts himself will be humbled, and he who humbles himself will be exalted."

Of course, by now you must know I do not perceive this parable as a Miss Manners or Emily Postian instruction guide for wedding banquets. Anytime I hear in the gospel "marriage" or "wedding," I hear the word "union" or integration of opposite parts. This parable is not just about social custom, but about a uniting of something that is not united. Union of separate parts is the marriage symbol. Here, I believe Jesus is teaching something deeper than dinner-party etiquette. Another hint of what this parable is about: anytime you hear "marriage" think of "union" or "reunion," and when you hear "feast" think of Eucharistic meal. Think of "union" in "marriage" and "communion" in "feast."

Alan Jones claims that most clergy are victims of the lethal combination of low self-esteem and high idealism. That uncomfortable ring of truth may be generalized for any of us who mean to do good, and more so, want to be recognized for doing good. I suspect that on hearing Dean Jones' statement, you, too, hear an uncomfortable ring of truth for your own life. Low self-esteem and high idealism may be a generalized description of a human split in self-consciousness. Denial of this human truth ultimately causes an overcompensation. Is it any wonder that so many of us who have low self-esteem and high ideals become the opposite and present ourselves as egocentric cynics? No one is adequate to this task, and yet, our task is greater than we can accomplish. So, too, we might generalize about each human being in his or her life's journey.

He who exalts himself will be humbled and he who humbles himself will be exalted. Do not confuse low self-esteem with humility. The word "humble" comes from the word "humus," or "earth." A humble person knows his dust nature. In mature spirituality, to be humble means to know and to accept one's own imperfection and to know and to accept such imperfection in another. To be humble means to accept one's own scars of imperfection and to accept the scars of another. One definition of love is the intimacy of sharing and accepting our scars. If we begin by accepting our lower nature first, then we are called up higher into an integration—a marriage, as it were—of our human and divine natures through such unconditional love. When we accept our place as imperfect, dust-natured people, we then are invited to the higher place of children, not of the earth alone, but children of the kingdom—the marriage of human imperfection and divine perfect love. When we accept this divine, unconditional, perfect love, we have a union—or marriage, if you will—with God. We come from the humble place into a higher place, called out of the animal kingdom of the dust into the glorious kingdom of being human. The higher place we are called is into humanity. This union casts out fear of being imperfect. It is the union, or marriage, found at the heavenly banquet.

The true grace of God is the gift of giving each of us our appropriate place. In the Kingdom of God, there is no hierarchy of better or worse. God's eyes do not rank order or keep score, but behold each of us as unique. Our vocation is to fulfill the possibility of our own uniqueness. Biologically, it is our destiny to be similar to every other human being on earth in our basic composition, and at the same time our DNA makes us a never-before and never-again special and unique organism with a distinct and chosen personality. Bernard Segal writes:

> God gave us all certain gifts, but it is up to us to decide how to use them in such a way that even the being who gave them to us will look down one day in admiration and say, "Humm, I never thought of it that way before."

Jesus calls us to know our place. We begin, not in low self-esteem, but in honest acceptance of our humble humanity. We then catch the gift of grace, the unconditional permission to become ourselves—the union of our human imperfection and God's perfect love in a marriage feast.

If we ever capture this graceful marriage of human imperfection and God's perfect love, we know both humility and exaltation, and they are one. Perfect love, God's love, casts out all fear; why in the world are we so afraid? It is a free gift—with no strings attached—you have your entire life to find your place. Most of us are too afraid to look. Low self-esteem and high idealism are integrated into a human being who is at peace to be in his own place, each of which is a union of proper humility and appropriate place of honor.

We spend so much of our lives trying to impress others with how wonderful we are, rather than simply living the wonder of who we are. This tension of trying to be perfect, do good, and be approved of by our appearance and action robs us of the joy of living with spontaneity. The true saints have never been perfect; a requirement for sainthood is imperfection. You have to be a miserable sinner before you can know true grace. The true saints are those who live life uniquely and with grace and humor.

Such graceful humor is so wonderfully revealed in Jenny Joseph's poem:

Warning

When I am an old woman I shall wear purple
With a red hat which doesn't go, and doesn't suit me.
And I shall spend my pension on brandy and summer gloves
And satin sandals, and say we've no money for butter.
I shall sit down on the pavement when I'm tired
And gobble up samples in shops and press alarm bells
And run my stick along the public railings
And make up for the sobriety of my youth.
I shall go out in my slippers in the rain
And pick the flowers in other people's gardens
And learn to spit.

You can wear terrible shirts and grow more fat
And eat three pounds of sausages at a go
Or only bread and pickle for a week
And hoard pens and pencils and beermats and things in boxes.

But now we must have clothes that keep us dry
And pay the rent and not swear in the street
And set a good example for the children.
We must have friends to dinner and read the papers.

But maybe I ought to practice a little now?
So people who know me are not too shocked and surprised
When suddenly I am old, and start to wear purple.

Jenny Joseph's poetic character knows that old is young and last is first. That humility is exaltation. Today we have a wedding feast—a re-union, a comm-union—a time in which your imperfection and mine is integrated in perfect unconditional love. At this banquet, there are no outcasts, there are no boundaries, and there are no barriers. At this banquet, we are all offered to be married once again to God in union with the Christ in each of us. Come just as you are. Come, wear purple with a red hat that doesn't go. Here, at this table, everybody has a place, and there is a place for you.

Amen.

❖ ❖ ❖

September 17, 1989
Luke 15:1–10

"Now the tax collectors and sinners were all drawing near to [Jesus]. And the Pharisees and the scribes murmured, saying, 'This man receives sinners and eats with them.' So he told them this parable."

Always leaning against the task of proclaiming Christ, I seek new ways to articulate who he is. Today I say what the Bible says: Jesus is the one who receives sinners and eats with them. This is how the religious leaders of his day described him, but with a different tone in their voice. This is the way religious leaders of our day ought to describe him with still another different tone and emphasis. Jesus Christ is the one who receives sinners and eats with them. Christ Jesus came into the world to save sinners. This is the best way to describe what is happening here today; we have come here to be received, to be accepted and to be found acceptable, and we have come to eat with Jesus.

The sinners to be received are all of us. And in particular, we are going to make a parable. The parable is to bring these lambs into the house and rejoice that they will never be lost, for through their baptism, they will always have a home and a place to eat.

When I was a little boy, my days were spent in discovery through play: war, cops and robbers, baseball, basketball, marbles, cowboys, kick the can, campouts, storytelling, experimentation, limit testing. Some days I strayed, not only from home, but from inherited values; I heard things, said words, thought thoughts, even enacted actions that broke rules, ran against the teachings of my teachers. But after a day of straying, at about dusk I always heard an accepting invitation from a shepherdess who called me her lamb. From the front porch she would call: "You boys come in, wash up, it's time to eat." And whatever soil had sullied my body or soul was received, washed away, and we ate. This is, of course, the ritual of the gospel of baptism and Eucharist. Today we wash up these children and the child in each of us, and we renew our bodies in this bath and our souls with this soul food from our shepherd.

Jesus is the one who receives sinners and eats with them. What else do we need to say regarding his being our Savior? A bath and a meal are the sacramental rehearsals of our faith. It is easier to make our faith complex than it is to make it simple. But making it simple does not make it easy. The most difficult doctrine of our faith is believing that we are totally acceptable to eat at Christ's table. Our intellect cannot bear such certainty. For to be human means to have a double vision. We see ourselves in the darkness of our own shame and misery. And we see ourselves in the light of pure desire for wholeness.

God has only the eye of unconditional love. God sees us as he created us: good! Very good! God knows that in order for us to come home, we have to leave home. He said to Abraham in Genesis 12:1: "Go from your country and your kindred and your father's house to the land that I will show you." That is the covenant that we are in. We leave wombs, gardens, homes, parents, values, ideals, boundaries, rules, groups. We leave because we are called to leave, in order to discover larger worlds, greater issues, and expanded selves. But we go grudgingly, because we know leaving means being lost, falling down, getting hurt, feeling abandoned. It means we will feel the loss of the safety of whatever home we are called out of. But God calls and nudges us out because unless we leave, we will never know the gain from losing, the getting up from falling down, the healing from the hurt, the being found in feeling lost, the coming home from leaving.

Simple, not easy. The Gospel's simplicity is acted out today. The disease (the dis-ease) is our anxiety in facing the unknown. The healing from our disease of anxiety comes from the known. Our Lord receives sinners and eats with them. Those who leave can always come home. One unscientific postscript: it is only God who can decide who is lost. Those of us in our egocentric attitudes are often too quick to assume who is lost. One assumption we always make is that the "them" are those, not we, surely. A lot of folk that we religion folk think are lost have found something for which we would give our kingdom to have. Let us not be so quick to judge who is lost. Some whom we see as "lost" may have found something we desperately seek. The parable need not be interpreted any further, only retold. Children, come home, wash up, it's time to eat.

Bring me those lambs. They are not lost because they have been found by a family that expects them to leave home. Encourages them to leave the country and their father's house in order to discover life more abundantly than you can discover it in the womb. They are not lost; they are adventurers, called into the adventure of living. Today we are christening them as one would break a bottle of champagne against the bow of a ship, launching them into the journey, because they are made to be lost. No matter where they go, or with whom, or when, they can always come home. We will greet them on the porch like the patient father waiting for the prodigal children, and we will say to them: come in, wash up, it is time to eat! Let us welcome them home. The water is here, so is the table for the food. Dirt and hunger are requirements for the holy sacraments. Our host is the one who receives sinners and eats with them.

The candidates for bath and meal will now be presented.

Amen.

1990

August 5, 1990
Romans 8:35–39; Matthew 14:13–21

In the July 23, 1990, edition of The New Yorker, Galway Kinnell has a poem entitled "Kilauea." July 23, 1990, is also the day my father died. Throughout my professional life, God has continued to provide occasional breadcrumbs of revelation, incarnations. The day my father died, on the airplane home, reading this poem was one of those breadcrumbs. This poem holds many of the circular thoughts engendered by such a traumatic transition.

Kilauea

Here is a stone with holes in it,
like a skull. It has furrows,
like my father's brow. Once
he could get up when he wanted and go
into an untouched future; when I knew him
he was sprinting to get to death
before his cares could catch up
and kill him. A small rainbow
that forms around me now curves in,
like the birth-forceps that hoisted me out
—witness the depressions in the temple bones—
until its two ends almost touch
my feet. Could it be that *I*
am the pot of gold? Both pots,
one inside the other,
like the fire leaping inside the steel drum the night workers hold out
    their hands to, in the icy air before morning,
or the pitch-black of speech about to be born through scarlet lips,

> or the child getting off her bicycle inside the old woman the priest has
>   told to get ready to die,
> or the father of Edinburgh rising early inside the son of Pawtucket—
>   to whom on Sundays after church he read the funnies, Scripture
>   in the father-tongue?
> Now the rainbow throws its double onto the air above it—
> as on those Sundays, when the first blessing was we were blessed,
> and the second, we knew we were blessed...

Even in the child's night of magic thought, he knows his parents' death will be of enormous dimension and precious meaning. All of life is a drama written through the action and dialogue between parent and child. The center of one's own conscious image is an imprint of such dialogue and event. Whose story is not written in response to one's parents' presence and absence?

Having spent some nine months listening intently to people's stories and their struggling efforts toward peace, I am more convinced than ever before that wholeness requires one reflecting consciously upon his own story, but more so, finding a place in a transcendent story that will free one to travel one's own way.

This Christian drama of life, death, and new life is my transcendent story—not written just for me, but written no less for me than any who ever lived. My life moves in a double rainbow, as my story is lived out in this humus, human earth, this sod, and at the same time, lived out in eternity within the sacred story. I am the pot of gold. I do not seek it elsewhere in some magic potion of quick cure, or in some superstitious religion, but in the mysterious paradoxes of my own life and death, blessing and curse, presence and absence, known and unknown.

Today's sequence hymn is my favorite hymn. It was sung at my ordination and my father's burial. It is from William Alexander Percy's poem and sets the paradox of our journey as life's disciples. Humus we are, rising up human, to live our lives by the sweat of our brow, the soil of our existence, from which we have come and to which we shall return:

> They cast their nets in Galilee
> Just off the hills of brown;
> Such happy, simple fisherfolk,
> Before the Lord came down.
>
> The peace of God, it is no peace,
> But strife closed in the sod.
> Yet, brothers, pray for but one thing—
> The marvelous peace of God.

Such a paradox it is to live the sacred and secular, the conflict and the peace, at the same space and time. Such a paradox to hear our sacred story and know it to be our own story.

We look no further than today's scripture lesson, a unique and poetic story of our primal truth.

Jesus withdrew to a lonely place. But the crowds followed. He had compassion on them and healed the sick. When it was evening, the disciples came to him and said, "This is a lonely place, send the people away to fill their hunger for themselves." Jesus said, "Don't send them away; you give them something to eat." They said to him, "We have only five loaves and two fish." Jesus said, "You have enough." And he thanked God for what they had, blessed it, broke it, and they ate and were satisfied. It was a breadcrumb; it was just enough to satiate those who were starved for life. They had enough to satiate the hunger in their midst; it took the wisdom of our Lord to get them in touch with what they already had.

The Psalm says, "They ate the bread of angels. He provided food enough." I know loneliness. Loneliness is a requirement for one to discover what is his alone. Hunger is a requirement to discover what is necessary for survival. Jesus is the One, in symbol and fact, who lived the paradox even unto the contradiction of the cross. He lived that of which he spoke. His transcendence comes to us even in the mundanity of death, in the transportation through time. The source of the mystery has given us a resource, a breadcrumb, and it is just enough. He lives in our story to transcend time and space, to be incarnate, to grant us our own selfhood and sufficient resources to become whole. The peace of God, it is no peace, but we pray but for one thing, the marvelous peace of God.

Having spent most of a year in the clinic, I have observed that the scientists have no more idea of what heals than do the theologians. Ordained people believe that since they have named God, they have captured his power. Doctors believe that once they can diagnose something, they have explained it. Neither is true. The scientific system has been set up to fill in the gaps between the unknown and the imagination—not at all different from the religious myth. We don't know about the unknown. There is a place yet for mystery and for human beings to grow up about their limitations and possibilities. I have come to some comfort that there is a place where science and spirituality can share a tradition of healing. We need a scientific system, but we also need a symbolic model, and we need the two to continue to talk to each other.

My own recent event of my father's death sets in motion my own psycho-spiritual dynamic. Having now lost both of my parents, I know that lonely place apart where only I can stand alone. I have not spent twenty years in the priesthood only to have my bluff called and soul shattered by the death of a parent. It was apparent in the beginning that this life was a time-limited experience. There are no exceptions. I don't want to be an exception, and although my father was exceptional, I don't have any fantasy that I would have wanted him to have missed his death. It must be the most spiritual time of life. He died suddenly, and suddenly I was in touch with how much a part of me he is and I of him, and how unique and different we are. It is my story, but it is not a special story. I also am a part of a greater story, a holy family, a sacred journey that does have incredible, mysterious meaning. In this holy family, I can rest assured that my archetypal needs can be met where they can only be met; that is, finally by me within my own soul. I have sufficient soul mates who struggle with me to help one another seek peace in this strife closed in the sod. The only healing comes from the source of all the mystery, for which the word "God" is not adequate. God comes to us in many names, in many places, in many faces.

Maturity tells us now that God comes to us in loss, hunger, loneliness, tribulation, distress, persecution, hunger, peril, and sword. These are not times when God is absent, but times when perhaps our own egos are sufficiently impotent to yield to a greater self and know a larger mystery within the narrow reality. That essential truth is something that Paul tells us can conquer all things through him that loves us. Paul was persuaded, as I am, that neither death, nor life, nor angels, nor principalities, nor powers, nor things present, nor things to come, nor height, nor depth, nor any other creature is able to separate us from the love of God which is in Christ Jesus our Lord. There are few things I know, but I know that is true.

Heaven is but a form of the word "home." My father and mother are home. But so am I. This place is my spiritual home. The church is where I first heard of God's unconditional love for me. I was taken there by my parents. I am still here. This Cathedral has been my home for a decade. It is nice to be home.

I am alone and yet in the midst of a holy family. I have come home hungry, yet I have just enough. I have come home conflicted, yet am at peace. I have come home imperfect, but am twice blessed. I am blessed and I know I am blessed. I thank God for the breadcrumb of the poem that I read on the day my father died.

> Here is a stone with holes in it,
> like a skull. It has furrows,
> like my father's brow. Once
> he could get up when he wanted and go
> into an untouched future; when I knew him
> he was sprinting to get to death
> before his cares could catch up
> and kill him. A small rainbow
> that forms around me now curves in,
> like the birth-forceps that hoisted me out
> —witness the depressions in the temple bones—
> until its two ends almost touch
> my feet. Could it be that *I*
> am the pot of gold? Both pots,
> one inside the other,
> like the fire leaping inside the steel drum the night workers hold out
>   their hands to, in the icy air before morning,
> or the pitch-black of speech about to be born through scarlet lips,

or the child getting off her bicycle inside the old woman the priest has
   told to get ready to die,
or the father of Edinburgh rising early inside the son of Pawtucket—
   to whom on Sundays after church he read the funnies, Scripture
   in the father-tongue?
Now the rainbow throws its double onto the air above it—
as on those Sundays, when the first blessing was we were blessed,
and the second, we knew we were blessed…

Amen.

❈ ❈ ❈

August 12, 1990
Jonah 2:1–9

One of the nice things about going to seminary, being from a small town in Oklahoma as I was, resting in that peaceful land between ignorance and innocence, is that your learning curve is so large. I arrived at seminary thinking that The Beatitudes were a singing group. You could always tell the religion majors in college, or those who hung around student centers like the Wesley Foundation, or the Baptist Student Center, or the Canterbury Club, because they were the ones with the ingratiating looks of recognition when the professor would say something in Hebrew. I had no idea what the Pentateuch was. When the professor used the German term for salvation history, which is *heilsgeschichte*, I thought I knew what it meant— at least, in Oklahoma I knew what it meant. In the Old Testament survey lecture, we came to the book of Jonah, out of which we have heard read this morning the prayer of Jonah in the belly of that great fish. When the professor said there is no evidence that it was a whale, it was just simply a great fish, one of those ingratiating religion majors said, "Well, what kind of a fish do you think it was, professor?" "Well, let's just agree it was a metaphorical fish." A friend of mine from a small town in Alabama leaned over and said, "They never got one of those in Mobile Bay!" Whether it was a whale or a metaphorical fish, it doesn't really make much difference because it is a story of incredible power and depth.

The story: Jonah was a prophet, a reluctant prophet. One called out by God for a mission. He was to go to the great wicked city of Nineveh and call the people there to repentance. Like many of us who receive a call, Jonah refused and fled to Tarshish. Nineveh and Tarshish are geographic anti-poles. Nineveh, to the east, is the large city and later capital of Assyria, the very nation that would destroy and carry off Jonah's people. The Assyrians were renowned for their power and gross cruelty. Nineveh is a city where power is a threat to Israel's existence and where evil is antithetical to God's will. Tarshish, on the other hand, lies somewhere in the far west and is a place where Yahweh is not known. Jonah, fleeing from God, sees Tarshish as a refuge beyond God's domain. Here, as always, are the opposites: a call to Nineveh to be a servant of God's calling in a place of difficulty and challenge, and a fleeing to Tarshish at the opposite end, a place of nonexistence.

Jonah "went down" to Joppa to catch a ship going to Tarshish. "Went down" is a description echoing the irony of an entry into a place where he thought he would escape God, only to eventually realize that entering the interior space is where one always encounters God.

When Jonah got on the ship, the Lord hurled a great wind upon the sea. The sailors were afraid and cried out, but Jonah went farther down into the innermost part of the ship and, like a good prophet, went to sleep.

The storm is a transparent metaphor for spiritual and psychic turmoil. Jonah, refusing to be what God was calling him to be, created a storm that made everyone around him uncomfortable. So it is when any of us flees our truth. It is not possible to have a psychic storm or a spiritual crisis in isolation. The crisis contaminates those closest to us and our storm threatens to disturb the calm of those around us.

Jonah went to sleep in the interior of the ship. Sleep may be an escape, but it may be a state for healing to take place. When in crisis or turmoil, consciousness cannot contain sustained conflict. Sleep creates an alpha state, where it is possible for the unconscious to communicate. It is natural for those in crisis, turmoil, or depression to sleep, to seek the shallow grave known as a bed, because it makes possible an opportunity for the unconscious to begin to heal through a dream, a vision, or a message. This is the psychological basis for the healing nature of prayer and meditation. When we are in conflict, we tire and desire a greater consciousness which is available to us in the unconscious. It would be easier for most of us if we would take conscious control of our own storms, pause to pray, and meditate. By doing so, one steps outside of one's normal state of consciousness in order to receive the information that is being blocked out by the ego, for the ego is so threatened by whatever it is that is critical. Crisis means change, and the greatest threat to the ego is the unknown. Sleep is the healthiest response to this critical period, this storm, this great psychic or spiritual crisis that comes to everybody at some time. Unfortunately, rather than dream or meditate, most of us tranquilize or anesthetize. We find some way to block out the pain of the transition from one state of existence to another, from inauthenticity to authenticity. (Authenticity is the concept which means, "I am being that which the author has authorized me to become.") When we have a conscious split between Nineveh and Tarshish, between God's call and our selfish desire for safety, we deny, and use drugs, alcohol, power, or any means available to avoid. This is the clinical definition of denial: to cope with the pain of a crisis by simply not recognizing it. Sleep can be an avoidance also, unless we are willing to hear the dream's message for our external life.

Jonah, like the New Testament prodigal son, awoke. He came to himself, came to a new consciousness, and took responsibility for his actions. Sleeping and awakening are like death and new life, or consciousness and unconsciousness. When he awoke, Jonah knew his distress was the cause of the danger. He then accepted the fact that his behavior had created the evil wind which threatened others. Jonah said an interesting thing: "In order to quiet the storm, take me and throw me into the sea; then the sea will quiet for you." He could have, upon waking and recognizing his responsibility, simply leapt into the sea to solve the problem. In that scenario, the only relationship that would count would be between Jonah and the Lord. By calling on others to throw him into the sea, he makes them a part of the process; he forces them to become involved. Therein they, too, participate in their own healing. This is the difference between suicide and sacrifice. By their participation and recognition of the consequences, the sailors have their own consciousness raised as well, so that they also, in a sense, wake up. Through his sacrifice, they might have new life. The parallel to Christian sacrifice and the well-known Savior of our tradition is transparent. Their committing his death gave them their life.

Jonah's descent has only begun. This is the nature of the journey for the human being: one test and trial after another. The scripture reads: the Lord appointed a great fish to swallow up Jonah; and Jonah was in the belly of the fish three days and three nights (a convenient period for consideration). The fish, of course, is a classic symbol of the unconscious. Therein is where we encounter our deep spiritual selves: our souls.

We must look beneath the water of consciousness into this elusive, jutting, difficult-to-catch consciousness that is just below the surface. There is no other way. To live on the surface, superficially, will not allow one to be in touch with the soul making. Soul making requires a crisis, a psychic storm to throw the ego into impotence so that one might seek a deeper existence, or die the death of nonexistence. Some still consider it easier to go to Tarshish than to jump into the unknown of the unconscious where the soul awaits. The belly of the whale, as it were, is the place where our ego is impotent, and we must look for deeper, greater resources than our life on the exterior can provide. This is the second womb gestation for our second birth. You can drive on Westheimer from Montrose Boulevard to Highway 6 and find nothing in any one of those strip shopping centers that will save you from this distress. "I called to the Lord; out of my distress, he answered me." The only way is to enter into the womb again, spiritually.

When will we learn that the hard way is the only way? When we enter into life, we come in the hard and narrow way. When we enter the new life of new awareness and new existence, we enter through the same hard and narrow way. Our greatest struggles are those that take place within the self, the deep, dark journey of the soul. The immature believe that the world is the source of our problems. The wise understand that we ourselves create our own struggles as the labor of our continual birthing.

Those struggles, those crises, those psychic storms where we feel nonexistent, are not the times when God abandons us. When the student is ready, the teacher appears. The teacher appears in the most unlikely places—people from whom and words from which you would never expect it to come. A woman taught me this year about grace. She was raised Anglican, but had never understood grace. While in her own deep, dark place, traveling her own deep, dark journey of the soul, in her own belly of the whale, she found herself watching a television evangelist—even though, she said, she found most of them distasteful (as do I). Yet, in her own Tarshish as she was watching Jimmy Swaggart on television, he leaned over that Plexiglas pulpit of his, with his lion-like mane of hair and large face, and looked at her (and through her to me), and said, "The grace of God! Don't even try to understand it!" When the student is ready, the teacher appears.

As the poet Rilke writes in his work, *Letters to a Young Poet*:

> We have no reason to harbor any mistrust against our world, for it is not against us. If it has terrors, they are our terrors; if it has abysses, these abysses belong to us; if there are dangers, we must try to love them. And if only we arrange our life in accordance with the principle which tells us that we must always trust in the difficult, then what now appears to us as the most alien will become our most intimate and trusted experience. How could we forget those ancient myths that stand at the beginning of all races, the myths about dragons that at the last moment are transformed into princesses? Perhaps all the dragons in our lives are princesses who are only waiting to see us act, just once, with beauty and courage. Perhaps everything that frightens us is, in its deepest essence, something helpless that wants our love.

The Jonah story is once again a voice and a vision of how life is. Between the opposites of Nineveh and Tarshish we dwell, running from what God is calling us to be. Storm and sacrifice are norms, not abnormal behavior. The deep, dark belly of the whale is the crucible of transformation that forces us to face even our own darkest parts and turn to the only true light that may be shining in a face where we never expected to see it. As Jonah confesses from the depths of his own soul: "Deliverance belongs to the Lord." Being a human being is an incredible journey. The difficulty and the trauma, the crisis, the denial, the running, the unconsciousness, are simply coping mechanisms as we journey to discover who it is that we are. When I talk about that which God is calling you to be, I do not mean to be ordained as a priest and go to Africa to save souls. Don't waste your time! There are more practicing Anglicans in Nigeria than there are in the British Isles. I mean being courageous in the face of the desire to turn and go to Tarshish. I am talking about being and doing that which is enlivening—come whence it will, cost what it may. I mean to account for something, to follow that which you know is yours and which nobody else can fulfill and nobody can take from you. It is doing the courageous thing. It is the willing of the one thing that you know you must have and be to fulfill your fullest expectations. Most of us are like Jonah: when called to Nineveh, we run. Yet the hound of heaven will force us time and time again to look, and will provide opportunity for us to grow.

What I like most about the book of Jonah is not simply its rich symbols of the psyche nor the drama of its mythological formula of the hero's journey, but the ending. Jonah does go to Nineveh, he does utter his prophetic word, the Ninevites do repent, and the Lord does save them and love them. But in spite of this spiritual crisis, his return and his success, he remains very human. Jonah pouts because God saved such a wretched people as the Ninevites. Because he becomes righteous in his journey, he also becomes self-righteous. And God had yet another lesson in store for him. Read it for yourself in chapters 3 and 4.

The journey to God is a never-ending journey, full of conflict, fear, death, and tragedy. The journey to God is never-ending, full of peace, joy, love, and new life. No matter what, we can make it no other way. Both are always true. But the grace of God which allows us to begin again at any time, to start over, to be—as it were—born again, even out of the fear and threat of disobedience, even out of being in the deep, dark journey of the soul, is always available to everybody. There are no God-forsaken places. There are no God-forsaken people. It is the grace of God. Don't even try to understand it.

Amen.

❖ ❖ ❖

August 26, 1990
Matthew 16:13–20

In today's Gospel, we have a richness of revelation. Jesus asks the disciples the fundamental question of the Christian religion: "Who do men say that I am?" They answer, "Some say John the Baptist, others say Elijah, and others Jeremiah or one of the prophets." He then turns directly to them with the penetrating and wholly personal question, "But who do *you* say that I am?" And Simon Peter replies, "You are the Christ, the Son of the living God." And Jesus answers him, "Blessed are you, Simon Bar-Jona! For flesh and blood has not revealed this to you, but my Father who is in heaven. And I tell you, you are Peter, and on this rock I will build my church…I will give you the keys of the kingdom of heaven…"

There is such richness here that the preacher must discipline himself to pare one kernel, for there is a lifetime of sermons in these seven verses. For instance, the incredible existential question of "Who do you say that I am?" that we each must answer when confronted with the question. There are a thousand ways to say "no," one way to say "yes," and no way to say anything else. The whole turn of that interesting phrase where the Greek, "You are Peter *(Petros)*, and on this rock *(petra)* I will build my church" is a change from the masculine to the feminine—*petra*, meaning "loose rock" —so that the Church is built on humanity; it is built on Peter's humanity, and yours and mine.

Although I have read this passage hundreds of times, this week I was, for the first time, struck curious by the statement, "I will give you the keys of the kingdom." What did Jesus give Peter that would provide entrance into the kingdom? I suppose, in the past my mind's eye focused on an image as in some ancient painting, with Peter holding a giant ring of keys. Such a literal mind leads nowhere but to close one's mind. What are the metaphorical keys? What did Jesus mean when he chose keys as a metaphor for what he had given Peter? And if he has given those keys to Peter, has not Peter passed them on, making them available to any human being?

Of course, I do not know the answer. But I like the question. As a matter of ironic process, when I ask myself the question, what are the keys to the kingdom, the answer to the question is questions. That is to say, that questions are the keys to the kingdom.

"What is the kingdom of heaven like, and to what shall we compare it?" was the question Jesus was asked to which his parables were the answers, and the parables, as answers, were always questions. The keys to the kingdom are the questions we ask. Most of us are much involved in questions about things that matter a good deal today but will be forgotten when answered. At the same time, we spend so little time in the intimacy of asking questions about things that matter always, life-and-death questions about meaning, purpose, and value. When we don't ask deep questions, we never discover the depths. I suspect that doubt and curiosity are among the most undervalued gifts of human nature. Our external consciousness, known as ego, seeks certainty in order to abet fear about the unknown. The soul, the center of depth consciousness, seeks the unknown, for therein is where truth dwells in an elusive mystery, known simply as the kingdom.

Frederick Buechner writes: "There is perhaps no stronger reason for reading the Bible than that somewhere among all those India-paper pages there awaits each reader, whoever he is, the one question which, though for years he may have been pretending not to hear it, is the central question of his own life."

Think for a lifetime on the first question asked in the Bible. In the creation story, God asks, "Adam, where are you?" That question must be asked by us every day in order to know where we are vis-à-vis the kingdom. Where are you with your vocation, marriage, spiritual journey, life? Where are you?

Questions are the keys:

Who is my neighbor?
Am I my brother's keeper?
How can a man be born when he is old?
Whither shall I go from thy spirit?
What is truth?
What does it profit a man to gain the whole world and lose his own soul?
What shall I do to inherit eternal life?
Whom shall I send?
Who do you say that I am?
Who are you?

I, for one, prefer the question to the answer. John Ciardi writes:

> It is easy enough to praise men for the courage of their convictions. I wish I could teach the young of this generation the courage of their confusions.
>
> We labor to teach the young rules of conduct that amount to convictions, yet which of us is really sure the convictions we peddle to our cubs? May it not be that we have made too much of conviction as an ultimate goal? Show me a man who is not confused, and I will show you a man who has not been thinking. He will be a man who has not asked enough questions.
>
> He will, in fact, incline to think that the reason for asking questions is to answer them. Is it? May it not be the greater merit of questions that they lead not to answers but to new questions, and the new questions to others, and they to others yet?
>
> I, for one, do not know how to live without more questions than I shall ever have the answers for…how could I think it less than a human disaster to throw away my questions in order to come to rest in nothing more than answers?
>
> Yes, I am confused, but I will prefer the larger confusion to the smaller certainty. The true force of education is nothing if it does not drive a man into more and more meaningful confusion. What man of recent times has been better confused than, say, Einstein? His engagement of the confusing universe was his act of mind, positive and creative and of life. What sane man can let himself despair of his mind's life-force?
>
> Let that be my plea to the young. The chances are they have already been taught more convictions than they will be able to live with unless they shut their minds. But let them be told at least once that the courage of one's convictions may in reality turn out to be the cowardice of one's mind, the retreat into easy and self-binding certainty. Where mind is the measure, there must be the courage to face one's confusions whole.

> It takes courage to engage a confusion deeply. It is at least a ponderable proposition that the courage to engage it is better than is that order of conviction that can survive only by refusing to consider seriously those questions an inquiring mind must find unavoidable.
>
> A good question is never answered. It is not a bolt to be tightened into place but a seed to be planted and to bear more seed toward the hope of greening the landscape of idea.

I do not personally rest on the broad upland of a system that includes a series of sure statements about the absolutes, but on a narrow, rocky ridge between the gulfs where there is no sureness of expressible knowledge, but the certainty of meeting for me what remains undisclosed.

I prefer the question to the answer, for the question is the quest. The knowledge we seek is not facts, but knowing. Who or what do you know? For whom or for what would you sacrifice all security in order to know? Knowing about something is not the same as knowing. Reading about an ox, writes Jung, is not the same as riding one. Such knowing requires a commitment of the soul. Such soul commitment is a quest. The key to the quest is the question. Who are you? Who am I? Who are we? Where are we going? What is that we seek that will unlock the mystery of who we are?

In former times when people were forced to move from one kingdom to another, they never asked, What is the geography of the kingdom? They never asked, What is the weather in the kingdom? They never asked, What are the people like in the kingdom? The only question they asked was, What is the king like? If they knew the nature of the king, they knew the nature of the kingdom. There is our key. Who is your king? Knowing the nature of the king will tell you the nature of the kingdom.

All the questions in the Holy Scripture lead to the singular answer: God is love. Jesus Christ is the King of Love. Knowing that reveals the nature of the kingdom. The questing thirst of every question is to drink from this well.

Quest is the spiritual journey. Our questions do not lead us to all knowledge, but they do lead us to knowing the unknown, revealed most particularly in life's greatest mystery: love.

Quest through every question. Therein and there through, you will find the key to a door that is never locked. Where are you vis-à-vis the kingdom? What cost will you pay to enter therein? The one cost we are clear about is that if you do not ask enough questions, you will never know the way.

Amen.

September 9, 1990
Romans 12:9–21; Matthew 18:15–20

Hear what our Lord Jesus Christ saith: "Thou shalt love the Lord thy God with all thy heart, and with all thy soul, and with all thy mind. This is the first and great commandment. And the second is like unto it: Thou shalt love thy neighbor as thyself. On these two commandments hang all the Law and the Prophets." There it is, rehearsed once again in all of its symmetry and simplicity, its mystery and complexity. The human being seeks, finally, at the deepest, quintessential level nothing more than an authentic relationship with God, with another, and with oneself. As much of a tragedy as an un-reflected life is, even those who have never seriously reflected upon their lives have played games with some degree of seriousness. Having played the game, and even though unaware of the metaphor, they know that grace comes hard, rises through the wrong move, the bad hand, or the final out. Grace emerges through the cheap in us, the petty, the childish. Grace is God's tenacious commitment that through unconditional love we will eventually be capable of participating in an authentic relationship. Jesus summed it up: love God, love another, and love yourself. Seek within each of those relationships something that is truly and fully human. Even though there is a real power within the world and within each of us that seeks to sabotage even our most precious love relationships, God's grace is the persistent hope that we will eventually see that God does not dwell in an abstract concept called heaven, but God lives in the midst of those who commit to a love relationship. Lovers who only seek one another will eventually discover the unbearable truth that we fear such intimacy and we create barriers that prevent the unbearable truth of our inadequacy.

Those who seek God in one another will play out the bad hand, the wrong move, or the final out and know that seeking God within in a relationship means that grace always deals a new hand, a new move, and another turn at bat. There is within God's love no end, just transitions and transformations, and always new beginnings.

Both the epistle and Gospel are replete with admonitions for forgiveness. "Repay no one evil for evil, but take thought for what is noble…" "Beloved, never revenge yourselves, leave it to God…" "Do not be overcome by evil, but overcome evil with good."

Paraphrasing Jesus' teaching in today's Gospel, he admonishes us to "talk it out," to stay with the conversation, when we are in disagreement. Phillip Lopate, in one of his essays, says, "Friendship is a long conversation." Stay with another until grace can prevail. And prevail it will. What is done in Christ's name is done through his graceful presence.

The human limitation is our humanity. Divided between good and evil, split between human and divine, torn between hope and fear, human beings are not capable of what they desire the most, for that which they most desire is what they most fear. And that feared desire is to be totally known by another. We cannot truly love another without truly knowing another.

Our fear is that when another truly knows us, that knowledge is a sacred ground of rejection. Rejection is our greatest fear. Our greatest fear from our beginning is the threat of non-being. We do not know who we are until another tells us. Being is dependent on another affirming our presence. We depend on parents, peers, friends, and lovers to bring us into being by their affirmation of us. To be rejected means to be as nothing. As Paul says, "Without love, we are nothing." Nothing is what we fear the most. That is why we rarely show another our hand, for we may not be bringing enough to the table to play. If I show you who I am, you might reject it, and it is I, and I am all I have. And I seek your love—for without love, I am nothing. That which I desire the most is that which I most fear.

Grace, which is God's unconditional love and belief in us, comes hard, rises through our dark side. Grace is the sun that rises through the opaque mist of our inadequacy. Human beings cannot have authentic love relationships without the presence of God's grace in the midst of the mist. God is love, and those who dwell in love, dwell in God and God in them. God is love. There is nothing else that we are about. It is for which we were born and that for which we would die. As our Lord Jesus Christ says, "Thou shalt love the Lord thy God, with all thy heart, and with all thy soul, and with all thy mind, and love thy neighbor as thyself." On this hangs everything.

I have seen and heard in my own life and in the loves of countless others, the bitter stories of human rejection. The childish parent who abuses a child. The desire and withdrawal of lovers who cannot find the courage to connect for fear of rejection. The friends who have argued and half believe that their hurt is more important, and that their better self, which will emerge through forgiveness, is not worth the wrong that committed the pain. I believe that if one seeks always the authentic presence of God in a relationship, the relationship will eventually be authentic.

I do not contend that all relationships are capable of authenticity at an equally deep level. Biology and biography set limits. Circumstance of personality type, interests, gifts, and liabilities may make some relationships always limited to a certain level of depth. It may not be humanly possible for certain persons to live together authentically. Some people are simply wrong for one another. Some people, because of mystery beyond our comprehension, have chemical elements which, when put together, poison the well of creativity that they seek from one another. I do not want to be lulled into some religious chauvinism that says anybody can live in a relationship. It is simply not true. We kid ourselves in some romantic idealism to hope for that which is impossible. Such incompatibility does not mean rejection or destruction, though it may mean honest recognition of limitation. Where people cannot transcend their own limitations in a relationship, it doesn't mean they cannot respect and forgive themselves and one another. It means that their human limitations put limits on their relationship. Honest acceptance of limitations may be the most authentic love.

Such graceful realization and acceptance, though, as Paul and Jesus teach, requires forgiveness. Jeffrey Skinner, in his book of poetry entitled *A Guide to Forgetting*, sums up this sermon in a powerful poem of forgiveness—not a poem that is easy to hear, but a poem that details the reality, the hard place where we must look for grace. The title of the poem is "The Last Poem to His First Wife."

> Sometimes, when I wake up tired, I think
> Of your hand coming from the back seat
> To slap my face, in our own car
> In front of our friends. They sat there
> Like thick, unread novels.
> And then I want those years back in my body.
> I want the silly mustache I grew in defense
> Erased from the photographs, whatever
> Boxes they moulder in. I want
> The walls I punched through replastered,
> And all the dark little hopes I kept from you
> Hammered out like bent nails.
> I want the nothing I wanted from you
> And the universe you wanted from me
> To mix and dissolve, once and
> For all. Lifted by mercy, we have fallen
> Into other lives, you to a black-haired child
> And a husband who works with his hands,
> I to a woman no different than
> My soul, two daughters God himself sighs over.
> I forgive you now, Elizabeth, I forgive us both—
> That sad young couple wrong for each other
> As salt and rain. I let go, here and forever,
> The grief we shared, calling it love.

This is not a sermon about marriage and divorce. It is about authentic relationships and seeking them. It is through the hard way that the grace of God comes, through the opaque mist of our humanity. We must forgive one another for our humanity if we are ever to enter into authenticity through the intimacy we seek. That is just the way it is. Hear what our Lord Jesus Christ says: "You must love the Lord your God with all your heart, and with all your soul, and with all your mind. That is the first and great commandment. And the second is like unto it: You should love your neighbor, and you should love yourself." The most insidious, difficult, destructive relationship we hold is the one with ourself. Self-rejection is at the center of all inauthentic relationships. They carry for us all of our anger, all of our hurt, all of our disappointment, because the hand that has come across to slap our face is our own. Can you find it within yourself to forgive yourself for your own imperfection? God has. It is the least you can do for yourself. You are inadequate and imperfect. If you will offer that, it will be just enough. Can you enter into a relationship with yourself? A love relationship? An unconditional relationship of love inspired by the God that dwells within you and unites you with yourself? If you are able to do that, you *will* love another as you love yourself.

Each of us knows, even in the un-reflected life, that grace comes hard. Grace is not necessary for those who are perfect, but for the rest of us. We pray for nothing more.

Grace is God's tenacious commitment that through unconditional love, we will eventually be capable of participating in an authentic relationship. An authentic relationship with God, an authentic relationship with another, and an authentic relationship with ourselves. Even this vague hope is stronger than our certain fear. Perfect love casts out fear. You need not be afraid. Complete love, authentic love, casts out all fear. We must learn, once again, that we are accepted, but we are not very good at accepting our acceptance. We pray but for one thing, this marvelous grace of God.

Let us pray: May the grace of our Lord Jesus Christ, and the love of God, and the fellowship of the Holy Spirit, be with us all evermore.

Amen.

❊ ❊ ❊

September 16, 1990
Romans 14:5–12

Paul writes in a subtle way today about wonder in life: "One man esteems one day as better than another, while another man esteems all days alike. Let everyone be fully convinced in his own mind. He who observes the day, observes it in honor of the Lord,…"

Paul's observation as to how we observe a day unveils a fundamental role in living a spiritual life versus living a profane or secular existence. Mircea Eliade, a scholar of profound, if little-known, influence, was a student and scholar of religious phenomenology. Eliade's entire corpus of writings on the human religious experience is based on the central role played in his distinction between the sacred and the profane by the religious experience of the human being. For Eliade, the key experience in archaic religious life was that of the heterogeneity of space and time in religious experience. Profane space and time was characterized by duration, disorientation, and deterioration. Sacred space and time, on the other hand, manifested an encounter with the eternal, the orienting center, and regeneration. Sacred space, in short, was the locus of regeneration, creativity, and transformation. The capacity to locate and utilize appropriately such transformative space was the special province of the religious leader in human culture.

To translate Eliade's thesis, he is saying that it is the province of the religious leader to point out the wonder in the midst of the horrible; to point out the sacred space and time in the midst of the profane; not to keep the two at contrast, but seek continually to see one through the other. That therefore was Paul's job and, in a smaller sense, my responsibility in this community; that is, to locate and bring to awareness that this life we have been given is a wonderful life. Perhaps the priest has no more fundamental, nor more important, task than to esteem life, to live it fully and abundantly, and then to proclaim, based on that experience, that it is good, that it is very, very good; not perfect, not enjoyable, not even understandable, but it is *good*. Good in the etymological understanding of the word "good"—not one being of moral superiority, meaning simply that something or someone is being what they were created to be: it is good. It is what it is supposed to be. Life is not to be enjoyed, it is to be experienced. The esteem of life is to experience it fully, to stand back and reflect upon it and to say, "By God, it is good!" The difference between the priest and the shaman is that the shaman experiences it, the priest represents it.

Stephen Jay Gould wrote a book last year that I read this summer. I read it on a screened porch, twenty feet from one of our great lakes, Lake Michigan. As this great body of water breathed back and forth at my feet, I read about the discovery of the Burgess Shale, tucked into the Canadian Rockies, eight thousand feet above sea level, in a small limestone quarry formed 530 million years ago. Less than a city block long and only ten feet high, the Burgess Shale holds the remains of an ancient sea that nurtured more varieties of life than can be found in all our modern oceans. Here lived dozens of creatures never seen before or since, and in this small section of shale, the creatures are perfectly preserved in awesome detail. The overt plot of the book is the misinterpretation and classification of these organisms by Dr. Charles Walcott of the Smithsonian Institution, and the reinterpretation and reclassification of these organisms years later by H. B. Whittington. Such an error and its correction has had a great influence on the history of science.

But the better plot for the shaman priest, and the more interesting nature of the book, is the more subtle theme addressed by Gould, found in the book's title, *Wonderful Life*. The title of the book expresses the duality of wonder about these organisms themselves. And the wonder of how different life would have been without them. This is, of course, the central theme in one of America's most memorable films, *It's a Wonderful Life,* and why Gould borrowed the title for his own book. If you remember from the film, Jimmy Stewart's guardian angel replays life's tape without him and demonstrates the awesome power of apparent insignificance in life. Is there any reason why each of us doesn't get up every day and realize that within that day there is no insignificance? Every heart beat and every breath drawn has within it the significance and wonder of life. Have you not read the beginning of the book where it says that the image of God dwells within you? What a wonder! How full you are of wonder. What a wonderful life! Not an enjoyable life, not a perfect life, but what a wonderful life! The paradoxes are overwhelming. To live in the midst of these paradoxes is wonderful.

It's a wonderful life, whether we ponder a prehistoric organism never known by our own consciousness and yet absolutely essential to bringing history to us today, or whether we ponder our own lives and those around us, and wonder what would life have been without me or without you. What would my life have been without you in it? Imagine your life without the people who have made up your life! It allows us to ponder the apparent insignificance and the awesome power found within the apparent insignificance. There is no insignificant event. Measure it out for yourself. We have a time-limited experiment called life. We can enumerate the days. To spend one more day without that which enlivens? To esteem all days as alike? Or to esteem that every day is the full history of humanity accumulated in that one twenty-four-hour experience. All that has ever been has been contributing to this one day. This twenty-four hours is the tip of an immense iceberg, and this day is the only day. Ponder that this is a wonderful life.

Paul writes: "One man esteems one day as better than another, while another man esteems all days alike. Let everyone be fully convinced in his own mind." How do you esteem your days? Are they profanely dull and gray, like pages of a book being silently flipped by a breeze of time, or are they wonderful, eternal moments, centered in life's abundance and full of mystery's creativity?

The priest's job is to proclaim life's wonder, to see the sacred in every space, and the eternal in every moment. The pleasurable province of the Church is to ritualize the life cycle and proclaim every act, every person, every day as an esteemed event of the advent of holiness. It is the particular character of the Church and its proclamation to remind you of your unique and special role in history as your vocation to play your part in the process of creation, becoming full and whole by your fullness and wholeness. Your life is not an accident of insignificance. It is a part of the entire universal drama.

We see life as a wonderful life. We see your life as wonderful. We see sacred spaces in profane places. We behold every event as a transformation. We celebrate every day as not duration and deterioration, but as creation and regeneration.

If Christ's life, death, and resurrection mean anything, they mean that you have a right to be and your becoming is a holy process. No less holy than all the process of which you are a part. Every cell is sacred, and the only sin is to refuse to live, abundantly. Christ came to bring life more abundantly. You are important. Narcissism says, "The world was created for me." Holiness says, "You were created for the world." God so loved the world that he gave himself to and for it. Why are we so afraid of it? And why do we attempt to deny it? It is wonder full; it is what it was created to be. It is very, very good!

Virginia Woolf, in *A Room of One's Own*, wrote: "I find myself saying briefly and prosaically that it is much more important to be oneself than anything else." That is the wonder. You have been given your life. It is yours: never before and never again. It is up to you. Nobody can live it for you, and nobody can live it the way you were created to live it. It is more important that you be yourself than anything else. It is a wonderful life, but you are your vehicle for living it. Saul Bellow, in *What Kind of a Day Did You Have?*, penned, "Of all that might be omitted in thinking, the worst was to omit your own being." When you consider the day, do you esteem it, and do you esteem it as wonderful and good? And what about your self-esteem? The chronic, evil, insidious sickness of being human is the inability to esteem ourselves. Do you esteem the day? The world? Your life?

It is the Church's job and my wonderful purview to proclaim that it is a wonderful life, and so are you!

Amen.

❖ ❖ ❖

September 23, 1990
Matthew 20:1–16

When I read one of Jesus' parables, more things occur to me than I can consciously contain. My thoughts are like scared monkeys jumping through jungle trees. Two thoughts settled this week sufficiently long enough for me to record them. The first being that these stories survived, not because of their truth alone, but because of who told them. Studies indicate that these parabolic formulae were not original with Jesus, but were out of the rabbinical tradition. The simple truth about parables is that they are simple truth. But in the case of Jesus' parables, they survived because he told them. One of the things that was said about Jesus is that "he taught as one who had authority." This word "authority" takes on a deeper implication when we look at the Greek word from which it is translated. The Greek word is *exousia*, which means that what he says is validated by his own being, not by any external credentials. If we could say anything about Jesus that would cause us a lifetime of theological pondering, it is that he was self-validating. What he said, he said not as an authority, but with authority, validated by his own being. He was not rehearsing words; he and his word were one. He was what he spoke.

What distinguishes Jesus from his apostles is that Jesus lived the life about which he spoke. Apostles speak about a life that they cannot possibly live, particularly without the grace of God. The apostles' word is not self-validating. To be an apostle, you have to have external credentials. It is not simply that we cannot practice what we preach, it is that what we preach is that our lives are validated by God's grace, not by our actions or words. Our authority is not our own, but the truth about which we speak. We each desire to do and be the truth (in Greek, the truth is a verb), but the truth is that our lives are validated by God's sovereign, unconditional love, not by our ordination, our actions, our accomplishments, our degrees, our wealth, our brilliance—not by our lives alone. Our lives are validated by God's sovereign, unconditional love.

That is what today's parable is about. Those workers who came in at the eleventh hour received the same payment as those who had worked all day. Those who had worked all day grumbled, "You mean you have made them equal to us?" Wow! Think about it. Who are "they"? Who are those who have come late? So it is. God's ways are not our ways. Let's say you are on the Gulf Freeway, going south toward Hobby Airport. In your pocket is a ticket for a trip that you had slavishly saved your frequent flyer passes for and you are getting away for the weekend. At about the Jefferson entrance onto the Gulf Freeway, you see that the line of cars is stretched all the way to Galveston. You left early, you had an hour to catch your plane, and every inch of traffic moving slowly down the Gulf Freeway increases your anxiety because it is a tick on the clock, and your long-awaited holiday is disappearing before your very eyes. Finally, within five minutes of your flight, you get just to the exit for the airport, and in your rearview mirror you see coming from miles back, on the shoulder of the road, a red Cadillac convertible. As it pulls alongside, you see that it is full of teenagers—drinking beer, shouting obscenities, wearing Day-Glo sunglasses—and they ask, "Can we get in front of you?" God's ways are not our ways. Of course you wouldn't let them in! God's ways are not our ways! You would grumble, "You mean you've made them equal to us?" These Johnny-come-latelies, these irresponsible people! The answer to that is, "Yes!" It is a scandal. This is a scandalous love that God has for us. It makes no sense to us, because we only occasionally get a glimpse of what this looks like. Some days we whine, some days we grumble. So much so, that we begrudge those who live a life we do not respect, and we are angry at a God who would reward a sinner with as much love as he affords the righteous. God validates all life by equal love, not by only loving those who work hardest, but by loving even those who take advantage of his generosity. Read the Old Testament lesson again about Jonah. He pouted and whined, "You mean you've made the Ninevites equal to the Hebrews?" Who are the Ninevites in your life?

Karl Rahner, a leading post-Vatican II, Roman Catholic theologian, in a reflection upon this parable, writes:

> The thing which God freely disposes of, the thing we cannot negotiate or calculate about with him, is ultimately our own selves. He bestows us upon us. Our own selves, just as we are: with our life, with our temperament, with our destiny, with our surroundings, with our time, with our heredity, with our family, with everything we happen to be and cannot change. And whenever we grumble and complain about others with whom God has dealt differently, we are really refusing to accept our own selves from the hands of God. The parable teaches us to say: we are those who receive the denarius—the late payment. We ourselves are the denarius...what we ultimately receive

from God is ourselves. This we must accept...we must accept God's gift of ourselves. Do you begrudge his generosity? This then is our life's work: to accept God's generosity. For everything that we are and have, even the painful and mysterious, is God's generous gift. We must not grumble at it but must accept it in the knowledge that when we do so, God gives himself with this gift. All of us, young and old, are really latecomers...and yet God is willing to give us everything if only we will accept it—ourselves, and himself and life without end...

Rahner is correct. Our lives are validated by God, not by our own actions, which brings me to my second thought. Even though our lives are not self-validating—that is, we are valid by God's grace, not by our own actions—the only way to accept this life we have been given is to live it, rather than apologize for it, read about it, or talk about it. We have been paid a life by having been given a life validated by God's grace. The only way to receive a gift is to use it. The only way to receive life is to live it, unashamedly.

John Updike, in his memoir entitled *Self-Consciousness*, writes about Christian living:

> During adolescence, I reluctantly perceived of the Christian religion I had been born into that almost no one believed it, believed it really—not its ministers, nor its pillars like my father and his father before him. Though signs of belief (churches, public prayers, mottos on coins) existed everywhere, when you moved toward Christianity it disappeared, as fog solidly opaque in the distance thins to transparency when you walk into it. I decided I nevertheless *would* believe. I found a few authors, a very few—Chesterton, Eliot, Unamuno, Kierkegaard, Karl Barth—who helped me believe. Under the shelter (like the wicker chairs on the side porch) that I improvised from their pages I have lived my life. I rarely read them now; my life is mostly lived. God is the God of the living, though his priests and executors, to keep order and to force the world into a convenient mold, will always want to make him the God of the dead, the God who chastises life and forbids, makes rules, and says no.

Updike has caught a glimpse as he has lived into the opaque fog. I love his summary: "I rarely read them now; my life is mostly lived." I don't think he meant used up or over. He meant that, rather than reading about life, he *lives* it!

The parables are a living word about God's scandalous love for us, invalid souls who cannot validate our lives except by accepting this amazing grace and sharing it with another. The only way to receive this life is to live it with the same radical boldness as the act of creating it. About the parables: perhaps the real faith statement is to say, I rarely read them...I mostly live them. If that were to ever happen, that would be some valid life to see. And now to my parable: maybe, rather than letting those teenagers cut in front of me, I'm going to get in the car with them.

Amen.

October 14, 1990
Psalm 23; Matthew 22:1–14

William Styron's book, *Darkness Visible: A Memoir of Madness*, has occupied much of my conscious and unconscious thought for the past week. It is the story of Styron's devastating descent into depression. The author, best known for his novels *Lie Down in Darkness*, *The Confessions of Nat Turner*, and *Sophie's Choice*, tells of his own deep, dark journey of the soul, through a despair beyond despair, which drew him to the edge of claiming his own life by creating his own death. In less than one hundred pages, he outlines through his own story how much and how little we know about depression and its devastating effect on the human soul. What we do know is that we should never again use the word "depression" in any casual sense, for anyone who has ever suffered from depression or anyone who has ever witnessed or tried to minister or treat someone in true depression knows that there is no darker state of being. For those who have sat and stared out a window for a year at a time, unable even to muster the energy to cope with the normal courses of pedestrian existence, depression is not an expression to be used to casually describe a low spot in someone's existence.

In simple terms, such mental illness is a mysterious combination of biology and biography that presents itself in general similarity, yet with particular uniqueness, to each victim. There evidently is some reasonable certainty that such near-madness results from an aberrant biochemical process, while at the same time, one's own life story will trigger, enhance, or exacerbate such a predisposition.

Given the chemically-induced systemic stress amid the neurotransmitters of the brain which causes a depletion of certain chemicals and an increase of other hormones, the endocrine system becomes vulnerable to one's own ego formation and ability to cope with extraordinary or even normal stress. The coping and adapting systems simply shut down. One is left unable to adapt or cope with the process of normal events of the human dynamic.

Styron writes about his descent to the edge as this illness took him beyond his own ability to function:

> Late one bitterly cold night, when I knew that I could not possibly get myself through the following day, I sat in the living room of the house bundled up against the chill; something had happened to the furnace. My wife had gone to bed, and I had forced myself to watch the tape of a movie in which a young actress, who had been in a play of mine, was cast in a small part. At one point in the film, which was set in late-nineteenth-century Boston, the characters moved down the hallway of a music conservatory, beyond the walls of which,

> from unseen musicians, came a contralto voice, a sudden soaring passage from the Brahms *Alto Rhapsody*.
>
> This sound, which like all music—indeed, like all pleasure—I had been numbly unresponsive to for months, pierced my heart like a dagger, and in a flood of swift recollection I thought of all the joys the house had known:...All this I realized was more than I could ever abandon, even as what I had set out so deliberately to do was more than I could inflict on those memories... And just as powerfully I realized I could not commit this desecration on myself.

Pay attention to the fact that his blessing he describes in this way: "This sound, which like all music—indeed, like all pleasure—I had been numbly unresponsive to for months, pierced my heart like a dagger,..." The word that came to him on the wings of those musical notes pierced his heart like a dagger, and that wound was the beginning of his healing.

After hospitalization, a combination of psychotherapy and experimentation with medication, Styron re-emerges into the light. He concludes his book:

> Since antiquity—in the tortured lament of Job, in the choruses of Sophocles and Aeschylus—chroniclers of the human spirit have been wrestling with a vocabulary that might give proper expression to the desolation of melancholia...The vast metaphor which most faithfully represents this fathomless ordeal, however, is that of Dante, and his all-too-familiar lines still arrest the imagination with their augury of the unknowable, the black struggle to come:
>
> > *In the middle of the journey of our life*
> > *I found myself in a dark wood,*
> > *For I had lost the right path.*

Styron's story contains a universal element. Though each of us may not be called to the psychotic edge of depression's evil destruction (and I pray to be delivered from that evil), each of us knows the dark wood and lost path of life's destined journey. Who among us does not know the "night of quiet desperation"? Who among us has not experienced what the Psalmist writes in today's Psalm: "Yea, though I walk through the valley of the shadow of death..."? Who among us does not share a biography of mistakes, losses, traumas, and illnesses that make a portion of our life self-rejecting? The vast metaphor of the dark wood is from the collective voice echoed from Job to Dante, from Abraham to Jesus, from Styron to me. We each know the dark wood.

Today's parable is from Jesus, the victim of Gethsemane's bloody sweat to his own forsakenness on the dark wood of the cross. In the parable, he tells of the king's invitation to the wedding feast. The righteous and healthy were too healthy to come, too righteous to be present at this feast, and they refused. So the king invited those rejected ones from the streets, both good and bad. The sinners, losers, harlots, and beggars were invited to the feast. Many scholars are wont to make this an allegory of the nation of Israel feeling too righteous to receive Jesus as Messiah, and therefore the Gentiles were invited into the Kingdom of God. It this is so, then this parable holds great historical relevance, but does not hold application to the journey of my own existence these two thousand years hence. But the story survives, because it tells me today that all parts of my own personality are invited and included at the feast in the Kingdom of God. I can bring all of me; my inferiority, my inadequacy, my inauthenticity, my pain, my loss, my illness, my depression are all acceptable at God's family table. As a matter of fact, one might even postulate that they are prerequisites—not that we don't all have them, but very few of us admit them publicly. Very few of us wear them as an outer garment of reality. One of the ways to become authentic is to admit publicly your inauthenticity.

This word is the voice of God that continually speaks amidst the great competition from the dark voices of inferiority that say, "You are not worthy!" This voice is the voice that came to William Styron late at night in the "sudden soaring passage from the Brahms *Alto Rhapsody*."

Some part of Styron knows that that was the voice of God, though he might express it in less pietistic terms. He does so in the conclusion of his story:

> One need not sound the false or inspirational note to stress the truth that depression is not the soul's annihilation; men and women who have recovered from the disease—and they are countless—bear witness to what is probably its only saving grace; it is conquerable.

It can take one to the edge, to the valley of the shadow of death, the deep, dark journey of the soul, and yet, if one will hang on, through the love and care of a doctor of the soul, and through the salvation that may come, encapsulated in medication, the word of God will come. It is our promise; it is our hope. A man that I trust and respect and admire and have great affection for, who himself was a victim of this deep despair and depression, told me that for years his favorite piece of scripture was in an unlikely place. It was in the raising of Lazarus, when Jesus went to his dear friend, who was holed up in a cave, bound up, and his sisters said, "You've come too late! By now he will stink, in the stench of his own withdrawal." And Jesus said, "Lazarus, come out!" And Lazarus came out! It must have been like the sound of a sudden surge of a Brahms' rhapsody. Then my friend said this is what happened to him. Finally, out of his own depression, Jesus said, "Loose him, let him go!" The only saving grace about illness is the incredible experience of getting well. Styron continues:

> For those who have dwelt in depression's dark wood, and known its inexplicable agony, their return from the abyss is not unlike the ascent of the poet [Dante], trudging upward and upward out of hell's black depths and at last emerging into what he saw as "the shining world." There, whoever has been restored to health has almost always been restored to the capacity for serenity and joy, and this may be indemnity enough for having endured the despair beyond despair.

The poet writes for us all, even all of us who have found ourselves amidst a dark wood and have lost the right path: "And so we came forth, and once again beheld the stars."

Why have we, as pilgrims wounded by life's reality, who have sat and listened for some rhapsody that would pierce our hearts and start our healing, trudged and trudged for centuries up these chancel steps to go to the banquet table for the heavenly feast, except to behold the stars? This holy table and its prepared feast invite us to bring all of our biology and biography, our body and soul, poor, crippled, blind, lame, and scarred, from every street and alley of our own interior dark wood. Like the surging sudden passage of the spirit's rhapsody, we are enlightened and enlivened to conquer the black struggle and emerge once again to behold the stars.

I cannot leave romanticizing religion or depression—romanticizing the hard wood, the cross, which is the way of life. I can say that the gift of this place to the world, and to the physicians and to the sick ones of every generation, is "don't give up hope!" Hope is that rope we cling to, and every human being who has ever lived and survived the deep, dark journey of the soul and the valley of the shadow of death has been delivered. Death for some may be the only way to get well. I have great empathy, even for those who have to, because of the hell of their own being, inflict their own death upon themselves. I believe by the revelation of God and by my own experience, listening for the sound of God in the vacant voices of those who struggle to stay alive, there are no God-forsaken events, no God-forsaken actions, no God-forsaken people. What needs to die, will die. But you need not kill your body. Just hang on. Eventually God will speak, in the sudden surge of a rhapsody somewhere. We don't know how it comes or how it leaves, but we do know why it comes and why it leaves. It is the journey of life for all of us. Eventually, the word will come. "Loose him. Let him go." My faith is not in some memorization of creeds or prayers. My faith is that for every one of us, the voice will come and give us that for which we have waited our whole lives. That is, to be free. Free at last. Loose him. Let him go.

Amen.

November 4, 1990
All Saints' Sunday
Ecclesiasticus 44:1; Matthew 5:1–12

Shortly after Canon Logan was called to be the Subdean of the Cathedral and while Canon Powell was still here as the Canon Residentiary, we had a baptism frenzy in this place. A group—a band—of people of Eastern European heritage, referred to popularly, although no longer pejoratively, as Gypsies, showed up on our doorstep with about twenty-five children to be baptized, most of them infants. These Gypsies held an interesting tradition: the parents didn't come to the baptism, but the relatives, many of whom were godparents, did. They would not give the real name of the baby until the moment of baptism, when the name the baby carried up to that time was changed. They couldn't tell anyone the name of the child. It had to be given by the godparents. And when the name was given, it was very difficult to pronounce, generally. These baptisms were done on Tuesday afternoons usually. With a lot of animated conversation, the group would come into the Cathedral, bringing as many as ten babies at a time, and a sort of pell-mell ecstasy would ensue, all of it ruled over by this short, round man, who had a clear symbol of his place in the community. He wore a large tie bar that had the king of hearts on it. As we would begin the baptisms, I would say, "Name this child." They would, and then we would baptize them in sequence. Although it was very difficult for the Subdean to make out the baptismal certificates when the old name was no longer relevant and he didn't even know who the parents were, it was even more difficult for the celebrant at the baptism, because when we came to the place in the ceremony where we named the child, we had no name! Following all this, the man with the king of hearts as his tie bar came up to me, pulled out a large roll of bills (all ones), said, "Father, a little sowthin' fer you," and handed me five of them! He then pulled from his pocket a handful of gold chains with a small gold cross attached to each chain. He wanted each of the babies to have one, and he said, "Father, would you bless these crosses in the holy water."

"I'm sorry, I don't have any holy water."

"You what?"

"I don't have any holy water."

"You a priest?"

"Yes, I am."

"Did you bless that water?"

"Yes, sir."

"That water's holy water!"

"I'll be darned if it's not!"

I was taught a lot about sacramental theology that day from the king of a Gypsy band.

"Did you bless that water?" "Yes, sir." "That water's holy water!"

That kind of inflation and deflation, seems to be the journey of the human psyche. Who among us has not had the fleeting, reoccurring fantasy of fame? The human psyche with its egocentric consciousness by some necessity seeks the exterior approval of the world brought by power and authority. Ego strength is a necessity for survival; it is a natural urge toward power. The problem with fame is that, from time to time, rather than being simply power or authority, it becomes inflated and must be deflated. And yet, like all power forces, it holds within it not only the creative energy of identity, but the destructive power of ego mania, as well. What is the difference between a strong ego and an inflated or "big" ego? (A big ego is when we take all of our power and authority and try to run everybody else's world.) It is an interesting balance that we seek: to try to be strong in our own identity, and yet at the same time, not be inflated and make others suffer by our inflation. A punctured pretense may be the most prophetic role of any human being for another. I think the best balance between inflation and deflation is the word "saint." Sainthood is the key. The Christian conceptual framework of sainthood holds within it a paradigm of balance, or integration of superiority and inferiority. Sainthood includes both the light and shadow of the human personality.

Paul Tillich writes: "The saint is a saint, not because he is 'good' but because he is transparent for something more than he himself is." In proper theological terms, a saint is one who is sanctified. Sanctified has at its etymological roots *sanctus*, which means "holy" or "consecrated." In that sense, all baptized persons are saints, for in baptism we are consecrated by water and the Spirit to be set apart to be transparent to something within us that is greater than our own ego. That something, at the center of our psyche, is called a soul. And God dwells within us as a primary force and fundamental resource for our soul making.

Being sanctified is a process of inflation and deflation, symbolized by the sacramental act of baptism. Baptism is a beginning, an outward and visible sign of what has begun within—the soul making. Becoming a saint is the process of inflation and deflation, of balancing the opposites, to become whole. Little by little, by the painstaking journey, and the taking of the pains incumbent within the journey, we seek to allow the holy to happen through us in our relationship with the world.

That holiness is the state of consciousness which knows that we are at one and the same time holy and human and find peace through the contradiction. That peace is the transcendent function that allows us to see ourselves as ultimately whole, while penultimately, very human and not very holy. We are confused, contradicted, painful, and incomplete.

When Ecclesiasticus says in this familiar line: "Let us now praise famous men, and our fathers in their generations," it is not a call to enumerate those who have distinguished themselves in history through power and authority. The famous people that Ecclesiasticus calls upon us to praise are the people who have no memorial other than their own struggle to allow their lives to be transparent to the something that is greater than themselves.

And yet, I believe that, in spite of the ego inflation attached to the phrase from Ecclesiasticus, the Christian journey is about each of us making a name for ourselves. A large part of our Christian tradition of baptism is "naming." Today the baptism ritual will call for the candidate to be presented by name—Christian name. In the 1928 liturgy, the priest, before he consecrated the child with water, said, "Name this child." Today when I baptize this baby, I will baptize him by name. His job is to become his name, to make a name for himself.

Saints know who they are. And equally important, they know who they aren't. Saints know they have a life to become. They know they do not have to control all of life. Saints know that there dwells within them something greater than themselves. They know from time to time they have to get themselves out of the way in order for the something to shine through them. Saints know that that "something" within is someone. They proclaim that the "someone" is the highest authority, higher than their ego or any other power. Saints know that they have a covenant and a promise that comes to them from the highest authority and dwells within their love. Saints know that that highest authority dwells within even the lowest human being. Saints know that they are both human and holy, and they try not to confuse the two, but seek to integrate both. Saints know that through baptism, we have been declared righteous (not self-righteous). They know that in the eyes of God they bring delight, and that even at their own displeasure at their inability to be holy, God takes pleasure in them. Our task is to become that which we were created and declared to be: saints.

The saint is a tireless swimmer who has escaped the drowning of baptism. The saint knows that we must continually escape the drowning. St. Therese proclaimed, "If you are willing to serenely bear the trial of being displeasing to yourself, then you will be for Jesus a pleasant place of shelter." We who are saints are always coming back to this font, climbing back in to be cleansed, toweled off, and refreshed with new self-esteem. Each time we seem satisfied, and we feel that we will never need to return. But guess what? Every time we promise never to need a return, we find ourselves swimming again with a guilty grin. And guess who is there to towel us off again? This is the nature of the sainthood journey. We are all swimmers, all within a hairsbreadth of drowning, and yet being able each time to climb back into the font, be toweled off and sent on our way, rejoicing.

So is the nature of sainthood. We are all water babies who swim again and again toward sanctification. Sanctification is a process of swimming toward wholeness. And as we swim, heaven is filled with all the saints who have swum before us, and they are a vast multitude who cheer us on our way. All Saints' Sunday proclaims that we are not alone. We are in a stream of saints who have so lived their lives that they have made a name for themselves, and at the same time allowed themselves to be lights reflecting the unconditional love of God that accepts all comers, accepts all saints.

Today, when you come to receive the holy meal, you will walk past a font filled with consecrated water. I have it from the king of hearts that it is holy water. Don't be afraid to reach in and take a drop on your finger and make the sign of the cross as a reminder that our sanctification has not ended, it has just begun again…

Amen.

❖ ❖ ❖

November 11, 1990
Matthew 25:1–13

Not only would it be very difficult to imagine the world without the primary resources of wind, water, earth, and fire, it would be very difficult to describe the world without wind, water, earth, and fire as similes for what the world is like, as it depends on these elements for resources. Two subtleties about today's Gospel: the word "marriage" suggests "union," which in Latin means *unus* or "oneness," so we have something about God and us marrying in this wonderful Parable of the Bridegroom and the wise and foolish maidens. In addition to the marriage metaphor, we have the symbol of fire used in an interesting way.

Even more subtle than the image of fire is the manner in which Jesus teaches us something about the developmental, collective consciousness of the emerging Christianity. Remember the Abraham-Isaac story. The story holds within it not only a lot of subplots, but through symbols, a statement about the evolving of the religious collective consciousness from polytheism (many gods) to monotheism (one god). In the old polytheistic mind-set, the gods were adversaries to human beings. Human beings had to appease the gods, or trick the gods, in order to get the resources the gods held. The Abraham-Isaac sacrifice story begins that way: one must sacrifice to win the gods' favor, but in this story, everything gets reversed. This is the subtle change in consciousness between polytheism and monotheism; the stage is set for the human sacrifice to appease the gods under the old system, when a new system is ushered in, and this time God provides the sacrifice. So God, in that symbolic story, is changed from an adversary to an advocate. The religious consciousness is changed from sacrifice to an angry god and tricking the god who holds the resources, to an advocate god who sacrifices on our behalf.

The pre-Christian Greek story of Prometheus will lead us to the wisdom of this story of fire. Prometheus, you will remember, tricked Zeus and stole fire for human beings. For this, he paid a great price. He was bound, as a sacrifice, to a mountain for the rest of his life, where the birds of prey eternally pecked at his liver. Contrast this story of Prometheus, who had to steal the fire in order for human beings to have this resource, with the story in our Gospel this morning. Jesus offers us freely the resource of fire. We do not have to trick or appease. It has been given to us. What he *does* say, in this story, is that human beings must use this resource wisely.

This is a confusing irony. If we take today's parable concerning the wise and foolish maidens on the literal level, then we are to keep oil flasks with us at all times to keep our lamps bright. Being the child of parents who were survivors of the Great Depression, I take this story at its most literal level: we should save these natural resources we've been given—not a bad lesson. A whole sermon could be created and directed toward the importance of saving our natural resources for time in the future rather than expending them now. However, I do not think that this was an economic theorem on how to save enough fossil fuel to run all of our machines in the future. This lesson says that we should be prepared, like good scouts, from now until the end. Such a prudent interpretation runs counter, and indeed is contradictory, to most of Jesus' other teachings.

If today's Gospel means we are to hoard oil or natural resources, what do we do with Jesus' other teaching? For instance, when earlier in Matthew's Gospel Jesus teaches, "Therefore I tell you, do not be anxious about your life, what you shall eat or what you shall drink, nor about your body, what you shall put on. Is not life more than food, and the body more than clothing? Look at the birds of the air: they neither sow nor reap…and yet your heavenly Father feeds them…Consider the lilies of the field, how they grow; they neither toil nor spin;…But seek first [God's] kingdom and his righteousness, and all these things shall be yours as well." Or how about his Parable of the Talents where he admonishes us to spend our talents rather than bury them in the ground? And again, what about the workers in the vineyard, whereby those who work only one hour are paid the same as those who work all day?

Perhaps given the central motif of our Lord's teaching, we should re-examine today's parable and ponder what he might mean by oil and lamp. He tells us that the bridegroom will come to each of us. Whether that is the ultimate end of time or the end of an individual's personal history, it makes no difference, for he is trying to tell us how to be prepared. The wise keep their lamps lit and the foolish don't. We are to prepare for our end by living a life with our lamps lit. This symbol holds a subtle clue that may be a true key as to how it is we are to live our lives. From another tradition, the Greeks held that Prometheus was a savior of humankind. Prometheus' greatest gift was that he stole fire from Zeus and gave it to mankind as a gift. What Jesus is teaching is about the gift of fire. It is given to us freely. We are to live our lives on fire. Fire, in this sense, means energy and light.

In order to prepare for death, we are to live on fire. We are to live with energy and enlightenment. That is the way to prepare for the coming of the bridegroom—that ultimate reunion. The human psyche is energy. Jesus' central teaching is that our human energy has been given to us as resource. You are a quantum of energy, and that is your resource for living. Live it energetically. Harness the energy and focus it and it becomes power, the power for warmth and awareness. God has given us some of God's self. In the Christian story, God gives us freely of his own energy. We have within us this primary source, this resource. This time, it is a gift; we didn't have to steal it. We don't have to spend our lives trying to trick God into giving us energy; it has been given to us freely. We own it, it is ours, and we are to be responsible for the discipline of harnessing it, through focus, into power for something creative, rather than losing it, undisciplined and unfocused, into something destructive. We do not have to have a Promethean trick to obtain our source of light. God has freely given to us our energy. We are to expend it in love and awareness. In summary, if you want to have a short gospel formula for how to prepare for death, it is to live. And how we are to live is to love and be aware. Any time spent pursuing something other than love and awareness is not wasted energy, but energy directed for something other than the Kingdom of God. Love and be aware. Fire and enlightenment. Even the newborn infant knows that warmth and light hold more life than the cold and dark.

For today, let us end with this image. The creation story gives us the image and should help us unlock today's parable. "In the beginning, God created the heavens and earth. The earth was without form and void, and the darkness was upon the face of the deep; and the Spirit of God was moving over the waters. And God said, 'Let there be light'; and there was light." And there still is, and that is what this parable is about. Light comes from the elementary resource of fire, and that energy source is within us. Yet, it is a metaphor for warmth or love and enlightenment or awareness. All the genius and glory are found in these simple poetic metaphors. "And there was light!" John begins his Gospel in our New Testament, where he reveals: "In him was life, and the life was the *light* of men. The light shines in the darkness, and the darkness has not overcome it." Life is light. Keep your lamps lit, or you will not be prepared for this end that is rushing upon you. How you live between now and then is not by hoarding resources, but spending the energy in love, warmth, and enlightenment—knowledge, wisdom! Love and be wise!

Today's parable is not about saving your oil or being prepared like a good scout. It is about using it to love and be aware. All the genius and glory of God are somehow represented by the simple paraphrase of today's Gospel. You have been given all you need to make a life between birth and death. It is symbolized in the gift of fire. Use your resources for warmth (love) and enlightenment (awareness). Whatever is cold and dark robs life, like a grave. Whatever gives awareness and warmth gives life, like a house with a light in the window and a fire in the hearth. Is your life such a house for yourself and others on a cold night? If not, it is a grave, and death has already come. Let your light so shine—so to speak...

Amen.

November 18, 1990
Matthew 25:14–15, 19–29

Today, following this Eucharistic celebration, the bishop of Texas, whom we welcome to his Cathedral today, will dedicate our new Jesse H. and Mary Gibbs Jones education building, the Huffington Courtyard, the Boylston Gallery, the Jeffers Gates, and the renovated Great Hall. This is a grand day and the culmination of years of planning, work, gifts, and talents of hundreds and hundreds of people. Our Visions Campaign, taking its text from the prophetic Old Testament word, "without a vision, the people perish," saw to it that our dream came true of a place for the people of God to begin a second 150 years in this vineyard. We are what we dream.

But even as we prepare to culminate this great project, I strongly empathize with the third servant in today's parable. He was the one who, out of fear, buried his talent in the ground. Five years ago, we began this project because the property at the corner of Prairie and Fannin, where the Jones building now stands, became available for purchase. This created an external crisis for us, which I believe was a mirror in the outer world of what was happening on the interior soul of the Cathedral. We had emerged from a time of trial, where sociological patterns had made downtown churches difficult to maintain. We had struggled to give ourselves away in downtown Houston in order to discover who we were. We had come to the place where viability questions had turned to questions of vitality. What was the soul of the Cathedral to become in the decade of the eighties? The word "crisis" means turning point. The availability of the corner became a call to grow in vitality. This was clearly in the mind of faith a gift and a call from God. But it was, like any journey of faith, a frightening call—a true crisis. The word "blessing," I remind you, comes from "mark of blood." It was a blessing.

The leadership of the Cathedral, after much brooding, decided to take our talent and try to be faithful and venture out and grow. Did we have the resources to respond to the call? It was a time of deep anxiety. What kept echoing in my ears were the lines from Eliot's poem, "The Journey of the Magi":

> A cold coming we had of it,
> Just the worst time of the year
> For a journey, and such a long journey:
> The ways deep and the weather sharp,
> The very dead of winter.
> …There were times we regretted…
> With the voices singing in our ears, saying
> That this was all folly.

The time to set in place our long-range plan for a new education building and renovated parish hall was just the worst time. The depression in Houston had reached its lowest point. And at that point was when we ventured out. I empathize with the third servant who decided to take his talent and bury it in a vacant lot. The fear and anxiety that captured me will always be a part of my memory. I kept thinking of the distinction of the difference between being a "fool for Christ" versus being "a damned fool."

It would be too easy to romanticize the journey of the Visions Campaign and building projects, but to do so would be to repress and deny the sacrifice, the sacrifice that is a part of the blessing—the giving up, the risking, the offering, and the sacrificial giving of more people than can be named. Long hours of study, protracted meetings, compromised decisions, disappointments, organizational committees, late-night phone calls, sleepless nights, and always the fear and anxiety of failure. It doesn't take much wisdom, though, to see that this journey of Christ Church Cathedral from a crisis to a celebration is but a collective metaphor for the individual spiritual journey. My prayer is that what we accomplished through a faith response to a crisis can be a model for each of us as we respond to crises in our own lives.

It is not a coincidence that the Parable of the Talents rolled up on our lectionary as today's Gospel. Our dedication today is not a prideful backslapping of self-congratulatory hubris, but a humble witness to faith. The Christian faith, as inspired by the Holy Spirit, is a journey whereby we offer our talents to God, and it is God who gave us the resources as an image of his primary source and calls us to offer them, and through the inspiration of his Spirit, they are multiplied. In Christianity, the formula reads, if you risk in God's name, there is no way to fail. All losses will be transformed into gain if we seek to respond to God's call. Even though the world may deem one foolish, there *is* a difference between a ship of fools who only know two words of response to God's call: "yes" and "thanks."

Today, we have not come to self-congratulate. We have come to say "thanks"—thanks to everyone who said "yes" when asked to contribute time, talent, and treasure. We have come to say thanks to God for calling us and blessing us through crisis to grow and then inspiring us through the Holy Spirit to find the resources to make a response.

In Spanish, the word for thank you is *gracias*. The root for *gracias* is grace, and all about us is grace: undeserved favor. All of life is gift. God delights when we receive the gift and give it away, for it is in giving that we receive. And all we have come together today to say is *gracias*. Thanksgiving. Grace. We have come today to say grace over these buildings.

And now to the future. These new spaces will be consecrated today as sacred spaces. Our bishop will set them apart to serve the people of God in God's name. It is not our church, it is Christ's church. Let us dedicate these spaces to be places of hospitality. The words "hospital," "hospice," and "host" come from the root word, *ghosti*; it is, surprisingly, also the root of the word "guest." Host and guest are the same word. This sacred space is a hospital, a hospice, where we learn how to live and how to die; sacred spaces where the hosts are guests and the guests are the hosts. Let us dedicate these spaces to be places where we welcome ourselves as those estranged strangers who need a safe place to learn, rest, eat, celebrate, and refresh.

Let us remind ourselves today that we must welcome all strangers as guests, for we hosts are also guests. Let us further remind ourselves that in welcoming the strangers we have welcomed Christ. "In as much as [we] have done it unto the least of these, [our] brethren, [we] have done [it] unto [Christ]." And at the same time, we know that Christ is both guest and host. This is his house. Today at our family meal, you will receive Christ as host. He is guest when we welcome strangers, and he is host to the heavy laden.

Please remember to say "yes" to the invitation to journey with Christ, and "thank you," *gracias*, for the grace of the invitation.

To all that has been, we are grateful for the ability to cast out fear by saying "yes," and for the grace, we say "*gracias*."

Amen.

✣ ✣ ✣

November 25, 1990
Christ the King Sunday
Matthew 25:31–46

Preaching a sermon is like weaving a pattern on an invisible loom—publicly. I've been preaching for twenty years, and I have never failed to draw each thread tightly into place and fashion the pattern I started out to fashion. But you must realize that the pattern from here looks very different from what it looks like out there, and even though I know exactly where I am going and where I will end up, it may not look the same to you. So maybe we had better reverse roles. I realize that it is your job to take the threads to weave them together and get the pattern. Therefore, if it doesn't turn out so well, don't blame me. For too many years, I've been quoted as "having said…," when that wasn't at all what I said.

Today, I take three threads and at no time will my tongue leave my mouth as I weave these threads together on an invisible loom, making a pattern of the Gospel read today.

Thread one: God is subtle, not devious. The Hebrews were very wise in their writing of the creation story in the book of Genesis, because what they did was to reveal to us in the beginning what God has done as Creator. He has entered creation and has hidden himself therein. So thread one is that God has hidden himself in creation, not in a devious way, but in a mysterious way. God is in creation, and our journey is to seek God in creation and within the creature.

Thread two: I've been disturbed a bit about the reporting on President George H. W. Bush's visit to Saudi Arabia. Thanksgiving morning, I was watching the national news as it reported on the president's visit. It seemed, from the commentator, that the total motivation for the visit of our president to the troops on Thanksgiving was to enhance his approval rating. What is the approval rating on our president's action in Saudi Arabia? The entire motivation of the president of this nation is for my approval? I think the implications of that are absolutely scandalous. My accusation is not toward the president, but for those who are interpreting his actions. I do not fear that they may be wrong. This says much about us as human beings. How much of our motivation is for approval rating? The entire journey of the consciousness of the ego is to seek approval in order that we may find our place in time and space. Will Mommy and Daddy like me? Do my friends approve of me? The primary motivation in the external kingdom is for approval, come whence it will, cost what it may. The confusion of consciousness for most of us human beings is that we confuse approval with love. We assume that if people approve of us, they love us, and if people disapprove of us, they do not love us. When, indeed, some of the most important prophetic, outrageous, courageous actions in all the world have been met with great disapproval. Had it not been for the one who ran contrary to expectations, we would be mired and stuck in places that lead nowhere. Is the entire motivation of our behavior in order to gain approval? Leaving thread two and returning quickly to thread one, what is it that we seek in life? Is it approval? Or, is it God? Thread one begins to be woven with thread two. What do you seek in life? What have you given up for your approval rating? What kingdom do you exist in when you seek approval?

Thread three: Jesus was very concerned that his disciples' righteousness exceed that of the Pharisees. The Pharisees' righteousness was self-righteousness. You remember the Pharisee and the publican. The Pharisee said, "I give all my money to the church, I say my prayers, and I follow all of the rules, and"—thread three begins to be woven in with thread two!—"I gain approval from all of those people from whom I seek approval by following all of the laws, and doing exactly what the culture says I must do, and among all, I am the most self-righteous!" The poor publican said, "Lord, have mercy upon me, a sinner." Jesus posed the question, "Which of the two was the more righteous?" And he said, the one who knew who he was and didn't try to be something he wasn't, and who didn't seek approval from his peers, but sought God. Thread three is now woven with threads two and one. Seek ye first the kingdom of heaven, and all things shall come to you. Don't just seek approval, seek God. Jesus said that not everyone who says Lord, Lord shall inherit the kingdom of heaven, but those who do God's will. God has implanted God's self in creation, and our job is to reunite with God as we seek God everywhere and anywhere. Rather than seeking the approval of those in the external world who are concerned that our behavior make their life easier, we must be sure that our righteousness exceeds just making life easier. Our righteousness must be honest self-evaluation: seeking the truth—come whence it will, cost what it may—not simply seeking approval.

Now to the Gospel lesson for today. Don't pay too much attention to this business about the sheep and the goats. Not because it isn't important, but because it is a simile that doesn't fit cattle ranchers like us. We don't know much about separating sheep and goats. One was more valuable than the other, and one got cold at night, and they had to watch out for them. They were the goats; they weren't as valuable. Don't get hung up on moralizing on whether you are a sheep or a goat. The fact of the matter is that you are both! The kernel of the Gospel is when Jesus says, "And the King shall answer and say unto them, 'Inasmuch as ye have done [it] unto one of the least of these my brethren, ye have done [it] unto me.'" You seek him in the sick, not for the approval, but the experience, the ironic experience of finding God in sickness. You clothe the naked, not in order to get external approval, or Nobel Peace Prizes (the Pharisees were interested in that monkey business); you clothe the naked because, in the shame, you will find God. Visit the estranged and imprisoned—not in order to get a plaque on your wall, but because the irony is that in the imprisoned, you will find Christ. Feed the hungry, not in order to obtain sainthood, but because it is in the hunger that you will find God.

Thread one says that God has hidden God's self in creation. Thread two says that we should seek God, not approval. Thread three says we must exceed the Pharisees in our righteousness and not seek God in external approval, but seek God wherever God has hidden God's self. Jesus tells us today that if you seek God in the most unexpected places, that is where the righteousness shall come. You must seek God in the darkness, in the sickness, in the imprisoned, in the estranged, in the naked, and inasmuch as you have done that, you have found God.

That is somewhat the pattern of things. From where I see them.

Amen.

December 9, 1990
Advent II
Mark 1:1–8

There are two primary ways to view life. One is a straight line, alpha to omega—a movement from one point to another, linear. Another is to view life as a circle. There is nothing new under the sun. What is, is what has been and what will be. A straight line and the circle give us two ways to prepare for Advent. One is John the Baptist, preparing the way and a path. The other is Mary, opening and waiting. "Prepare ye the way of the Lord"—that is one way. The other way is, "Now the birth of Jesus Christ took place in this way." Two ways. Both inform us of our Advent journey. What is the way to prepare for the way?

It seems an appropriate Advent question to meditate on the way. The early Christians were known as "the people of the way." Today's Gospel lesson from Mark recounts, "Behold, I send my messenger before thy face, who shall prepare thy way; the voice of one crying in the wilderness: 'Prepare the way of the Lord, make his paths straight.'" Matthew, in his Gospel, writes: "Now the birth of Jesus Christ took place in this way." On Advent II, let's consider the way from two directions. First, what is the way? And secondly, what was the way that God showed us the way?

The way is the path through the mystery of life to life's essential, inscrutable meaning. The way is the path into the Kingdom of God. The way is the return home, to the place we have never been before. The way is into life's deepest truth. The way is to union with the one who is the way, God. The more we know about the way, the less we need to know. We just know.

John the Baptist's vocation was to prepare the way. Jesus' vocation was to show the way, to integrate the circular (now, then, and always) and the linear (the time to come). Our Advent task is to prepare by getting everything out of the way that is keeping us from entering the way and continuing on our path. Take an Advent image. Look at your life and imagine a path ahead of you. What is there in your way that is keeping you from moving? What obstacles, what duties, what impediment or detriment is keeping you from moving on your way along the way? It may be subtle, or it may be obvious.

R. S. "Buck" Abraham, my dear East Texas friend, tells a story of his father who was hit by a train. In court, while trying to recover damage claims, the attorney for the defense asked Mr. Abraham, "Sir, were you driving your car with the windows up, your air conditioner on, and your radio turned up? Is that the reason you did not hear the train whistle?" Mr. Abraham replied, "No, sir. It was a cool spring day, and I had the windows down and no air-conditioning on. I only bought the radio for my wife. I never listen to it. The train whistle never blew. First thing I saw was this great big ol' engine crushing into me as it came out from between a line of old boxcars. Next thing I knew, I was lying upside down in a turned-over car with the train engineer staring down at me." The defense attorney asked, "What did you do then?" Mr. Abraham replied, "I said, 'For Christ's sake, will you get this train out of the way so I can get to work?'"

There are subtleties in our way, but for the most part, they are obvious. You must decide what must be cleared from your path before you can go on your along the way. Advent is the time to do so.

I find it ironic that at this season of preparation, we spend our time, not meditating on what is in our way, but collecting more things which weigh heavily against the way. Jesus said this about the way: "Enter by the narrow gate; for the gate is wide and the way is easy, that leads to destruction, and those who enter by it are many. For the gate is narrow and the way is hard, that leads to life, and those who find it are few." This is the season to get things out of the way rather than accumulate more. How proud are we of how we use Advent? I wonder if Santa could get his bag of consumer goods through the narrow gate. Ponder the way and what is in your way as your Advent discipline.

A second direction to consider the way is the way God showed us. Matthew says, "Now the birth of Jesus took place in this way." The way God showed us is that things happen unexpectedly. God showed us that the way is full of irony, paradox, and surprise. If "it was odd that God should choose the Jews," how much more surprising that the way he entered history was through a scared, teenage, Jewish girl who wasn't married. God is always a surprise. We learn to expect the unexpected, the extraordinary in the ordinary, the miraculous in the mundane. In this way of thinking, we image life as being all around us and all within us.

Isn't it ironic that the hallmarks of the way are surprise, humility, rejection, humiliation, and death? The way to the truth, the way of life, is the way of the cross. Isn't it a paradox that the full life is the life given up for another? Isn't it ironic that the abundant life is the life of abandonment? This circular view of life—Mary's receptivity—is to become a container for life, an open "yes" to all of the irony, surprise, and paradox; to be open to all of the curvaceous ways on which God can lead us. The way it happened is the way it is. The joy to the world is that all the things we have acquired are not essential and that which is required is a free gift. The way is through union with another. The way is through reunion with yourself. The way is reunion with God. And the way is grace. It is important to pay attention to both ways: alpha-to-omega straight path and the circle. To get everything out of the way and to pay attention to receiving everything as being the way. A "no" to anything that is in my way; a "yes" to being a container of all things. Christianity is mysterious and miraculous in its image. The circle, which includes and encompasses all of life receives it and births it; and the line, which is precise gets everything out of the way except that which is essential to life. This is our Advent image.

What is keeping you from loving? Love is the way. The love of God for Mary and Mary's willingness to be rejected and humiliated for love; and her baby boy grew to be rejected and humiliated for love. This is where we come from. This is where we are going. This is the way.

There is a long tradition of thought called Taoism. It is not so much a religion, but a way to think about things—or better still, a way not to think about things. It, too, is called "The Way." It is possible to integrate some of this ancient thought pattern into our own religion. The fundamental writing of Taoism is entitled *Tao Te Ching*, which can translated as "The Book of The Way."

> Look, and it can't be seen.
> Listen, and it can't be heard.
> Reach, and it can't be grasped.
>
> Above, it isn't bright.
> Below, it isn't dark.
> Seamless, unnamable,
> it returns to be the realm of nothing.
> Form that includes all forms,
> image without an image,
> subtle, beyond all conception.
>
> Approach it and there is no beginning;
> follow it and there is no end.
> You can't know it, but you can be it,
> at ease in your own life.
> Just realize where you come from;
> this is the essence of wisdom.
>
> —Chapter 14, *Tao Te Ching*

I think I want both. I want to know the way, and I want to get everything out of the way. I want to be the way: doing and being, the rhythm of Advent. Be the straight line, be the circle, be one with the story. Be with John the Baptist, the one who proclaims the way, and in Mary, the one who becomes the way. We seek God, God seeks us. This is the way.

Amen.

❖ ❖ ❖

December 16, 1990
Advent III
John 3:23–30

As St. John the Divine writes about St. John the Baptist, he could not have done so without this continuing metaphor of light and dark. Even here before you on the Advent wreath is one candle now awaiting the sacred fire to light, to complete the cycle, the Advent story. Where are you, vis-à-vis Advent and Christmas?

"Have any good books read you lately?" That question, attributed to W. H. Auden, is not unlike the tourist who, looking at art in the Louvre, commented to the docent, "I don't think the art here is so great." The docent replied, "My good man, the art here is not on trial, you are."

This reversal of responsibility might also be applied to our Advent journey through our sacred story. The question I ask of you this morning is not "What do you want for Christmas?" but "What does Christmas want from you?" How does the Advent story read you? Every time

I read this Gospel passage, I am read by John's clarity about who he was not.

"There was a man sent from God, whose name was John. He came for testimony, to bear witness to the light, that all might believe through him. He was not the light, but came to bear witness to the light...And this is the testimony of John, when the Jews sent priests and Levites from Jerusalem to ask him, 'Who are you?' He confessed, he did not deny, but confessed, 'I am not the Christ.'"

Two more times they asked him who he was. Who are you? Who are you? Now let this story begin to read you. If you were read by this story, what would your answer be? Suppose a tribunal of some ecclesiastical authority came to you and asked you three times: Who are you? What would your answer be? You remember the man who, out of his dark existential anxiety, cried out, "Who am I?" and a voice came back saying, "Who wants to know?"

Being read or on trial by Advent means to struggle with the question: "What does Christmas want from me?" James Hillman says about dream interpretation that one must realize that the dream comes to us by night because it wants something from us. He says it is as if a stranger bangs on your door at night. When you go to the door, you don't say, "I wonder what you mean." You ask, "What do you want from me?"

Christmas wants something from you this year. It is the reversal of the responsibility. Rather than waiting for Christmas to come and bring you something, the responsibility is up to you. Christmas wants something from you this year. What does Christmas want from you? It wants to know who you are. John knew who he was. He was to bear witness to the light. And he knew several things about light: light required fire; fire requires dead wood and tinder to ignite the sacred fire; and that light warms, enlightens, purifies, and destroys. He also was clear that he couldn't be the light. He could only allow such to shine through him. He did not need to be the Christ to proclaim the Christ. The priests and Levites came to him and said, "Who are you?" He confessed, he did not deny, but confessed, "I am not the Christ."

"John was a man sent from God," says the sacred scripture. "He came for testimony, to bear witness to the light, that all might believe through him. He was not the light, but came to bear witness to the light." The fundamental question for human beings is, "Are you God or not?" If you can decide that, you can get on about the task of being human. "Who are you?" they said. "I am not Christ. God knows, I am not Christ," he said. "I'm just trying to be transparent enough that this sacred fire can light and that I can reflect it." Most of us are trying to do it perfectly; therefore, we never do it! Whatever it is. "It" is the thing you want to be with, as in "with it!" Or "to get it together." We all know what "it" is because that is what struggling to be born is. That is what Christmas wants from you.

Christmas wants us to allow the sacred fire to finally be lit. Christmas wants us to realize that we don't have to be the Christ in order to live. We live because there was a Christ, and we need not confuse our roles. This is the time for you to prepare to finally begin to live. The wood is chopped and stacked. The fireplace is open. The tinder is awaiting only a spark. It is so scary because dead wood won't burn; it takes tinder. We are so afraid of the flame. The bearer of light, John the Baptist, was born to prepare for the fire to light and enlighten.

Christmas wants us to be born. Only you and God know what must be ignited in you. John Updike wrote in his autobiographical statement, *Self-Consciousness*: "I had learned from Kierkegaard and Barth to say the worst about our earthly condition, which was hopeless without a scandalous supernatural redemption." Each of us is judged or read by John the Baptist, who set the world on fire by this scandalous claim that the one born in Bethlehem must be born in us.

Such a birth requires our death. In order for such love to be born in us, we must give up trying to be Christ and submit to his redeeming us from an empty life. We must die to trying to be perfect and allow perfect love to ignite within us. Perfect love casts out all fear. Maybe what Christmas wants from us is to quit being so afraid. Hemingway wrote in his war writings: "I was very ignorant at nineteen and had read little and I remember the sudden happiness and the feeling of having a permanent protecting talisman when a young British officer I met when in the hospital first wrote out for me, so I could remember them, these lines: 'By my troth, I care not; a man can die but once; we owe God a death…and let it go which way it will, he that dies this year is quit for the next.'"

What does Christmas want from you? We owe God a death. This is what Christmas wants. There will be no birth until we die to whatever is our barrier to birth. Maybe that which will light our sacred fire is for the first time to love and praise this world into which we have been born. To thank God for being born. We are privileged in this complex interval of light to have been born at all, and to be in the same story at the same time. Perhaps we must die to our fear of living.

For some, it may mean letting go of the memory or relationship that is keeping us in the dark. For others, what must die is the blame of the past for the darkness of the present. Whatever your darkness, John came today to bear witness to the light. And this year, the Gospel will read you. This year, Christmas wants something from you, and only you must decide who you are and who you are called to be. It is going to have something to do with death, birth, and sacred fire.

The word "nostalgia" means pain of the past. Some of the most nostalgic days of my life have been during the last decade, driving away from here on Christmas Eve, with the exhaustion of the labor of the birth, ritualizing the sacred story, and the hopes and fears of all the years. Several years ago, I wrote a poem entitled "The Years Are Many Now." Held within this is something of what Christmas wants from us.

This is the timorous season.
Irreversible continuum of time
Star crossed thoughts of Christ-
Mas Eve driving home alone.

The incense of sky is stippled
Silent lights. The streets
Are wet with ash. Now shadows
Dream misty joy and lonely

Grief. A crocus to be delivered
As a midnight sachet sits
Beside me now lush
And come of age. Eyes

Are apertures, every sight
A memory and a dream. The
Silhouettes intersect to
Circulate the intervals and

Oscillate the time as birth
And when alone to know
That every year, and there
Are many now, moves us closer

To the shameless sunrise coming
From a sleeping source resting
Still in a rough-hewn bed waiting
For the sacred fire to light.

One never quite knows what that spark will be. What Christmas wants from you is to be prepared for that fire to come and burn the dead wood, ignited by the tinder, even knowing that ash may result. But without the dead wood being burned (and the ash as a result), there would be no fire, no warmth, no light or enlightenment. This is the year for the sacred fire to finally light.
Amen.

✤ ✤ ✤

December 23, 1990
Advent IV
Luke 1:26–38

In his *Visions Seminars*, C. G. Jung speaks:

> Wisdom begins only when one takes things as they are...when we can agree
> with the facts as they are; only then can we live in our body on this earth...

each person has something specific to accept...let us just say that the thing we have to accept is whatever we want to escape.

So here is Mary, in her body on earth, given this scandalous message by way of proposal from the angel Gabriel, "Hail, O favored one, the Lord is with you!" The rubric of the wily nature of the Holy Spirit is embossed forever in this sacred story. In her book *Wisdom of the Psyche*, Ann Belford Ulanov suggests that "the Holy Spirit is always a surprise, and not always a gentle one." Mary was asked to accept something so outrageous and odious that surely some part of her wanted to escape. We hear her say, "How can this be?" God desired to take up residence in Mary. God wanted Mary to house God; to receive into her womb a revolution. Rather than escape, she held the spirit, not fleeing, not solving, not denying, but pondering it, looking upon it, making space for it. She refused to make life in her own image, but simply to obey. Wisdom begins when we take things as they are.

There is a force loose in creation that seeks to order chaos. Creation, re-creation, Christmas, all are the same: ordering chaos. Order means to make known through an arrangement. Chaos originally meant "empty." To order chaos is to "fill the empty." Now, we who seek a Christmas we can believe in might look and listen to the lesson from Mary: be available for the Holy Spirit to fill our emptiness. Frederick Buechner writes:

> It is well to remember because it keeps our eyes on the central fact that the Christian faith *always* has to do with flesh and blood, time and space, more specifically with your flesh and blood and mine, with the time and space that day by day we are all of us involved with, stub our toes on, flounder around in trying to look as if we have good sense. In other words, the truth that Christianity claims to be true is ultimately to be found, if it's to be found at all, not in the Bible, or the church, or theology—the best they can do is point to the truth—but in our own stories.
>
> If the God you believe in as an idea doesn't start showing up in what happens to you in your own life, you have as much cause for concern as if the God you don't believe in as an idea does start showing up.

God is as present in our stories as he is present in Mary's story. Mary's story *is* our story. God in Christ is filling our emptiness. Before our emptiness can be filled, we must not try to escape the fact that each of us carries a vacancy that can only be filled by God. And yet, such an emptiness will be filled, not in abstract, or in general, but in particular, in our own flesh and blood, time and space existence.

Perhaps rather than expecting one event to be our fulfilling, we could ponder the fact that our life is that for which we have waited. There may be an event or more that we fashion into a single story to symbolize our life, but life is God's gift which is designed to fill our empty lives. Your life is God's gift to fill an empty life. "Let us just say that the thing we have to accept is whatever we want to escape." Escape from life is the greatest sin. Emerson wrote: "No one suspects the days to be gods." Perhaps wisdom's truth is that our days are God's surprise. The Christmas we await is a daily event.

Plato penned:

> What if the man could see Beauty Itself, pure, unalloyed, stripped of mortality and all its pollution, stains, and vanities, unchanging, divine,…the man becoming, in that communion, the friend of God, himself immortal;…would that be a life to disregard?

Have you disregarded your life, as if it was not yours to live? The life led to escape life is not a life lived in the Spirit. A life lived only as a biological function is a life of greed; it requires more and more. The life lived in the Spirit requires less and less; time is ample and life's passages sweet. This is Christmas—the accepting of the gift of life as that which fills an empty life.

Like the man riding on an ox looking for an ox, we search in vain. Like a woman wearing glasses looking for her glasses, we do not see what is before us. Do we not know life when our life from which we have tried to escape is that which we must accept? Each of us is given ourselves and another. We must know our own life and that of another. Thoreau said it another way: know your bone. "Pursue, keep up with, circle round and round your life…Know your own bone; gnaw at it, bury it, unearth it, and gnaw at it still."

Teilhard de Chardin wrote: "The world is filled, and filled with the Absolute." Today we ponder Mary, filled with the Absolute. And what of us? The emptiness we each know is filled with days, and the days are filled with activity, business, distraction, and we remain empty. Unless we can begin to see that life is what happens to us while we wait for life, we will write our story unlike Mary. When Gabriel comes to us and tells us that God wants to be born in us, we will say "no." Not by a word, but by an empty life, never lived, closed, vacant, and dead.

Christmas is a gift. The Christmas gift to you is your birth. You are a fact. "Wisdom begins only when [we take] things as they are…when we can agree with facts as they are; only then can we live in our body on this earth. Each person has something specific to accept…let us just say that the thing we have to accept is whatever we want to escape."

If you have accepted your life as your gift, you know Christmas. If you seek to escape your life, this year may be your year to be born again. As Mary said, "Let it be unto me according to your word."

Amen.

December 30, 1990
John 1:1–18

If Christmas is for children, then the doctrine of the incarnation is for adults. One of my favorite stories is a simple story, but carries much complexity beneath it, like some kind of intricate netting. It is the story of the young curate who went to see the dying parish priest. He had been the rector of that parish for some thirty years, a priest for fifty, and the young curate went to him and said, "Father, before you die, could you please impart to me some wisdom of your years in the parish?" The priest said, "Just remember that people are neither as happy nor sad as they appear, and there aren't many adults." This doctrine of the incarnation is for adults.

I have for a number of years collected some "hallmarks of maturity." These are sentences that are based on my own sense of issues or questions that must be dealt with before one can enter adulthood. Some of these hallmarks of maturity are: "One must decide whether he or she is God nor not; one must be able to hold a paradox consciously; one must know one's own possibilities and limitations; one must be able to delay gratification; one must be able to retard instinct and impulse; one must have someone or something for which one would give one's life; one must be able to live at the edge of death and keep a sense of humor; one must find meaning in general, purpose in particular, and a place to belong."

Today, I add another to the list: "One must decide whether the task is to escape life or enter it." One must live the incarnation. Life, as I have said for years, may be viewed as lived between a birth we did not request and a grave we cannot escape. How do we respond in general and to each decision in particular? Do we escape or enter?

The doctrine of the incarnation as espoused in the prologue to John's Gospel is the Christian model for our response to life. God entered the world in flesh, full of grace and truth. God in Christ gives us the model of how it is that we are to live as adults in this world: enter it!

One of the most insidious heresies of Christianity is the popular notion that religion is a way to "cope with life," which is in truth a euphemism for a strategy of escape. The spiritual danger of drug and alcohol abuse is not the physical danger and destruction alone, but that such abuse is a statement that the task of life is not to enter it, but to escape from it. One can be as addicted to religion as alcohol as a way to escape life. In some ways, they both are equally destructive.

Clearly, if there is any message at the Christmas incarnation, it is that God entered life fully and the mature person finally decides that the key to life is to live it rather than fear it. The fearful continually seek and search for ways to postpone, avoid, escape, or evade life. The mature cope with life by living it. This is the model given us by God in Christ.

Perhaps this is the message of the incarnation: life is not a strategy of escape, but a call to enter into the experience as fully as possible. Life is not to be enjoyed but experienced. Wisdom from every corner of life reminds us that problems, crises, and decisions are not barriers to growth, but resources for growth. One of the problems with adolescents who have spent their adolescence stoned is that they have a retarded emotional development. They haven't had to solve any problems. They have gone through the difficulties of life stoned. A stone has very little awareness and no growth. If we cope with these realities through evasion or escape, we miss the possibility of growth, which evidently is the purpose of the problem.

The aphorism concerning a crisis, "The only way to get through it is to go through it," presumes that in going through, one will discover awareness and resources that simply could not be discovered in any other way.

The clear irony about entering versus escaping is that resources appear that can only come through the crucible of crisis and the difficult decisions that must be made. The way out is always the way through: entry, not escape. Patience is a virtue until it becomes avoidance. Fear is appropriate, for without such, there is no courage. Courage without fear is ignorance. I remind you, "decide" comes from the same root as "homicide" and "suicide." To decide is to enter, not to decide is to escape. The fear is the recognition of the pain inflicted on others and self when we must decide to enter rather than escape.

Much of the time, what we don't understand is that we create our own crisis because some part of us knows that that is the only way to health. Jack Sanford writes:

> We are like Naaman the Syrian, whose story we find in the fifth chapter of the Second Book of Kings. Naaman was a Syrian general afflicted with leprosy, who went to the prophet Elisha to be cured. When Elisha told him to bathe seven times in the Jordon River, he was disdainful. Why should he bathe in the muddy old Jewish River Jordon when the waters of his own country were so much purer? Just the same, he did it and was cured.
>
> So it is with us. There must be some more glorious way of curing ourselves than bathing in our own muddy waters.

We muddy our own water, and in so doing, we are forced to seek a new clarity. We create our own crises in order to grow up.

If the world was a problem for God, it was one he created himself and he chose to enter it in the flesh. He entered it through birth, knowing that wherever there is birth, there is blood. Such grace and truth is the enabling model for our response to life.

The New Year begins in but a few hours. Each of us will face life-threatening and life-making decisions housed in some crisis. Will we cope through escape and avoidance? Will we remain mediocre because mediocre people are always at their best? Or, will we enter in and discover life at a new depth? This incarnation is for adults. Will we take superficial resources as a strategy of escape, or will we discover new resources through the crucible of crisis? Will we choose to enter into the enfleshment of it—into the blood of it—into the new birth of it? This incarnation is for adults. God has given us the choice, but at the same time, an undeniable model. The Word became flesh and dwelt among us. In him was life, and the life was the light of men. The light shines in the darkness, and the darkness has not overcome it. Will we take the easy way out, the road most travelled? Or will we look for the Christmas gift, the new resource, in the crucible of the true crèche?

Jesus was born to bear the message that life is a gift. The gift of life is life. We are promised that nothing in life will defeat us if we enter into life fully. Christianity is not about a strategy to avoid life and find a way to life after death; it is a gift of life after birth, before death. If the purpose of Christianity is to avoid death, we have not yet had one success, not even our Lord. Christianity is about overcoming the fear of death. Perfect love casts out all fear. What in the world are you afraid of? Not living is what I am afraid of; having come to the edge of death and having nothing to laugh about. When we learn to love life, we love God. For we know that God so loved the world that he gave his only begotten son, to the end that all that believe in him should not perish…even in crises, or decision making, but continually be given new life through every death, now and forevermore. Christmas may be for children, but the incarnation is for adults.

So, what will you right now write? As a gift, Christmas has handed you your own personal pen. You are asked to write your own autobiography. Every decision this year will be your life. Are you going to escape another year and avoid it, or are you going to be born? That is the Christmas message for children and adults alike.

Amen.

1991

January 6, 1991
Isaiah 60:1–6, 9; Matthew 2:1–12

Today's Old Testament lesson and the Epiphany Gospel hold within them two sayings about which I have changed my mind. The first is from Isaiah: "Arise, shine; for your light has come, and the glory of the Lord has risen upon you." I used to hate to hear this passage. Not in the sense of theological disagreement. As a matter of fact, I didn't even know that it came from Isaiah when first I detested its utterance. I'm not even sure the utterer of this passage ever knew he was quoting scripture.

When I was growing up, my father had the task of awakening my brother and me for school. Sleep has always been the one thing I do well. On those cold winter' mornings, I hated the sound of my father's beaming voice as he came striding down the hall from the kitchen, "Boys, arise and shine."

"Arise and shine; for your light has come, and the glory of the Lord has risen upon you." I must admit, even now, I prefer Isaiah's verse to my father's voice. Be that as it may, I love this line. The prophetic word is that the time has come to get up—arise and shine—for your light has come. It is not unlike what Jesus said to that poor soul lying by the pool at Bethesda all those years, expecting somebody else to come and get him up. Jesus said, "Do you want to get well?" "Yes, I do." "Then, get up!" said our Lord Jesus, mild and gentle. Likewise to Lazarus, who had withdrawn into the stench of his own death. Jesus said, "Lazarus, come out!" "Rise, shine, it is time to get up!" This is the feast of the Epiphany. Epiphany means "manifestation" (at hand: manna fest) or "appearance." The light of the world has come in Christ—your light; it should light some fire in you—it's time to arise and shine.

The second saying about which I have changed my mind is the term "stargazer." Where

I grew up a "stargazer" was one who was somewhere between indolent and irrelevant. A stargazer was one whose head was full of dreams or in the clouds! He or she was impractical and unproductive. The Protestant ethic had no room for a stargazer. The stargazers in today's Gospel are now known as wise men. In fact, these magi were dream interpreters, men of mystery, astrologers, priests. Had it not been for stargazers, the truth would not have been seen. They saw something others did not see. It was something very different, in fact, from what King Herod saw. Herod saw a threat; they saw light. They looked beyond the horizon and took a journey of faith, a fool's errand for the world. But in the world of faith and imagination, they knew that life could only be discovered at its fullest by following wonder. In the Kingdom of God, the wise are foolish, and the foolish wise. When I grew up, I devalued stargazers, but now I am one.

Two simple messages: "Arise and shine" and "Follow the star." Having a belief in God is less a position and more a journey, less a reality and more a relationship. A belief in the mystery of God is the reason we get up in the morning. It is a conviction that there is meaning in general and purpose for me in particular. Faith in God is that there is a place for me. The star in the East is the thing we must follow in order to discover ourselves, even if it means that, in order to follow the star in the sky, we occasionally stub our toe on earth. One cannot stargaze without stumbling over stones. This is the nature of the journey of faith. In the journey of the world, the admonition is: "Drive carefully—the life you save may be your own." Following the star, the admonition is: "The life you save is the life you lose."

"Arise and shine." "Follow the star." No wonder there are so few who follow wonder. The world does not reward stargazers. And yet, the Holy Scripture and sacred story are full of those who left security to seek mystery. Abraham just said "yes" to God's call to leave his father's house and go to a place that God would show him. Moses just went when the bush burned and told him to go to Egypt. Peter threw down his net when called to follow the star. Paul left his former life when the epiphany blinded him and opened his eyes. Where are the stargazers today?

Urban T. Holmes, in his book *Ministry and Imagination*, maintains:

> If the church is to be open to the presence of God in Christ now, it has to live a life of imagination. It has to embrace intuition and wonder to enter the epiphany of God. In our western culture, God is surely present, but we have made so little of imagination, intuition, and wonder that the ability to discern God's presence in our midst has been retarded.

The magi went on a journey. Such a journey is a costly journey because it is foolish to the world; it is the wise who wonder. What these wise men found was that they were no longer at ease in the world. The curse, or dark side, of the blessing of the journey is that you are no longer at ease in the world. They found that they must use their freedom to make a transcendent journey, not just a geographical one. The journey had only a direction, no map. Follow the star. But having said "yes," having got up and gone, having followed the star into the crucible of the crèche, they were no longer at ease in the world. They went home another way. Eliot wrote it this way:

> But had thought they were different: this Birth was
> Hard and bitter agony for us, like Death, our death.
> We returned to our places, these Kingdoms,
> But no longer at ease here, in the old dispensation,
> With an alien people clutching their gods.
> I should be glad of another death.

Let us not romanticize the journey of the stargazers like some paltry Hollywood plot. The journey is the difference between life and death. It is dramatic. To stay home, to stay in bed, is to save your life and lose it. To journey is to lose your life and find it.

This Epiphany morning, our heavenly Father is striding once again down the hall beaming: "Arise and shine."

Will we stay asleep or follow the star? The choice is always ours. Let me hasten to remind you; it is a matter of life or death.

Amen.

✤ ✤ ✤

January 13, 1991
The Baptism of Our Lord
Mark 1:7–11

The very part of the world out of which this story of Jesus' baptism comes, exists in great crisis this day. Perhaps no world crisis has been more greatly and publically evaluated, commented upon, and documented than the decision that the world leaders will be making in the next two days. What the world little awaits is my personal opinion about that. The light of the gospel tells us three things: one is that human beings never are off the hook of decision making, and that we are given generally not decisions just about good and evil, but decisions about greater good and lesser evil; secondly, we ought always to seek peace; and thirdly, that we are to pray for our enemies. Rather than my trying to preach some prophetic word, we will pause in silence for a moment, as a people huddled together, confused and frightened about how critical this decision is. We pray for the president of the United States and those in authority who are going to be our circle of leadership making these decisions. We want always to pray for peace, and due to Jesus' admonition, we must pray for those who call themselves our enemies. In silence, let us focus our prayer and reflection upon this critical time and look at it as a fact. At the same time, it is a metaphor for a conflict that we find in our own selves and within our own families, and let us be reminded that we must seek healthy solutions. Let us pray…

Perhaps the best thing I can do for all of us today is to preach the gospel, the gospel of love. Today is the "Baptism of Our Lord" Sunday. In much of my decade of preaching in this place, my theological emphasis has been on what I believe to be the three basic needs of the human being. Those needs are: to search for meaning in general, purpose in particular, and a place to belong. Meaning in general has to do with the search for a sense that there is a source to the mystery of the universe and if anyone or anything is in control of it. Further, to find that this universe is ordered for a purpose. Purpose in particular means that my individual life has a significance and particular intent that connects and serves the meaning of the whole. A place to belong means that I experience the acceptance and affirmation of another and others that give experience to meaning and purpose for my own life.

It may appear that a copious amount of my emphasis has been focused on the second need, purpose for the individual. Much of my concern *is* for the individual becoming that unique creature he or she was created to be and to become; to respond to the call to become that person whom God calls us to be. Individuation through awareness of our own personalities is, I believe, much of the enabling function of Jesus. Christ re-presents the possibility for authentic existence for everyone, and for me in my own life. His becoming who God called him to be is the representation to us to become ourselves as fully as Jesus became the Christ.

And yet, at the same time, we must be clear that the word "individual" is not to be confused with the word "isolated." The word "individual" means: that which is so sufficiently whole that it cannot be divided, cannot be broken up by conflicts, decisions, crises, or trauma—that there is a core, the heart of the heart, something that cannot be fractured or divided by life's realities. This must not be confused with "isolated," meaning not belonging to another or to others. Belonging to another or to others is a necessity of one's individuation. Both are always true at one and the same time.

Belonging is a fundamental part of what baptism is about in Christianity. Today is the Feast of the Baptism of Jesus. Mark's Gospel describes Jesus' baptism in such simplicity: "In those days Jesus came from Nazareth of Galilee and was baptized by John in the Jordan. And when he came up out of the water, immediately he saw the heavens open and the Spirit descending upon him like a dove and a voice came from heaven, 'Thou art my beloved Son; with whom I am well pleased.'"

From the beginning of his journey Jesus knew he belonged. He was pleasing to his parents. Mary was told that she would house something sacred. She treated him as a holy child; she held him as if he were sacred gift. From the beginning of his adult life he was told by God: "You are my beloved in whom I am pleased." No wonder Jesus was able to become who God created him to be. With such an affirmation from his very source, how could he not have the self-confidence and courage to accomplish his unique life? You are my beloved, in you I am well pleased. I delight in you. I relish your presence. I love you no less than I love my own life. I find you pleasing in my sight. Jesus knew he belonged there. Such affirmation and approval are ingredients of belonging, and necessary for individuation. We each desperately need to know this if we are going to be courageous enough to reach an individuation—a place that has a solid core, a place that cannot be divided by the slings and arrows of this world.

The baptismal rite is complex and mysterious. But through it, we begin our belonging to a community of affirmation and approval. Baptism tells us what God told us in Christ, "You belong here, you are loved, you are accepted and acceptable."

In his book, *Who Needs God*, Harold Kushner cites the panic in recent years that parents and religious leaders were experiencing as a result of so many young people being attracted to cults. Kushner's explanation was that the cults offered to rejected young people acceptance and community, bonding and belonging. Faced with an outside world that was constantly judging and rejecting, these young people were ripe for anyone who would promise to love them and give them a place to belong. (For example, "My father is always after me to improve my grades so I can get a better job and make more money," or "My phone never rings because I don't have the kind of body boys notice.") Kushner states, "What was lacking in our churches and synagogues that sent our young people so far afield in their search for community was for people who would love and accept them, rather than judge them."

The Christian church is supposed to be a community of acceptance and affirmation, a place to belong. The gospel is the "Good News." The good news is that at your baptism the heavens opened and God said about you, "You are my beloved child, in whom I am well pleased."

This Cathedral place must always be a place where we can search openly for meaning in general, purpose in particular, and find a place to belong.

God made us complex and such complexity creates confusion. In our freedom, we make bad choices and mistakes. Sometimes our only mistake is that we want desperately to be loved, to belong. This is no mistake, it is our nature. When we seek to follow our nature, we will ultimately find God, for that is also our nature.

This is the only requirement for belonging to the church—that is, to seek God—to seek God in others, and to seek God in yourself. This seeking will allow you to be found.

From the beginning Jesus was empowered, for he knew he was God's child. His mother told him and his father told him. You are a child of God. We are well pleased in your being here. You belong here. We accept you, we affirm you. We approve of you. No wonder he was the Christ! Our catechism teaches this simple truth in these simple words: "Holy Baptism is the Sacrament by which God adopts us as his children and makes us members of Christ's Body, the Church, and inheritors of the kingdom of God." Holy Baptism is the sacrament by which God adopts us as his children and says, "You are my beloved child, in whom I am well pleased." You (have/are) nothing to be embarrassed or ashamed of. You are a child of God.

I pray that this Cathedral church will always be a place of belonging. A place where the children of God can know that in us God is well pleased. And further, and finally, be a place where people who are searching for affirmation, acceptance, and approval will find a community who will accept and love them rather than judge them. God has already passed judgment, the judgment is over, and I have good news. His judgment is "You are my beloved child, in whom I am well pleased."

Amen.

✤ ✤ ✤

January 20, 1991
John 1:43–51

Pinned like a butterfly to a black widow's web, I am today caught between my opposite attitudes of idealism and cynicism.

The fact that we are embroiled in a world-threatening war demands from me a response on the nature of human's warring and destructive side, and humankind's nature of creative love.

All in a word, we have in today's Gospel Nathanael echoing our own cynicism: What good can come out of Nazareth? And at the same time, Jesus accepting him, inviting him into a creative love relationship, saying, "Behold, an Israelite indeed, in whom is no guile!"

The idealist in me says, "Out of every evil act will emerge a good." The cynic in me counters, "What good can come out of a war with Iraq?"

I am reminded of Kierkegaard's profound statement in his book, *The Concept of Dread*:

> He who is educated by anxiety and dread is educated by possibility...When such a person, therefore, goes out from the school of possibility, and knows more thoroughly than a child knows the alphabet that he can demand of life absolutely nothing, and that terror, perdition, annihilation, dwell next door to every man, and has learned that profitable lesson that every anxiety which alarms may the next instant become a fact, he will interpret reality differently...

Education for the human means facing up to his dark side and coming to terms with the results of such reality. We are at war. Human darkness which seeks to destroy calls out our ambiguous nature which also seeks to create. The cynical view is a voice which must be heard, "What good can come from this destruction?" But, too, the voice of hope must be heard. At times of terror, we must look beyond our nature to some invisible mystery, for humans are incapable of solving the human predicament.

In spite of our creativity, the economic network of supply and demand, now met by systems of preservation and planning—in spite of communication systems of instant information; in spite of transportation systems that make the world one commuter community—are still fighting, like animals, over territorial rights.

Through one man's obsession to control by force, visited with a maniacal attempt to deny his humanity, seeking immortality through dominance, we are brought back to the primitive solution of war. When reason fails, we are still left with the instinctual solution of bringing death to our enemy.

Science has not saved us from ourselves. Science has brought us a more sophisticated mask for our mortality, but has not eliminated our urge to destroy, which is equally as strong as our urge to create.

Elie Wiesel, the writer who survived a Nazi concentration camp, summed it all up in a wistful remark during a TV interview: "Man is not human." I would qualify Wiesel's conclusion with a faint hope, stating, "Man is not *yet* human."

This war must deflate any human hubris that we have evolved out of our animal nature and are able to save ourselves through our own ingenuity. We are still vicious and frightened creatures who have not secured a victory over our limitations by our scientific accomplishments. It is self-deception to blame others or to mask panic as reasonable. We still must look beyond ourselves. The only solution we have found to defeat an enemy is to destroy him. If there are no other solutions, then we must once again confess that we cannot save ourselves from ourselves. Such confession re-creates the possibility that we will learn once again the dreaded lesson that our significance is not based on our accomplishment, but on the absolute, infinite grace of God, which allows us to exist in spite of our inhumanity.

Pinned like a butterfly to a black widow's web, I must recognize that I am both the innocent butterfly and the dark spider. The web is my paradoxical nature. My plea is that I cannot save myself. Educated by such terror, I pray for a new possibility, that this warring nature will not be a waste, but another opportunity to invite a transcendent revelation which will lift us beyond the human narcissism that presumes we are beyond our own mortality.

Otto Ranke wrote:

> All our human problems, with their intolerable sufferings, arise from man's ceaseless attempts to make this material world into a man-made reality... aiming to achieve on earth a "perfection" which is only to be found in the beyond...thereby hopelessly confusing the values of both.

We always live in two worlds. The kingdom of the world is at war. We humans still suffer the results of our inhumanity. Perhaps war was the best solution to the dark spider who sought to enslave another people in his web of egomania. But, let this war remind us that in the Kingdom of God, we must allow love to be the only solution, for it is only God's unconditional love which reigns in God's Kingdom that can make the world tolerable and redeemable. What good can come out of Nazareth? What must come is an invisible kingdom that transcends our paradox and clarifies our confusion of how to live in this world in love.

Let us not give in to our cynicism, allowing its voice. Let us not be seduced by the hubris of our humanistic idealism that we can save ourselves. Let us visit a new possibility that one day the kingdom of the world and the Kingdom of God will be so integrated that we will study war no more, and the lion will lie down with the lamb, and the butterfly with the black widow.

Amen.

✤ ✤ ✤

February 3, 1991
Mark 1:21–28

In a recent PBS series on the 1960s, the first segment of the three-part series entitled "Seeds of the Sixties" concluded that the three dominant American cultural values given to children in the 1950s were: 1. Obey authority, 2. Do not express emotions, 3. Conform. In other words, the message was: Follow those who have gone before you. Do as they do, quietly. Be outstanding, but don't stand out. This is a difficult prescription. These seeds planted in the '50s bore contrary fruits in the '60s.

The question of authority has always been a primary issue for individuals and societies. As I am fond of saying, "The first question asked by the infant ego once a child bears the birth canal is, 'Who's in charge here, and what are the rules for making it?'" Authority for ego development is essential. The developing ego consciousness must have boundaries or it cannot survive or prosper. In this childhood developmental phase, parents and parental figures are the authorities (church, school, government, home). In adolescent years, the authority is passed from parents to peers. Whereas before, the parents were authorities on behavior boundaries, values, and decisions, peer groups become the teenage authorities. Somewhere between twenty-one and death, life has a natural way of creating such problems, complexities, crises, and conflicts that one's own internal self or soul is called upon to create an individual who must, finally, take authority and responsibility for his or her own life.

I am struck once again by Jesus' life as an enabling model for our own lives. In today's Gospel, Mark describes Jesus in this way: "And they went into Capernaum; and immediately on the sabbath he entered the synagogue and taught. And they were astonished by his teaching, for he taught them as one who had authority…"

Next in sequence after he had taught "as one who had authority," he delivered a man from an unclean spirit "and they were all amazed…'What is this? A new teaching! With authority he commands even the unclean spirits…'"

He taught with authority and he commanded with authority. Here is the striking irony. This man held no external authority. He was not a holder of office. He was not a parent. He was not credentialed by any *outside* authority. In Jesus' life, his authority was all internal. As a matter of fact, the external authorities of his time found him to be one who would not follow authority. He broke laws and traditions, and was ultimately put to death because his internal authority was such a threat to the external authority. If Jesus' vocation was to live his life seeking approval, he failed his task. If his vocation was to become the Christ, he succeeded.

The fear, of course, with this kind of conversation is that if authority is not upheld, authority's opposite will raise its head and reign. The opposite of authority is anarchy, which is the absence of any authority. This was not the case with Jesus. He knew that God, or the Holy Spirit dwelling within, was the ultimate authority. Jesus' teaching was replete with calls to being responsible to our freedom. His summary of the law was not that of an anarchist, but one who knew that love was the greatest freedom and greatest responsibility. What Jesus did was hold up the opposites of authority and anarchy and create a tension that called for a transcendent worldview to emerge, which is known as autonomy. In the creative tension between selflessness and selfishness, selfhood emerges. We are not to live only for authority, or to live as anarchists, but to live autonomously.

Jesus taught as one who had authority, not in outward office, but in internal resource. It seems to me that a primary responsibility of the spiritual formation is to develop such sufficient internal resources that one can live independent of his twofold temptation—of living only for the approval of others, or living only for the gratification of his own desires—by becoming himself in authentic relationship to others. Development of such internal resources is the true education for living. Such life work, though, requires commitment to knowing one's self and the discipline to work toward discovery of the authority within.

There is in Bruce Larson's book, *Dare to Live Now*, an important and simple story that illustrates this point.

> A letter was found in a baking powder can wired to the handle of an old pump
> that offered the drinking water on a lengthy, seldom-used trail across the

Amargosa Desert in Nevada: "This pump is all right as of June, 1932. I put a new sucker washer into it and it ought to last five years. But the washer dries out, and the pump has got to be primed. Under the white rock I buried a bottle of water, out of the sun and cork end up. There's enough water in it to prime the pump, but not if you drink some first. Pour about one fourth, and let it soak the leather. Then pour the rest in medium fast and pump like crazy. You'll git water. The well has never run dry. Have faith. When you git watered up, fill the bottle and put it back like you found it for the next feller. (signed) Desert Pete. P.S. don't go drinking the water first. Prime the pump with it and you'll git all you can hold."

What a metaphor. The internal resources are there. They never run dry. The discipline to work and use one's God-given ingenuity to prime the pump and delay gratification is the art. And, of course, to put back what you have learned so the next fella can drink is the greatest responsibility.

Jesus held the tension between external authority and selfish anarchy. His authority was in his autonomy as a child of God. He got in touch with the wellspring within. We are called upon to seek our own internal resources not in order to be like Christ, but in order to become ourselves as authentically as he became that unique Christ he was called to be. He is the authority who enables us to take authority and responsibility for our own lives. It is difficult to model one's life on Christ, but it is even more difficult for one to live his own life as authentically and autonomously as Christ lived his. This is our gift. This is our challenge.

Amen.

February 3, 1991
Ordination Sermon
The Reverend Paul David Fromberg to the Sacred Order of Priest

The Welsh poet-priest, R. S. Thomas, touches the current parochial nerve with dead accuracy. Put the following truths in an urban setting and they would ring the same. This is the hard landscape of the person set apart as priest.

> The priest picks his way
> Through the parish. Eyes watch him
> From windows, from the farms;
> Hearts wanting him to come near.
> The flesh rejects him.
>
> Women, pouring from the black kettle,
> Stir up the whirling tea-grounds

Of their thoughts; offer him a dark
Filling in their smiling sandwich.

Priests have a long way to go.
The people wait for them to come
To them over the broken glass
Of their vows, making them pay
With their sweat's coinage for their correction.

He goes up a green lane
Through growing birches; lambs cushion
His vision. He comes slowly down
In the dark, feeling the cross warp
In his hands; hanging on it his thought's icicles.

'Crippled soul' do you say? Looking at him
From the mind's height; 'limping through life
On his prayers. There are other people
In the world, sitting at table
Contented, though the broken body
And the shed blood are not on the menu.'

'Let it be so,' I say. 'Amen and amen.'

The priest is the pebble in the Church's shoe. It has never known quite what to make of us, and we have been its constant, irritating, incarnate reminder of the conflict between its contradictory natures of the human and the divine.

Frederick Buechner writes that the visible Church (the institution) and the invisible Church (the body of Christ) should be thought of as two circles. "The optimist says they are concentric. The cynic says they don't even touch. The realist says they occasionally overlap."

So it is with the sacramental priesthood and the person who carries its outward sign. To be a priest is to carry the cruciform sign of the divine paradox, the one who represents Christ at the holy table and the one who himself is a redeemed sinner. Jesus says in John's Gospel within his sheep and shepherd metaphor: "For this reason the Father loves me, because I lay down my life, that I may take it again. No one takes it from me, but I lay it down of my own accord."

The priest, for reasons more complex and complicated than consciousness alone can divine, offers down a life of such contradiction, a life of such whirling complexity, a life of such mixed motive, and does so for Christ's sake. That life laid down is taken again and used by God as a symbol of how it is that we gain our lives by losing them for Christ's sake. Living into the impossible task of ordained priesthood makes possible the priesthood of all believers. Such a duality of circular symbols keeps conscious God's inexplicable generosity of providing us with two paradises—one of his unconditional love for the humanity he has created, and the other for the everlasting spirit he has implanted within our eternal soul.

There is the dual focus of what the priest represents and what the priest does. The priest represents an image of what Christ's vocation was, and that is to represent the possibilities of authentic human existence. There is also the focus of what the priest does. What doing priestcraft entails is symbolized by the Bible and the altar. The priest as preacher and teacher is to keep the sacred story alive. By the priest's presiding at the holy table, the priest is to keep the mystery present. The pastoral office of the ordered priest is to represent Christ's love in care and concern for all people, caring alike for young and old, strong and weak, rich and poor.

Furthermore, and perhaps most importantly, the priest is to experience the mystery he represents. Joseph Campbell distinguishes the shaman from the priest. "The priest," he writes, "represents; the shaman, experiences what he represents." There must always be a shamanistic principle present for a complete priest. The true priest must enter into the darkness of his own soul before he dares enter the dark place of another. The priest must wrestle with his own evil in the desert of his own soul if he is to enter such with another. The priest as shaman must enter hell, and then pray to be given safe return so that he may live to tell about it. It is only the wounded physician that can heal. The teacher can only take the student as far as he himself has gone. And then there is the world, which little understands. The world from its own view doesn't know the difference between a fool for Christ and a damned fool.

Seminary prepares, but the practice of priestcraft is the only teacher. The priest must wet his own face with the tears of grieving parents at the loss of a child and taste their salt. The priest must kiss the parched lips of a person dying of cancer and breathe hope into a laboring soul. The priest must hear the confession and know the terror that must be incomparable in the psyche of an unmarried teenage girl who is torn with the choice of what to do with the life she has growing in her womb. The priest must listen to the young man or woman caught in the torturing choice between serving the cross and the flag. The priest must listen to the wounded human beings who have been scarred by unlimited freedom and limited information, and the pain of responsibility of choices made or refused, or loves that were loved or cast out.

The priest must be the object of projection from the confused and repressed. The priest will be too human for some, too holy for others, and contradictory for all. The priest is the pebble in the Church's shoe, for we are the constant reminder of the contradictory natures of the human and divine, seeking to be in the same place at the same time.

And all at the same time, such a vocation is a most wholesome life of wonder and experience. Since we left the safe garden of paradise, we have sought through God-inspired intelligence, memory, and imagination to obey the call to the mindless, inexplicable bliss of being a child of God. The priest is the paradigm of God's love for his children; sometimes the prodigal, sometimes the older brother or sister, but no less a child of God. The priest is finally, among all human beings, the absolute unabashed lover: the lover of God, the lover of others, and the lover of his own soul. Love is his life and his meal.

Another priest-poet, George Herbert, writes of the priestly call of love:

> Love bade me welcome; yet my soul drew back,
>   Guilty of dust and sin.
> But quick-eyed Love, observing me grow slack
>   From my first entrance in,
> Drew nearer to me, sweetly questioning,
>   If I lack'd anything.
>
> "A guest," I answered, "worthy to be here:"
>   Love said, "You shall be he."
> "I the unkind, ungrateful? Ah, my dear,
>   I cannot look on thee."
> Love took my hand, and smiling did reply,
>   "Who made the eyes but I?"
>
> "Truth, Lord; but I have marr'd them: let my shame
>   Go where it doth deserve."
> "And know you not?" says Love, "Who bore the blame?"
>   "My dear, then I will serve."
> "You must sit down," says Love, "and taste my meat."
>   So I did sit and eat.

So now, Paul, stand in our midst. I charge you in the name of the source of the mysterious integration of the human and divine to boldly, steadfastly, and without fear be a priest. Be the present and heroic presence of love in the midst of this complex and confusing world. Be one who stands. Be a priest. Be what God is calling you to be. Be yourself. And be yourself for another. Be yourself for yourself. Give yourself away for something greater than yourself. For God's sake, give yourself away. That is when you'll begin the discovery of who you are. And you will be a priest. Give yourself away for love's sake. You have a long way to go. Priests have a long way to go. The people wait for you to come to them over the broken glass of your vows, but go inspired by the Holy Spirit. Be an unabashed lover. Go into the dark and feel the cross warp on your hands and bid them in the name of love to eat. Be a priest. Be a priest.

Let it be so. I say, amen and amen.

February 24, 1991
Lent II
Mark 8:31–38

    I guess I remain Christian because the gospel is not about life, it is life. The Gospel today reminds us that after transfigurations or transformations, our ego consciousness wants to stop and declare life a victory. But not so, this dynamic journey which makes a life. As soon as Jesus has won from the disciples the acknowledgement that he is the Messiah at the Mount of Transfiguration, Jesus, in today's passage, clarifies his duty as the Christ and the implications of the cross for his disciples: "If any [one] would come after me, let him deny himself and take up his cross and follow me. For whoever would save his life will lose it; and whoever loses his life for my sake and the gospel's will save it." A footnote: the Greek word in the text for "life" is "psyche" translated as "soul" in earlier English versions, but as "life" in the Revised Standard Version. Ponder soul. Soul making requires a cross.

    Jesus' life giving and soul making came to us via a crucifixion. His cross was literal, ours is metaphorical. About such attempts to lessen our commitment to soul making, C. S. Lewis writes in his book, *Miracles*:

> Some people when they say that a thing is meant 'metaphorically' conclude from this that it is hardly meant at all. They rightly think that Christ spoke metaphorically when he told us to carry the cross: they wrongly conclude that carrying the cross means nothing more than living a respectable life and subscribing moderately to charities.

Soul making is an awareness that crosses are borne as crucibles and their function is to form a soul which is of sufficient strength to journey through eternity. This life, if it is about anything, is about soul making. This crucible, this cross we are to bear, is a fire in the soul and burns away the impurities. Such core building, or soul making, comes like a wound, where the proud flesh, burned away, is trimmed by the healing surgeon (as Eliot called our Lord), and healing comes from the inside out. The cross is a metaphor, but no less terrifying than the literal fact of being torn in four by the weight of life.

    This descent from the Mount of Transfiguration or transformation to the cross is the journey of the sun. Borne from the dark horizon to its apogee, and then an inevitable descent into darkness before its return can be rekindled by the dark. Such was Jesus' journey from his Bethlehem stardom to the trudging up the mount and his descent to Jerusalem and three-day deeper descent before his Easter sunrise. Lent is the time to consider the descent, the fall, the entering into the deep, dark journey of soul making.

    In Robert Bly's *Iron John*, a book about masculine psychology, he writes of this descent.

The mark of Descent, whether undertaken consciously or unconsciously, is a newly arrived at lowliness...The lowliness happens particularly to men who are initially high, lucky, elevated...[this is] what the ancient Greeks called *katabasis*.

There is something more than a little frightening about this Drop. Our ego doesn't want to do it, and even if we drop, the ego doesn't want to see it. The sounds in "katabasis," harsh and abrupt, feel right for this trip.

What I am saying, then, is that the next step in initiation for men is finding the rat's hole. The rat's hole is the "dark way,"...

When "katabasis" happens, a man no longer feels like a special person. He is not.

It is as if life itself somehow "discharges" him. There are many ways of being "discharged": a serious accident, the loss of a job, the breaking of a long-standing friendship, a divorce, a "breakdown," an illness.

Bly goes on to quote C. G. Jung:

It is said that whenever a friend reported enthusiastically, "I've just been promoted!" Jung would say, "I'm very sorry to hear that; but if we all stick together, I think we will get through it." If a friend arrived depressed and ashamed, saying, "I've just been fired," Jung would say, "Let's open a bottle of wine; this is wonderful news; something good will happen now."

This descent, evidently, is a necessity for growth, for transfiguration—a crucible for change. It does not always have to be as dramatic as an outer-world trauma. If done consciously, as in a spiritual journey or psychoanalysis, it may be the horror of facing one's own dark, shadowy nature. Depression is a *katabasis*; as is ennui, as the French call a dark sense of meaninglessness. Lostness may be the mood of such a descent.

Whatever the affect or effect, it is a wounding. This cross-wound that we must descend into and carry is the making of a soul.

It must be remembered that this wound is the same wound that St. Thomas needed to see in the hands of our Lord and in his side. We are assured as we take our own soul making, soul wounding, that our Lord, too, is wounded. But we also know from the experience of Christ's wounds, that these scars are doors. Christianity requires us to be wounded; that is, to give up our ego need to measure our worth by net worth, or the need to measure our meaning by our competence or accomplishment. We must be willing to give this up in order to enter into the fullness of life that is not opulent, but is abundant. Whether it be an outer-world breaking or an inner-world losing, the wound is a door. We exit from superficiality through the wound.

The way down is the way out. It is, from the Mount of Transfiguration to the wound of the cross, that which opens and allows exit. The way down doesn't require poverty, homelessness, or physical harm, but it does require a conscious fall and giving up of everything which formerly was held as important, and entering into our own basic woundedness. Such a conscious journey is cross bearing and, at the same time, soul making. Each of us knows, at some level of our existence, where it is we must go. We also know, at some level of consciousness, the barriers to our own journey. We also know that the way is not necessarily up the success ladder; that it may be down into the deep, dark recesses of our own soul. Clearly, if I read the gospel right, we are called to that.

Today Jesus makes us an invitation to follow him. Here are the rules: deny your (old) self and take up your cross. Whoever would save his life will lose his soul; and whoever loses his life for my sake and the gospel's will gain his soul.

This is the invitation of one who actualizes in his life what he requires of his followers. He accepts the wound, the *katabasis*, and exits his old life through it.

He is the Wounded Healer, who both inflicts and heals the wound. This is our Lenten truth; this is our Lenten journey. There are other ways, but this is the way God has called us. I remind you: there are a hundred ways to say "no," one way to say "yes," and no way to say anything else.

Amen.

※ ※ ※

March 17, 1991
Lent V
John 12:20–33

Today we hear from John's Gospel that "[some Greeks] came to Philip…and said to him, 'Sir, we wish to see Jesus.'"

Since the time of Alexander the Great, the prevailing culture of the whole Eastern Mediterranean world had been Greek. When the Romans gained control of the area, they made no effort to supplant this heritage. So Jewish writers, and Jewish Christians like Paul, frequently used the term "Greek" to stand for any Gentile. In all likelihood, these Gentiles were representatives of the class of Gentiles known as "God-fearers," people who were seeking to know the God of the Jews, but did not have a Jewish background. And they had heard of Jesus and the claims his disciples had made about Jesus, and they wanted to see him. I suppose these Greeks were much like the secular agnostics of our day.

Indulge me in a fantasy. Suppose such seekers came to you today wanting to see Jesus, what picture would you paint? Because you were wearing a cross, or had been seen leaving the Cathedral, or, for some other reason, you were identified as a Christian, some secular humanists sought you out to see Jesus; what would you show them?

Were you to build a portrait of Jesus, would you not create him in your own image?

I suppose some of us would sketch a portrait of a sort of prep school or Ivy League Jesus: bright, attractive, probably blond, blue-eyed, athletic, wise beyond his years, urbane, and witty. "Yes, of course," we would say, "he was of a good family...an extraordinary birth, you know, marvelous, divine...earnest, loyal, dedicated, powerful, victorious...a leader." Perhaps we would bring them a compact disc of the choir from St. Paul's, London, singing Handel's *Messiah*, sip chardonnay, and reflect that, "He was one of us, you know."

Some might draw another portrait from their own image. "He was poor, from questionable birth, held no job. He spent his time with the lame, blind, prostitutes, beggars, rejected, outcasts, sick, hungry. He himself was excluded by the ruling class, rejected, inferior, punished, jailed, crucified. He came to poverty to be one of us, you know."

Some might draw a portrait of a prophet. "He was a rebel who overthrew the hypocritical oppressors who exploited the working class. He was a voice of justice in a culture of superficiality and opulence. He gave liberation to the oppressed. He set the captives free. He was a guerilla warrior who sided with members of the underclass in their struggle against the unjust system of occupation. He was one of us, you know."

Others would read Jung. "He was a heroic symbol from the collective unconscious. He was a mythological figure of the archetype of the self. He constellated the paradigm of the essence of the psyche. His Christ symbol was the universal integration of the opposites found in the human predicament of the reconciliation of the human situation from this birth we did not request to a grave we cannot escape. He freed us to be human. He was human like one of us, you know."

Yet others would proclaim him as judge. "He came to eradicate sin. He came to save us from our sinful natures. We are weak, miserable sinners, unworthy, and tainted by the original sin of Adam and Eve. He came to judge our sin and save us from our own sinful nature. Without him all men die and are destined for hell. You must accept him as your personal Lord and Savior. Only those who do so will be saved. All others will be sentenced to eternal damnation. If you just accept him as Lord and Savior, your whole life will be changed, and when the end of the world is at hand, those who have accepted Christ will go to heaven, and those who haven't will go to hell. Don't you want to be one of us? He was, you know."

What would you say if one who was seeking to see Jesus came to you? Each of us has created a Jesus in our own image. Is there any way to portray Jesus apart from our own subjective need? Maybe that is the genius of the revelation. No portrait can capture the dynamic Christ. Whatever God's purpose was, it is true that each of us must experience the Christ for ourselves. In so doing, we must confess that our image is subjective, limited, and incapable of comprehending such power.

Whatever the objective truth, presuming there might be one, we must seek to see Jesus in our own experience. We must be willing to see the Christ in our own toils, conflicts, sufferings; we must be open to seeing him in our loves and ecstasies, in our decisions and choices. He is, as Schweitzer has written, "an ineffable mystery, they shall learn in their own experience Who He is."

The error is not in our own subjective prejudices, as we attempt to articulate who he is. Our error is in not looking for him ourselves, wherever he may be. The true tragedy is not in our inadequate attempt to describe him, but in assuming that he can only be seen in one way—the way we see him. The true heresy is to have lived and never seen that God was present in Christ in all that we do. The ultimate loss would not be in misrepresenting Christ, but in missing his presence in the person who seeks him.

My greatest fear is not in my having seen Christ in my own way; my greatest fear is in not having seen him at all. My only proclamation is that I have seen him; I have seen him with my own eyes. For those who wants to see him, they may. They will see him in their own experience, and it will be as valuable and available as mine.

Amen.

❖ ❖ ❖

March 24, 1991
Palm Sunday
Mark 14, 15

I suspect, since the time consciousness dawned on humankind, there have been conversations about dreams. For years, and with particular emphasis this year, I have studied dreams. Dream interpretation is a mysterious art; it is not a science. I do not do glib dream work. Even the dream conversation at breakfast with children leaves me silent, as such is private and sacred and deserves more than casual conversation. Telling dreams in public is a dangerous practice, for not only are the dreams for the dreamer alone, but one might just reveal something of a private nature that is devalued or perhaps desecrated by careless conversation.

Even with such an ardent disclaimer concerning public telling, some dreams demand to be told. They evidently belong to the collective. This dream came to me within months after my father's death. He appears to me, as if he has just gotten out of bed. He looks like I have seen him for so many mornings in my span of life. His hair is white and silken, slightly tousled. He is wearing his robe, always too short of sleeve, and those house shoes with the backs ridden flat by years of clopping down dark hallways. His face is a cameo. He looks at me and his eyes twinkle—eyes which always, under thick brows, looked soft and slanted. He smiles a knowing smile and says, "All of those things you are worried about don't matter."

That was it. In less time than a digital clock can turn a number, the dream appeared and vanished—in no more than ten words. These words of hope and peace came to me from my soul's nightclub of the unconscious. This message came to me in the voice of a man who had quoted to me only years earlier from Thoreau, "The mass of men lead lives of quiet desperation." This word appeared out of the face of a man who for his entire life had struggled against his own sense of failure, having sat at his desk in the dining room of a small rented house for years, posting his books and trying to squeeze his expense account for enough extra to make ends meet. This word came from my father who couldn't muster enough hope or meaning or peace to assuage my mother's chronic, and at times dysfunctional, depression. In his voice, the words came, "All of the things you are worried about don't matter."

If dreams compensate consciousness with messages, then it doesn't matter whose voice that was. If it was my father complex, an archetype image of the self, or God, or some chemical reaction to something I ate, those words are mine. David Hume, the Scottish philosopher, asks, "Did you dream God spoke to you, or did God speak to you in a dream?" Finally, the distinction makes no difference, for the words come.

Today we begin a tattered tradition of remembering and rehearsing Holy Week, the week of passion. Our family's story will be told in all its ancient and dramatic ritual. Palm Sunday, Maundy Thursday, Good Friday, Holy Saturday, and Easter will pour down the awareness of another year. The words of the passion narrative are as familiar to us as our own hands. They are words, and they come to us as if from a dream: Gethsemane. A sorrowful soul. This cup. Willing spirit, weak flesh. Judas. Kiss of death. Chief priests. "Are you the Christ?" Denial. Twice-crowing cock. Pilate. "Are you the King of the Jews?" Barabbas. "Crucify him! Crucify him!" Strike. Spit. Strip. Mock. Simon of Cyrene. Divide. Separate. Cast lots. "My God, my God, why hast Thou forsaken me?" Torn curtain. Mother Mary. Linen shroud. Tomb.

These are the nights of quiet desperation for the human masses: betrayal, denial, anguish, horror, death. And yet, even now, a dream shuffles down the hall in worn but comfortable words. The father's voice begins to utter an Easter dream. The heaven-sent vision of our future will not fade.

Amen.

March 29, 1991
Good Friday

Even now, with the crucified one hovering over the ache of a threshold beneath an ash-pale sky, we must question all life's meanings in this silence of a closing door.

In the thickening silence, the light narrows and disappears behind the door without a knob. It can never again be opened from life's side.

The Austrian philosopher Ludwig Wittgenstein once declared: "Death is not an event of life. Death is not lived through." Whatever it is about one's life that is unfinished, never known, not yet experienced, remains and disappears unknown.

The sweet boy who never knew a lover, never knows. The little girl who never birthed a baby doesn't enjoy her own fruit. The unfinished novel is not written. The unbuilt house is never built. The unspoken words, held in the secret of the heart, are never uttered. The nursing home holds the blank stare of the old woman who did not act to claim her own life for fear; she now has no life left to fear. The middle-aged man who never knew his soul has sold his soul to the outer world and cannot now avoid the closing door.

Our religion, in spite of the nature of the human, does not deny death, but hangs its reality and inevitability before us as an ironically sacred limit; such a life limit. Though each person must live under the sovereign caprice of death's unpredictability, we each live under its undeniable inevitability.

What energy does this life limit add to life before death? Does it stew and boil in bubbled vapor called anxiety, or does it become a numinous spirit that creates a life lived in all its authentic wonder? Who decides? The little girl who dies unfruitful may have lived a more fruitful life than the wasted woman of eighty who never lived. Quantity and quality question one another.

This cross is not a barrier, but it is a limit we must face. Its annual presence on Good Friday provides us the opportunity to evaluate our life and account for the question, "Have we lived?"

This cross always stands as reminder in the forefront of our consciousness that a life postponed is a life of impossibility. Such a cross demands us to question not human nature, but God's nature. What kind of creator would be such a destroyer? God, who is the creator of a covenant of love and the giver of a promise of eternity, is also a God who allows horror, hate, and death. The giver of the mystery of love allows the love to disappear with the light of death's one-way door. Who among us does not know the voice of forsakenness? And who, this day, will speak the mystery that is as dark as it is light.

The quickened voice of panic runs through our souls like our breath coming and going and our blood branching through fluttery veins. What are we to make of this journey and the one who had bequeathed us such authenticity and its dark twin, absurdity?

Too many passionate words have attempted to romanticize the death of Jesus as if it is only a ceremonial preface to Easter's celebration. The human ego is haunted by such horror and denies its reality, no less than Peter denied his love for the dying one. The cross is not a piece of decorative art, but a gibbet of humiliation.

What must be pointed out, what must be seen, is that Jesus was crucified. Everything he had said and done was nailed to his cross. He who had considered the lilies of the field hung on a barren wasteland. Those he had healed could not prevent his pain. The woman he had saved could not save him. The law he had overcome had overcome him. He was suffering all the sacred moments of his life and doing so utterly and finally alone.

If there is a mythological nature about this sacred story of Jesus Christ, the Crucifixion is its grounding in history at a particular time, a particular place. This point between the virgin birth and mysterious resurrection is not doctrine, theory, or mythology. This death is as real as any and every death ever known. Jesus of Nazareth suffered under Pontius Pilate, was crucified, died, and was buried.

If we are to receive the grace of this act, we must first consider its disgrace. To rush too glibly to the empty tomb would devalue what is to come, and its prerequisite—death. Such hastening around the grave too quickly covers the trail of blood. Without this blood, there is no birth. There is something offensive about an Easter that has no Crucifixion. There is something scandalous about excitement without despair. Such would be a whitewashing of Black Friday. The more I have lived this story and mystery, the less satisfactory is the automatic resurrection. I need resurrection too desperately to have it glibly paraded around as if it is an automatic reward. I need life too desperately not to have to struggle through the deaths. I need life to be such that death can be transcended, transformed, and accepted. An automatic resurrection is a magic act—no suffering, no reality, no need of redemption, no blood, no birth. A glib Easter is a pretense that we understand what is impossible for us to understand. What we do know is that if death isn't real, neither is the resurrection.

Having now established objective premise, let me invite a subjective response. Death, in its inescapable reality, posits an objective point toward which all life moves. What, this day, is your subjective response? Will you live your life in denial? Will you postpone living until death robs you of life? What of the loves not known, words not spoken, houses not built?

We should remove the signs from all the chapels in Christendom that read: "Enter, Rest, and Pray" and replace them with: "Enter at Your Own Risk." You who have come today have been confronted by the truth of death, its reality, and its inevitability. What will be your response today? Will you wait another year? No response will be your response, for which you will now be responsible. I bequeath unto you this day full responsibility for your own life. This horrible burden of freedom I bequeath to you, through God's gospel, directly into the forefront of your own consciousness. Nobody else now is to blame. Your own impotence shall not be projected onto improper parenting! You are free! Free to live and free to die.

Let me encourage each of us, and let me judge myself. For in addition to looking objectively at the cross and making a subjective response, we must know that we cannot know our own soul until we enter the valley of the shadow of death. If we are to meet God in our own soul, we must die to whatever is keeping us from this meeting. Death is where we meet God. We must confess that abundance can only be known through abandonment. And resurrection requires death. To experience new life, resurrection means that we need to enter the place of death. We need to enter the cross. We *need* to need resurrection. Otherwise, it is devalued as some automatic, natural response. Resurrection is not natural, death is. Are you prepared by your own commitment for the supernatural surprise? We need to need resurrection before we receive it. We need to make the individual journey to that place of death at the center of each of us and be willing to die whatever deaths are necessary as prerequisites for this life that is promised.

Resurrection is such a universal human longing that it must be within us. Why death is a prerequisite is as mysterious as why life is a gift. If this is true for us, then this story tells us that it is also true for God. God dies. How can this be? This is the nature of God to die and rise again. Now we see the rhythm of creation and creature in the death and resurrection of the creator. Having faced the truth and its painful horror of loss, we can face the freedom. Being free to live means we are free to die.

The original sin that is atoned in this death is our fear of freedom. The freedom death brings is in its permission to live fully now. Our sin is our fear of freedom and the discipline and responsibility that freedom brings.

We don't naturally want this freedom. We are only able to have it because God wants us to have it. Our nature is to collapse back in fear and have a paradise lost. God in Christ has made it possible for us to live now. God in Christ has not overcome death, but has overcome the fear of death. We have absolutely nothing to fear, for now we know that death brings life. We are free to live and die and live and die, again and again, and every loss is healed by the gain, and every gain is greater than that which is lost. I bequeath unto you this day full of possibility for your own life. There may be those among us here today who will not return next year. Will he and she live this year?

Some of us *will* return next Good Friday. Will we have spent another year having not lived? I bequeath unto you this day the responsibility for the answer to that question—directly, clearly, into your own soul. I give you, in the name of Jesus Christ, responsibility for your own life.

Amen.

March 31, 1991
Easter Day
Mark 16:1–8

Is it irony or paradox that the fullness of the Christian gospel is found in the emptiness of a tomb? Whatever it is, today's lesson from Mark's Gospel gives us a sparse and open narrative. The mysterious, angelic young man tells the women who always come to bring spices, "Do not be amazed; you seek Jesus of Nazareth, who is crucified. He has risen, he is not here…" The fullness found in emptiness may be paradox and irony, but by the Gospel account, it was surprise. The witnesses were "amazed," "astonished," and "afraid."

So, too, we who have been trained to fill ourselves are surprised to hear that emptiness is the good news. "More is better," reads the American script. Our ego instinct is to satiate and gratify our appetites. If one drives from Montrose Boulevard to Highway 6 on Westheimer, one will see the American filling stations. Strip shopping centers full of restaurants, stores, shops, and boutiques, with a sort of galleria climax midway, complete with ice rink.

Such a surprise! The fullness is to be found in the emptiness. If God were to re-create the world, wouldn't it be logical that he would re-create out of nothing? Such emptiness re-creates possibility. It leaves little certainty, but that something totally new can emerge leaves little doubt.

A Zen monk once told Morton Kelsey, "We think there is something to Christianity, but we don't think Christians know what it is." The resurrection *is* the gospel. What we know is that since God left the tomb, it means that there is a new creation and that new life can begin again at any time. I like the metaphors from nature: the butterfly emerges from the cocoon, the knuckled bud springs forth into bloom after a dead winter, the egg breaks forth with the fluffy chick. But these metaphors fall short and trivialize, because the resurrection is not natural; it is a shock, a surprise, amazing, awe-full, fearful. We expect the chrysalis to become a butterfly, we expect the knuckled bud to bloom, but it is unexpected and supernatural that we can begin a new life at any time. Resurrection means a new worldview, whereby eternity breaks into history and numinous energy swells. It does not simply make the old new, but creates the never before, the not yet, and the unimaginable. Easter is not natural. Nature is cruel in its predictability and objectivity. All things die. It is the natural consequence. Easter is subjective surprise.

Easter has created a new order; it is called the Kingdom of God. In the Kingdom of God, surprise is the natural order. Jesus warned us of the new order. In the Kingdom of God, the Samaritans are neighbors. In the Kingdom of God, rebellious children come home. In the Kingdom of God, mustard seeds are great. In the Kingdom of God, those who work one hour are paid in full. In the Kingdom of God, the last are first, the poor are rich, the king serves.

Easter life is what the Zen monk saw that we may not see. Easter life is caprice. Easter life is not predictable, for kings ride donkeys, beggars are kings, treasurers rust, water is wine, stables are palaces, and emptiness is fullness.

We are an Easter people. We expect the unexpected. Grace is surprise. The covenant is comedy. When we least expect new life, it walks into our old life and transforms it. Easter people don't have to wait for eternity, for now history houses the fullness of time, from the timelessness of an empty tomb. Surprise! Surprise! Surprise!

Amen.

✤ ✤ ✤

June 2, 1991
II Corinthians 4:5–12; Mark 2:23–28

> Heavenly Muse, Spirit who brooded on
> The world and raised it shapely out of nothing,
> Touch my lips with fire and burn away
> All dross of speech, so that I keep in mind
> The truth and end to which my words now move
> In hope. Keep my mind within that Mind
> Of which it is a part, whose wholeness is
> The hope of sense in what I tell. And though
> I go among the scatterings of that sense,
> The members of its worldly body broken,
> Rule my sight by vision of the parts
> Rejoined. And in my exile's journey far
> From home, be with me, so I may return.
>
> —Wendell Berry, "Remembering"

An experience of synchronicity is where an unconscious pattern crosses the threshold of consciousness to constellate an experience of truth. It appears to the ego as coincidence, but in fact, it is the revelation of something significant that needs to be metabolized. Such is the event of today's epistle and Gospel, two of my favorite pieces, appearing on this Sunday. The first one is from St. Paul. In summary, Paul writes to the church at Corinth: "For what we preach is not ourselves, but Jesus Christ as Lord…we have this treasure in earthen vessels, to show that the transcendent power belongs to God and not to us. We are afflicted in every way, but not crushed; perplexed, but not driven to despair; persecuted, but not forsaken; struck down, but not destroyed; always carrying in the body the death of Jesus, so that the life of Jesus may also be manifested in our bodies…So death is at work in us, but life in you."

Therein rests so much of my own priesthood and personal faith: that the love of God for us is simply stronger than any death. There is given in the human soul such an energy of life that nothing can separate us from this love of God. My one commitment to the troubled and suffering, without and within, is that no matter what, we may be "afflicted in every way, but not crushed; perplexed, but not driven to despair; persecuted, but not forsaken; struck down, but not destroyed." Paul, from his own experience considering life to be a crucible whereby souls are made, writes: "For I am persuaded, that neither death, nor life, nor angels, nor principalities, nor powers, nor things present, nor things to come, nor height, nor depth, nor any other creature shall be able to separate us from the love of God, which is in Christ Jesus our Lord."

This is the essence of my own existential faith. Nothing, not even we, ourselves, can separate us from God's love. And then today's Gospel, from St. Mark, provides the basis of my theological system. One Sabbath Jesus and his disciples were walking through the grain fields, and as they made their way, the disciples began to pluck ears of grain. And the Pharisees said to Jesus, "Look, why are they doing what is not lawful on the Sabbath?" and he said to them, "The sabbath was made for man, not man for the sabbath."

My theological system rests on that premise; that we have not been given a religion of rules, but a gift of grace, which is the fundamental essence of human freedom. This gift of grace has no strings attached; it is free, ours for the taking; there is absolutely no way to mess it up! We have been given this incredible gift of grace, which below us is a safety net and above us is an umbrella, and we dwell in the midst of this grace, this free gift. We resist this freedom, but there is something within us that knows God wants freedom from us. God does not want automatons, he wants people of autonomy.

Such an image of life. Jesus and the disciples were not on the highway, the expected path. They were not travelling the known way, but were walking where no one had walked. They were walking through the grain fields, making their own way. They were hungry, and they plucked this free gift before them. The religious of true spirituality simply do the obvious. They ate; they saw the grain as gift. The Pharisees were the priests of the time. Priests are infamous for trying to perpetuate the institution that gives them their authority; they were, therefore, afraid of these rules being broken. They were a part of a religion which attempted to offer rules and guidelines for human behavior in every situation. The rule was: no work on Sunday. The disciples, going their own way through the grain fields (my guess is that they were skipping along, barefooted!) broke the expected rules. The Pharisees rebuked them, and Jesus retorted: human beings are free. The Sabbath was made for us, and we are celebrating it! We were not created for the Sabbath. Jesus took the law off of stone tablets and placed it in the freedom of our own souls. Jesus taught simply: act responsibly in love. Love God, love neighbor, and for God's sake, love yourself. (And, if you get out on Sunday, skip through fields of grain!)

These two images—nothing can separate us from the love of God, and God in Christ has set us free to take responsibility for our own lives—summarize my essential theology and faith. And all of this is enacted within a covenant and a promise. The covenant is God's unfailing love, and the promise is that if we go our own way, we will discover what God is calling us to be, and in so doing, we will discover God in our own uniqueness. All the sins and mistakes are necessary to our development. Our souls are formed by suffering. The world is the sacred grove wherein we will discover God. We need not fear the world, for God created it for us, and we for it. And as we develop ourselves, we are developing a cosmos. Our gift to the world is to become ourselves. We are both heirs and victims of this birth we did not request and this grave we cannot escape. Between this yes and no, we fashion a life. Our life has been given to us to live. We are the only ones who can live our lives, and the truest faith response is to live fully, abundantly, and authentically. We are to live our own lives as authentically as Christ lived his. When I die, God won't ask me, "Why didn't you live your life as Christ?" but will ask, "Why didn't you live your life as Pittman?" I pray and plan to live my life as Pittman so that when I see God face-to-face, I will know I attempted to be what God created me to be. If I have abused such freedom, I expect that God's grace will transform my transgressions into a soul worthy to enter his presence. The first half of life is biography, but at some point in life, we are handed the pen and are told that from here on our life is autobiography. God's grace and our freedom are the resources from the primary source, and all we need for the human journey. If we will just go our way through the grain fields, there will be plenty of fruit.

Whatever has happened in the last ten years in this place, it has been because we opened this sacred space to the world about us. We were not afraid of the world. We opened those iron gates and these oaken doors and we said, "Come in!" We opened ourselves to one another and tried to be honest, and accepting, and affirming. We took seriously that one gains one's life by giving it away. We lived our lives in ways that allowed others to come as they were, with no apologies, conditions, or requirements, and to struggle to become whoever they were called to be. If you are doing it in love, it will be responsible. We attempted to say that we are not stuck, that we are not prisoners, that we have choices. We tried to say we have the freedom to choose. We tried to accept human limitations and seek human possibilities. We attempted to be believable and authentic. We sought to tell the story of Jesus and to tell our own story. We tried to cry when we hurt and laugh when joy surprised us. We laughed at ourselves and acknowledged our own faults. We attempted to live the paradox and seek the transcendent function that would integrate the opposites. We mourned the death of loved ones, celebrated the birth of new ones, we blessed love and cursed bigotry. We never sought perfection, but always prayed for wholeness. We have also tried to remember that the angels fly because they take themselves lightly.

When time was born from the womb of nowhere, this was our time to be together. And this is our time to depart. Soon, another leader will be called among you. He or she will be under the singular obligation to be himself or herself. Success is relative, and comparisons are odious. The new dean will be just the right person to create a new personality. Your openness will be a necessity for a new era to develop. Please acknowledge this importance of differences and be as affirming with the new dean as you have been to me. In the interim, there remains an excellent and abundant source of ordained and lay leadership. You *now* have all you need to be the people of God. I will make one final declaration as I leave: there will be no interim between deans. You do not need me or him or her; you have all you will need to be the people of God at Christ Church Cathedral. Let us declare that there will be no interim, just the continuity of the peculiar people of God in this place, laughing and playing together, ritualizing the life cycle and celebrating the fact that all of life is a gift. Whoever comes to take the office of dean will be just another gift.

I thank God for calling me here. I have discovered things here I could never have discovered any other place. I thank you for allowing me to be myself here. I did not claim to be perfect, never had that as a desire; to the contrary, it seems to me that imperfection is the only way to wholeness. I thank God for not allowing me the comfort of complacency and for calling me to a new context for my priesthood and personhood.

For all that has been, I say "thanks," and to all that is to come, I say "yes!"

Amen.

ABOUT THE AUTHOR

J. Pittman McGehee is an Episcopal priest and Jungian analyst in private practice in Houston, Texas. He is former dean of Christ Church Cathedral in Houston. He is widely known as a lecturer and educator in the field of psychology and religion, as well as a published poet and essayist. He is the author of *The Invisible Church: Finding Spirituality Where You Are* (Praeger Press, 2008), and *Raising Lazarus: The Science of Healing the Soul* (2009).

Made in the USA
Charleston, SC
16 April 2011